D1117629

SENIORPLOTS

SENIORPLOTS

SENIORPLOTS

A Book Talk Guide
for Use with Readers Ages 15–18

By JOHN T. GILLESPIE
and CORINNE J. NADEN

R. R. BOWKER
New York

Published by R. R. Bowker Company
a division of Reed Publishing (USA) Inc.
Copyright © 1989 by Reed Publishing USA
All rights reserved
Printed and bound in the United States of America

Library of Congress Cataloging-in-Publication Data

Gillespie, John Thomas, 1928–
    Seniorplots : a book talk guide for use with readers ages 15–18 /
by John T. Gillespie and Corinne J. Naden.
      p. cm.
    Includes indexes.
    ISBN 0-8352-2513-5
    1. Young adult literature—Stories, plots, etc. 2. High school
libraries—Book lists. 3. Young adults—Books and reading.
4. Teenagers—Books and reading. 5. Book talks. I. Naden, Corinne
J. II. Title. III. Title: Seniorplots.
Z1037.A1G524 1989   88-27333
809'.89283—dc19   CIP

ISBN 0-8352-2513-5

Contents

Preface   ix

Introduction   xi

1. Growing Up   1
   Baldwin, James. *If Beale Street Could Talk*   1
   Greenberg, Joanne. *Simple Gifts*   5
   Hamilton, Virginia. *A Little Love*   8
   Kerr, M. E. *Night Kites*   13
   MacLean, John. *Mac*   18
   Marshall, Catherine. *Julie*   21
   Naylor, Phyllis Reynolds. *The Year of the Gopher*   25
   Simon, Neil. *Brighton Beach Memoirs*   29
   Townsend, John Rowe. *Downstream*   33
   Townsend, Sue. *The Adrian Mole Diaries*   37

2. Interpersonal Relations   41
   Bridgers, Sue Ellen. *Sara Will*   41
   Brooks, Bruce. *Midnight Hour Encores*   45
   Cormier, Robert. *Beyond the Chocolate War*   50
   Crutcher, Chris. *The Crazy Horse Electric Game*   55
   Dorris, Michael. *A Yellow Raft in Blue Water*   59
   Fox, Paula. *The Moonlight Man*   65
   Guest, Judith. *Ordinary People*   69
   L'Engle, Madeleine. *A House Like a Lotus*   73
   Plain, Belva. *The Golden Cup*   78
   Porte, Barbara Ann. *I Only Made Up the Roses*   82

3. Challenging Adult Novels   87
   Brin, David. *The Postman*   87
   Conroy, Pat. *The Prince of Tides*   92
   Dickens, Charles. *Hard Times*   96

Gordimer, Nadine. *July's People*   100
Hugo, Victor. *The Hunchback of Notre Dame*   104
Morrison, Toni. *Beloved*   108
Twain, Mark. *Puddn'head Wilson*   113
Tyler, Anne. *A Slipping-Down Life*   117
Walker, Alice. *The Color Purple*   121
Welty, Eudora. *The Optimist's Daughter*   126

4. Stories of Other Lands and Times   131
    Bradshaw, Gillian. *The Beacon at Alexandria*   131
    Gordon, Sheila. *Waiting for the Rain: A Novel of South
        Africa*   136
    Miller, Arthur. *The Crucible*   139
    Myers, Walter Dean. *Fallen Angels*   143
    Pullman, Philip. *The Ruby in the Smoke*   147
    Solzhenitsyn, Alexandr. *One Day in the Life of Ivan
        Denisovich*   153
    Stewart, Mary. *The Wicked Day*   156
    Walker, Margaret. *Jubilee*   160

5. Possible Worlds   165
    Asimov, Isaac. *Foundation*   165
    Clarke, Arthur C. *Rendezvous with Rama*   168
    Heinlein, Robert A. *Stranger in a Strange Land*   172
    Johnson, Annabel, and Johnson, Edgar. *The Danger
        Quotient*   177
    McCaffrey, Anne. *Moreta: Dragonlady of Pern*   181
    Sleator, William. *Singularity*   186

6. Fantasy   190
    Brooks, Terry. *Magic Kingdom for Sale—Sold!*   190
    Hilton, James. *Lost Horizon*   195
    Mahy, Margaret. *The Tricksters*   198
    Murphy, Shirley Rousseau. *Nightpool*   203
    Vonnegut, Kurt, Jr. *Cat's Cradle*   207

7. Adventure Stories   212
    Alexander, Lloyd. *The El Dorado Adventure*   212
    Crichton, Michael. *Sphere*   216
    Forsyth, Frederick. *The Day of the Jackal*   221

Higgins, Jack. *Solo* 224
Paulsen, Gary. *Hatchet* 227

8. Suspense and Mystery 232
   Avi. *Wolf Rider: A Tale of Terror* 232
   Clark, Mary Higgins. *Weep No More, My Lady* 236
   du Maurier, Daphne. *Rebecca* 240
   Francis, Dick. *Bolt* 245
   Rendell, Ruth. *Heartstones* 249

9. Sports in Fact and Fiction 253
   Allen, Maury. *Jackie Robinson: A Life Remembered* 253
   Kinsella, W. P. *Shoeless Joe* 257
   Malamud, Bernard. *The Natural* 260
   Plimpton, George. *The Open Net* 265
   Voigt, Cynthia. *The Runner* 269

10. Interesting Lives and True Adventure 274
    Angelou, Maya. *All God's Children Need Traveling Shoes* 274
    Brown, Peter, and Gaines, Steven. *The Love You Make: An Insider's Story of The Beatles* 277
    Dahl, Roald. *Going Solo* 281
    Herriot, James. *The Lord God Made Them All* 285
    Lawick-Goodall, Jane van. *In the Shadow of Man* 289
    Lopez, Barry. *Arctic Dreams: Imagination and Desire in a Northern Landscape* 292

11. The World Around Us 298
    Finnegan, William. *Crossing the Line: A Year in the Land of Apartheid* 298
    Hawking, Stephen W. *A Brief History of Time: From the Big Bang to Black Holes* 302
    Hofstadter, Richard. *America at 1750: A Social Portrait* 306
    Terry, Wallace. *Bloods: An Oral History of the Vietnam War by Black Veterans* 309
    Wilford, John Noble. *The Riddle of the Dinosaur* 313

12. Guidance and Health 318
    Alexander, Sue. *Finding Your First Job* 318
    Benedict, Helen. *Safe, Strong and Streetwise: The Teenager's Guide to Preventing Sexual Assault* 321

Booher, Dianna Daniels. *Coping: When Your Family Falls Apart* 324

Gale, Jay. *A Young Man's Guide to Sex* 328

Leana, Frank C. *Getting into College* 332

Author Index 337

Title Index 355

Subject Index 373

Preface

The earlier Juniorplots series (by John Gillespie) gives assistance in book selection and introducing books to audiences of approximately 12 to 16 years of age. The present volume, *Seniorplots*, is intended to be a companion volume extending coverage for readers through the senior high school years—roughly ages 15 through 18.

In choosing the 80 books to be highlighted, a serious attempt has been made to cover a variety of topics and interests at various reading levels and abilities. Therefore, a few titles like those by Lloyd Alexander and Avi could also be read and enjoyed by a slightly younger audience. And, titles like Toni Morrison's *Beloved* and Nadine Gordimer's *July's People* will challenge the most perceptive of adult readers. In addition to contemporary fiction, other genres are represented—the classics, plays, biographies, general nonfiction, and several old favorites like Daphne du Maurier's *Rebecca*. A basic criterion for book selection was that each had to be recommended for purchase in standard bibliographies and/or reviewing sources.

The 80 plots in *Seniorplots* have been divided into 12 subject and genre areas representing a variety of reading areas popular with late adolescents. They are (1) Growing Up (stories involving personal maturation, coming of age, encountering adult problems, assuming new responsibilities), (2) Interpersonal Relations (adjusting to new social situations, reviewing relationships with family and friends), (3) Challenging Adult Novels, (4) Stories of Other Lands and Times, (5) Possible Worlds (science fiction), (6) Fantasy, (7) Adventure Stories, (8) Suspense and Mystery, (9) Sports in Fact and Fiction, (10) Interesting Lives and True Adventure, (11) The World Around Us (science, history, current events), and (12) Guidance and Health (occupational and educational guidance, personal and developmental problems). Sometimes arbitrary decisions had to be made because some works could logically fit into more than one category. For example, David Brin's novel of our earth's devastation by a nuclear holocaust, *The Postman,* could be classed as science fiction but instead was placed in a more general area, Challenging Adult Novels.

The individual titles are analyzed under six headings:

1. *Plot Summary.* Each plot briefly retells the entire story. The summary includes all important incidents and characters, while trying to retain the mood and point of view of the author.

2. *Thematic Material.* An enumeration of primary and secondary themes that will facilitate the use of the book in a variety of situations.

3. *Book Talk Material.* Techniques are given on how to introduce the book interestingly to young adults. Passages suitable for retelling or reading aloud are indicated, and pagination is shown for these passages for the hardcover and, when available, the paperback editions.

4. *Additional Selections.* Related books that explore similar or associated themes are annotated or listed with identifying bibliographic information. Approximately ten titles are given per book.

5. *About the Book.* Standard book reviewing sources (for example, *Booklist*) are listed with dates and pages of reviews. Also, listings in *Book Review Digest* and *Book Review Index* are given when available so that additional reviews can be located if needed.

6. *About the Author.* Standard biographical dictionaries (for example, *Something about the Author* and *Contemporary Authors)* were consulted to locate sources of biographical information about the author. When this section does not appear, no material was found. However, the user also may wish to consult other sources, such as periodical indexes (*Readers' Guide, Education Index, Library Literature*), jacket blurbs, and material available through the publisher.

The detailed treatment of the main titles is not intended as a substitute for reading the books. Instead, it is meant to be used by teachers and librarians to refresh their memories about books they have read and to suggest new uses for these titles.

This volume is not meant to be a work of literary criticism or a listing of the best books for young adults. It is a representative selection of books that have value in a variety of situations.

The authors have had many helpers, but special thanks is given to Mary Lee Graeme for help in locating delinquent titles and to Bette Vander Werf for assistance in manuscript preparation.

Introduction: A Brief Guide to Booktalking

by John T. Gillespie

There is basically just one purpose behind booktalking—to stimulate reading and a love of literature through delivering tantalizing, seductive introductions to books. There are, however, often many different secondary purposes, for example, to introduce specific authors, titles, or themes of books; to develop a specific aspect of literary appreciation; to further a particular school assignment; to present yourself to students; or to encourage visits to and use of the library.

Book talks generally fall into two main categories, informal and formal. The informal book talk consists of the spontaneous introduction to books that goes on every day in the library with single or small groups of students often in reply to such questions as "Could you suggest some good books for me to read?" The formal book talk is explored here in this brief introduction.

Before preparing a specific book talk, three "knows" are helpful. First is to know your audience as well as possible. By this is meant such factors as age and grade levels, the range of abilities and interests, and levels of maturation and sophistication. Second is a knowledge of books. This comes in time through reading about books, in book reviewing journals and other secondary sources, but more importantly from reading the books themselves. It is wise to begin a card file with brief notes on each book read. Although these are never as detailed as the coverage of each title in *Seniorplots*, certain topics should be covered. Basically these are: a brief plot summary; a list of a few key passages, particularly at the beginning of the book, that would be suitable for retelling or rereading to an audience; a note on the major subjects or themes covered; and other related book titles that come to mind. As this file grows it can be used to refresh one's memory of books and thus save rereading time and also serve as a source to create new book talks by "mixing and matching" titles to create a variety of interesting new combinations of titles and themes.

Third is a knowledge of the many aids, such as *Seniorplots,* available to help in preparing and delivering a book talk. Some of the most valuable aids are described at the end of this introduction.

Before choosing the books to be presented, a preliminary framework should be established. First, the physical conditions should be studied (place, time, purpose, number of attendees). Second, the length of the talk should be determined. Most book talks have a time length of 15 to 25 minutes depending on such factors as the number of books to be introduced and the attention span of the audience. An average length is about 20 minutes. In a classroom period of 40 to 45 minutes this allows time for housekeeping chores (for example, announcements, attendance taking), the book talk itself, browsing through the books presented and additional titles, checking out books, and so on.

Deciding on the number of titles to be presented is next. Some booktalkers like to give short one or two minute "quickies" whereas others feel more comfortable spending longer periods, perhaps five minutes, on each title supplying more details of plot or character and perhaps retelling or reading a key self-contained incident. Still others mix both techniques. The conditions of the book talk and the preference of the booktalker in the end determine the style used. Also, if a large number of books is to be introduced, a bibliography can be prepared and distributed to students to prevent confusion and give them reading guidance for future visits to the library. This bibliography should contain names of authors, titles, and a brief "catchy" annotation for each.

In preparing the talk, a connecting link or theme should be decided on. This could be as general as "Books I think you would enjoy reading" or "Some titles old and new that are favorites of young people your age" to something more specific as American Civil War novels or family crises as portrayed in fiction. The more specific topics are often suggested by a classroom teacher and are assignment-oriented. Regardless of the nature of the theme or subject, it supplies a structure and connecting link to produce a oneness and unity to the book talk. It is used to introduce the talk, act occasionally as a bridge from one book to the next, and serve as a conclusion to round out the presentation.

Next choose the books themselves. Although this seems an obvious point, each book should have been read completely. The ultimate outcome or denouement in a book will often determine the material to be presented in introducing the book. Lacking this knowledge, the book-talker might misrepresent the contents or give an inaccurate or incorrect interpretation. One should believe in the value of each title to be presented—feel that the book is worthy of being introduced and that it will supply enjoyment and pleasure to the intended audience. The booktalker does not necessarily have to dote on each title; for example, many readers dislike a particular type of book like fantasies yet the booktalker must introduce examples of the genre. It is sufficient that one choose good books that will enlighten and entertain the audience regardless of the personal preference of the presenter. Be sure the selection represents the interests and reading levels of the group—some difficult, some average, some easy; some old titles, some new; some fiction, some nonfiction; and so forth.

Having chosen the theme and the books to be introduced, the method and content of each book introduction should be determined. There are several ways of introducing books. The most frequently used is a brief description of the plot to a certain climactic moment. Words of caution: do not give away too much of the plot, stick to essential details (for example, avoid introducing subplots or subsidiary characters), and try not to overwork this technique or else students will find the "cliff-hanger" endings ultimately frustrating. The second method is by retelling or reading a specific self-contained incident or incidents that give the flavor of the book. This is sometimes the most satisfying for the audience because a "complete" story has been told and yet one hopes a desire for more has also been implanted. One must be very cautious about reading from the book and use it sparingly only when the author's style cannot be produced otherwise. Some booktalkers eschew entirely reading from the book and instead memorize the passages because reading from the book interrupts the immediate eye contact with the audience and can lessen or destroy the rapport one has with the group. Therefore, passages to be read must be chosen very carefully, and should be short and fulfill a specific purpose when simple retelling will not suffice. A specific interesting character can be introduced fully and placed within the context of the book. This is a suitable technique for booktalking such works as *Goodbye Mr. Chips* or *Breakfast at Tiffanys*. Using the setting or atmosphere of the novel is a fourth method. Science fiction or fantasies with their often exotic, fascinating locales lend themselves frequently to such introductions.

Make sure you are honest in interpreting the book. To present, for example, *The Red Badge of Courage* as an exciting, action-filled war story is both a disservice to the book and a misrepresentation to the audience.

Some people write down their book talks and memorize them; others simply prepare them mentally. A rehearsal, however, is necessary to test pacing, presentation, timing, and sequencing. Perhaps friends, family, or colleagues can be an initial test audience. Tape recorders, or better yet, video recorders are also helpful in preparation. Though rehearsals are necessary, always try for sincerity, naturalness, and a relaxed atmosphere in the delivery. Because initial nervousness can be expected, be particularly careful to know thoroughly the beginning of the talk. Once one becomes used to the audience and the surroundings nervousness usually disappears. Introduce the theme quickly in a way that bridges the gap between the experience and interests of the audience and that of the contents of the books you wish to introduce. Be sure to mention both the author and the title of the book (often twice—once at the beginning and once at the end of the presentation), show off the book (dust jacket and covers can help sell a book and supply a visual reminder of the book), and then display the book (usually by standing it up on the desk). Try to adhere to principles of good public speaking—include the entire audience in your eye contact; don't fidget, rock, play with elastic bands or create other distractions; speak slowly with good intonation and use pauses effectively; and move quickly from one book to the next.

Fortunately there are many excellent guides to help one become a good booktalker. Joni Bodart, a master booktalker, has written extensively on the subject. Bodart's *Booktalk! 2* (Wilson, 1985), an update of *Booktalk!* (Wilson, 1980), gives extensive guidance in preparation and delivery of book talks and supplies many brief examples. A sequel, *Booktalk! 3* (Wilson, 1988), gives additional sample book talks. Bodart also writes a regular column on booktalking for *VOYA* (*Voice of Youth Advocates*). Bodart's 30-minute videotape *Booktalk* (also available from Wilson) supplies both tips and actual presentations.

Hazel Rochman, staff reviewer for young adult books on *Booklist*, also has a fine book and videotape on booktalking (both released in 1987). They are called *Tales of Love and Terror: Booktalking the Classics Old and New*, and are available from the American Library Association as are two old standbys on the subject by Elinor Walker, *Book Bait* (ALA, 1988) and *Doors to More Mature Reading* (ALA, 1981). Some general books on teenage literature such as Alleen Pace Nilsen and Kenneth L. Donelson's

Literature for Today's Young Adults (Scott, Foresman, 1985) also contain valuable sections on the subject. Also suggested are my own Juniorplots series of book talk guides. They are *Juniorplots* (Bowker, 1967), written with Diana Lembo and containing an introduction on booktalking by Doris Cole; *More Juniorplots* (Bowker, 1977), with a special section on booktalking by Mary K. Chelton; and *Juniorplots 3* (Bowker, 1987) coauthored with Corinne J. Naden.

1

Growing Up

In late adolescence, teenagers are confronted with the same problems of early adolescence, now compounded by such factors as the necessity to assume new responsibilities and take part in adult decision making. These novels explore various ways of reaching different kinds of maturity—physical, emotional, sexual, and spiritual.

Baldwin, James. *If Beale Street Could Talk*
   pap., NAL, $3.95

When James Baldwin died in 1988, American literature lost one of its best contemporary writers, and the black people one of its most articulate spokesmen and advocates. Since his first novel, *Go Tell It on the Mountain* (Doubleday, 1953, $13.95; pap., Dell, $4.95), appeared in 1953, his voice in American letters has been a commanding one. *If Beale Street Could Talk* comes roughly midway in his output. Its title is also that of a famous blues song, and its story is a movingly painful one of black survival in spite of prejudice and injustice. It was originally published in 1974 and is enjoyed by mature readers in the senior high grades.

Plot Summary
   Fonny is 22 and Tish is 19. They are black; he is in jail for a crime he didn't commit, and she has just found out that she is pregnant.
   So begins James Baldwin's powerful love story, of two young people who have made a world for themselves with each other. They may be beaten by the poverty and the bigotry and the harshness of life in the streets of the city, but they are not beaten down. They have found each other, and it is enough for them . . . or so they desperately hope.
   Tish and Fonny have been friends for a long time, and it is only fairly recently that they have realized that they are in love. They are poor, as

1

are their families; both of them work and Fonny struggles at night to wrest beautiful forms from the wood and stone he tries to carve. On the night they discover their true feelings for each other, Fonny takes Tish back to her family's home to tell them of their plans to marry.

Tish's family is happy with the news. Her mother, father, and sister like Fonny, and they realize the depth of the young couple's feelings for each other. The reaction is not quite the same in Fonny's household. Although his father, Frank, is genuinely delighted with the coming marriage, Fonny's mother and sisters—whom Tish suspects do not even like Fonny—react as though Tish is beneath their consideration.

Nonetheless, the young couple makes plans by first trying to find an affordable loft that they can rent in the city so that Fonny might continue his sculpture and they might have a place to live.

And, almost miraculously, they do find a place. Unfortunately, it happens to be in a city neighborhood where the bigoted policeman Officer Bell is often seen. One evening when Fonny defends Tish against the unwarranted attentions of a street punk, Bell almost pulls Fonny off to jail. He is stopped by the protests of a witness who defends Fonny and swears that Tish is telling the truth. The officer leaves Fonny alone, but as Fonny later tells Tish, "He's out to get me."

Although the words make Tish uneasy, she cannot believe them. Fonny has never been in trouble with the law, has never been on drugs, has never been arrested.

But Fonny's words seem all too true when he is later picked up, on a charge of rape. He has been picked out of a lineup by a young woman. She claims that the rapist was dark-skinned; dark-skinned Fonny is put into a lineup with three light-skinned men. The woman claims he is the one.

So Fonny is now in jail, where he learns that he is to be a father. Desperately, Tish assures him that her family and his father are trying to get him out.

To that end they hire a white lawyer, who discovers that the woman who accused Fonny has disappeared. The family tries to get together more money, and the lawyer finds out that the woman, Mrs. Rogers, has gone off to Puerto Rico.

Tish's family and Fonny's father band together by working extra jobs to try to raise money for Fonny's defense. Tish struggles to keep her job as her time of delivery grows nearer and she struggles to keep Fonny from growing ever more desperate behind bars.

In an attempt to change the testimony against Fonny, Tish's mother, Sharon, goes to Puerto Rico to locate Mrs. Rogers, who is now living with a young man named Pietro Alvarez. Sharon finds him and pleads with him to help her. He refuses. But Sharon does locate the woman and tells her that she has named the wrong man. Despite her pleas, she is refused.

Nothing Tish's mother can do will persuade Mrs. Rogers to change her mind. Saddened, she returns to New York, only to learn that the young woman has had a miscarriage and has been taken to an asylum. All hope that she would change her testimony is lost.

Without the principal witness, Fonny's trial will be postponed. This news devastates his father. Sometime later Frank is found, up the river, in the woods, sitting in his car with the doors locked—and the motor running.

Tish has not been feeling well all day. Now her father brings her the terrible news about Frank. She opens her mouth, but she can only think of Fonny. She screams and cries, and her time has come.

Thematic Material

This love story is harsh and realistic as it deals with two young people who are frightened but brave, vulnerable, and proud as they try to deal with the realities of a life lived in poverty and discrimination. Their love for each other is particularly haunting as circumstances close in on them, and they cling to each other as a way to ward off their pain and fright. The story is told with great simplicity and dignity. Also compelling is the picture of black family members who share a loving relationship with each other and who stand up for each other in times of stress and desperation. Their realness and their caring come through, even as the net around Fonny and Tish grows tighter and more hopeless.

Book Talk Material

The obvious depth of feeling between these two young people is a good introduction to this modern love story. See: Tish first notices Fonny and accidentally hits him in the head (pp. 11–14); their "first date" (pp. 21–32); and the night Fonny asks Tish to marry him (pp. 93–96). Also, the relationship among members of Tish's family can be used to initiate a talk on how family strength can overcome the harshest of obstacles; see Tish's family handles the news of the baby (pp. 38–41); the family spends the evening together (pp. 48–52); and Tish's father reacts to the marriage (pp. 103–111).

Additional Selections

A young Caribbean girl challenges her mother's authority and grows to adulthood in Jamaica Kincaid's *Annie John* (Farrar, 1985, $11.95; pap., NAL, $5.95).

Fourteen-year-old Rainbow has to move in with a foster mother when her real mother deserts her in Alice Childress's *Rainbow Jordan* (Coward, 1981, $9.95; pap., Avon, $2.50; condensed in *Juniorplots 3*, Bowker, 1987, pp. 16–20).

Coming of age in the 1950s is hauntingly recaptured in Lloyd Kropp's *Greencastle* (Freundlich, 1987, $17.95).

Joyce Thomas has written three novels about Abby growing up. In the first, *Marked by Fire* (pap., Avon, $2.25), she overcomes the trauma of a physical assault and a broken family. The second, *Bright Shadow* (pap., Avon, $2.25), continues the story and it is completed in *Water Girl* (pap., Avon, $2.50).

Ralph Ellison has written the classic novel of the black man trying to find his identity in a white-dominated America in *Invisible Man* (pap., Random, $3.95).

A black student struggles against prejudice in Ann Fairbairn's *Five Smooth Stones* (Crown, 1966, $10.95; pap., Bantam, $4.95).

There is conflict in the black community when the pastor's illegitimate son appears in Ernest J. Gaines's *In My Father's House* (Knopf, 1978, $13.95; pap., Norton, $5.95).

Two fine novels about growing up Hispanic are *Pocho* by José Antonio Villarreal (pap., Doubleday, $3.95), a story set in depression Santa Clara Valley in California, and Myron Levoy's *A Shadow Like a Leopard* (Harper, 1981, $8.95; pap., NAL, $1.95), about streetwise Ramon Santiago.

About the Book
Booklist, July 1, 1974, p. 1179.
Horn Book, October 1974, p. 158.
Library Journal, April 1, 1974, p. 1057.
New York Times Book Review, May 14, 1974, p. 1.
See also *Book Review Digest,* 1974, p. 53, and *Book Review Index,* 1974, p. 25.

About the Author
Commire, Anne, ed. *Something about the Author.* Detroit: Gale, 1976, Vol. 9, p. 15.
Ethridge, James M., and Kopala, Barbara, eds. *Contemporary Authors* (First Revision). Detroit: Gale, 1967. Vol. 1, pp. 44–45.

Evory, Ann, ed. *Contemporary Authors* (New Revision Series). Detroit: Gale, 1981. Vol. 3, pp. 49–52.
Wakeman, John, ed. *World Authors 1950–1970*. New York: Wilson, 1975, pp. 107–109.

Greenberg, Joanne. *Simple Gifts*
Henry Holt, 1986, $15.95, pap. $7.95 (same pagination)

Joanne Greenberg is perhaps best known for her largely autobiographical first novel, *I Never Promised You a Rose Garden* (pap., NAL, $2.95), written under the name of Hannah Green. It tells the deeply disturbing story of a young girl's battle against schizophrenia. Since then Greenberg has written many other novels suitable for young adults, including *In This Sign* (pap., Henry Holt, $5.95), a story that tellingly probes the inner world of the deaf. *Simple Gifts* is a good-natured, often humorous and tender story of a backwoods family and how sudden affluence affects it. It is read and enjoyed by senior high students.

Plot Summary

To be sure, the Fleuris are not your average American family. And it's not just because they live on an isolated ranch in Colorado, or because the place is, to be honest, somewhat in need of repair. After all, the Fleuris are poor and there just isn't money for improvements. And it isn't just that they sell moonshine to the local jail, or keep an illegal herd of Texas longhorns in the mountains. It's more than just the Fleuris themselves; some of the townsfolk regard them as eccentric, even shiftless, and perhaps not quite all there. And perhaps they are misfits, but if so, they are totally engaging.

The father is Akin Fleuri, a rather gruff, secretive individual, not given to many words, but given to the odd habit of going into what the family calls his "sleeps," periods during the day when he just lies down and goes to sleep for a spell, whatever he's doing.

Mother is Mary Beth, a charming eccentric who dreams of champagne parties with Japanese lanterns strewn about the ranch and who oftentimes mixes up sugar and flour when cooking and whom the children regard with bemused love and affection.

The oldest is Robert Luther, 18, patient, hard-working, and dreaming of the unheard-of possibility that he can go to college. Next comes Kate, 15, smart, charming, and attractive, who also hopes that somehow extra schooling is in the future. The two youngest are Louise, 12, the smartest in school and the family writer, and Kate, 6, whom her mother thinks of as the fairy child.

Into the family one day comes Mr. Kelvin from SCELP—the Social, Cultural, and Ethnic Life Placement program. He has a novel idea. He wants to turn the Fleuri ranch back a century so that visitors can come and sample life as it was lived by the original homesteaders in 1880. The Fleuris will have to dress and live as the homesteaders did when visitors are around; in return, the ranch will be repaired and put in good working order. The program will pay for the visitors' food and lodging and the visitors will help on the ranch so that the program will pay for itself. All this is part of a new government effort to preserve authentic homesteads.

Although the children are enthusiastic right away, father Fleuri definitely is not, being somewhat worried about the moonshine and the illegal cattle. However, with the entire family against him, he finally gives in, and the program begins.

At first things seem to go smoothly. In fact, mother Fleuri, who was used to being shunned by the townspeople, one day finds herself the center of attention in the market as she tells of how they have returned the ranch to the 1880s and of the people visiting from all over the country.

The first visitors are a stockbroker and an agent from New York and their three children. The Fleuris are sorry to see them go. And there are the Lewises who became somewhat emotionally and physically aroused witnessing the Fleuris butcher steers. And there is Dr. Van Houghton who figures out what father Fleuri's "sleeps" mean. He diagnoses them as narcolepsy, a brain disorder, and the doctor is amazed at the four healthy, bright children born into this family. Meantime, the doctor's wife introduces Robert Luther to the wonders of love.

The Fleuris and their "city" visitors have many misadventures, but all in all the program seems to be working well, except that Mr. Kelvin, who started it all, is unhappy. The Fleuris are just costing him far too much money, for clothing, and repairs, and supplies, and what all. His complaints fall on deaf ears, although finally the Fleuris suggest a big Fourth of July picnic at the ranch for all those involved in the SCELP program so that they can see just what is going on.

That proves to be the biggest mistake of all. First a big panel television

truck comes up the road to take in the happening, and then, somehow—
and the Fleuris never are sure how—the illegal cattle get loose and stam-
pede the picnic, knocking over the television truck and lots of people.

Miraculously, no one is killed, although some people are injured, including Mr. Kelvin, who collapses from the shock of it all. But that ends
the project. The visitors stop coming, the townspeople go back to regarding the Fleuris as eccentric or worse, and the Fleuris themselves, although never quite the same again, figure that they have been fairly
successful; they had gone back and had been as clever and strong as the
real pioneers. Louise decides to write the whole experience down in
poetry.

Thematic Material

This is a fun, offbeat story of an eccentric family with a great deal of
charm and spunk, and a loving, close relationship among the members.
It also shows how a good idea can sometimes work too well, and that
"authentic" isn't necessarily "real."

Book Talk Material

The individual thoughts and feelings of the family members are a
good introduction to this amusing story of life and love in a group of
eccentrics. See: Jane talks about Mr. Kelvin (pp. 18–23); Kate muses
about the program and worries about how visitors will respond to her
mother (pp. 30–31); mother, Mary Beth, regards the entire family as a
kind of miracle (pp. 58–62).

Additional Selections

Joanne Greenberg explores the world of the blind and deaf through
the viewpoint of 25-year-old John Moon in *Of Such Small Differences*
(Henry Holt, 1988, $18.45).

Alternating between hilarity and tragedy, Marianne Gingher's *Bobby
Rex's Greatest Hits* (Atheneum, 1986, $17.95) tells how the heroine of a
pop song handles her life after its release.

A young farm boy remembers his family and bizarre relations in the
seriocomic *I Am One of You Forever* by Fred Chappell (Louisiana State
Univ., 1984, $14.95). *My Name Is Aram* by William Saroyan (Harcourt,
1950, $8.95) tells humorous anecdotes about an Armenian-American
family.

When Maria inherits millions from her father she creates an ideal community only for teenagers in Julian F. Thompson's *The Taking of Mariasburg* (Scholastic, 1988, $12.95).

An unwanted and persecuted dwarf finds her destiny in rural Montana during the 1940s in Jeanne Dixon's *The Tempered Wind* (Atheneum, 1987, $13.95).

A small Gerogia town is scandalized by the humorous doings of a grandfather at the turn of the century in Olive Ann Burns's *Cold Sassy Tree* (Ticknor, 1984, $16.95; pap., Dell, $6.95).

In Mary-Ann Tirone's touching but very funny novel *The Book of Phoebe* (Doubleday, 1985, $14.95; pap., Dell, $5.50), a Yale senior goes to Paris to have her illegitimate baby.

A bumbling British agent tries to seduce a Russian chess player in Marc Lovell's *Good Spies Don't Grow on Trees* (Doubleday, 1986, $12.95).

Stella Gibbons's *Cold Comfort Farm* (Peter Smith, n.d., $12.95; pap., Penguin, $3.95) is the English comic classic about the dizzy Starkadder family.

About the Book
Book Report, November 1986, p. 28.
Booklist, February 1, 1987, p. 837.
Library Journal, August 1986, p. 80.
New York Times Book Review, October 12, 1986, p. 38.
School Library Journal, September 1986, p. 152.
VOYA, August/October 1986, p. 144.

About the Author
Colby, Vineta, ed. *World Authors 1975–1980.* New York: Wilson, 1985, pp. 299–301.
Harte, Barbara, and Riley, Carolyn, eds. *Contemporary Authors* (First Revision). Detroit: Gale, 1969. Vol. 5, p. 476.
Metzger, Linda, ed. *Contemporary Authors* (New Revision Series). Detroit: Gale, 1985. Vol. 14, pp. 203–205.

Hamilton, Virginia.   *A Little Love*
Philomel, 1984, $10.95

During her career in writing juvenile literature, Virginia Hamilton has received all the major national awards in this field. For example, *M. C. Higgins the Great* (Macmillan, 1974, $10.95; pap., Dell, $2.50; condensed

in *More Juniorplots,* Bowker, 1977, pp. 195–199), received both the Newbery Medal and the National Book Award, and *Sweet Whispers, Brother
Rush* (Philomel, 1982, $10.95; pap., Avon, $2.25; condensed in *Juniorplots 3,* Bowker, 1987, pp. 166–170), was given the Coretta Scott King
Award and the Boston Globe–Horn Book Award.

A Little Love and the book that follows it, *A White Romance* (Philomel,
1987, $14.95), were both written for an older audience than her previous
books. In *A White Romance* she expands into new territory by exploring
drugs, the rock scene, and premarital love relationships set against a
high school background. Both are suitable for readers in grades 9
through 12. *A Little Love* takes place in an Ohio town during late spring
1982.

Plot Summary

Sheema Hadley is 17, fat, black, and full of anxieties. She cries frequently and for no apparent reason. Many of her worries are somewhat
vague, like a fear of being incinerated when the Bomb drops; others are
more concrete, like the emptiness she feels about the absence of both her
father, Cruze Hadley, a man she knows only from photographs, and her
mother, Guida, who died before Sheema's days of remembering. Some
of this emptiness is filled by her vast consumption of food, as well as by
her loving grandparents and by her equally loving boyfriend, Forrest
Jones, who lives with his divorced tyrannical father. Sheema met Forrest
shortly after she transferred for this, her junior year, to Harrison Joint
Vocational School, where she and Forrest are both studying food services. Sheema was always conscientious but very slow in school, particularly in reading, but in her new school she is doing well and particularly
enjoys the classes on food preparation conducted by Miz Sherman.

Sheema has been raised by Granmom and Grandpa Jackson, both of
whom are now in their late seventies and, though forced to live very
frugally, are still happily married. Sheema thinks that her grandfather
might be guilty of some philandering because he spends much of his free
time at a storefront senior center. Granmom, who is becoming increasingly forgetful, prefers to stay home, watch her stories on afternoon
television, and visit with old friends like Miz Iris Tibbs.

On a typical school day, Sheema suffers taunts about her weight when
she enters the bus. She sits alone until Forrest enters. Although the two
share the same classes, they try to remain apart until after school when
they usually go for a ride in Forrest's old Dodge. After making dinner

for her grandparents, Sheema will do a little homework and go to bed, but often in the middle of the night she steals out to meet Forrest and in his car and on some deserted roadway, he parks and they make love.

Granmom often tells Sheema that she has inherited her father's hands. He was a sign painter and like him, her hands are those of an artist, long and slender. Sheema becomes obsessed with a desire to find her father and persuades Forrest to help her search for him when school is out.

One afternoon Granmom shows Sheema an album of drawings and plans for signs her father had left behind. This later produces such a barrage of questions from Sheema that her grandparents tell her the truth about her past. Her mother died of hemorrhaging immediately after Sheema's birth, and Cruze, hearing of his wife's death, left town without ever seeing his child, although he occasionally still sends money for her support. Sheema is devastated by the news. She believes she is responsible both for her mother's death and her father's departure. Under this burden of guilt and stress, she begins to skip school, staying in bed most days and having spells of inconsolable sobbing. The combined pressures of her grandparents and Forrest force her, however, to return to school in time for the end of school exams.

Now Sheema increases preparation for setting forth with Forrest to search for her father. When Granmom begins attending the senior center and entering into its activities, she feels less apprehensive about leaving the old woman behind.

On the Monday after exams, Sheema bids her grandparents good-bye and leaves with Forrest in his Dodge. Together they have $600, $100 of which was given to Sheema by her grandparents together with a note stating that Cruze's last address was Jellico, Tennessee. After a day's drive they arrive in Jellico but find no trace of him in the telephone book. They continue south hoping to see some of his artwork on highway signboards. As the excitement of their quest increases, so does Sheema's appetite. She consumes mountains of burgers and fries.

On the banks of the Tennessee River one evening, they pause to see in the distance the lights of the 1982 World's Fair in Knoxville. Before they can find a cheap motel, the car has a flat tire and they are terrified of having to ask for help in the completely white middle class neighborhood where they are stranded. One resident, however, calls a towing service and the driver, a black man named Sam, takes them to his garage where he also has a room that they rent for the night.

In the morning Forrest purchases two new tires from Sam, who also supplies them with valuable information, because he had in the past used the service of Cruze Hadley and knows that he now lives in Dalton, Georgia.

The two press on. In the Dalton phone book they find an entry for Cruze Signs Pro-Art and proceed to that address. Outside the house they see a woman playing with two children, and inside the adjoining studio they see a dignified man, whom Sheema recognizes as her father, conducting an art class. They enter the studio and as Cruze approaches them, Sheema's eyes well up with tears and she murmurs, "You could've called."

Although Cruze is cordial and welcoming, Sheema knows that in his life devoted to his work and a new wife and family, there is no place for her. She and Forrest leave. On their way home, Forrest proposes marriage and she accepts for a date after they graduate.

The Jacksons are delighted to see their granddaughter return so soon, and Sheema is also glad to be back, now somehow freed from the nagging tensions and questions about her past and her father. She senses a peacefulness within her—a restfulness that almost miraculously has even lessened her appetite.

Thematic Material

This is a story of a pathetic girl wracked with fears and conflicts looking for the security of a family and father she has never known and the inner peace she achieves through completing her quest. It is also the story of two trusting innocents and the purity of their love, a kind of love that is mirrored in the lasting marriage still shared by the grandparents. Many sorts of family relationships are explored, particularly that of a daughter with her father and grandparents. Bulimia and its causes are explored and the author has produced a convincing picture of students in a vocational high school setting.

Book Talk Material

An introduction to Sheema and her problems should interest readers. Some useful passages are: Miz Sherman's class learns about lettuces (pp. 27–31); Sheema and Forrest talk after school (pp. 44–49); Granmom and Miz Tibbs watch television (pp. 59–66); Sheema leaves the house at night to meet Forrest (pp. 80–91); she examines her father's portfolio (pp. 111–114); and she learns about her parents (pp. 118–124).

Additional Selections

In Walter Dean Myers's *Motown and Didi: A Love Story* (Viking, 1984, $12.95), two Harlem teenagers fall in love and try to beat the drug culture surrounding them.

Two unalike black girls form a friendship in Harlem in Rosa Guy's *The Friends* (Henry Holt, 1973, $10.95).

In Walter Dean Myers's *Crystal* (Viking, 1987, $12.95), a black teenage model must decide the limits to which she will go to further her career.

Misfits Rita Formica and boyfriend Arnold Bromberg find love and early marriage in Barbara Wersba's trilogy whose titles are *Fat* (Harper, 1987, $11.25), *Love Is a Crooked Thing* (Harper, 1987, $11.70), and *Beautiful Losers* (Harper, 1978, $11.95).

A 32-year-old bridgeworker and a homeless 16-year-old girl find love in Phyllis Naylor's *Unexpected Pleasures* (Putnam, 1986, $17.95).

In Rosa Guy's *My Love, My Love; or, the Peasant Girl* (Holt, 1985, $12.45) there is a tragic love between a peasant girl and a rich mulatto on a Caribbean island.

A 23-year-old failed rock musician, *Cooder Cutlas* (Harper, 1987, $13.95), has an affair with a 17-year-old girl in the novel by Elizabeth Bales Frank.

A 17-year-old black student's life changes when his older brother, a heroin addict, returns home in Sharon Bell Mathis's *A Teacup Full of Roses* (pap., Penguin, $3.95).

In the nonfictional *Runaway* by Lucy Irvine (Random, 1987, $18.95), a rebellious English girl flees a painful family situation.

About the Book
Booklist, June 1, 1984, p. 1392; June 15, 1986, p. 1529.
Bulletin of the Center for Children's Books, September 1984, p. 6.
Horn Book, September 1984, p. 597.
School Library Journal, October 1984, p. 167.
VOYA, December 1984, p. 263.
See also *Book Review Digest*, 1985, p. 673, and *Book Review Index*, 1984, p. 306; 1985, p. 265.

About the Author
Block, Ann, and Riley, Carolyn, eds. *Children's Literature Review*. Detroit: Gale, 1976. Vol. 2, p. 103–107.
Commire, Anne, ed. *Something about the Author*. Detroit: Gale, 1973. Vol. 4, pp. 97–99.

de Montreville, Doris, and Crawford, Elizabeth D., eds. *Fourth Book of Junior Authors and Illustrators.* New York: Wilson, 1978, pp. 162–164.

Estes, Glenn E., ed. *American Writers for Children since 1960: Fiction (Dictionary of Literary Biography,* Vol. 52). Detroit: Gale, 1986, pp. 174–184.

Kirkpatrick, D. L., ed. *Twentieth-Century Children's Writers* (2nd edition). New York: St. Martin's, 1983, pp. 353–354.

Nasso, Christine, ed. *Contemporary Authors* (First Revision Series). Detroit: Gale, 1977. Vols. 25–28, p. 299.

Senick, Gerard J., ed. *Children's Literature Review.* Detroit: Gale, 1986. Vol. 11, pp. 54–95.

Kerr, M. E.   *Night Kites*
Harper, 1986, $11.50, pap. $2.75 (same pagination)

In her young adult novels, M. E. Kerr often uses locales that are similar to places where she has lived. *If I Love You, Am I Trapped Forever?* (Harper, 1973, $12.89; pap., Dell, $2.25) is set in an upstate New York town, Cayuta, not unlike the author's hometown of Auburn. Brooklyn Heights, the location of her residence at the beginning of her writing career, is used as the setting of her first young adult novel, *Dinky Hocker Shoots Smack* (Harper, 1972, $12.89; pap., Dell, $2.95). She has also frequently used, as in *Night Kites,* Seaville, New York, a thinly disguised version of East Hampton, the author's present home. Once a whaling port in post-Revolutionary times, it is now a fashionable resort town for New Yorkers, close to Montauk Point at the tip of Long Island. The conflict between the life-styles and values of the affluent transients and the year-round residents has provided background material for Kerr's *Gentlehands* (Harper, 1978, $11.89; pap., Bantam, $2.50; condensed in *Juniorplots 3,* Bowker, 1987, pp. 48–52) and more recently *Fell* (Harper, 1987, $11.95). In the latter, a young teenager, John Fell, one of the have-nots, loses his high school sweetheart because of class differences and therefore readily accepts a tantalizing proposition to change places with the scion of one of Seaville's posh families and attend exclusive Gardner School. In contrast to her other novels, *Night Kites* is the darkest in tone. It deals essentially with a series of painful losses experienced by the teenage hero during a three-month period. Those include the loss of friendships and love relationships, as well as the imminent loss of his beloved older brother to AIDS. It is recommended to readers in grades 9 to 12.

Plot Summary

Erick Rudd, the narrator, is 17 and beginning his senior year at Seaville High. His father, Arthur Rudd, is a partner in the successful New York investment firm of Rudd and Lundgren. During the week Mr. Rudd lives in the city, some three hours away by car, but spends free moments with his wife and their son in their country house. The other member of the family is Erick's adored older brother, Pete, age 27. Pete is a private person, something of a loner, who dropped out of his Ph.D. program at Princeton and, much to his father's distress, is now teaching languages in a private school, living in a sublet Greenwich Village apartment, and aspiring to write science fiction. Erick often remembers that when he was only five his brother made him a night kite with little battery lights on it. To Erick, Pete has always been like that kite in the night sky—solitary, independent, and unafraid.

Erick's steady girlfriend is Dill, short for Marion Dilberto, an "all-American" girl—popular, dependable, ethical, and a good student. His best friend from childhood is another classmate, Jack Case, who like Erick is a disgruntled virgin. Jack is infatuated with his new girlfriend, Nicki Marr, and hopes that with her he will soon change his sexual status. Nicki is perhaps the most complex of the group. She lives alone with her father, Cap Marr, owner and proprietor of a seedy hotel complex, Kingdom by the Sea, named by Annabelle, Nicki's deceased mother, a psychic who claimed to be a descendant of Edgar Allan Poe. Nicki has a reputation for being fast, punky, and like Erick's brother a loner, and she has an encyclopedic knowledge of rock music and its stars. She has had a series of hoods as boyfriends, like Walter Ruski—Ski for short—who dresses in leather and rides a Kawasaki. Although she is trendy, unconventional, and sometimes vulgar, she cannot be considered trash, just different and more honest than her classmates. At present she is fond of Jack, but she does not share his ardor or yearnings.

Pete returns home for a weekend and announces that he might have sold one of his literary works. He attempts to be his usual affable self with Erick and his admiring mother and continues to exchange barbs with his somewhat stuffy, conformist father, but he is obviously very ill and has lost a great deal of weight. This he attributes to a dysentery infection.

To celebrate Jack's eighteenth birthday, Nicki has suggested to Erick that the two couples spend a weekend in New York at his father's apartment and attend a Bruce Springsteen concert. Mr. Rudd vetoes having both couples stay alone at this place. On the sly before he returns to the city, Pete offers his apartment and even arranges for them to purchase tickets to the show. The trip into town is somewhat stressful because Dill and Nicki have little in common, and Dill resents the attention Nicki pays to Erick. During the afternoon Dill takes Erick to Washington Heights to visit her Aunt Lana, who has conveniently lied about Dill's home for the weekend so that the two can stay together. When they return to Pete's apartment Erick's father is there. Pete has been in the hospital for tests, but is expected back in the apartment the next day. Therefore, Mr. Rudd escorts all four to his home.

In spite of all this, the concert is a great success with Nicki's performance in the audience a near rival to Springsteen's on stage. Back at the apartment, Jack gets tipsy and falls asleep, and Dill goes to bed. When Nicki and Erick are alone, she grabs him and kisses him passionately. Within seconds Mr. Rudd enters and asks Erick to join him in the study. He has terrible news. After swearing Erick to secrecy, he tells him that his brother has AIDS. He also learns that Pete is a homosexual. Erick is stunned. The only homosexual he has ever known is the local undertaker, Charlie Gilhooley, the target for derision and recently the center of a fag-bashing incident.

The next day Erick visits Pete. His brother talks about being gay, how he had told their mother only a year ago, but that his homosexuality had always been a secret part of his life, to the point of even naming his dog, now ancient and about to be put to sleep, Oscar, short for Oscar Wilde. Although Pete remains in New York, his illness is an all-pervasive presence in the family in Seaville, each trying to understand but none able to accept.

As well, Erick finds to his disgust and guilt that there is a growing mutual attraction with Nicki. She uses every possible opportunity to be with him. Unsuspecting Jack comes one Saturday night to talk to Erick about Nicki's growing coldness. Unfortunately he sits on a newly painted chair and must strip to his shorts. In an act of compassion, Erick puts his arm around his friend. Mr. Rudd enters and immediately jumps to the wrong conclusion.

The next morning a resentful Erick explains his innocent situation to his father. A violent quarrel erupts and Erick leaves his parents and hitches a ride to Kingdom by the Sea, hoping for solace from Nicki. He receives more than that. After bathing nude in the hotel's swimming pool, they make love in her bedroom. Before leaving, Erick kisses her passionately outside the hotel. In the distance they see Jack staring at them from his car.

Erick has lied to both Dill and Jack. In an attempted reconciliation during the annual ring dance to which he has taken Nicki, Erick approaches Jack who punches him out, almost breaking his nose.

Unable to live by himself, Pete is forced to move to his parents' home. In spite of attempts at secrecy, soon the community knows of Pete's illness. Many are openly hostile and uncomprehending, including Nicki, who breaks off the relationship with Erick. He is crushed and alone but will survive—besides there is still Pete to care for.

Thematic Material

This novel depicts a young man's coming to terms with his own and his brother's sexuality. It is a book about terminations, of life (even their dog is put to sleep), friendship, and love. It explores many aspects of boy–girl and parent relationships. A spectrum of attitudes about homosexuality, from open hostility and incomprehension to full acceptance, is depicted. This is also the first young adult novel to deal honestly with AIDS and the conflict within a family torn between attitudes about gays and love of a family member. The concepts of loyalty, guilt, and family solidarity are also explored. Rock music and its stars form a backdrop to much of the action.

Book Talk Material

Introducing Erick and his friends until he learns of Pete's condition should interest readers. Some specific passages are: Erick and Pete fly the night kite and discuss their father (pp. 12–16); the trip to New York (pp. 17–21); the concert (pp. 76–79); Mr. Rudd tells Erick about Pete and AIDS (pp. 86–88); and Pete and Erick talk about the meaning of being gay (pp. 94–100).

Additional Selections

In Gloria Miklowitz's *Goodbye Tomorrow* (Delacorte, 1987, $13.95), Alex, a teenager who is diagnosed with AIDS from a blood transfusion, confronts a variety of reactions from friends and family.

Chris Oyler in *Go Toward This Light* (Harper, 1988, $15.85) tells of the suffering and death of her nine-year-old hemophiliac son from AIDS.

In the novel by Alice Hoffman, *At Risk* (Putnam, 1988, $17.95), 11-

year-old Amanda has AIDS, and reactions are varied in her small New England community.

In a humorous novel with serious messages about AIDS and homosexuality, a teenager gets to know his gay uncle in Ron Koertge's *The Arizona Kid* (Little, 1988, $14.95).

Some nonfiction books on AIDS are: John Langone's *AIDS: The Facts* (Little, 1988, $17.95, pap. $8.95); *AIDS*, edited by Lynn Hall and Thomas Modl (Greenhaven, 1987, $13.95; pap. $6.95), and Paul Harding Douglas's *The Essential AIDS Fact Book* (pap., Pocket, $3.95).

Robin Gregory, age 17, finds she has leukemia but gains strength from fellow patient Rick in Jean Ferris's *Invincible Summer* (Farrar, 1987, $12.95).

Brotherly love is depicted in Tim Rumsey's *Pictures from a Trip* (Morrow, 1985, $15.95), a rowdy novel in which two brothers in their twenties set out across Montana.

In Robert Lehrman's *Juggling* (Harper, 1982, $11.25), a high school student suffers through first love and rejection from the soccer team.

About the Book
Book Report, January 1987, p. 36.
Booklist, April 1, 1986, p. 1135.
Bulletin of the Center for Children's Books, May 1986, p. 169.
Horn Book, September 1986, p. 597.
New York Times Book Review, April 13, 1986, p. 30.
School Library Journal, May 1986, p. 104; September 1986, p. 47; March 1987, p. 120; September 1987, p. 129.
VOYA, June 1986, p. 80.
See also *Book Review Digest,* 1987, p. 1002, and *Book Review Index,* 1986, p. 401; 1987, p. 417.

About the Author
Commire, Anne, ed. *Something about the Author.* Detroit: Gale, 1980. Vol. 20, pp. 124–126 (under Marijane Meaker).
de Montreville, Doris, and Crawford, Elizabeth D., eds. *Fourth Book of Junior Authors and Illustrators.* New York: Wilson, 1978, pp. 210–212.
Kirkpatrick, D. L., ed. *Twentieth-Century Children's Writers* (2nd edition). New York: St. Martin's, 1983, pp. 428–429.
May, Hal, ed. *Contemporary Authors.* Detroit: Gale, 1983. Vol. 107, pp. 332–336 (under Marijane Meaker).
Nilsen, Alleen Pace. *Presenting M. E. Kerr.* Schenectady: Twayne, 1986.
Sarkissian, Adele, ed. *Something about the Author: Autobiography Series.* Detroit: Gale, 1986. Vol. 1, pp. 141–154.

Who's Who in America: 1986–1987 (44th edition). Chicago: Marquis Who's Who, 1986. Vol. 2, p. 1902 (under Marijane Meaker).

MacLean, John. *Mac*
Houghton, 1987, $12.95

This is an unusual, disturbing novel by a relative newcomer to the field of young adult literature. With restraint and tact, the author tells of a boy's sexual molestation by a medical doctor. It is narrated by Mac, an average youngster who daydreams about sex, plays soccer, and suffers bouts of self-doubt, and is divided roughly into two parts; the first, until the medical examination, and the second, when the story resumes several weeks later. It is suitable for readers in grades 8 through 12.

Plot Summary

Mac certainly qualifies as your all-American 14-year-old: curly haired, likable, gets good grades, on the high school soccer team, has lots of friends and a loving family, and the new girl in school, Jenny of the beautiful dark hair, seems to like him.

Actually, things couldn't be better. Tongue-tied though Mac is, Jenny actually stops to talk to him, and stupid as he sounds to himself, they actually make a date to go to the dance together. Wonder of wonders, thinks Mac, he's on top of the world. About the only boring event coming up is the stupid physical exam that all the soccer players have to take to qualify for the team. . . .

So, if things are so wonderful for the all-American boy, how come they suddenly change? Mac flunks some classes, punches out one of his friends, ignores the beautiful Jenny, and is sarcastic and rude to his family. He just doesn't feel good about anything anymore, not about school, or Jenny, or himself. And certainly not about his family. Where before Mac had regarded his funny family—his mother is a practicing lawyer and his father takes care of the house—which includes six-year-old twin boys, as warm and special; now they only annoy him.

No amount of concern from his family or from Jenny, or even from the school principal, who learns of his inattentiveness and rudeness in class, seems to make any difference to Mac. He just doesn't care.

The principal finally sends Mac to a counselor. But the two just don't hit it off. So the principal calls in Mac's family and he is given an ultimatum. Either he tries another counselor or he goes to see the principal every day. Sullenly, Mac chooses another counselor.

Mrs. Resnick turns out to be red-haired and somewhat different than Mac had imagined. At their first session, they spend the time driving in her car and end up eating pancakes. She doesn't even ask Mac about anything—not that he was going to talk anyway. But what kind of a counselor is this, he wonders.

Then Mrs. Resnick asks him to draw up a list of questions she should ask him, just so she doesn't step on his toes since he doesn't want to talk about anything. Mac thinks the counselor is off her rocker. And when she cancels an appointment with him, he really gets mad.

Although Mrs. Resnick has Mac slightly off guard by this time, he is still as tormented as before, still as sullen and argumentative. It is as though this fun-loving boy had just disappeared and another taken his place. But Mrs. Resnick is not so oblivious to what is troubling Mac as he would believe. One day when Mac shows up for their meeting, she introduces him to a male doctor, a Dr. Amidon. Leaving Mac alone with the doctor, Mrs. Resnick tells him there are just some things that perhaps she and Mac can't talk about—like issues of sex and sexual identity.

As the counselor leaves the room and Dr. Amidon stands in front of him, suddenly Mac begins to scream and call for her. When Mac comes to, Mrs. Resnick is beside him. She tells him that it is time that they talk. "Somebody's really hurt you, Mac," she says, "worse than I thought."

Painful as it is, Mac's secret is uncovered. He was sexually molested by the doctor at the soccer physical. Since that time he has been frightened and angry, not sure if the assault meant that now he is gay, not sure what his friends would think of him if they knew, not sure what his family would say, not sure if Jenny would still like him.

With warmth and compassion, Mrs. Resnick tries to tell Mac that he has no guilt in the terrible thing that happened to him. That just like women who are raped, he, too, is a victim. It was not his fault. It is never the child's fault, she says.

Frightened to admit the truth at first, Mac listens as Mrs. Resnick tells him that his parents must be called and told the truth. He does not want them to know, but when they do come and, after learning the truth, treat him with the love and understanding they have always shown, one part of the terror dies away.

To help him on the road to healing, Mrs. Resnick introduces him to other youngsters who have suffered similar experiences, and he learns how they have coped with the same feelings he has been going through.

Then Mac must endure the questioning and taking of his statement by a social worker. Without the help of his counselor, he does not feel he could endure it. But he does, and perhaps his statement will save other children from the terrible thing he has suffered.

And, of course, there is Jenny. But Mac must find the courage to do this on his own. Standing with her in the cold, next to the ice-filled river, Mac tells her what happened to him.

"Why didn't you tell me?" she says. "You could have talked to me."

It will take time, and perhaps Mac will never be quite the light-hearted boy of a few months back, but he is well on the way to being all-American "Mac" again.

Thematic Material

The sexual abuse of children is the all-too-prevalent and terrifying theme that is handled with dignity and understanding in this very believable story of a young boy sexually assaulted by the doctor who is supposed to be examining him. The character changes in Mac are believable as the reader, given a hint of what has occurred at the beginning, follows Mac in his hurt and fright as he battles alone in a now-alien world. The family relationships are warmly portrayed, as is the feeling of "first love" between Mac and Jenny.

Book Talk Material

Mac's experience in the examining room and the changes in his personality can be used to begin a discussion of sexual abuse of young children, what safeguards children can take to protect themselves, and what they should do if they suffer such a devastating experience. See: Mac meets Jenny before the soccer physical (pp. 18–20); Mac makes Jenny laugh (pp. 23–29); the physical (pp. 48–50); Mac talks about his dream (pp. 56–59); he fights with his mother (pp. 64–67); and the first meeting with Dr. Resnick (pp. 95–99).

Additional Selections

A Mexican teenage waif and an alcoholic American sergeant make an unlikely pair in Gary Paulsen's *The Crossing* (Watts, 1987, $11.95).

Two adults become involved in helping a 16-year-old victim of child abuse in Judith Guest's *Second Heaven* (Viking, 1982, $14.95; pap., NAL, $3.95).

An abused eight-year-old forms a friendship with a recluse during World War II in London in Michelle Magorian's *Good Night, Mr. Tom* (Harper, 1982, $13.70, pap. $3.95).

For mature readers, use Sylvia Fraser's true account of her father's physical abuse, *My Father's House: A Memoir of Incest and of Healing* (Ticknor, 1988, $17.95).

With the help of a nurse, a teenage epileptic escapes from a mental ward in the nonfiction *Rusty's Story* by Carol Gino (pap., Bantam, $3.95).

Jennings Michael Burch tells of three years of his life as an emotionally and physically abused child in *They Cage the Animals at Night* (NAL, 1984, $14.95, pap. $3.95).

A lonely girl becomes victim of her father's sexual abuse in Patricia Hermes's *A Solitary Secret* (Harcourt, 1985, $11.95), and in Hadley Irwin's *Abbey, My Love* (Atheneum, 1985, $11.95; pap., NAL, $2.50), Chip discovers his girlfriend has been sexually abused by her father.

An unhappy family life drives teenage Geri into alcoholism in Sandra Scoppetone's *The Late Great Me* (pap., Bantam, $2.95).

Lynn B. Daugherty's nonfictional *Why Me?* (pap., Mother Courage, 1985, $7.95) has as a subtitle "Help for Victims of Child Sexual Abuse (Even If They Are Adults Now)."

About the Book
Booklist, October 1, 1987, p. 244.
Bulletin of the Center for Children's Books, December 1987, p. 70.
Horn Book, March 1988, p. 209.
School Library Journal, November 1987, p. 116.
VOYA, October 1987, p. 203.
See also *Book Review Index*, 1988.

Marshall, Catherine. *Julie*
McGraw, 1984, $15.95

Catherine Marshall's first book was *Mr. Jones, Meet the Master* (o.p.), a collection of her husband's sermons when he was chaplain to the U.S. Senate from 1947 to 1948. She also wrote about her husband after his death in *A Man Called Peter* (pap., Avon, $4.50). Her first novel was

Christy (McGraw, 1968, $14.95; pap., Revell, $4.50), a fictionalized account of her mother's experience as a teacher in the mountains of Tennessee. It begins in 1912 and with religious overtones deals with such crises as school discipline problems, a typhoid epidemic, bootlegging, and an awakening romance. *Julie* is her second novel. Marshall died in March 1983. Both *Christy* and *Julie* are enjoyed by girls in the high school grades.

Plot Summary

This story, set in the depression years of the 1930s, concerns an 18-year-old high school senior and struggling journalist in a small, flood-prone town in western Pennsylvania. Julie Paige Wallace, her brother, Tim, and sister, Anne-Marie, travel with their parents to the small town of Alderton, where their father has bought the town newspaper, *The Sentinel.* Kenneth Wallace, who has left the ministry and suffers from malaria, has taken the money initially set aside for the children's college education to start a new life for the family. After school hours, Julie is to become his assistant.

Almost from their arrival in late summer 1934, Julie and the Wallace family realize that Alderton is dominated by two presences: the Yoder Iron and Steel Company, which controls much of the labor and wealth in the town, and the dam, which holds back the waters of Lake Kissawha and overlooks the unappealing little mining community.

For Julie, there is a third "presence" as well in the person of Randolph Wilkinson, a wealthy Englishman who is the assistant manager of the Hunting and Fishing Club on the lake. Julie experiences love at first sight, although Randolph shows nothing beyond a friendly interest in her.

Life is not easy for the Wallace family and money is scarce for everyone in the years of the Great Depression. But more and more Julie grows to love her work at the newspaper and, with her father's reluctant assent, takes on more and more reporting assignments.

Julie often hears stories in the town of the frequent floodings and destruction, and more sinister stories of faulty repairs to the dam or incompetent construction. But such stories are denied or ignored by the officials of the Hunting and Fishing Club, who discourage any trespassing around the area of the dam.

But the following April the Wallace family experiences the horror of a flood firsthand as, after many days of rain, the surrounding rivers and creeks overflow their banks and spill into the town. Luckily for the family, the newspaper survives the damage with its press intact, although money is more scarce than before, and Julie must put aside her dream of college, at least for the present.

After the town of Alderton puts itself back together, the Wallace family becomes more involved, both personally and through the newspaper, in the affairs of the community, coming in conflict with both the officials of Yoder Iron and Steel, when their sympathies fall with the oppressed workers, and with those who resist all efforts to ascertain the true strength of the dam. However, they learn from a classmate of Julie's, Bryan McKeever, the grandson of the board chairman of Yoder Steel who is also head of the Hunting and Fishing Club, a possible reason why so many powerful townspeople resist all efforts to find out the true state of affairs at the dam. According to Bryan, Yoder has for years been dumping hot slag from the mill along the banks of the area's rivers and creeks. The slag hardens to rocklike consistency and decreases the river channels, making the likelihood of floods that much greater.

These issues also cause friction between Julie and Randolph, who now acknowledge their feelings for one another, even though the Englishman draws back from involvement, but find themselves on "different sides of the fence." However, Rand's conscience proves stronger than his family ties and he is instrumental in unearthing a lost file concerning the construction of the dam. It shows that an engineer's report pointed up three major defects to the dam, defects that Thomas McKeever had promised to correct but had not.

When Julie's father, with his daughter present, confronts McKeever, the official threatens *The Sentinel* with destruction if the facts are printed. And, indeed, the newspaper offices are severely damaged, but the editorial is printed anyway. And although *The Sentinel* is now threatened with extinction, the townspeople rally behind Julie's father.

But the fight between McKeever and Wallace becomes almost academic on September 21, 1935, when after another period of heavy rain, the dreaded news comes to the newspaper office. The dam has broken above Alderton! It takes just 27 minutes for the waters of Lake Kissawha to spill some 500 million tons of water into the valley. Reminiscent of the horrendous Johnstown Flood of 1889, the little mining community suffers a dreadful toll. Besides the great destruction, among the dead are Julie's brother, Tim, and Thomas McKeever.

After the flood, the community tries to rebuild. Randolph becomes the new partner in the newspaper. Tom McKeever, Jr., is expected to recognize the steelworkers' union, and Julie receives an education fund that enables her to enter Penn State to begin her college education.

The story ends when the narrator, Julie, many years later returns home with her family to visit her now elderly father. She and Randolph have married and have a son and a grandson. A modern concrete dam now controls the floodwaters above Alderton, and Julie Wallace Wilkinson is an established writer.

Thematic Material

This is a period novel about family life, about growing up and assuming responsibility, about falling in love. The close family relationships are well presented as is the moral fiber of the parents and of the time. Julie is shown as an intelligent young girl who keeps her family ties and responsibilities in perspective as she strives to fulfill her own career goals and romantic dreams.

Book Talk Material

The flood sequences may serve as an introduction to this book (see pp. 61–74, 76–78). Also of interest are Julie's reactions as romance begins to enter her life; see Julie daydreams about Randolph (pp. 97–98); the formal dance with Bryan McKeever (pp. 175–181); and the kiss (pp. 196–203).

Additional Selections

A doctor's wife cannot adjust to the lonely pioneer life in Nebraska in Pam Conrad's *Prairie Songs* (Harper, 1985, $10.89, pap. $2.95).

Frances Nolan's girlhood in early twentieth-century New York is recounted in Betty Smith's *A Tree Grows in Brooklyn* (pap., Harper, $4.95) and continued in *Tomorrow Will Be Better* (pap., Harper, $2.50).

Nineteen-year-old Pauline enrolls in a journalism school in Paris and falls in love in Janine Boissard's *A Time to Choose* (Little, 1985, $15.95; pap., Fawcett, $2.50).

In pioneer America, a 25-year-old woman moves west to marry a man she has never met in Margaret A. Robinson's *Courting Emma Howe* (Adler, 1987, $16.95).

Two girls exchange identities in Joan Aiken's light romance *If I Were You* (Doubleday, 1987, $16.95).

Modern women journalists and their problems are highlighted in *A Place in the News* by Kay Mills (Dodd, 1988, $17.95).

A white settler takes in a Cree boy despite community opposition in Luke Wallin's *In the Shadow of Wind* (Bradbury, 1984, $12.95).

A young woman who has grown up in a Kentucky mining town remembers the man responsible for her father's death when he begins courting her mother in *Good-bye and Keep Cold* by Jenny Davis (Watts, 1987, $12.95).

Ruth Gordon has an excellent collection of love poems in *Under All Silences* (Harper, 1987, $12.95).

About the Book
School Library Journal, January 1985, p. 92.
VOYA, February 1985, p. 329.
See also *Book Review Index,* 1985, p. 412.

About the Author
Commire, Anne, ed. *Something about the Author.* Detroit: Gale, 1971. Vol. 2, p. 182.
Evory, Ann, and Metzger, Linda, eds. *Contemporary Authors* (New Revision Series). Detroit: Gale, 1983. Vol. 8, p. 346.
Kinsman, Clare D., ed. *Contemporary Authors* (First Revision). Detroit: Gale, 1976. Vols. 17–20, pp. 477–478.

Naylor, Phyllis Reynolds. *The Year of the Gopher*
  Atheneum, 1987, $13.95; pap., Bantam, $2.95 (same pagination)

Naylor has written an amazing number of books for young people. Now numbering more than 50, they range from picture books to novels for junior to senior high students. In the latter categories are such highly acclaimed works as *A String of Chances* (Atheneum, 1982, $11.95; pap., Fawcett, $2.25), in which a young girl must reevaluate her values while spending a summer with her cousin, and *The Keeper* (Atheneum, 1986, $12.95), about a boy's relations with a father who becomes incapacitated. *The Year of the Gopher* takes place in Minnesota and is narrated by the hero, 17-year-old George Richards. Readers in grades 8 through 12 will identify with this plucky hero who decides to defy parental wishes and not attend college after high school graduation.

Plot Summary

On the surface at least, it seems as though 17-year-old George T. Richards is part of the all-American, midwestern, just-about-perfect family. His grandfather was a lawyer, his father is a lawyer, his mother is a teacher, his older sister is at Cornell, and George, in his last year of high school in Minneapolis, is busy filling out forms for all the "best" colleges in the East.

There are a few flies in the ointment, however. Trish, a sophomore at Cornell, has become engaged to Roger Blake Trenton, III, and is also nursing an ulcer, overachiever that she is. George's father, as George well realizes, sort of expects George to become a lawyer, too, even though George is not at all sure what he wants to do, or even if he wants to go to college at all. Then there is his younger sister, Jeri, with whom he doesn't communicate and with whom he can't get along, even though George realizes that it's sort of tough for her to follow in the footsteps of "perfect" Trish. And there is Ollie, the youngest and of whom George is genuinely fond; Ollie who frets over his schoolwork, but no matter how hard he tries just can't seem to keep up with the other "brains" in the family.

Little by little during that last year of high school the Richards family draws apart, as George becomes more and more rebellious and his parents push harder and harder for him to decide what he wants to do. When all his applications come back rejected from the eastern colleges (George sort of thinks he wants to go to the University of Minnesota anyway), his parents soon discover that he had made sure he wouldn't be accepted anywhere else by answering the application questions in a "smart aleck" manner. The great family "to-do" that follows prompts George to insist that he will not go to college at all.

Now practically no one in the family is speaking to each other. And when George is accepted at the University of Minnesota, he reluctantly turns it down because he has to stand by his word. He decides instead to go to work and show his parents that he can do what he says he will do.

After graduation George gets a job as a general handyman in a garden nursery; in other words, a "gopher." He likes the work, but he still isn't sure what he wants to do with his life. To complicate matters, he gets involved in a romantic relationship with Maureen, a classmate who has always had a crush on him. Although he enjoys this new awakening interest, George reluctantly admits to himself that he is just using Maureen; he doesn't really care for her. Trouble is, he just can't bring himself to break it off. And at work, an older woman seems to have the eye for him, too. Not knowing how to get out of that situation, George decides to quit his job and become a messenger, another "gopher" position.

George does finally find the courage to break off with Maureen, and he begins to date Anne, a girl he met at the nursery. He feels comfortable with her and able to talk about the things with his family that bother him.

It is after George's grandfather has a stroke, from which he will recover, that things begin to come together for the Richards family. George realizes from the conversation he overhears between his father and his aunt concerning where and how his grandfather will recuperate that his father had probably felt much the same as George does when he was young. George learns that his grandfather had chosen his father's career for him, just as George's father had tried to choose his. And George realizes that everyone goes on making mistakes throughout his or her life as one tries to find out what's best for oneself and for those one loves. Being grown up doesn't give you all the answers.

This new outlook allows George to try to find some answers of his own. With a new understanding, he tries to communicate with his sister, Jeri, and he tells his parents that, if the University of Minnesota will take him again, he plans to go there to study to become a school counselor. When Ollie then announces that he has decided to study to become a forest technician, George holds his breath. Can his father accept the fact that neither of his sons will follow in his footsteps?

But when his father remarks, "Maybe we've got enough lawyers in this family," George figures they might make it after all.

Of course, no one had figured on Jeri, who calmly tells them that she has decided to go to Radcliffe, and *she* just might end up being the lawyer!

Thematic Material

This is a story of a boy's coming of age, sexually and emotionally, and of how a family's relationships must grow and change as the children in the family grow up and become independent. George is portrayed as a likable young man who is genuinely confused about his future and the handling of his relationships with other people. All the family members are shown to be real people with real concerns and problems: the parents reluctant to let go of their authority and their own personal needs, the children unsure of themselves and rebellious, fighting to stand on their own, but afraid as well. A loving family story told with warmth and humor.

Book Talk Material

Readers will enjoy George's affectionate conversations with and concern for his brother, Ollie (see pp. 5–6, 59–61, 69–70, 77, 122–127). George's feelings about the growing estrangement of his family may start a discussion on what both parents and children have to do to keep a family happily together (see pp. 15–16, 20–22, 43–46, 47–50, 57–61).

Additional Selections

High school senior George Farina loses both his steady girlfriend and contact with his family in Harry Mazer's *City Light* (Scholastic, 1988, $12.95).

Two high school romances flourish and die in Bruce Hart and Carole Hart's *Breaking Up Is Hard to Do* (pap., Avon, $2.95).

James wants to be an artist but his parents object in Dennis Haseley's *The Counterfeiter* (Macmillan, 1987, $13.95).

A UCLA freshman is invited by an attractive fellow student to be her posslq (person of opposite sex sharing living quarters) in Eve Bunting's *Will You Be My Posslq?* (Harcourt, 1987, $12.95).

A teenage girl falls for an older man in Merrill Joan Gerber's *Marry Me Tomorrow* (pap., Fawcett, $2.50).

A high school senior moves to the country to help his family be reestablished on a farm in Alden R. Carter's *Growing Season* (Putnam, 1984, $13.95, pap. $2.25).

An assortment of wacky people pursues five children and an adult with a suitcase full of money in Rex Benedict's *Run for Your Sweet Life* (Farrar, 1987, $10.95).

Two unlikely companions are in danger of flunking out of college in W. E. Butterworth's *Flunking Out* (pap., Scholastic, $1.95).

Teenager Palmer has a crush on Liana, but they are competing for ownership of an old mansion in Peter Silgbee's *Love among the Hiccups* (Bradbury, 1987, $12.95). Also use Michael French's *Soldier Boy* (Putnam, 1986, $13.95; pap., Berkley, $3.95).

About the Book
Book Report, September 1987, p. 41.
Booklist, March 1, 1987, p. 1008.

Bulletin of the Center for Children's Books, May 1987, p. 175.
Horn Book, July 1987, p. 472.
School Library Journal, May 1987, p. 116.
VOYA, June 1987, p. 81.
See also *Book Review Digest,* 1987, p. 1347, and *Book Review Index,* 1987, p. 558.

About the Author
Commire, Anne, ed. *Something about the Author.* Detroit: Gale, 1977. Vol. 12, pp. 156–157.
Holtzer, Sally Holmes, ed. *Fifth Book of Junior Authors and Illustrators.* New York: Wilson, 1983, pp. 227–228.
Nasso, Christine, ed. *Contemporary Authors* (First Revision). Detroit: Gale, 1977. Vols. 21–24, p. 634.

Simon, Neil.   *Brighton Beach Memoirs*
Random, 1984, $10.95

This is the first title in Simon's semiautobiographical trilogy dealing with the making of a playwright. In the second, *Biloxi Blues* (Random, 1986, $11.95; pap., NAL, $5.95), the hero, Eugene Jerome, is in an army training camp where he humorously encounters the trauma of basic training and the effects of anti-Semitism. The third, *Broadway Bound* (Random, 1988, $11.95), returns Eugene to Brooklyn, where with his brother he begins his writing career. One of Simon's earliest successes, *Come Blow Your Horn,* though less autobiographical, continues the story of a budding writer. All these plays are suitable for senior high school readers.

Plot Summary
This two-act play, set in the lower middle-class neighborhood of Brighton Beach, Brooklyn, New York, is narrated by Eugene Morris Jerome, a bright 15-year-old who is destined to become a writer but who is currently torn between his desire to be a New York Yankee and his lust for girls.

It is the depression year of 1937. Crammed into the small frame house, not too far from the beach, are Jack and Kate, Eugene's parents, Eugene's older brother, Stanley, Kate's sister, Blanche, and her two daughters, Nora, 16 and adored by Eugene, and Laurie, who secretly annoys him because she has a "heart flutter" and never has to do anything around the house. Blanche and the girls moved in with the Jeromes after her husband died. The house is crowded, but the families manage to get along.

But on this day in September, the Jerome household is rife with crises. First, Nora comes home from dancing class to announce that she is quitting school for a career on Broadway. A producer came to the school and practically assured her that she will get a part in an upcoming show. Blanche is highly skeptical. After some sharp words it is decided that when "Uncle Jack" comes home, he will give an opinion on this matter. Uncle Jack is very fond of his niece, so Nora is confident of her success.

Then Stanley comes home and confides to Eugene that he has lost his $17-a-week job. This is a large part of the Jerome family income. Actually, Stanley has not lost his job—yet. He defended a black worker and in doing so insulted the boss; Stanley has been told to write a letter of apology by the next morning or lose his job. Stanley, remembering how has father has always told him to stand up for his principles, has no intention of writing the letter.

Eugene is sympathetic, but his mind soon wanders off to wishing that somehow he could see his cousin Nora without clothes on. Stanley confides that he actually accomplished this miracle by barging into the bathroom one day quite by accident. Eugene is overcome with envy.

Father Jack arrives home that night, looking tired and worn out as indeed he might be from working two jobs to support his extended family. But he does manage to deal with the two crises, although not to everyone's satisfaction. He takes a walk down to the beach with Nora, who returns home to announce that Uncle Jack thinks she should finish school. Everyone agrees but Nora.

He is more successful with Stanley, however, telling his son that he is proud of him for standing up for his principles and defending a co-worker. But he also announces that the Jeromes can't afford principles right now. Stanley decides to write the letter.

The second act takes place a week later, but there are a number of changes. Nora and Blanche are not speaking, and Nora has taken to spending most of her time away from the house, dating someone whom Eugene considers a creep. And, in fact, Eugene has decided that perhaps he isn't in love with Nora anyway.

But the biggest change, and greatest worry, is that Jack has had a mild heart attack, and has been ordered to rest in bed for two or three weeks.

Besides being worried about him, Kate is disappointed because this means they can't go to the annual dance at the Commodore Hotel. She had been looking forward to it, and was going to take Blanche along so that she might meet some eligible men from Jack's company. Blanche didn't want to go anyway, and in fact has a date with the man across the street (whom Kate screams is a drunk) for that very evening.

Meantime Stanley comes home with another problem. Trying to make more money for the family, he took his pay and gambled—and lost it all.

But Laurie comes home with a letter given to her by the mother of the man across the street. It seems he was in an auto accident (drunk again, Kate says) and is in the hospital. From this incident, Kate and Blanche get into a terrible argument, each venting her frustrations of worry and fear for the future on the other. Blanche vows to leave the Jerome household.

Stanley tells Eugene that the only thing he can do is join the army. He packs his clothes and leaves without telling anyone else.

Nora returns home to find her mother is leaving. The two finally have a heart-to-heart, and although Nora still wants to take the job with the Broadway producer, she understands her mother's concern and why she said no.

The atmosphere of reconciliation spreads, and Kate and Blanche talk over their problems, deciding that when Blanche is ready for her own home, Kate will help her find it—but it shouldn't be too far away.

Then, surprise of surprises, Stanley returns home. He has decided that his father and the family need him more than the army does. He confesses his gambling to his father, who understands what his intentions were and promises that after dinner the two of them will go out in the backyard, and he'll teach his son the right way to play poker.

The Jerome family is back to relative normalcy. As they sit down to dinner, except for Eugene who is still upstairs, they get a letter. It is from London. Jack's cousin has just escaped from Poland with his wife, mother, and four children. They will be arriving in New York . . . they have no place to go. The Jeromes begin to make plans.

Kate calls for Eugene to come down to supper. "Be right there!" he yells. At the moment, he is preoccupied. Stanley, on his return home from not joining the army, has given his brother a postcard that has paralyzed Eugene Morris Jerome into total inaction. Eugene has finally seen a naked lady.

Thematic Material

This is a funny, warm story of an American family during the depression years, and of a young boy on the brink of adulthood. It speaks of closeness and love between parents and children, of admiration of an older sibling, and of the first stirrings of sexual feelings in a teenager. Eugene is presented as a bright, amusing, almost 15-year-old who alternates between considering himself quite wise and acting like the boy he still is.

Book Talk Material

Conversations between Eugene and family members are good introductions to his character and the other Jeromes, and they point up the closeness of the family unit beneath all the bantering and bickering. See: Eugene and his mother argue about going to the store (pp. 18–19); Eugene hears that Stan may lose his job (pp. 23–28); Eugene and his mother discuss liver (pp. 46–47); and Stanley tells a wide-eyed Eugene all about girls, boys, and puberty (pp. 54–60).

Additional Selections

A 16-year-old Jewish misfit learns about sex from older women at a summer camp in New York of the 1930s in Julius Fast's *What Should We Do about Davey?* (St. Martin's, 1988, $14.95).

History and personal values mix in a story of a childhood in New York during the 1930s, E. L. Doctorow's *World's Fair* (Random, 1985, $14.95; pap., Fawcett, $4.95).

Six recent plays written by teenagers for the Young Playwright's Festival are included in *The Ground Zero Club and Other Prize-Winning Plays*, edited by Wendy Lamb (Dell, pap., $3.50).

Memorable speeches from 80 films are included in *The Actor's Book of Movie Monologues*, edited by Marisa Smith and Amy Schewel (pap., Penguin, $5.95).

Ah! Wilderness, Eugene O'Neill's romanticized view of adolescence, is included in *Nine Plays by Eugene O'Neill* (Modern Lib., 1941, $9.95), and *Three Comedies of American Family Life*, edited by Joseph Mersand (pap., Pocket, $3.95), includes *I Remember Mama, Life with Father*, and *You Can't Take It with You*.

Two other selections enjoyed by teen readers of plays are Ira Levin's thriller *Deathtrap* (Random, 1979, $7.95) and Agatha Christie's *The Mousetrap and Other Plays* (pap., Bantam, $4.50).

The theory and practice of playwriting are discussed in William Packard's *The Art of the Playwright* (Paragon, 1987, $14.95, pap., $12.95).

About the Book
Booklist, July 1984, p. 1511.
VOYA, December 1984, p. 276.
See also *Book Review Index,* 1984, p. 650; 1985, p. 565.

About the Author
Nasso, Christine, ed. *Contemporary Authors* (First Revision). Detroit: Gale, 1977. Vols. 21–24, pp. 800–805.
Wakeman, John, ed. *World Authors 1950–1970.* New York: Wilson, 1975, pp. 1311–1313.

Townsend, John Rowe. *Downstream*
Lippincott, 1987, $12.89

John Rowe Townsend is a prolific and much-respected English writer of books for children and young adults. This title refers to the journey that young people must take on the road to becoming adults.

Plot Summary
Alan Dollis, soon to be celebrating his seventeenth birthday, has moved with his father and mother from their row house in north London to a country home close to King's Eaton, a small town still within commuting distance to the big city. It is now late June. In the autumn Alan is to enter, as a senior, nearby Kinrose, a posh boys' school. Alan's father, Geoffrey, now 46, is a charming, still very handsome freelance artist, and his mother, Kath, is a practical-minded, down-to-earth housewife. Unfortunately, their marriage seems now to consist of a series of petty squabbles that usually result from Geoffrey's extravagant and often irresponsible actions, particularly those involving money.

A windfall arrives from Geoffrey's agent in the form of a check for £1,108 and a penny—royalties on illustrations used by an American publisher. To escape the quarrel that erupts about how this should be spent, Alan walks to Hal Aubrey's boatyard, retrieves the family's newly acquired rowboat, and heads downstream on the bucolic river Wendell. His father waves to him from the bank and the two decide to spend the afternoon on the river. In a narrow inlet they see perched on a platform a deserted ramshackle boathouse. After docking the punt, they find a "For Sale" sign close to the country lane that forms the inland boundary of the property. Alan's father is intrigued. At the office of the estate agent posted on the sign, Geoffrey impulsively offers £1,108 for Ebenezer's Path, the name of the plot, and is surprised when the offer is accepted. Back home, Kath is furious when she learns of the purchase and blames both Alan and her husband for this latest extravagance.

Alan invites his former girlfriend, Wendy, to visit him from London. Together they refurbish the cabin and repair the roof. Alan begins to find a new and different attraction toward Wendy and one day during a work break tries to make love to her. She refuses anything beyond kissing. Aroused and angry, Alan sulks. The next day, Wendy returns home.

Geoffrey is pleased with the boathouse restoration and rewards Alan with a driving lesson in his red Jaguar. However, the son's nervousness coupled with his father's impatience produces far from satisfactory results.

To boost Alan's sorry grades in German, the Dollises hire sight unseen a tutor named Mrs. Briggs who is to come twice a week from the neighboring town of Eastminster. Alan imagines her as a frumpy, fat, middle-aged woman, but instead a shapely, 23-year-old blonde divorcée named Vivien appears. She also possesses an open, engaging personality. For Alan it is infatuation at first sight. Mr. Dollis has a more sobered reaction, but nevertheless also expresses his approval.

As the tutoring progresses, Alan's obsessive attraction toward Vivien increases and whenever she is near him, he feels euphoric. As a seventeenth birthday present, Alan receives a schedule of lessons from a local driving school and Vivien good-naturedly volunteers to supplement these by giving Alan extra driving practice in Dad's Jag. Mr. Dollis obliges by instructing Vivien in the controls.

When there is only one week of classes left, Alan begins to panic at his impending loss. On one of his outings he takes Vivien for a boat ride. He tries haltingly to express his feelings toward her. She gently but firmly discourages him, but unable to control himself, he begins kissing her wildly and suffers the embarrassment of a premature ejaculation. On their drive home, Vivien tactfully tries to comfort Alan and explains that his emotionalism is a natural part of the growing-up process.

The next week Vivien makes excuses and does not appear for the last lessons. Coincidentally, Mr. Dollis is called to London on these days for business conferences.

Alan enters school and becomes acquainted with a fellow senior, Derek Prouse, who lives only a few miles away. But Alan's mind is still filled with thoughts of Vivien.

One day while his father is in London, Alan accidentally misses the school bus and decides to pay a surprise visit to Vivien. He goes to the train station to retrieve his father's car and finds that it isn't there. Alan bikes to the boathouse instead and to his surprise, he sees the red Jag parked by the wharf. Peeking through the window of the boathouse, he sees Vivien asleep in his father's arms. He is stunned by this discovery and experiences both anger and a sense of betrayal.

The next time his father is absent "in London," Alan skips school and returns to Ebenezer's Path. Breaking down the door of the boathouse, he interrupts his father and Vivien making love. In the angry scene that follows, Alan calls his father a bastard and Vivien a whore. Geoffrey physically attacks his son, but Vivien is able to separate them.

Although he says nothing to his mother, Alan feels increased hatred and disgust toward his father.

One day while home from school with a cold, Alan overhears a telephone conversation between Vivien and Geoffrey. They are making plans to spend Bonfire Night of Guy Fawkes Day together at the boathouse.

Alan plots revenge. He tears down the boathouse and with some of the wood lays the makings of a fire on the bank. With cast-off clothes and straw, he creates two figures—effigies of Vivien and his father—and labels them GD and VB.

Telling his mother that he is planning to attend a party at Derek's, Alan bikes to the property. When his father and Vivien appear, he lights the fire and the effigies. There is another angry confrontation that is interrupted by the arrival of Alan's mother. She had gone to Derek's to leave a parka for Alan and traced him to the boathouse. Vivien and Geoffrey leave together. When Alan tries to tell his mother the truth, she tells him that she was aware of Geoffrey's infidelities. This was just the latest of many she has accepted in the past. Without bitterness she tells Alan that he has been responsible for breaking up his own home.

Kath expresses confidence that Geoffrey will return when he misses the comforts of his home and the affair with Vivien is over.

The acrimony and anger that Alan possessed disappear. He accepts an offer from Derek to help construct a new boathouse. For Alan, this is only the beginning of the rebuilding process.

Thematic Material

This novel deals honestly with a boy's sexual awakening and the conflicts and confusion it brings. The classic situation of a teenager infatuated with an older woman is well handled, as is a son's growing awareness of his own father's sexuality. Father-son conflicts are candidly explored, including the feeling of competition—over love for the same woman—that often characterizes these relationships. The novel depicts a loveless marriage and how husband, wife, and son adjust to it and the effects of marital infidelity on this family. Fundamentally, however, this is a coming-of-age novel about a painful incident on the road to manhood.

Book Talk Material

There are a number of fine incidents worth reading or retelling: the arrival of the check (pp. 3–6); exploring Ebenezer's Path (pp. 18–24); buying the property (pp. 24–31); the incident with Wendy (pp. 46–52); Geoffrey gives his son a driving lesson (pp. 62–65); Vivien arrives (pp. 68–74); and the incident with her in the boat (pp. 96–102).

Additional Selections

After a quarrel with his father, Richard strikes out on his own in the comic English novel by Jean Ure, *The Other Side of the Fence* (Delacorte, 1988, $14.95).

Eugene is 15 and hopelessly in love with unattainable Della in Paul Zindel's *The Amazing and Death-Defying Diary of Eugene Dingman* (Harper, 1987, $12.95).

Bess copes with the news that her brother and best friend, Margaret, have had sex in Phyllis Schieber's *Strictly Personal* (pap., Fawcett, $2.75).

A high school senior's parents separate and he loses his virginity in Joseph Olshan's *A Warmer Season* (McGraw, 1987, $15.95).

When his mother leaves with another man, Evan escapes into an affair with an older woman in Charles Crawford's *Split Time* (Harper, 1987, $12.95).

In Norma Klein's *My Life as a Body* (Knopf, 1987, $12.95), a 17-year-old girl falls in love with a handicapped classmate.

Quarrels with his father and his first sexual experience are pivotal occurrences in the life of Ditto, a young English adolescent, in Aidan Chambers' *Breaktime* (Harper, 1979, $12.70).

A senior high student mourns the death of a father in the coming-of-age adventure novel *Travelers* by Larry Bograd (Lippincott, 1986, $11.70).

Paul Hemphill's mature nonfictional work *Me and the Boy* (Macmillan, 1986, $16.30; pap., Ballantine, $3.95) is subtitled "A Journey of Discovery; Father and Son Discover America and Each Other."

For better readers, C. L. Sulzberger in *Fathers and Children* (Arbor, 1987, $19.95) traces famous paternal relationships from Alexander the Great to the Kennedys.

About the Book
Booklist, July 1987, p. 1673.
Bulletin of the Center for Children's Books, May 1987, p. 179.
Horn Book, July 1987, p. 474.
School Library Journal, August 1987, p. 99.
VOYA, June 1987, p. 84.
See also *Book Review Digest,* 1987, p. 1875, and *Book Review Index,* 1987, p. 765.

About the Author
Commire, Anne, ed. *Something about the Author.* Detroit: Gale, 1973. Vol. 4, pp. 206–208.
de Montreville, Doris, and Crawford, Elizabeth D., eds. *Fourth Book of Junior Authors and Illustrators.* New York: Wilson, 1978, pp. 328–330.
Evory, Ann, ed. *Contemporary Authors* (First Revision). Detroit: Gale, 1979. Vols. 37–40, pp. 557–558.
Kirkpatrick, D. L., ed. *Twentieth-Century Children's Writers* (2nd edition). New York: St. Martin's, 1983, pp. 770–772.
Riley, Carolyn, ed. *Children's Literature Review.* Detroit: Gale, 1976. Vol. 2, pp. 169–175.
Sarkissian, Adele, ed. *Something about the Author: Autobiography Series.* Detroit: Gale, 1986. Vol. 2, pp. 271–286.

Townsend, Sue. *The Adrian Mole Diaries*
Grove, 1986, $14.95

Sue Townsend's books about Adrian Mole were great successes in the United Kingdom, selling more than 5 million copies, and even spawned a West End play and a television series based on the diaries. They deal with two and one-half years in the life of an English boy as he passes through darkest adolescence, and overcomes school and family crises with the help of his girlfriend, Pandora. This volume combines *The Secret Diary of Adrian Mole, Aged 13 3/4* (pap., Methuen, $5.95; pap., Avon, $3.95) and *The Growing Pains of Adrian Mole* (pap., Avon, $3.50). They are enjoyed by both adults and teenagers.

Plot Summary

The center of this story, set in England, is Adrian Mole, a pimply faced, nearly 14-year-old who is, above all, a worrier. He worries about nearly every facet of his existence, all of which he confides to his diary, whose entries make up this hilarious book. And from the entries, it would seem that there is a lot to worry Adrian.

Mainly, he worries about himself: his terrible complexion and the fact that certain parts of his body don't seem to keep still, as well as the fact that his voice fails him at embarrassing moments, and that he certainly must be the only virgin in his class. He worries about his parents; Adrian is an only child and his mother and father are about to break up. His parents are a bit unconventional anyway, so Adrian always worries that he isn't getting the proper nutrition. He worries that Britons don't show the proper respect for the forthcoming marriage of Lady Diana Spencer, and he worries because his 89-year-old, chain-smoking friend Bert is about to go off to a nursing home.

Adrian also worries about his career. He is convinced that he is turning into an intellectual. But since he remains undiscovered by the world at large, he sends off letters and poems to the BBC on brightly colored stationery, and, surprisingly, receives some rather interesting replies, which Adrian interprets in his own way.

There is, however, a brighter side to Adrian's existence. There is Pandora, a new girl in his class. Adrian is in love. And even though, as he admits, she is of a "higher social class," it seems that Adrian's feelings of devotion are returned. Adrian soon discovers, however, that being in love with Pandora does not change his virgin status.

With his diary entries reflecting both the pretensions of daily life and the confusing world of the adolescent, Adrian lurches through his rocky existence, meeting disaster at every turn and in between wilting for love of Pandora. His parents do break up—for a time—and Adrian suffers through his mother's affair with "creep Lucas" and his father's dalliance with a "stick insect." But when his parents are reunited, Adrian is soon in for another shock. He is going to be a brother; as though he doesn't have enough problems, he moans.

But surprisingly to Adrian, "Rosie" quite captivates him, and with the commotion nearly always constant in his house and between his parents, he often finds himself taking care of the infant; he checks her pulse frequently to make sure she is breathing properly.

Adrian is also fairly well occupied outside of his home life, too. His friend Bert, at 89, gets married to Queenie, who later has a stroke and dies. Bert is in a wheelchair, so Adrian takes care of him (and his dog) a lot (with Bert complaining loudly all the while). The Moles' own dog gives him lots of trouble, too. He is always knocking over something or at the vet.

As if all this weren't enough, Adrian Mole must contend with having his tonsils out, rejections of his poems from the BBC, being picked on by a class bully, a short sojourn with a "gang," which Adrian finds not to his liking, a very rocky romance with Pandora, and a visit from a rather obnoxious American acquaintance. But somehow one gets the feeling that the irrepressible Adrian Mole will carry on for dear old England, and all the intellectuals out there.

Thematic Material

The entries in Adrian Mole's diary are sometimes touching in their naiveté and deeply affecting as the young man pours out his worries and his feelings about a life that does seem rather fraught with crises, imagined and real. They also, in their details, reveal the intimate life of a working-class English family somehow bumbling through. But most of all, the entries are very funny; from his constant complaints about his family's lack of a proper diet, to his rather calm acceptance of his parents' "drinking problems," to his inability—for all his new-found intellectualism—to ascribe the "correct motives" to the meanderings in opposite directions of his parents and their love/hate relationship, Adrian is a funny, wonderful character that readers of almost any age will enjoy.

Book Talk Material

A few of Adrian's diary entries will give the comic flavor of this book and point up the "extent" of his worries; see the dog in trouble (pp. 14–15), Adrian discovers his intellectual nature and writes a poem (pp. 17–

18), Adrian visits Bert (pp. 24–25), Adrian breaks out (p. 44), and Adrian faces divorce (pp. 45–46).

Additional Selections

A 15-year-old college freshman plans to oust the school's administration in the humorous *Simon Pure* by Julian F. Thompson (Scholastic, 1987, $12.95).

Jardine is convinced that life is out to get him in Gordon Korman's *A Semester in the Life of a Garbage Bag* (Scholastic, 1987, $12.95). Also use Korman's *Son of Interflux* (Scholastic, 1985, $12.95).

An English teenager writes a pulp romance while exploring his own sexuality in June Oldham's *Grow Up, Cupid* (Delacorte, 1987, $14.95).

Peter Cameron has written 14 funny but touching stories about young adults today in *One Way or Another* (Harper, 1985, $15.95, pap. $5.95).

Tim sends anonymous love letters with unexpected results in Constance C. Greene's *The Love Letters of J. Timothy Owen* (Harper, 1986, $11.25).

A big city Catholic school is the setting of John R. Powers's very funny *Do Black Patent Leather Shoes Really Reflect Up?* (pap., Warner, $2.95).

An English working-class boy takes up ballet but is more interested in girls in Jean Ure's *You Win Some, You Lose Some* (Delacorte, 1986, $14.95; pap., Dell, $2.95), a sequel to *What If They Saw Me Now?* (Delacorte, 1984, $14.95; pap., Dell, $2.50).

By contrast to Adrian Mole, growing up in a 1980s English working-class milieu with its grinding problems is the subject of Janni Howker's *The Nature of the Beast* (Greenwillow, 1985, $10.25; pap., Penguin, $4.95), Robert Swindells's *Staying Up* (Oxford, 1988, $13.95), and Gillian Cross's *Chartbreaker* (Holiday, 1987, $12.95).

About the Book

New York Times Book Review, May 25, 1986, p. 9.
School Library Journal, February 1987, p. 37.
VOYA, December 1986, p. 222.
See also *Book Review Index*, 1987, p. 766.

About the Author

Commire, Anne, ed. *Something about the Author*. Detroit: Gale, 1987. Vol. 48, pp. 217–218.
May, Hal, ed. *Contemporary Authors*. Detroit: Gale, 1987. Vol. 119, p. 381.

2

Interpersonal Relations

ADOLESCENTS as they reach adulthood face new problems in getting along with people, particularly as their relationships are constantly changing and often bringing with them new and different conflicts. These books explore a variety of social situations with emphasis on those involving parents and friends.

Bridgers, Sue Ellen. *Sara Will*
    Harper, 1985, $14.95

Sue Ellen Bridgers has had an outstanding record of successes as a writer of young adult fiction. All of her first five novels, including *Sara Will*, have been named in the American Library Association annual list of "Best Books for Young Adults." Immediately preceding *Sara Will* was *Notes for Another Life* (Knopf, 1981, $9.95; pap., Bantam $2.50, condensed in *Juniorplots 3*, Bowker, 1987, pp. 9–12), about two teenagers, a brother and sister, who are raised by grandparents when their father sinks gradually into insanity and their mother leaves home for employment. Immediately after *Sara Will* was *Permanent Connections* (Harper, 1987, $13.70), about 17-year-old sullen, uncommunicative Rob who is sent to North Carolina to help on his uncle's farm after Uncle Fairlee has broken his hip. Bridgers's novels are quiet and slow moving but deal with the bonds of extended families and the power of love. *Sara Will* is adult in tone and chronicles among other plots the coming out of isolation of a fiftyish spinster. In it three generations interact as the story flows from past to present. It is recommended for students in grades 10 through 12.

Plot Summary
    Living out her pleasant, serene days between youth and old age, Sara Will Burney, who has not cut her hair in 40 years and keeps a 1965

Mustang in the garage, is, for the most part, content. True, her widowed sister, Swanee Hope, has come back to the family home to live with her—and Swanee does watch rather a little too much television to suit Sara Will—but, all in all, life is suitable.

Sara Will prides herself on "keeping up" the small cemetery that has been neglected by the rural community, where many of the Burneys now rest. And she nurses a heartache that stems from the long-ago death of her sister, Serena, whose grave Sara Will cannot visit because, through a TVA dam project, the part of the cemetery where Serena is buried is now cut off from the rest by water. Sara Will has long been nagging officials to erect the land bridge they promised, but it has never come to pass, and Serena's grave lies unattended. This disturbs the calmness of Sara Will's existence.

Then one day her calm existence is further disturbed in a way Sara Will could never have imagined. Fate Jessop, brother of Serena's husband, arrives in a beat-up truck with his niece, Eva—a teenager, unwed, and the mother of Rachel. Pleasant-mannered Fate, suffering inside from an accident that cost him the use of one arm, has never quite gotten over the fact that his wife ran off with another man. But since Eva showed up on his doorstep, pregnant, and with no place to go, he feels a sense of protection toward the young girl and a sense of family. So when Michael, who is not the father of Rachel but desperately wants to marry Eva, became overzealous in his pursuit, Fate packed up his niece and the baby and took off for the out-of-the-way home of Sara Will.

Swanee Hope is delighted with the visitors, but Sara Will extends only the barest of courtesies, allowing them to stay overnight—after all, where can they go?—and then reluctantly stretching the stay until the weekend. Where Swanee gives her heart immediately to the baby and to the troubles of Eva and the kindness of Fate, Sara Will remains stiff and apart, wishing only that these intruders leave her to her serenity.

As if the house is not crowded enough, Michael shows up, still pursuing Eva, who wants nothing to do with him. Caught between his parents, who demand that he return home and go to college, and his love for Eva, he, too, despite the growing frustration of Sara Will, joins the household.

Sara Will is perplexed, for suddenly she feels powerless to run her own life, and more devastating to her are her growing feelings for Fate. When Eva, who shows signs of maturing, asks Sara to allow them to stay for a longer period until she is ready to return to her parents with the baby and go back to school, Sara Will reluctantly agrees.

In subtle, quiet ways, these six people of different ages and different outlooks settle down to become a family. Where before, Thanksgiving and Christmas were wearisome holidays to Sara Will, they take on new meaning this year. And where before she resisted all change, she now finds herself sympathetic to the concerns of Eva and the baby and to the plight of Michael, and she also finds herself falling in love with Fate.

Things come to a climax for Sara Will when she allows Fate to take her precious Mustang into town, and he has an accident. Sara Will packs up, leaves them, and goes into town to wait for the car to be fixed. But she knows in her heart that she is just running from Fate.

During the days that Sara Will spends in town waiting for her car to be repaired, she reflects on her life and comes to realize that the pain she has suffered from the deaths of people she loved has made her afraid to live, afraid to care. When a note comes from Fate saying that he should be the one to leave but cannot because it would break his heart to leave her, Sara Will goes home.

The coming together of these people has changed all their lives: Swanee Hope decides to visit her son in California, whom she has not seen in a long, long time; Eva decides to go home with the baby, and realizes that Michael may be more important to her than she realized; Michael learns that, although he hopes things will work out for them to be together, what he really wants is what's best for both; Fate puts his hurts away; and Sara Will gives her heart as she and Fate are married.

But there is one more bond for Sara Will to break. Fate fixes up an old boat, and although Sara Will is terrified of the water, she allows herself and the others to be taken across the water to the grave of Serena. And it is there that Sara Will puts aside her grief at last and takes her place among the living.

Thematic Material

This is a story of love and how people deal with the loss of it. Swanee Hope embraces people easily as she tries to compensate for the death of her husband and the indifference of her son; young Eva feels smothered by the overzealousness of her suitor; Michael cannot understand that Eva might not share his feelings; Fate disguises his hurt by refusing to acknowledge the truth of his first wife's actions; and Sara Will has let the pain of her grief frighten her out of living. This is also a family story, as strangers come together and slowly learn to care about one another even as they are learning to be themselves. It shows that giving love is the surest way to receive it.

Book Talk Material

The strong character of Sara Will is the key to this sensitive story, and readers will notice the subtle changes that this "new family" begins to work on her. See: Sara Will reacts to Fate's arrival (pp. 14–19); Sara Will goes to the cemetery (pp. 63–72); and she reflects on her life (pp. 116–119). Also enjoyable are the scenes where this oddly matched group begins to become a family; see Thanksgiving Day (pp. 129–134) and they all go out to dinner (pp. 146–154).

Additional Selections

Jonny, suffering from his sister's death, befriends an old lady with Alzheimer's disease in Margaret Mahy's *Memory* (McElderry, 1988, $13.95).

In Norma Fox Mazer's *After the Rain* (Morrow, 1987, $11.75), Rachel tries to understand and love her difficult 83-year-old grandfather.

Elizabeth is growing up in a small Canadian town and gradually discovering herself in Isabel Huggan's *The Elizabeth Stories* (Viking, 1987, $15.95).

In *Illumination Night* by Alice Hoffman (Putnam, 1987, $18.95), several inhabitants of a rural community including a rebellious teenager help one another.

Sarah and Abel, two young Shakers, are in conflict over their love in Jane Yolen's *The Gift of Sarah Baker* (pap., Scholastic, $1.95).

The pangs and humor of first love are captured in Brigitte Downey's *Nellie* (St. Martin's, 1984, $12.95) set in a remote Irish village.

A lame girl and a wandering naturalist find love in southern Appalachia in Mildred Lee's *The People Therein* (Houghton, 1980, $10.95; pap., NAL, $1.95).

When his brother is killed in a mining accident during the 1920s, Sammy di Cantini learns about responsibility in Jay Parini's *The Patch Boys* (Holt, 1986, $15.95).

James Agee's *A Death in the Family* (pap., Bantam, $3.95) is the moving story of the effects of a father's death on the family.

Hunter's Horn by Harriette Arnow (pap., Avon, $2.50) is a beautifully written novel about life in the great Smokies.

About the Book
Booklist, January 1, 1987, p. 602.
Library Journal, January 1, 1985, p. 98.
VOYA, December 1985, p. 318.
See also *Book Review Index,* 1985, p. 87.

About the Author
Bowden, Jane A., ed. *Contemporary Authors.* Detroit: Gale, 1977. Vols. 65–68, p. 79.
Commire, Anne, ed. *Something about the Author.* Detroit: Gale, 1981. Vol. 22, p. 56.
Estes, Glenn E., ed. *American Writers for Children since 1960: Fiction (Dictionary of Literary Biography,* Vol. 52). Detroit: Gale, 1986, pp. 38–41.
Evory, Ann, ed. *Contemporary Authors* (New Revision Series). Detroit: Gale, 1984. Vol. 11, pp. 89–90.
Holtze, Sally Holmes, ed. *Fifth Book of Junior Authors and Illustrators.* New York: Wilson, 1983, pp. 47–49.
Sarkissian, Adele, ed. *Something about the Author: Autobiography Series.* Detroit: Gale, 1986. Vol. 1, pp. 39–52.

Brooks, Bruce. *Midnight Hour Encores*
Harper, 1986, $13.89

Bruce Brooks's first young adult novel, *The Moves Make the Man* (Harper, 1984, $13.70, pap. $2.75; condensed in *Juniorplots 3,* Bowker, 1987, pp. 235–238), was a Newbery Honor Book and the winner of the Boston Globe–Horn Book Award, in which Jayfox, a cheeky, incoherent black student tells about his friend Bix, who is troubled after his mother's mental breakdown, and about his love affair with basketball. *Midnight Hour Encores* is also a first-person narrative told by Sibilance T. Spooner, age 16, and is about her search for identity and self-discovery by traveling cross-country with her father to meet the mother who deserted her at birth. The author uses the world of music, both performing and composing, as a backdrop (Sib is a musical prodigy), and appears to be as at home here as on the basketball court. The novel is suitable for readers in grades 7 through 12.

Plot Summary
The relationship between father and daughter, and mother and daughter, are very much in the forefront in this offbeat story of a very

"eighties" 16-year-old meeting her definitely "sixties" mother for what to her is the very first time.

Sibilance T. Spooner and her father, Taxi, of Washington, D.C., do not have what might be called a usual father-daughter relationship. For one thing, Sib is not your usual daughter. She is a genius—a recognized (including by her) genius of the cello. She is tall, sarcastic, lonely, smart, and devoted to her passion for being the best at what she does. Taxi is not the usual type of father either. For one thing, he let Sib change her name when she was eight years old; her hippie mother had named her Esalen Starness Blue.

Taxi last saw his wife when Sib was less than a day old; on that day Taxi took his daughter and left California for the East Coast. But every year since Sib has been old enough to understand, he has asked her if she wants to meet her mother. No big fuss; he just asks the question. And Sib has always said no. This year, Sib surprises Taxi, and herself, by saying yes.

But Taxi, as Sib knows, cannot do anything easily. Not content to put Sib on a plane for San Francisco, Taxi is determined to show his daughter what life was like for such people as her mother during the sixties. He wants her to understand, Sib realizes, why her mother "abandoned" her and was willing to let a day-old baby go off with her husband—never to be seen again. Toward that end, Taxi searches for and finds a Volkswagen bus from the sixties, fixes it up for their trip (including space for Sib to practice her cello), tosses Sib's clothes into an old duffel bag, collects records from that era, and the two start off on a trip cross-country, aimed at educating Sib about the "Age of Aquarius."

Sib takes the proposed trip with a good deal of sarcasm and above-it-all amusement. However, as they travel cross-country she does learn much about the young woman who was her mother—a young woman who was wrapped up in the lore of native American tribes, who put her day-old child into a leather papoose and hung her on a stick, who went in for very private kinds of meditation, who felt that if her husband and baby stayed with her, she would never be "self-realized," and who was very much "into macramé."

Outwardly she scoffs, but inside, despite herself, Sib is somewhat fascinated.

As they travel along and Sib learns about her mother and about the youth of the sixties, she and Taxi compose what she calls a tone poem to the Age of Aquarius—"The Morning Years." They also stop to see an old and dear friend of her father's from that era. This woman, too, abandoned her child, Sib learns—didn't any of these hippies want their children, she wonders. But she watches also with fascination as she begins to learn not only about her mother and her mother's generation but about what kind of a man her father was and now is.

Sib learns, for instance, what it meant for her father to care for her when she was baby. A newspaperman, he devised a sort of "briefcase" so he could, and did, take her along on interviews when there was no one to leave her with. How much trouble can a baby be, Sib asks—a bottle now and then? She begins to learn just how much time and patience and caring are required. Good old Taxi, Sib thinks, a little surprised.

And then the tour through the sixties is over, and they are in San Francisco. Despite herself, Sib is apprenhensive about meeting her mother. At first, Taxi wants her to go in alone, but she persuades him to accompany her. What they see is a small woman with very bright blue eyes who says, "Hello, Cabot" to Taxi, as though she had seen him yesterday. He says merely, "Hello, Connie." To Sib she says, "Your father was afraid that if he let me know you were coming, I might disappear."

In just a few minutes Sib realizes that her mother is welcoming her, and that her father is not included, which he knows. Taxi brings in her belongings and leaves. However, he tells her that he will see her at the audition. Although she is scheduled to attend Juilliard in New York in the fall, Sib is to have an audition for a scholarship at the Phrygian Institute in San Francisco. She learns that her mother is on the board of directors of the school. Connie has become very successful in real estate.

Over the next few days this child of the eighties and former hippie of the sixties come to know each other; Connie explains to her daughter that she was not ready to be a mother 16 years ago. But Sib isn't buying that so easily. As she says, "I'm only bothering because I like you. I didn't expect to bother—to try to understand . . . now I've got a lot of things to work out very fast."

Despite what went before, mother and daughter are drawn to each other, and it is as though Sib knew from the start that she would stay with her mother when this journey ended.

And then it is time for the audition. Sib plays before the members of the institute and she knows she has never been better. And once during her playing she notices a dark figure dead center in the very back row, where Taxi always sits at her recitals.

After the thunderous applause has died down, Connie meets Taxi as he is leaving. "Quite a finish, wouldn't you say?" she asks.

Thinking she means the Szymanowski piece Sib ended with, Taxi agrees. But, no, Connie does not mean the Szymanowski piece; it seems that Sib played an encore, after Taxi had left. "I never stay for her encores," he explains.

"You mean you were going back to Washington and leaving her with me?" Connie asks.

To which Taxi replies, "I assumed you two had arranged that."

Taxi learns from an almost angry Connie that the encore Sib played for the distinguished group at her audition was the "tone poem" he and Sib had composed on the trip cross-country; she called it "The Peace and Love Shuffle." For that the institute very nearly dumped her—very nearly, but it didn't. Taxi asks if Sib knows that she is in. Connie replies that Sib left the stage immediately afterward and they can't find her.

Saying good-bye and exacting a promise from Connie that if Sib wants to see him, she will send her, he boards the old Volkswagen bus for the trip home. Some 15 minutes later, out on the highway heading east, Taxi hears the first of the cello chords. In only a few seconds he has pulled across two lanes to a screeching stop and is hugging the girl playing the cello in the back of the van.

Thematic Material

Midnight Hour Encores is a story of relationships, of family love, and of the vast differences that can occur from one generation to the next. Sib's genius sets her apart from other girls her age, and she is portrayed as a young woman in many ways older than her years, traveled, smug, worldly, and yet inside lonely and eager for the love of the woman who abandoned her. It is only through her meeting with her mother and her experiences on the trip cross-country that she begins to see her father for the caring and loving parent he has always been. Both mother and father are portrayed as believable people who make no apologies for themselves. This is also an interesting portrayal of the sixties generation, the Age of Aquarius, which although only two decades past, may seem impossibly far away to young people of today.

Book Talk Material

Descriptions of the generation of the sixties may spark a conversation to compare the so-called hippies with teenagers of today—their differences in values and outlook on life. Would a young mother and father in the 1980s act as Sib's parents did? See: Taxi and Sib look for records (pp.

44–62); Taxi talks about Sib's mother (pp. 83–94, 131–141); and they visit an old friend (pp. 145–153).

Additional Selections

In Colby Rodowsky's *Julie's Daughter* (Farrar, 1985, $12.95), a 17-year-old girl meets the mother who deserted her as a baby.

When her mother returns, 16-year-old Leemi vows to reject her in Patricia Calvert's *Yesterday's Daughter* (Scribner's, 1985, $15.95; pap., Avon, $3.50).

After he attacks his cruel stepfather, a teenager sets out to live with his grandfather in David Small's *The River in Winter* (Norton, 1987, $16.95).

Three siblings decide to go it alone when their parents leave their Brooklyn home for a scientific expedition in Karin N. Mango's *Somewhere Green* (Four Winds, 1987, $13.95).

Chelsea questions the price of friendship in Richard Peck's *Princess Ashley* (Delacorte, 1987, $14.95).

Peter falls under the spell of a preacher and runs away with him in Cynthia Rylant's *A Fine White Dust* (Bradbury, 1986, $11.95; pap., Dell, $2.75).

After Oliver's beloved grandfather dies, he turns to Charlotte with demands on their relationship she finds difficult in Nancy Bond's *A Place to Come Back To* (Atheneum, 1984, $13.95), a sequel to *The Best of Enemies* (Atheneum, 1978, $11.95).

Fifteen-year-old Harry Eastep is determined to lose his virginity soon in Ed McClanahan's *The Natural Man* (Farrar, 1983, $11.50; pap., Penguin, $4.95).

College freshman Jennifer spends a summer on a Massachusetts island with her dying mother in Lisa Grunwald's *Summer* (Knopf, 1986, $15.95).

About the Book

Book Report, January 1987, p. 34.
Booklist, February 1, 1987, p. 837.
Bulletin of the Center for Children's Books, November 1986, p. 43.
Horn Book, January 1987, p. 58.
New York Times Book Review, January 4, 1987, p. 33.
VOYA, December 1986, p. 213.
See also *Book Review Digest,* 1987, p. 233, and *Book Review Index,* 1987, p. 100.

Cormier, Robert.   *Beyond the Chocolate War*
Pantheon, 1985, $11.95; pap., Dell, $2.95 (same pagination)

In an interview printed in the March/April 1985 issue of the *Horn Book* magazine, Robert Cormier states that he wrote the sequel to *The Chocolate War* (Pantheon, 1974, $12.95; pap., Dell, $3.95; condensed in *More Juniorplots*, Bowker, 1977, pp. 28–32) to answer the many questions asked him about what eventually happened to the many memorable characters he created in the first book. Like its sequel, *The Chocolate War* takes place in a parochial boys' day school, Trinity High, situated in Monument, a drab mill town in mid-Massachusetts. Brother Leon, a sinister, ambitious man, is acting headmaster and engineers a fund-raising activity of selling boxes of chocolates. Because his eventual promotion rests on the success of this sale, he enlists the help of the Vigils, a powerful, secret student society. Although Carter is the president of the organization and Obie, the secretary, the real power lies in the hands of another senior, the suave, ruthless Archie Costello, the assigner, or the officer who conceives and assigns ingenious hazing tasks for new members. Before assignments become official, Archie must undergo the black box test in which there are five white balls and one black one. Should he draw the black ball, he must fulfill the assignment himself. However, in his three years as assigner, he has drawn only white ones. A newcomer in school, Jerry Renault, though friendless except for Roland Goobert, nicknamed the Goober, becomes famous when he refuses to sell the chocolates. The remainder of the novel deals with his unsuccessful crusade to fight the power structure led by Brother Leon and the Vigils. At the end he is beaten to a pulp by the school bully, Emile Janza, and sent to the hospital. All these characters appear in the sequel, plus several others who play only minor roles in the first book. For example, Tubs Casper is mentioned as trying to keep the proceeds of his chocolate sales to buy a bracelet for his girlfriend. Obie is the Vigil who brings him into line. David Caroni is also introduced as a sensitive, nervous boy who is so obsessed with maintaining his grade A average that he becomes an easy blackmail target for Brother Leon, who deliberately gives him an F in order to obtain information about Jerry Renault's activities in exchange for possibly adjusting the grade upward. Both books are read by junior and senior high students.

Plot Summary

It is now April in the same school year of the fall chocolate sale. Brother Leon has been named headmaster of Trinity, the Vigils continue their insidious covert activities, led by Archie, who has a protégé in a sophomore named Bunting who, with his stooges, Harley and Cornacchio, forms the next wave of the Vigil leadership. Both Carter and Obie have lost some interest in the group, particularly Obie who is infatuated with Laurie Gundarsen, a student in the neighboring public high school.

After spending several weeks in the hospital, Jerry was sent to recuperate with relatives in an idyllic small Quebec town. He has returned to Monument to live with his widowed father before returning to school in the fall. Goober is filled with guilt, first for abandoning Jerry and his fight for justice, and second for indirectly causing the nervous breakdown of Father Eugene during Goober's unwilling execution of a Vigil assignment.

There is a new boy in school, a loner named Ray Bannister, an amateur magician who is building a large model guillotine for a trick he knows will be his masterpiece.

Archie has devised a brilliant new assignment. On the day the bishop is scheduled for his annual visit to the school, all but one of the students will be absent. Carter is the only Vigil not enthusiastic about the scheme. Ray Bannister is selected to be the lone student (Archie again chooses the white ball) and Obie is sent to inform him. At Ray's home Obie is given a demonstration of magic tricks and is particularly impressed with the guillotine and its mechanisms.

Archie expresses a certain displeasure at Obie's preoccupation with Laurie. Eager to curry favor with his mentor, Bunting, with Harley and Cornacchio, one night raids Obie's car while he is parked in a deserted area petting with Laurie. Disguised by the dark, Cornacchio forces Obie's head under the car while Bunting and Harley attack Laurie. Only her quick kick to Bunting's groin prevents a rape before the three attackers escape into the night.

Obie's only clue to their identity is a glimpse of his assailant's shoe from under the car—a brown loafer with slashed instep and dangling brass buttons. Laurie is devastated by the assault and refuses any further contact with Obie, who vows revenge.

Goober tries to resume his friendship with Jerry, but with disappointing results. Jerry is now distant and psychologically damaged from his ordeal, and Goober is still wracked with guilt, particularly after he learns about Brother Eugene's death. Goober, sickened by the Vigils' activities, decides to transfer next year to another school, but Jerry, particularly after once again being beaten up for no apparent reason by the thug Emile Janza, knows he must return to Trinity to confront this evil once again.

The Vigil assignments continue. . . . Tubs Casper, though already 45 pounds overweight, is commanded to gain 20 more, and further plans are made for the bishop boycott. Carter is so upset at the possible consequences for the school should the plan be implemented that he secretly writes a warning note to Brother Leon, who coincidentally has just learned that the bishop has canceled his proposed visit.

Leon tells Archie about the note. Through his usual clever snooping, Archie forces a confession from Carter and threatens terrible reprisals.

Obie spots the telltale loafer at school and corners Cornacchio, who to save his own hide implicates Archie. Obie's attentions now focus on settling the score with the assigner. He elicits the help of Carter and together they substitute black for white balls in the assignment box so that Archie must accept the assignment of Fool during the school's annual Fair Day. This involves a possible dunking during the day, sitting in the water game chair while customers fire baseballs at the target. In the evening he must place his head on the block while Ray Bannister and his assistant, Obie, demonstrate the guillotine trick.

David Caroni is also planning for Fair Day. A perfectionist given to bouts of extreme depression, he has already seriously contemplated suicide because of Brother Leon's unfair F grade. On Fair Day, he, too, plots revenge. Armed with a large butcher knife, he confronts Brother Leon in his study. A passing faculty member, however, disarms him, and David flees. Distraught, he later kills himself by jumping from a railroad bridge.

Meanwhile Obie's plan to humiliate Archie at the fair misfires. Everyone is so intimidated and fearful of reprisals that the water game is shunned and Archie remains as dry and impudent as ever. However, Obie knows that the evening's activities will be different.

After a cabbage is sliced for effect by the guillotine and Archie's head is placed on the block, Ray surreptitiously changes the controls and Obie, also secretly, reverses them back to the slice position. The blade falls.

Fortunately for Archie, Ray has a second safety mechanism in place should the first fail, and again he escapes unharmed.

Archie knows Obie wanted him dead and in a confrontational scene, Obie blames Archie for perpetrating all the cruel and heartless acts of the Vigils. Archie retaliates by stating that if there is guilt, all must share it; no one forced Obie or Carter or any of the others to participate in any of these acts.

At the next school assembly, Brother Leon pontificates hypocritically about David's death. Suddenly a large rotten tomato is hurled and hits him in the face. The next day the thrower, David Mollaran, is elected president of the senior class.

Thematic Material

Henry Kissinger once said that power is the ultimate aphrodisiac. The actions of the Vigils and Brother Leon bear this out as well as power's corrupting strength. As in the earlier novel, evil goes essentially unpunished, although the symbolic tomato is a ray of hope. Cormier has stated that his central theme for these books is "terrible things happen because we allow them to happen." As Archie points out, Obie and the other Vigils could have simply said no. That is, individuals must be responsible for their own actions. Other themes include the meaning of friendship, the effects of peer pressure, the consequences on others of misusing positions of power, the corrosive nature of revenge-seeking, reaching maturity, and the abhorrent nature of raw violence.

Book Talk Material

The discussion of the power structure at Trinity High should interest readers. Some important passages are: planning the boycott (pp. 12–16); Goober visits Jerry (pp. 57–62); David contemplates suicide (pp. 70–75); Leon shows the anonymous note to Archie (pp. 76–82); Bunting describes the attack (pp. 89–95); and Tubs receives his assignment (pp. 112–119).

Additional Selections

Two boys in Mexico form an ultimately destructive friendship in Michael Schmidt's *Green Island* (Vanguard, 1982, $11.95; pap., Dell, $4.50).

A group of youths tainted with the power that evil brings is the subject of William Butterworth's *The Butterfly Revolution* (pap., Ballantine, $2.95), and three teenage boys try to blackmail their teacher in Charles Craw-ford's *Letter Perfect* (pap., Pocket, $1.95; condensed in *Juniorplots 3,* Bowker, 1987, pp. 28–32).

Frank and his fellow Obnoxious Jerks challenge their high school conformists, both students and faculty, in the humorous *The Obnoxious Jerks* by Stephen Manes (Bantam, 1988, $13.95).

In *Here at the Scenic-Vu Motel* by Thelma Hatch Wyss (Harper, 1988, $11.95), 17-year-old Jacob and six other teenagers must live in a motel when no school bus is available.

Roger's sophomore year is disrupted by the arrival of twins in Randy Powell's touching and often funny first novel *My Underrated Year* (Farrar, 1988, $12.95).

An adult novel of life in a boys' prep school is James Kirkwood's *Good Times, Bad Times* (pap., Fawcett, $2.95).

A boys' school on the eve of World War II is depicted in John Knowles's *A Separate Peace* (Macmillan, 1960, $13.95; pap., Bantam, $2.95). A sequel is *Peace Breaks Out* (pap., Bantam, $3.50).

A group of boys turns to savagery when marooned on a tropical island in William Golding's *Lord of the Flies* (Coward, 1962, $13.95, pap. $3.95).

In the adult novel *The Dancing Men* by Duncan Kyer (Holt, 1985, $14.95), a family secret jeopardizes a U.S. presidential hopeful's chances.

About the Book

Booklist, March 15, 1985, p. 1038.
Bulletin of the Center for Children's Books, April 1985, p. 143.
Horn Book, July/August 1985, p. 451.
New York Times Book Review, May 5, 1985, p. 34.
School Library Journal, April 1985, p. 96.
VOYA, June 1985, p. 128.
See also *Book Review Digest,* 1985, p. 339, and *Book Review Index,* 1985, p. 142.

About the Author

Campbell, Patricia J. *Presenting Robert Cormier.* Schenectady: Twayne, 1985.
Commire, Anne, ed. *Something about the Author.* Detroit: Gale, 1976. Vol. 10, p. 28; updated 1986. Vol. 45, pp. 58–65.
Estes, Glenn E., ed. *American Writers for Children since 1960: Fiction* (*Dictionary of Literary Biography,* Vol. 52). Detroit: Gale, 1986, pp. 107–114.
Evory, Ann, ed. *Contemporary Authors* (New Revision Series). Detroit: Gale, 1982. Vol. 5, pp. 130–132.

Holtze, Sally Holmes, ed. *Fifth Book of Junior Authors and Illustrators.* New York: Wilson, 1983, pp. 86–87.

Kirkpatrick, D. L., ed. *Twentieth-Century Children's Writers* (2nd edition). New York: St. Martin's, 1983, p. 203.

Senick, Gerard J., ed. *Children's Literature Review.* Detroit: Gale, 1987. Vol. 12, pp. 144–155.

Crutcher, Chris.   *The Crazy Horse Electric Game*
Greenwillow, 1987 $10.25; pap., Dell/Laurel Leaf, $3.25

During the early 1960s and before, one of the mainstays of the so-called junior novel was the sports story, with such representative writers as John R. Tunis, Duane Decker, and Joe Archibald. Although interest in sports has certainly not diminished, fiction on the subject has all but disappeared. Chris Crutcher seems to be leading a renaissance in this genre with already such fine novels to his credit as *Running Loose* (Greenwillow, 1982, $10.25; pap., Dell, $2.95) and *Stotan!* (Greenwillow, 1986, $10.25; condensed in *Juniorplots 3*, Bowker, 1987, pp. 238–243). *The Crazy Horse Electric Game* uses baseball and basketball as background sports, but it is principally the story of a courageous boy's struggle to conquer a physical disability and to make the necessary adjustments toward his family and friends that this disability brings. It covers a two-year period in the life of Willie Weaver and is recommended for grades 9 through 12.

Plot Summary

In the small town of Colo in eastern Montana, 16-year-old Willie Weaver is the local sports hero. Not only does he excel as the pitcher and ace batter on the Samson Florals baseball team, named after its sponsoring flower shop, but he also plays football well in school and dabbles in basketball. His commitment to sports is partly because he loves the games but also because he is obligated to continue an illustrious family reputation. The local sports field is named after his grandfather, a star athlete at Notre Dame, and his father, Big Will, whom Willie idolizes, was named Most Valuable Player when he lead his university football team to victory in the Rose Bowl during the early 1960s.

Willie's mother, Sandy, is also a firm supporter, although much of her zest for life was destroyed when her only other child, six-month-old Missy, died of SIDS (Sudden Infant Death Syndrome) in her crib four years ago. A lingering, vague guilt haunts her, although she was not responsible for the death.

Willie's friends include his loving girlfriend, Jenny Blackburn, herself a fine basketball player, Johnny Rivers, the catcher on the team and irrepressible master of word plays, and Petey Shropshire, another teammate.

The biggest game of the baseball season is against the Crazy Horse Electric team for the Eastern Montana American Legion Championship. By the top of the ninth, Willie has pitched an exemplary game and the Samson Florals are ahead 1–0 because of Willie's triple in the fifth. Crazy Horse's big gun, Sal Whitworth is at bat with one out and one on base. With supreme nonchalance, Willie catches Sal's fly ball with his back to the plate and flips the ball to second for the third out. Willie is lionized by the town and later his teammates present him with a cane, the head of which is baseball-shaped and inscribed "Willie Weaver 1, Crazy Horse Electric 0."

The Weaver family plus Jenny and Johnny go to nearby Salmon Lake for the last picnic of the autumn. With Big Will at the controls of their boat and Jenny spotting, Willie begins water skiing. He misjudges a move, loses control, and a ski tip cracks open his skull. His father panics, but Jenny saves him from the water and applies mouth to mouth resuscitation.

Willie's brain damage partially paralyzes one side of his body and causes halting pauses in his speech. He now begins using in earnest the cane his teammates gave him.

Willie wants to withdraw completely from life, but his father, troubled by his own guilt, forces him to return to school where he is sickened both by his own condition and by the pity of his friends. Things deteriorate further when Willie's first experience with acid at a party produces such a violent reaction that he must be taken to an emergency ward. Although his understanding therapist–counselor, Cyril Wheat, is of some help, Willie's father's impatience with his lack of progress, the discovery that Jenny has a new boyfriend, and his parents' quarreling over his condition force Willie to a drastic decision. He packs his bag, collects all his money, and heads for the bus station.

He first gets a bus to Spokane and then catches another to California. Outside the Oakland bus station he is jumped by Kam and his gang of Chinese punks called Jo Boys, beaten up, and robbed of all his money. A black bus driver named Lacey Casteel finds him and reluctantly takes him home to nurse his wounds. Lacey is not as respectable as he appears. His main source of income is as a pimp for his stable of prostitutes. Willie nevertheless appreciates Lacey's hospitality and acts as his housekeeper in exchange for room and board. Lacey enrolls him in an alternate school, OMLC High (short for One More Last Chance), where he will earn his tuition by performing janitorial work. This school is operated by a dedicated black director, Andre Porter, and is inhabited by such problem kids and public school dropouts as Warren Hawkins, a streetwise teenager known as Hawk; Jack, a superactive youngster who is also called the Telephone Man because of his avowed occupational goal; and Angel, an attractive black girl who earns money as one of Lacey's stable.

Willie, something of a misfit himself, is accepted by these students on his own terms. He becomes a special protégée of the physical education teacher, Lisa, who gives him specific exercises for his problems, enrolls him in Nautilus training at a local gym, and persuades her lover, Sammy, a Japanese-American Tai Chi expert, to give Willie lessons in oriental movement and martial arts.

Under this specific individual attention, Willie's condition improves as the months pass, and eventually he is back to normal. His home life with ill-tempered Lacey is, however, less satisfying. One evening Lacey attacks Angel unmercifully. Willie intervenes, using his cane with such violence that Lacey must be admitted to the hospital. Willie later apologizes and is accepted back by Lacey, who in an emotional scene confesses to Willie that in one of his former bouts of manic violence he had brain-damaged his only son. His helping Willie is an act of contrition and he now regards the boy as a surrogate son.

Jo Boys, the neighborhood gang that had attacked Willie months before, begin vandalizing the school. When Hawk beats up their leader, Kam, they plan revenge. One evening when Willie is alone in the basement, they enter and set fire to the school. Surrounded by flames, Kam spots Willie and attacks him, but Willie knocks Kam down with his cane and drags him to safety and an eventual jail term.

Through community efforts, the school is rebuilt and Willie and his friends graduate. Uncertain of what he will find, he boards a bus and heads for Colo, Montana. His reception is generally far from cordial. His father, now divorced, has become a mean alcoholic who grudgingly talks to his son; his mother has remarried and though she is overjoyed to see her son, she now has a new husband and baby—a new life that doesn't include Willie. Even Jenny is filled with spite and recriminations about his absence. Willie, sensing that his true home is now elsewhere, buys his dad's old motorcycle and heads back to Oakland.

Thematic Material

Although there is enough sports action to qualify this as a sports novel, other themes predominate. The delicate structure of family ties is examined, as well as one boy's struggle to overcome physical and emotional handicaps. Father-son relationships are also explored as are the often debilitating effects of guilt. Life on the seamy side is portrayed realistically but with emphasis on values and human dignity. Other important themes are courage, friendship, interracial relationships, the nature of pity, and attitudes toward the handicapped.

Book Talk Material

After introducing Willie, his family, and friends, one or more of the following passages could be used: the Crazy Horse Electric game (pp. 19–24; pp. 26–32 pap.); Johnny tells a whopper in English class (pp. 27–30; pp. 34–38 pap.); Willie's water skiing accident (pp. 42–45; pp. 50–52 pap.); the party and drug taking (pp. 52–59; pp. 59–67 pap.); and Big Will loses his temper over Willie's disabilities (pp. 73–77; pp. 81–85 pap.).

Additional Selections

A high school soccer star with cancer finds self-help on an archaeological dig in Jan Greenberg's *No Dragons to Slay* (Farrar, 1984, $10.95, pap. $3.45).

A Mexican-American family, gangs in Los Angeles, and 14-year-old Chato are featured in Danny Santiago's *Famous All Over Town* (Simon, 1983, $14.95; pap., NAL, $7.95).

A group of misfits helps save a threatened buffalo herd in Glendon Swarthout's *Bless the Beasts and Children* (pap., Pocket, $2.95; condensed in *More Juniorplots*, Bowker, 1977, pp. 226–228).

Tony Ross is an exchange student in Japan but finds he can't leave his family's problems behind in David Klass's *Breakaway Run* (Dutton, 1987, $13.95).

A prize sheep dog is separated from its master in a story of love and courage, *Nop's Trials* (Crown, 1984, $14.95; pap., Warner, $3.95), by Donald McCaig.

Matt's mother and sister are killed by a drunken driver and he must adjust in Marc Talbert's *Dead Birds Singing* (Little, 1985, $12.45).

John Locke is hired to escort a rich, spoiled teenager around Italy in Jack Barnao's exciting *Hammer Locke* (Scribner's, 1986, $13.95; pap., Ace, $3.50).

David Guy's *Second Brother* (NAL, 1986, $14.95) is about a high school freshman's growing up in the shadow of an over-achieving older brother.

Ray Maloney's novel *The Impact Zone* (Delacorte, 1986, $14.95; pap., Dell, $2.95) explores a delicate father-son relationship.

Ted Conover gave up his comfortable existence to become a railroad hobo and found that people have much in common in *Rolling Nowhere* (pap., Penguin, $5.95).

About the Book
Booklist, April 15, 1987, p. 1275.
Bulletin of the Center for Children's Books, May 1987, p. 165.
School Library Journal, May 1987, p. 108.
VOYA, June 1987, p. 76.
See also *Book Review Digest,* 1987, p. 408, and *Book Review Index,* 1987, p. 174.

About the Author
Commire, Anne, ed. *Something about the Author.* Detroit: Gale, 1988. Vol. 52, p. 31.
May, Hal, ed. *Contemporary Authors.* Detroit: Gale, 1985. Vol. 113, pp. 103–104.

Dorris, Michael.   *A Yellow Raft in Blue Water*
Henry Holt, 1987, $16.95; pap., Warner, $7.95

This highly original first novel contains the story of three generations of lonely, complex native-American women. The first narrator is Rayona, a 15-year-old half-Indian, half-black; the second, her mother, Christine; and last, the grandmother, who is known in the family as Aunt Ida. Each story complements the others by adding extensions in both plot and time, and new dimensions to the characters already introduced. The locales are the Pacific Northwest, chiefly the Seattle–Tacoma area, and an Indian reservation in Montana. Using a reverse chronological order, the novel extends from the present to the closing years of World War II. Some of the language and incidents are sexually explicit but always presented maturely and in keeping with the author's narrative purpose. It is a wonderful reading experience for mature readers in the senior high school grades.

Plot Summary

Rayona's visit to her Indian mother, Christine, in a Seattle hospital is interrupted by the arrival of her black father, Elgin. As long as Rayona can remember, her parents have had a life of separation, numerous sexual affairs, heaving drinking, and short-lived reconciliations. Rayona, who has lived a pillar-to-post existence with her mother, longs for the security and stability of the middle-class families she sees on television.

Christine is so insulted by her husband's indifference to her condition that when he leaves, she grabs her medicine, dons a candy-striper's uniform, and leaves, meeting Rayona in the parking lot. At first she mutters intentions of suicide, but instead they return home in Christine's beat-up Volare after a delay caused by an empty gas tank.

The next day without explanation, Christine orders Rayona to pack all her belongings—they are moving to the Indian reservation in Montana where Christine's mother, Aunt Ida lives. Rayona's only previous visit there was many years before when she was taken to the burial service of Christine's only brother, Lee, a much-beloved young man who was killed in Vietnam. By using an expired credit card to purchase gas and food for the trip, the two arrive at Aunt Ida's. The old lady shows such hostility toward her daughter that Christine grabs her two plastic bags and hitches a ride from a passing motorist, leaving her daughter behind.

Rayona is an enterprising, independent girl, but she is miserable living with Ida, a taciturn, solitary woman who speaks only an Indian language that Rayona fortunately knows. At the reservation school she is taunted and insulted because of her mixed parentage by her Great-Aunt Pauline's son, Foxy Cree, and his girlfriend, Annabelle Stiffarm. In desperation she accepts the help of a do-gooder priest, Father Tom Novak, who offers to take her as a representative of his God's Squad to a Teens for Christ jamboree in Helena. On the way they stop at Bearpaw Lake State Park, where she sees a beautiful yellow raft in the peaceful waters of the lake. She swims to it, but when Father Novak tries to do the same, he develops a cramp and Rayona must pull him onto the raft. Here the priest becomes so sexually excited that he begins rolling around on top of Rayona. Fearful that she will tell others about his misconduct, he gladly encourages, with a gift of money, her plan not to return to the reservation but to continue to Seattle.

She pauses at a gas station in the park and meets the owner–operator, Norman "Sky" Dial, who takes her to his trailer to meet his wife, Evelyn, the cook for the park workers. They manage to get Rayona a job gathering litter in the park and she moves in with the Dials. She tells them a fanciful story that her parents are rich and presently vacationing in Switzerland and that she has their permission to have her own adventure. They find her story unconvincing until they see the scrap end of a letter in Rayona's possession signed "Mother and Pop" wishing her well and stating how much everyone including the dog Rascal misses her. Actually this is only a discarded piece of paper Rayona found in the park but saved because it represents the kind of life and family she would like.

Rayona fits in well and is loved by the Dials. She envies and admires from afar the beautiful and talented white lifeguard and college student Ellen De Marco.

Rayona's masquerade ends abruptly when Mr. and Mrs. De Marco visit Ellen, and Evelyn overhears them speak of their dog, Rascal. Rayona blurts out the truth, and far from being angry, they volunteer to help the girl find her mother, whom Rayona believes is now living on the reservation with Lee's old friend, a mixed breed named Dayton Nickles.

A big Indian rodeo is planned in Havre, and Rayona is convinced that someone there will have news of her mother. The three set out. There Rayona meets drunken Foxy, who persuades her to ride in his place in the bronc-busting event. She consents because the horse she is scheduled to ride, Babe, belongs to Christine's boyfriend, Dayton. She narrowly escapes death and is thrown three times, but for her courage and tenacity she wins a special prize as the "roughest, toughest, clumsiest cowboy in the event." When she claims the prize, a silver-plated buckle, her identity is revealed. Dayton appears to take her and his horse back home. She says good-bye to Sky and Evelyn and is soon reunited with her mother, who she realizes is very ill. In Dayton's comfortable house, mother and daughter again try to create a home.

In Christine's story we are first back in the 1960s on the reservation. She is in her teens and completely in the thrall of her handsome, charming brother, Lee, four years younger than she. As Lee grows into adolescence, he forms a close friendship with Dayton, which arouses Christine's jealousy, and he also becomes involved in the native-American civil rights movement. As his eighteenth birthday approaches, he announces that he will flee the draft and will not fight in a white man's war in Vietnam. But Christine goads him with accusations of cowardice until he relents and enlists.

With Lee, her chief interest in life, about to leave the reservation, Christine makes a hasty decision and, without telling sullen Aunt Ida, leaves for Seattle and freedom. She moves from one menial job to another and has a series of male companions. On the day she learns that Lee is missing in action, she wanders into a bar and meets a black soldier, Elgin Taylor. They have a tempestuous love affair. Christine becomes pregnant and they marry. Rayona is born the same day that news reaches Christine that Lee is officially considered dead.

As time slips by, Christine's marriage and her life disintegrate into sessions of drinking, quarreling with Elgin, and one-night stands. Only once does Aunt Ida visit her. Ida insists that Christine accompany her to a hospital in Seattle to see a dying relative, Clara, who is the younger sister of Ida's mother.

Christine's health deteriorates and she is sent to the hospital where the doctor tells her that she has only six months to live. Desperate to provide for Rayona, she hurriedly leaves Seattle and deposits her daughter with Aunt Ida at the reservation. Her mother's hostility arouses Christine's anger, and she leaves and moves in with bachelor Dayton, who realizes that she is desperately sick. He tends her as he would a sister.

Although Christine misses her daughter, she feels that separation at this time is necessary. However, when Dayton returns from a rodeo with Rayona in tow, she somewhat begrudgingly allows a little joy into her life at this, their last reunion.

Ida's story reveals a dark family secret. During the last years of World War II, her mother, suffering from a lingering heart disease, sends for her younger sister, Clara, a vivacious, fun-loving girl, to help run the household on the reservation. Ida worships her aunt, and later when it is revealed that she is pregnant by Ida's father, to avoid a scandal she volunteers to accompany Clara to a convent in Denver, wait out the pregnancy with her, and then bring back the baby as her own.

Christine is born and Ida returns to face the shame and censure of the reservation community. Clara, who is now revealed as a shallow, selfish woman, tries to have the baby adopted, but Ida steadfastly retains custody of the child.

When her mother dies and her father wanders off the reservation, Ida takes in as a companion and lover the once-handsome Willard Yellow Dog, now grotesquely scarred from war wounds. She becomes pregnant, but tells no one. Willard undergoes facial surgery that restores his good looks. Ida, knowing that he once again will be the catch of the reservation, lets him go and later bears his son, Lee. In isolation she raises her family and eventually sees each leave her: her daughter for a dissolute life in Seattle and her son to his death in Vietnam.

Thematic Material

This is a story rich in incident, but is essentially a novel of character. The novel has created three tough, indomitable women who will remain in the reader's memory long after the book is finished. It contains many themes, such as the crippling effects of rejection, the tragedy of betrayed love, the need for belonging, and the gutsy fortitude required to endure life's problems. It examines the defenses that people develop to help them survive but that often create barriers to honest relationships. The gritty stubbornness and pride that each of these women has developed both shield and divide them. It tells of three women's coming-of-age ordeals, and of the complexity of family relationships, particularly those involving mothers and daughters. In these contrasting stories, the unity of time and the multiple shades of truth are explored. Though the novel deals with emotions that transcend race, it also gives an unforgettable portrayal of native-American culture on the decline, past and present life on the reservation, and a glimpse of racial prejudice.

Book Talk Material

An introduction to the three overlapping life stories in the book will interest readers. Some important passages: Christine and Rayona join a video club (pp. 18–21; pp. 18–22 pap.); the trip to Aunt Ida's (pp. 23–28; pp. 25–30 pap.); Rayona joins the God Squad (pp. 38–42; pp. 41–45 pap.); the raft at Bearpaw Lake and the incident with Father Tom (pp. 54–59; pp. 58–64 pap.); and finding the scrap of letter and its consequences (pp. 74–80; pp. 80–86 pap.).

Additional Selections

Three generations of Palestinian Christian women are featured in the family saga *Daughters* by Consuelo Saah Baehr (Delacorte, 1988, $18.95).

In the pre-whiteman Plains Sioux culture, a young girl grows to womanhood in Ella Cara Delorio's *Waterlily* (Univ. of Nebraska, 1988, $18.95).

Another three-generational novel is Berlic Doherty's *Granny Was a Buffer Girl* (Watts, 1988, $13.95).

A Cree boy grows to maturity with whites in Hal Borland's *When the Legend Dies* (pap., Bantam, $2.95), and a white boy is raised Indian in Conrad Richter's *A Light in the Forest* (Knopf, 1953, $13.95; pap., Bantam, $2.75).

Navajo culture forms a backdrop for a series of excellent mystery stories by Tony Hillerman including *Skinwalkers* (Harper, 1987, $15.45, pap. $3.95) and *A Thief of Time* (Harper, 1980, $15.95).

A multigenerational novel featuring an Indian rodeo rider is Craig Lesley's *Winterkill* (Houghton, 1984, $14.95).

In *House Made of Dawn* (pap., Harper, 1977, $3.95) by N. Scott Momaday, a troubled misfit cannot find peace either on the reservation or in the city. Also use Jamake Highwater's historical trilogy about an Indian family beginning with *Legend Days* (Harper, 1984, $11.70).

For a slightly younger audience, Norma Johnston in *The Potter's Wheel* (Morrow, 1988, $11.95) unravels a plot that brings daughter, mother, and grandmother together.

In the nonfictional *The Last Algonquin*, by Theodore L. Kazimiroff (Walker, 1982, $14.95; pap., Dell, $7.95), Joe Two Trees, unable to live in a white man's world, retreats to an island off New York City after the Civil War.

About the Book
Booklist, March 1, 1987, p. 946.
Library Journal, May 1, 1987, p. 82.
New York Times Book Review, June 7, 1987, p. 7.
VOYA, August 1987, p. 119.
See also *Book Review Digest*, 1988, and *Book Review Index*, 1987, p. 206.

About the Author
Locher, Francis C., ed. *Contemporary Authors*. Detroit: Gale, 1981. Vol. 102, p. 154.
Metzger, Linda, ed. *Contemporary Authors* (New Revision Series). Detroit: Gale, 1987. Vol. 19, p. 173.

Fox, Paula. *The Moonlight Man*
Bradbury, 1986, $12.95

Paula Fox's brilliant literary career has encompassed fiction for children, young adults, and adults. Among the many awards she has gathered for her books is the 1974 Newbery Medal for *The Slave Dancer* (Bradbury, 1973, $10.95; pap., Dell, $2.25; condensed in *More Juniorplots*, Bowker, 1977, pp. 82–86). In *The Moonlight Man* she explores the complex relationship of a father and daughter when the girl gradually realizes that the father she has worshiped has very real feet of clay. The book is suitable for readers in grades 9 through 12.

Plot Summary

Catherine's father, the writer Harry Ames, could be described in many ways—debonair, charming, undisciplined, irresponsible, and even undependable. These latter characteristics were now uppermost in Catherine's mind. Since the end of the school year, on June 7, three weeks ago, she has been waiting to be picked up by her father at her school, the Delraida Boarding and Day School in Montreal. He has promised her a seven-week stay with him at his home in Rockport while his second wife, Emma, is visiting Virginia. Catherine has heard nothing from him and is frantically making excuses to the headmistress, Madame Soule, and the only remaining faculty member, a frequently tipsy history instructor called Madame LeSueur.

Catherine's mother, Beatrice, and her father divorced when she was three years old, and from that time until last year Catherine has been living alone with her mother, an editor in a New York publishing house, in an attractive apartment on the West Side of Manhattan. Last year her mother married Carter, an academician, and Catherine was allowed for the first time to attend a boarding school.

Catherine is now 15—well liked, intelligent, and mature beyond her years. She has made many friends at school and has a special relationship with a 19-year-old sophomore at McGill named Philippe Petit, who is at present spending the summer in a remote Quebec logging camp.

Even after the three weeks' wait, she desperately hopes to hear from her father, a man she scarcely knows except for a few whirlwind visits to New York when he dazzled her with his erudition and ebullience. Carter and her mother are traveling in Europe, or Madam Soule would certainly have tried to contact them. But time is running out for Catherine. When it appears that reaching her mother is her only alternative, she receives a call from Harry Ames from Nova Scotia. After mumbling ill-formed excuses about overimbibing plus minor writing and marital problems, he invites Catherine to spend time in Nova Scotia where he has rented a cottage close to the ocean for a month.

Within two days of her arrival, she discovers a hitherto hidden side to her father's personality. He invites two local townspeople, Farmer Glimm and a bus driver named Conklin, to their cottage where the three proceed to get so roaring drunk that at 5:00 A.M. Catherine has to drive them home in her father's station wagon along unfamiliar dirt roads with her father passed out in the back seat. She is furious, but the next day her father, now contrite and hung over, is again sufficiently disarmingly engaging to win her over. As a sign of forgiveness, she shaves her father, whose hands are so shaky he can scarcely hold a coffee cup. Though completely washed out, he nevertheless enchants the cleaning woman, Mrs. Landey, when she arrives.

Gradually, their lives become more routine. Because of Catherine's objections, her father, under great strain, seriously limits his drinking. One day they go fishing with the local minister, a dour, severe man named Reverend Ross. The combination of unsuccessful fishing plus Ross's indifference to his blandishments eventually bore Ames and he becomes sullen. On another occasion Catherine is disappointed and perhaps a little jealous when she discovers her father flirting with Mrs. Conklin, the wife of his drinking partner. Catherine realizes that her father seems to have a limitless need for admiration and attention.

Through these experiences and their many days alone, Catherine at last becomes acquainted with this enigmatic man, her father. He is a man of contradictions: on the outside a published novelist when in his early twenties, brilliant, witty, suave, and self-assured, but inwardly now a pathetic 50-year-old hack writer whose charms are running thin as his alcoholism increases. In spite of these failings, Catherine still loves and respects her father. She is also still enchanted by his knowledge of literature, foreign countries, and the finer things in life. He thrives on this adulation, but during times of stress in their relationship he seems to regard her as the personification of his own conscience.

A few days before leaving, Ames befriends a young Royal Canadian mounted policeman, Officer Macbeth, who in his off-hours agrees to take him on a tour of the local bootleggers. Catherine accompanies him and is horrified to notice that at each still, while she remains in the car, her father is once again drinking uncontrollably. Before he finally passes out, she is disgusted to see him on all fours, barking like a dog.

With Macbeth's help, she gets him home, but when his breathing becomes erratic, Catherine drives to Reverend Ross for his help. Together they get Ames to bed after fits of violent vomiting.

The next morning her father is subdued but haughty and seemingly unrepentant. This angers Catherine so much that she screams, "You're nothing. You're just a drunk, you bastard!" He grabs her and holds her until she says she will forgive him. Their last days are at first strained, but gradually the two begin once more to talk and even laugh together.

Catherine is met in New York by her mother, newly arrived from Europe. Under questioning, Catherine protects her father and does not mention his three-week silence or his drinking bouts. But she inwardly wonders about the future of her relationship with him now that they know one another so well. Particularly distressing were his parting words. His reply to her "See you" was a kiss and "Not if I see you first."

Thematic Material

This novel explores father and daughter relationships from the perspective of the young girl. Throughout the novel the differences between exterior appearances and inner reality are explored. It probes the shattering disillusionment and disenchantment of discovering weaknesses in someone previously adored to the point of worship. That this involves one's father—the man that every son or daughter wants to admire and be proud of—makes the story doubly poignant, particularly in contrast to the many tender moments that Catherine shares with her father. The reluctant recognition and acceptance of the flaws in her father's character are well portrayed. The description of an alcoholic and his subterfuges is truthful and uncompromising. Catherine emerges as a strong, admirable person who though saddened by these experiences has matured and grown in independence as a result. The author has also interestingly and often amusingly portrayed small-town life in rural Nova Scotia.

Book Talk Material

An introduction to Catherine's dilemma while waiting for her father, and a foreshadowing of events to come, should interest prospective readers. Some incidents of importance are: the long-awaited phone call from her father (pp. 12–16); driving her father's drinking companions home (pp. 21–27); and the morning after (pp. 29–35).

Additional Selections

A daughter is unable to please her father whom she wants to love in Cyra McFaddan's *Rain or Shine* (Knopf, 1986, $16.95; pap., Vintage, $4.95).

Kate resents being dominated and overshadowed by her famous artist father in Zibby Oneal's *In Summer Light* (Viking, 1985, $12.95; pap., Bantam, $2.95; condensed in *Juniorplots 3*, Bowker, 1987, pp. 82–85).

Michael, who is grieving the death of his father, falls in love with Courtney, whose father is a recovering alcoholic, in Stephen Schwandt's *Holding Steady* (Henry Holt, 1988, $13.95).

In Julie Reece Deaver's first novel, *Say Goodnight Gracie* (Harper, 1988, $12.95), Morgan painfully adjusts to the death of her dear friend Jimmy.

An old man remembers an unloving father in *Isaac Campion* by Janni Howker (Greenwillow, 1987, $10.25).

Seventeen-year-old Ariel wants to escape from her domineering, cruel father in Lynn Hall's *Flyaway* (Scribner's, 1987, $12.95).

Catherine's father has committed suicide and she blames the women in his life, including herself, in Jean Thesman's *The Last April Dancers* (Houghton, 1987, $13.95).

After her father's death, Olivia reviews their relationship in Paul Fleischman's *Rear-View Mirrors* (Harper, 1986, $10.89; condensed in *Juniorplots 3*, Bowker, 1987, pp. 45–48).

A father wants to reestablish contact with his three sons in Doug Finn's *Heart of a Family* (Univ. of New York, 1984, $14.95).

Five teenage brothers steal their alcoholic father's car hoping to escape his abuse in Joyce Sweeney's *Center Line* (Delacorte, 1984, $14.95).

About the Book
Booklist, April 15, 1986, p. 1220.
Bulletin of the Center for Children's Books, April 1986, p. 147.
Horn Book, May 1986, p. 330.
New York Times Book Review, March 23, 1986, p. 48.
School Library Journal, April 1986, p. 96.
VOYA, August 1986, p. 142.
See also *Book Review Digest*, 1987, p. 615, and *Book Review Index*, 1986, p. 257; 1987, p. 259.

About the Author

Block, Ann, and Riley, Carolyn, eds. *Children's Literature Review*. Detroit: Gale, 1976. Vol. 1, pp. 59–60.

Commire, Anne, ed. *Something about the Author*. Detroit: Gale, 1979. Vol. 17, pp. 59–60.

de Montreville, Doris, and Crawford, Elizabeth D., eds. *Fourth Book of Junior Authors and Illustrators*. New York: Wilson, 1978, pp. 135–136.

Estes, Glenn E., ed. *American Writers for Children since 1960: Fiction (Dictionary of Literary Biography*, Vol. 52). Detroit: Gale, 1986, pp. 143–156.

Locher, Frances C., ed. *Contemporary Authors*. Detroit: Gale, 1978. Vols. 73–76, pp. 214–215.

Guest, Judith.   *Ordinary People*
pap., Ballantine, $3.95

To publishers, the term "over the transom" refers to the arrival, directly from an author, of an unsolicited manuscript. Such an event usually produces nothing more than a rejection slip, but with *Ordinary People* it began a Cinderella story almost unheard of in publishing circles. The book when published in 1976 became a best-seller in both trade and paperback editions, as well as a selection of four major book clubs.

The story concerns a family of three normal, seemingly typical people who live comfortably in the upper-middle-class suburban community of Lake Forest, Illinois. They are 41-year-old Cal Jarrett, a successful tax attorney, his lovely wife, Beth, and their 17-year-old son, Conrad (Con). All three, however, are beset by a debilitating residue of guilt and sorrow resulting from two rarely mentioned tragedies in their lives: the accidental death of an older son, and the resultant suicide attempt by Con six months later. The novel, told in brief, abrupt episodes, covers one year and details the shifting relationships and adjustments that these traumatic events ultimately cause in the lives of these "ordinary people." It is read and enjoyed by both adults and mature teenagers.

Plot Summary

When Conrad Jarrett awakens on the morning of September 30, he realizes that it is a special day for him because it is exactly one month since he was sent home after eight months of treatment in a mental institution following a suicide attempt. Assessing his situation, he wonders if he is really making progress.

At school Conrad has always been a perfectionist, a straight A student driven to excel. Since his return, he has tried to regain this academic record as well as resume his extracurricular activities in choir and swimming. However, the old motivation somehow is lacking, and having lost a year, he finds it difficult to relate to his old friends like Joe Lazenby and Dick Van Buren, who are now seniors. Even Kevin Stillman, the acknowledged bane of everyone's existence, is unduly annoying.

In many ways, Con has an ideal father in Cal. He is attentive, generous, but in his desire to prevent a relapse, often overly solicitous toward his son. Cal has undergone many vicissitudes in his life. He is a self-made man who though orphaned at 11 and brought up as a public ward, managed to graduate from law school and establish a successful tax practice with his close friend and partner Ray Hanley. On the other hand, Cal's mother was raised without want in a solid middle-class environment. Since Conrad's return she has continued her efficiently well-organized life of meticulous housekeeping, golfing, bridge, and other social events as though nothing has happened. Behind her cold matter-of-factness and independence Conrad feels an objectivity bordering at times on indifference.

In spite of a veneer of normality and outward cheerfulness, each of the three is alone, separated from the others by a private world of sorrow and silence involving the death over a year before of Jordan, nicknamed Buck, the light-hearted, carefree older son who was drowned when the boat in which he and Con were sailing capsized during an unexpected storm on Lake Michigan.

Over breakfast, Cal casually but calculatingly suggests that Con should heed his hospital doctor's recommendation and begin seeing a local psychiatrist, Dr. Berger. Later that week when Conrad visits Dr. Berger, he is confronted by a man who resembles a slightly mad, undersized gorilla who makes rotten coffee. Though obviously eccentric, Berger so impresses Conrad with his candor, humor, and relaxed attitude that the boy begins seeing him twice a week. Dr. Berger tries to ease Conrad's tensions and self-generated pressures by persuading him to give up his after-school swimming classes. Conrad delays telling his parents about this change, but unfortunately at a women's meeting, Beth learns about it from Joe Lazenby's mother. That evening she accuses Conrad of being deceitful and unfeeling, in that he has needlessly caused her embarrassment and humiliation in front of her friends. Cal defends his son and the couple quarrel. Beth openly expresses the resentment she has inwardly felt since Conrad's return concerning the amount of attention Cal showers on his son at the expense of her own feelings and concerns. This becomes the leitmotif of many quarrels in the future.

For Christmas, Cal decides to give Conrad a very special gift, an automobile. After the traditional turkey dinner with Beth's parents, Ellen and Howard Butler, Cal presents his son with the keys to a new LeMans. Conrad reacts in a dazed way and does not show the expected gratitude and excitement. Later that evening Beth again accuses Cal of overindulging their son while neglecting her.

At the same time that the Jarretts' marriage is floundering, Conrad's fortunes prosper under Berger's tutelage. The psychiatrist's success in freeing Conrad from his prison of passivity and guilt often brings unexpected results like a fist fight with Kevin Stillman, in which Conrad is the victor. On a more constructive note, Conrad begins a friendship with Jeannine Pratt, a new girl in town whom he first meets at choir practice. During the spring, their dating becomes more frequent and through their mutual exchange of love, Conrad feels for the first time the responsibility of having someone depend and rely on him.

To help pacify Beth, Cal takes her for a weekend to Dallas to visit with her brother and sister-in-law. Unfortunately their short vacation ends with more recriminations when Beth again accuses Cal of indifference and apathy.

While his parents are away, Conrad stays with his grandparents. Although he is able to successfully weather his grandmother's well-intentioned nagging, on Sunday night after reading of the suicide of Karen Aldrich, one of his close friends and copatients at the hospital, he is once more thrust into an emotional crisis during which he courageously and unflinchingly relives both his suicide attempt and the death of his brother. The next day in a painful session with Dr. Berger, he confronts and explodes the guilt myth that somehow he should have saved his brother's life.

By the end of the summer, the Jarretts decide on a trial separation while Beth goes to Europe to sort things out. On the other hand, Conrad has so grown in confidence and self-understanding that he checks himself out from Dr. Berger's care. In thinking of the many changes the year has brought to his family, he realizes that "it is love, imperfect and unordered that keeps them apart, even as it holds them somehow together."

Thematic Material

The author seems to be saying that in this life there really aren't any "ordinary people." Conrad's quote about the paradoxical effects on family love provides an important theme. Another is that sorrow, though often destructive, can lead to greater self-understanding. The author has captured beautifully the doubts and anxieties of adolescence. Conrad's recovery is convincingly told and the sessions between the boy and his "hip" psychiatrist are revealing and entertaining. As well, they are bound to challenge a teenager's conventional image of a "head shrink."

Book Talk Material

A discussion of Conrad's feelings about the constructive and destructive elements in love (p. 245) could serve as an introduction. Other passages of interest are: Conrad's first visit to Dr. Berger (pp. 35–41); his visits with Karen (pp. 49–54); Beth confronts him about dropping swimming (pp. 100–104); and the quarrel on Christmas Day (pp. 117–119).

Additional Selections

John fights parental authority and a distorted black self-image in James Baldwin's 1953 novel *Go Tell It on the Mountain* (pap., Dell, $4.95).

Fifteen-year-old Karen has a love affair and learns about adult relationships when visiting her unconventional aunt in Lowry Pei's *Family Resemblances* (Random, 1986, $16.95).

When a 15-year-old boy commits suicide, everyone asks why in Fran Arrick's *Tunnel Vision* (Bradbury, 1980, $10.95; pap., Dell, $2.75).

Teenagers Buck and Kate cannot believe that their dearest friend, Trav, is suicidal in Richard Peck's *Remembering the Good Times* (Delacorte, 1985, $13.95; pap., Dell, $2.95; condensed in *Juniorplots 3,* Bowker, 1987, pp. 90–94).

Some fine nonfiction titles on teenage suicide are *A Time to Listen: Preventing Youth Suicide* by Patricia Hermes (Harcourt, 1987, $12.95); *Teenage Suicide* by Sandra Gardner (Messner, 1985, $9.79); and Peter Sioracchini's *The Urge to Die: Why Young People Commit Suicide* (pap., Penguin, $5.95).

A brother and sister are sent to their uncle's ranch in the tragic novel by Jean Stafford, *The Mountain Lion* (pap., Dutton, $5.95).

After his father's death, 19-year-old David Marks tries on paper to capture their hostile relationship in Barbara Wersba's *Run Softly, Go Fast* (pap., Bantam, $3.95).

A 16-year-old girl adjusts to the death of her mother in Barbara Girion's *A Tangle of Roots* (pap., Berkley, $2.50).

Sibling rivalry and a hazardous backpacking trip are featured in Thomas Baird's *Walk Out a Brother* (Harper, 1983, $12.70).

About the Book
Booklist, June 15, 1976, p. 1572.
Horn Book, October 1976, p. 528.
Library Journal, May 1, 1976, p. 1142.
New York Times Book Review, July 18, 1976, p. 14.
School Library Journal, September 1976, p. 143.
See also *Book Review Digest,* 1976, p. 479; 1977, p. 540, and *Book Review Index,* 1976, p. 178.

About the Author
Locher, Frances, ed. *Contemporary Authors.* Detroit: Gale, 1979. Vols. 77–80, pp. 200–201.
Metzger, Linda, ed. *Contemporary Authors* (New Revised Series). Detroit: Gale, 1985. Vol. 15, pp. 170–174.

L'Engle, Madeleine.   *A House Like a Lotus*
Farrar, 1984, $12.95

In an earlier novel by Madeleine L'Engle *The Arm of the Starfish* (Farrar, 1965, $11.95; pap., Dell, $3.25), readers met 16-year-old Adam Eddington, a marine biology student who is bound for a remote island off Portugal to help Professor O'Keefe in his starfish research. During the flight the professor's 12-year-old daughter, Polyhmnia, or Polly, disappears, thus beginning a tale of international intrigue with, as in others of L'Engle's tales, a healthy moral point of view. Adam reappears in *A Ring of Endless Light* (Farrar, 1980, $11.95; pap., Dell, $2.95; condensed in *Juniorplots 3,* Bowker, 1987, pp. 63–67), and Polly, now 17, is the heroine of *A House Like a Lotus.* She is a bored, insecure teenager who welcomes friendship with an older female artist, Max Horne. The story, told in flashbacks, handles a lesbian incident that is traumatic for Polly with sensitivity and restraint. This novel about degrees of love and friendship is somewhat philosophical in tone and enjoyed by thoughtful readers in grades 9 through 12.

Plot Summary

Polly O'Keefe is on her way to Athens; she is to spend three weeks at a conference in a village called Osia Theola, where she will be a "gofer." This experience has been set up for her by her friend Max. But as Polly arrives in Athens where she will spend a couple of days before the conference, she is sick at heart with the betrayal she feels from the person she has adored.

At 16, Polly is the oldest of seven children born to two scientists. Although their home is now on Beene Seed Island in South Carolina, the O'Keefes have lived in and traveled to exotic places mostly pursuing her father's work as a marine biologist. Tall for her age and intelligent, Polly is slow to make friends among her peers and does not enjoy her high school years or living on the island in general . . . until Max comes into her life.

Max is Maximiliana Horne, a rich and talented artist who has returned to her mansion home on the island with her longtime companion, Dr. Ursula Heschel. Max opens Polly's eyes to culture—reading aloud from books of ancient history, religion, and poetry—and awakens her heart to an understanding of people; Max makes Polly see that the high school teacher she detests may be lonely and uncertain and reaching out.

For Max, Polly becomes the daughter she never had; for Polly, her adoration of Max grows to near worship. But two flaws appear in this impossibly idyllic situation. Polly senses that something is wrong with Max's health, and with the aid of her friend Renny, a young intern at the local hospital, she learns that Max is dying; she contracted a parasite on a South American trip. There is no cure—the disease affects the heart muscle—and Max has returned to the island for her last days. Polly also learns that there is talk about Max and her friend Ursula, and now about Polly for spending so much time with them. Polly learns that Max and Ursula have been lovers for 30 years.

Shocked at first, Polly talks with her mother, who tells her that she doesn't feel particularly curious about Max and Ursula's personal lives, that they have opened a world of ideas to Polly, and that she should not let vicious gossip destroy a true friendship. Polly eventually talks to Max and learns the truth. Max makes no apologies for her relationship with

Ursula, but she tries to explain to Polly, and she tells her that she loves Polly as she would a daughter.

One night when Ursula must be away, Polly stays with Max because she should not be alone in her condition. Drinking to ease her pain, Max becomes drunk and slurry in speech and manner, to Polly's horror, and reaches out for her. Polly runs away, shocked and feeling betrayed. She goes to her friend Renny, and they make love, although both later realize that it will never happen again for them.

No amount of talk, even of Ursula's pleading for her to understand what Max is going through, will change Polly's mind. She refuses to talk about it, even to her parents.

Now in Athens, upset and confused and waiting for her aunt and uncle, who are late in arriving, to join her, Polly meets a wealthy young man named Zachery who seems to be "bumming" around Europe. Zachery is attracted to her, but Polly refuses a romantic relationship with him.

When Polly gets to the conference, she meets a number of fascinating, warm people, especially a young man named Omio from the island of Baki. She feels attracted to Omio and senses that he cares for her in return.

Zachery arrives at the conference to spend a few hours with Polly and they go out in a kayak, which overturns, and they are nearly drowned. Omio saves them.

As she is recovering from the ordeal, Polly thinks back to a conversation she had with her uncle before she left for Athens. It was about Max. He tells her that she had made Max into a god and that now she will not let Max be even a little human.

When Omio gives her a farewell present as a gesture of friendship, Polly is shocked to learn that he is married and has a child. But when she thinks it over, she realizes that his warmth and caring was that of a friend, nothing more. And when Zachery calls her, she realizes that she likes him but doesn't love him and that it is often difficult to understand what love really is. And she begins to understand that Omio had never promised her more than friendship; it was she who was grasping for more.

Would she have never wanted to have met Max, she asks herself. Would she have never wanted to have all those wonderful times, all the wonderful things she had learned from this intelligent, caring, dying woman? Perhaps that one moment when Max was drunk and not herself was terrible, but does that erase all the good ones? To cut Max out of her life would be to cut out a part of herself.

With this new understanding, Polly places a call to the United States, and to Max. "I love you," she tells her. And when Max says, "Forgive me," Polly adds, "Me, too, forgive me, too." When Polly tries to add that there is so much to tell Max when she returns, the line is cut off. But it is all right. . . . Polly has said what she needed to say.

Thematic Material

This is a complex, sensitive story dealing with relationships, those that are common in society, as husband and wife, child and parent, and those that are uncommon and generally not discussed, such as two women who are lesbians. The subject is handled with great sensitivity and understanding, as is the adoration young Polly feels for the older woman. Polly is portrayed as an above-average teenager who is still having difficulty dealing with her emotions; her parents are shown as people who try to give their children decent values by which to live; and Max and Ursula appear as two intelligent, contributing members of society who live their lives in dignity.

Book Talk Material

Polly's relationships with people and how they grow and develop are the keys to this sensitive novel. See: Polly learns of her forthcoming trip (pp. 14–15); Polly meets Max and Ursula (pp. 29–36); Polly meets Zachery (pp. 42–48); Max and Polly talk about love (pp. 83–84); Polly hears about the rumors (pp. 102–113).

Additional Selections

In college Liza Winthrop recalls how she met and fell in love with Annie Kenyon in Nancy Garden's *Annie on My Mind* (Farrar, 1982, $11.95, pap. $3.45).

Seventeen-year-old Lucille helps her parents and pregnant sister in her South Carolina home in Josephine Humphrey's *Rich in Love* (Viking, 1987, $16.95).

In Isabelle Holland's *Summer of My First Love* (pap., Fawcett, $2.26), Sarah finds she is pregnant by a Polish-American boy.

Jody's younger brother disappears and her family is falling apart in Susan Beth Pfeffer's *The Year without Michael* (Bantam, 1987, $13.95).

A young teenager befriends a hideously disfigured veteran in Margaret Rostkowski's *After the Dancing Days* (Harper, 1986, $13.95).

A young Japanese girl questions the beliefs of her people in a novel set after World War II, Hisako Matsubara's *Cranes at Dusk* (Dial, 1985, $15.95).

At 18, Pauline faces such problems as her older unmarried sister's pregnancy and the death of the juvenile delinquent friend of her younger sister in Janine Boissard's *Christmas Lessons* (Little, 1984, $15.95), a continuation of *A Matter of Feeling* (pap., Fawcett, $2.50).

Seventeen-year-old Paul Waterford matures after the death of his younger sister in a plane crash in John Wain's *The Free Zone Starts Here* (Delacorte, 1984, $13.95).

Brad is horrified to see his beloved grandfather become a victim of Alzheimer's disease in *Doc* (Harper, 1985, $13.95) by Richard Graber.

About the Book
Booklist, December 1, 1984, p. 518.
Bulletin of the Center for Children's Books, December 1984, p. 70.
Horn Book, January 1985, p. 58.
New York Times Book Review, February 17, 1985, p. 25.
School Library Journal, December 1984, p. 91; April 1985, p. 49.
VOYA, April 1985, p. 49.
See also *Book Review Digest*, 1985, p. 938, and *Book Review Index*, 1985, p. 369.

About the Author
Block, Ann; and Riley, Carolyn, eds. *Children's Literature Review*. Detroit: Gale, 1976. Vol. 2, pp. 129–134.
Commire, Anne, ed. *Something about the Author*. Detroit: Gale, 1971. Vol. 1, pp. 141–142; updated 1982. Vol. 27, pp. 131–140.
Estes, Glenn E., ed. *American Writers for Children since 1960: Fiction* (*Dictionary of Literary Biography*, Vol. 52). Detroit: Gale, 1986, pp. 241–249.
Ethedge, James M. *Contemporary Authors* (First Revision). Detroit: Gale, 1967. Vols. 1–4, pp. 582–583.
Evory, Ann. ed. *Contemporary Authors* (New Revision Series). Detroit: Gale, 1981. Vol. 3, pp. 331–332.
Fuller, Muriel, ed. *More Junior Authors*. New York: Wilson, 1963, pp. 137–138.
Kirkpatrick, D. L., ed. *Twentieth-Century Children's Writers* (2nd edition). New York: St. Martin's, 1983, pp. 467–469.

Plain, Belva. *The Golden Cup*
Delacorte, 1986, $17.95; pap., Dell, $4.95

Belva Plain was often asked by her family to tell them about her grandmother who had emigrated alone from Europe at age 16 to seek a new life in America. From these stories came the inspiration for *Evergreen* (Delacorte, 1978, $19.95; pap., Dell, $4.50), the romantic saga of Anna Friedman, a young Jewish girl who rises from the position of a poor Polish-born house servant to that of a wealthy dowager. Many of the characters introduced in *Evergreen* reappear in *The Golden Cup*, and the story of the Werners and the Roths is continued further in *Tapestry* (Delacorte, 1988, $19.95). These best-selling popular entertainments are enjoyed both by adult women and senior high school girls.

Plot Summary

Henrietta De Rivera first sees Daniel Roth as she watches one of the all-too-common tenement fires of the late nineteenth century in New York City. Out walking with her young nephew Paul, she is fascinated by the heroism of the reckless young man who rescues an old woman from the blaze. Through her uncle, Hennie learns that Dan is a teacher and known as a radical, a young man who ridicules many of the conventions that Hennie's Sephardic Jewish family reveres. Uncle David also tries to tell her that he believes Dan to be a man who "runs after women."

But warnings from her family do no good, and Hennie and Dan begin to see each other over a period of nearly two years. Hennie watches Dan's flirtations, but tries to put them out of her mind, telling herself they are harmless and "just the way he is." Then she senses that Dan is no longer interested in her and is seeing someone else; just about that time Hennie discovers she is pregnant. And so they are married.

Their son, Freddy, is born and Hennie and Dan settle down to greet the twentieth century. When Freddy is still a young boy, they take another child into their home to raise; Leah is the daughter of Hennie's friend, a factory worker who died of tuberculosis, as did so many young women who were forced to spend long hours in unsanitary and deplorable working conditions in the late nineteenth and early twentieth centuries.

Hennie is desperately in love with her husband, and their passion for each other does not diminish, even though Dan carries on affairs without her knowledge. And some of his radical views touch her, too; Hennie

Roth becomes a suffragette and a fighter for social justice, much to the dismay of her conventional family.

When both Freddy and Leah are still quite young, they discover, each in his or her own way, that Dan is unfaithful. Leah, being a stronger figure than the sensitive Freddy, confronts Dan, who is visibly shaken by the experience and vows that such conduct will end. He does, indeed, send a letter to the woman he has been seeing and breaks off the affair. But neither Freddy nor Leah can forgive him.

Hennie's nephew, Paul, grows up and marries Mimi, even though he is in love with a servant girl, Anna. When talk of World War I begins, Paul and Freddy express interest in enlisting, but such talk is loudly decried by both Dan and Hennie, who scorn battle even in the cause of nationalism and patriotic fervor.

Nonetheless, both Paul and Freddy do go to war. But before Freddy leaves college and goes overseas, he startles his parents by secretly marrying Leah. About this time, Dan, who has always been a "tinkerer, an inventor of sorts," is offered $20,000 for the government's use of his radio direction-finder. Outraged that his brother-in-law would allow his invention to go to war, Dan refuses the money, and Hennie agrees, even though on Dan's salary as a teacher the Roths have never been well off.

But things change for the Roths when Freddy loses both his legs in Europe. He returns home, a bitter, defeated young man, to Leah and his young son, Hank. Soon after his return, Dan goes to see his brother-in-law and requests the money earned from his invention, which he uses to buy Leah and Freddy a beautiful home.

Sometime later Hennie, restless and saddened by her son's condition and obvious unhappiness, cleans out some old files of her husband's and comes upon a reply to the letter he had sent to the woman with whom he was having an affair years before. Shocked and embittered, she orders him to leave the house, which he does.

More tragedy is in store for Hennie when Freddy takes his own life. When Hennie learns that Leah had been having an affair and that Freddy had discovered it, she refuses to see her again and calls her the murderer of her son.

Despite all efforts by Paul and others to change her mind, Hennie refuses to have anything to do with either Dan or Leah. But, finally, with Paul as an unwilling third party, Dan forces her to hear the truth. First he tells her that she is too rigid and unforgiving, and then he tells her that Leah took a lover, not because of Freddy's condition, but because, in fact, Freddy's interest was not in women, something Dan had long suspected of his son.

At first, Hennie is too shocked and horrified to listen. But eventually she comes to terms with Leah's actions, with her son's feelings, and with her husband's weaknesses, and she calls Dan to return.

The Golden Cup ends with the family members together. World War I is over, and everyone happily tells each other that they have seen the last of war, that the spirit of the German people will quickly rebuild their devastated country, and all will be well . . . Paul wonders why he considers the thought naive. . . .

Thematic Material

This novel of an earlier period points up the social injustices of the times—including the deplorable working conditions for men, women, and children in the factories of the city—and the complacency of the middle class, who cling to conventions and mores in the face of impending change. It vividly portrays the powerful themes of bigotry and injustice, and of insensitivity to the plight of the poor. It is also a sensitive picture of the world of the Jewish immigrant in turn-of-the-century New York. Another important theme is the picture of a woman far ahead of her time, who struggles to control her own life in a period when women were not expected to think for themselves. Young women of today can relate to Hennie Roth as she tries to reconcile her beliefs and her conscience with the demands of her heart and a difficult marriage.

Book Talk Material

Working conditions in the late nineteenth and early twentieth centuries and the status of women are important points for conversation. As well, some of the author's descriptions of life in turn-of-the-century New York can serve as an introduction. See: the tenement fire (pp. 4–8; pp. 10–14 pap.); New Year's Eve, 1899 (pp. 72–81; pp. 115–127 pap.); hired toughs break up a strike (pp. 86–89; pp. 131–135 pap.); Dan challenges the family's complacency (pp. 110–129; pp. 180–203 pap.); and World War I begins (pp. 223–226; pp. 356–360 pap.).

Additional Selections

Richard Peck's adult novel about a rich woman and her maid is *Amanda/Miranda* (pap., Avon, $2.95).

A liberated woman faces motherhood in Margaret Drabble's *The Mill-stone* (pap., NAL, $6.95), and Elizabeth F. Hailey's *A Woman of Independent Means* (pap., Avon, $4.50) follows the career of Bess Steel Garner, a completely twentieth-century woman.

Growing up in the 1930s and conflict with her Jewish faith are experienced by the heroine of Chaim Potok's *Davita's Harp* (Knopf, 1985, $16.95).

Nell Dobell falls in love with a young Jewish singer in Hitler's prewar Europe in Rosemary Harris's *Summer of the Wild Rose* (Faber, 1988, $11.95).

For a younger audience, Judie Angell tells about a young Jewish immigrant girl and her struggles in *One Way to Ansonia* (Bradbury, 1985, $11.85; pap., Pacer, $2.50).

The nonfictional *World of Our Fathers* by Irving Howe (pap., Simon, $12.95) tells about Eastern European Jews and their voyage of opportunity to the United States.

In turn-of-the-century Amherst, an 18-year-old girl is being forced into a loveless marriage in Susan Terris's *Nell's Quilt* (Farrar, 1987, $12.95).

A Jewish boy grows up in New York's slums in the early twentieth century and is terrified of his father in Henry Roth's *Call It Sleep* (Cooper Square, 1934, $20.00; pap., Avon, $4.50).

Life in early twentieth-century Warsaw is detailed in Isaac Bashevis Singer's *In My Father's Court* (pap., Farrar, $5.95; pap., Fawcett, $2.50).

About the Book
Booklist, September 1, 1986, p. 3.
New York Times Book Review, September 28, 1986, p. 27.
See also *Book Review Index*, 1986, p. 580.

About the Author
Locher, Francis C., ed. *Contemporary Authors*. Detroit: Gale, 1979. Vols. 81–84, p. 557.
Metzger, Linda, ed. *Contemporary Authors* (New Revision Series). Detroit: Gale, 1985. Vol. 14, pp. 375–376.

Porte, Barbara Ann. *I Only Made Up the Roses*
Greenwillow, 1987, $10.25

Barbara Ann Porte, a former children's librarian, has written a number of picture books for young children. This is one of her few forays into the world of teenage literature. It is narrated by 17-year-old Cydra, who gives the reader a guided tour of her loving extended family of mixed races. It is episodic in nature, with each chapter consisting of a separate short story. Such topics as life cycles, family relationships, and racial prejudice are touched on in this warm, beautifully realized novel for readers in grades 8 through 12.

Plot Summary

Cydra, at age 17, considers herself a "well-adjusted person." But as she writes, " . . . sometimes I envy Perley [her nine-year-old brother]. His origins, less obscure than mine, are easier to explain." Cydra's mother wants to know what she means by "obscure." And her father wants to know, "explain to whom?"

Cydra's meanings, however, become more and more obvious to the reader through the stories she tells of her family, stories that make up the entire book. And one of the stories explains the "origins," hers and her brother's.

For starters, her brother's name is Perley Robert Williams. Cydra's last name is James. The man Cydra calls Daddy, and loves deeply, is her stepfather, who married her mother when Cydra was about eight years old. Daddy is an engineer, and her mother is an artist. But the fact that she has a stepfather and a half-brother is not what sets this family apart. What does set them apart somewhat is that Mrs. Williams is white, and Mr. Williams is black.

In truth, Cydra is remarkably well adjusted, although, as she recounts, there was a time when she wished that Daddy didn't take such an avid interest in her schooling. Despite herself, her stomach would turn over and her head would pound when she waited for him to walk in the door on Open School Day or PTA night. "Don't worry, Cyd," said Daddy, "all children are embarrassed by their parents sometimes."

And Daddy was right. At 17, Cyd is mortified to remember those feelings.

Many of Cydra's stories of her family, both sides, recount the death of her grandfather, her father's father, and their trip to Virginia to the funeral. The Williams family, educated and comfortably well off, is filled with marvelous characters. There was Granddad himself, never, as far as Cydra can remember, without a coat and tie, and Grandmother, who some time after Granddad's death takes off for a trip to Senegal (because she can't bear the thought of the upcoming Thanksgiving holiday in the house without him) and invites Cydra to go along on her next trip, which she thinks will be to China.

There is Daddy's oldest sister whose real name is Henry George, but whom everyone calls Aunt Sister. Sister's Great-Aunt Helen earned a teaching degree from Howard University. And there is Cousin Tineen who is going to be a lawyer, and Uncle Ben who has a farm in South Carolina.

Although it takes some time, Cydra feels that the entire family adjusts well to Granddad's death. It is then that Daddy starts to "act strange." Suddenly he has become a historian and their home a living history lesson. Daddy, who had gone to private black schools in the South, starts coming home and tacking up lists on the kitchen wall. One list might contain pertinent facts about the continent of Africa and others about important black people in American and world history. And the lists aren't all of it. There are books to read—novels, and histories, and poetry—and memorable black people to learn about. When Perley and Cydra speak to their mother about their father's peculiar actions, she tells them that he is just "adjusting to the death of his father."

And indeed, their mother seems to be right, for in time the history lessons stop, the lists come down. Perley decides that Daddy "must have adjusted."

But Daddy's history lessons are not forgotten by either Cydra or her brother. And, as she later recalls, they come in handy in an American history course she takes in her pre-med college course. The professor turns out to be a black woman, and a lot of what she teaches is news to Cydra's classmates. But to Cydra, it is all just another list.

The title *I Only Made Up the Roses,* made up of Cydra's narrations, comes from the time when Cydra, age eight and just before the birth of Perley, decides that she wants to know her "real" father. She cannot remember ever seeing him and he appears to her only as a somewhat stocky man in an old army snapshot. He is a salesman, and at Cydra's insistence, though he has never shown any interest whatsoever in seeing her, promises to take her to dinner the next time he is in New York.

On the appointed day, she is dressed in her best and waiting in the apartment for her "real" father to arrive. He never does, although he does telephone to say that business has him tied up and he just can't make it.

Cydra is still sitting on the chair all dressed up when Daddy comes home. He asks how she is and she starts to cry, despite her attempts not to. "My father doesn't love me," she tells him, and in reply Daddy says to her, "This is important. I love you. I love you very much. I will never stop loving you. You can count on that forever."

Then Daddy leaves a note for her mother, and he and Cydra go out to dinner by themselves.

Later, in school Cydra is assigned an essay to write. She writes about a young girl who has a date to go to the prom with a prince. The prince promises to send her white roses, but they never arrive. When the girl finds out they have been delivered to the apartment across the hall, she retrieves her roses. But the prince never arrives. The next morning the roses are dead. The girl presses them, but they turn moldy and have to be thrown out. She never hears from the prince again, but she doesn't care any longer. She learns that he isn't a real prince after all and later she finds out that proms aren't always all they're cracked up to be.

Cydra gets a "C" on the essay. It is interesting, says the teacher, but it was "supposed to be autobiographical."

Cydra doesn't explain, even though she thinks it deserves an A. After all, she only made up the part about the roses.

Thematic Material

Barbara Ann Porte has written a wonderfully warm story, told through the eyes of the teenage daughter of a family that happens to be "interracial." Although both the white and black relatives are obviously fairly well off and educated people, they are not above the same reactions and hurts and prejudices of everyday folk. The black side of the family has suffered prejudice and the pain of bigotry; the white side of the family was not pleased with Cydra's mother's decision to marry. But their somewhat unusual situation does not overwhelm them or put undue strain on their relationships. The parents are seen as people in their own right, living their lives with warmth and dignity, and teaching their two children to do the same.

Book Talk Material

What would it be like to be a white child in a family with a white mother and a black father? Or a child who looks black but has an obviously white mother? Various interactions between Cydra and family members can serve as an introduction to a discussion of these two questions. See: after Granddad's funeral (pp. 8–10); out on Uncle Ben's farm (pp. 15–20); the day at Aunt Sister's (pp. 24–33); Perley on names (pp. 34–47); and Cydra almost meets her "real" father (pp. 48–53).

Additional Selections

Susan's senior year plans are dashed when her older sister appears in Caroline B. Cooney's *Don't Blame the Music* (Putnam, 1985, $13.95; pap., Berkley, $2.50).

In Jean Ferris's *Looking for Home* (Farrar, 1988, $12.95), 17-year-old Daphne must decide the fate of her unborn illegitimate baby.

In Ouida Sebestyen's novel *Words by Heart* (Atlantic, 1979, $12.45; pap., Bantam, $2.50), a black family faces violent whites when they move to a small southern town in 1910.

Denny, a son of a mixed marriage, sets out on a cross-country trip to find his roots in Carolyn Meyer's *Denny's Tapes* (McElderry, 1987, $12.95).

Two fine novels about boys coming of age are Dallin Malmgren's *The Whole Nine Yards* (Delacorte, 1986, $14.95; pap., Dell, $2.95) and Stuart Buchan's *Guys Like Us* (Delacorte, 1986, $14.95).

A black man helps a group of German refugee nuns in William E. Barrett's *The Lilies of the Field* (Doubleday, 1962, $8.95; pap., Warner, $2.50; condensed in *Juniorplots*, Bowker, 1967, pp. 35–37).

A young brother and sister become rivals in the world of ballet in Rumer Godden's *Thursday's Children* (pap., Dell, $2.95).

A black teenager is caught up in racial tensions in his middle-class neighborhood in Bernie MacKinnon's *The Meantime* (Houghton, 1984, $11.95).

Prominent young adult novelists have contributed original short stories to Donald R. Gallo's *Sixteen* (Delacorte, 1984, $14.95).

About the Book
Booklist, May 1, 1987, p. 1362.
Bulletin of the Center for Children's Books, June 1987, p. 194.

Horn Book, November 1987, p. 745.
School Library Journal, May 1987, p. 117.
VOYA, June 1987, p. 82.
See also *Book Review Digest,* 1988, and *Book Review Index,* 1987, p. 614.

About the Author
Commire, Anne, ed. *Something about the Author.* Detroit: Gale, 1986. Vol. 45, p. 168.

3

Challenging Adult Novels

Aʟᴛʜᴏᴜɢʜ there is a growing tendency to continue reading young adult novels well into the senior high grades, teenagers should increasingly be introduced to challenging, quality reading material at the adult level. In this cross-section, there are three classics of world literature—one English, one French, and one American—plus a selection from contemporary authors that represents some of the best writing being produced today.

Brin, David. *The Postman*
 Bantam, 1985, $15.95, pap. $4.50

David Brin, though a relative newcomer to science fiction writing, has already won every major award in the field. Trained as an electrical engineer and also a computer expert, he has a natural scientific frame of mind in approaching his material. One of his most famous novels, *Startide Rising* (Phantasia, 1983, $18.00; pap., Bantam, $3.95), is the story of a starship with a crew of humans and dolphins that crashes on an unknown world and faces danger from a hostile new environment and from attacking aliens. It was preceded by *Sundiver* (pap., Bantam, $3.50) and followed by *The Uplift War* (Phantasia, 1987, $22.00; pap., Bantam, $4.50). *The Postman,* by contrast, deals with our own world in the not unbelievable future. These novels are suitable for readers in the senior high grades.

Plot Summary
It is now 16 years after the beginning of the Doomwar of the mid-1990s. This global nuclear holocaust left vast areas of the world a radioactive wasteland, and most of what remained was destroyed during the three-year winter that followed the war. And what of the United States?

Most of the country is desolate and covered with deadly nuclear radiation. All aspects of modern technology and civilization have disappeared. In the western states, however, pockets of land, though not escaping the destruction of the war, emerged with safe atmospheres still capable of maintaining life. Many of the few people who survived in these areas have banded together into small isolated communities living lives similar to their pioneer ancestors of almost 200 years before. In addition to the natural vicissitudes that confront these settlers, their fragile communities are subjected to raids from bands of nomadic barbarians who live by rape, murder, and pillage. They are known as Holnists because they follow the neo-Fascist philosophy preached by the now-deceased survivalist Nathan Holn.

Gordon Krantz, who is now 34, was only 18 when Doomwar began. Even though he remembers the trauma of these years of destruction and despair while in the service, somehow he retains a belief in those ideals that once guided life in the United States. For the past 18 years, he has wandered from community to community, surviving by his natural instincts and his remarkable ability to hold audiences spellbound while retelling such tales as stories from Shakespeare's plays.

As Gordon enters what was once Oregon, a calamity occurs. His outdoor campsite is attacked by bandits, who steal his gear and supplies, including clothes, boots, shotgun and Geiger counter. While wandering in the wilderness, Gordon happens on the remains of a rusty postal service jeep. At the wheel, clad in a postman's uniform, is the skeleton of what had been a mailman, obviously another victim of the war. In desperation, Gordon dons the skeleton's clothes and shoes. At the next community, Pine View, Gordon once more enchants his audience, who because of his uniform begin to regard him as a postman. He becomes particularly friendly with the leader of the community, Mrs. Thompson, and willingly consents to sleep with a young married girl, Abbie, so that she and her sterile husband, Michael, can have the child they have always wanted.

Gordon leaves Pine View carrying letters from residents hoping to make contact with any other community of survivors. In the wreckage of a small town, he uncovers a valuable cache of medicines, but is forced to abandon it and flee when another murderous group of survivors appears.

In order to gain admission to the town of Oak Ridge, he fabricates a story that he is a courier from the Restored United States, with headquarters in St. Paul City (actually, Minnesota is a total wasteland), whose responsibility as general federal inspector is to organize a mail route prior to establishing other contacts with the East. They believe him, not only because of Gordon's persuasive powers, but also because his story gives them hope for a better future.

As Gordon moves from community to community gathering and delivering letters and establishing post offices, the mythology he has created about himself and his mission grows in detail and complexity. And though he loathes himself for these falsehoods, Gordon is unable to deprive these people of the comfort and security his message brings. He also hears rumors that in northern Oregon there is a community governed by a benevolent force known only as Cyclops.

In the ruins of what had been Eugene, Gordon overhears some Holnists reveal a plot to attack and occupy communities in the North. They leave behind their two captives—a young boy and his dying mother, whose last words are "North, take boy, warn Cyclops."

He learns that Cyclops's headquarters is in Cornvallis in the Williamette Valley. Here he finds a much higher level of prosperity and well-being than in other communities. Gordon still maintains his assumed identity, and before confronting Cyclops, he meets many of its Servants, including the attractive archfeminist Dena Spurgen. Cyclops is revealed to be a superintelligent computer saved from the war by its designer and companion, Dr. Lazarensky. Because Cyclops's advice has brought good times to the people of northern Oregon, he has become godlike in their eyes.

After Gordon warns Cyclops of the imminent Holnist attacks, he leaves Cornvallis. However, growing doubt concerning Cyclops's power forces him to return, and in a confrontation with Lazarensky, he discovers that Cyclops, like the Wizard of Oz, is actually a nonfunctioning computer whose messages are really the work of its Servants. Gordon and Cyclops have much in common.

Fraudulent or not, the world of Cyclops is still facing grave threats from the Holnists. Gordon decides to remain and offers his help. During the period of planning, he becomes increasingly attracted to Dena, with whom he has a love affair.

When the survivalists' savage raids begin, Gordon knows that Cornvallis is doomed without help from other neighboring communities. With several scouts accompanying him, he begins a perilous journey through

Holnist territory to seek men and supplies from George Powhatan, the powerful leader of a group that for years had successfully withstood survivalist raids.

Powhatan is sympathetic to their cause, but he refuses to commit his people to another bloody conflict. Disheartened, Gordon and his men leave. They are ambushed and Gordon, with young Johnny Stevens, is taken prisoner and brought by Colonel Bezoar to the Holnist leader General Macklin. He offers Gordon a position of power in his organization if he will persuade the people of Cornvallis to capitulate. Gordon refuses.

After a futile escape attempt during which Johnny is drowned, Gordon is once more thrown in prison where he is reunited with Dena, who has been mortally wounded leading a group of gallant female warriors in an unsuccessful attempt to rescue him. She dies in his arms.

When Powhatan learns about the courageous attempt of the women of Cornvallis, he is shamed into action. His men attack the Holnist stronghold and in single combat he kills Macklin and frees Gordon.

With the Holnist threat ended, Gordon packs his belongings and sets out alone. He heads south. After all, there are many post offices to be established in California.

Thematic Material

This is more than a fast-moving adventure story set in the future. In its many layers of symbolism, it explores such themes as the importance of ideals in life and the need for faith and hope. The conflict of belief versus truth is explored in the effects of the positive mythology of Gordon and the Cyclops and the destructive perversions of fact by the Holnists. The importance of ideals in life, the nature of liberty, the necessity to act against oppression and evil, as well as courage against adversity are important themes. Individual bravery and heroism are often depicted as the strength that comes with sharing and cooperation. Gordon is a believable character who, though beset with doubts, sacrifices his own well-being to fight for his ideals. This is also a cautionary tale about the awesome destructive power that humankind now controls and the catastrophic results should it be unleashed.

Book Talk Material

This book could be introduced by a discussion of the nature of life after a "limited" nuclear war. It is also filled with exciting episodes suitable for reading or retelling. A few are: Gordon's camp is attacked (pp. 5–10 pp. 4–9 pap.); he finds the jeep and its grisly contents (pp. 21–25; pp. 20–24 pap.); his discovery of a house containing medicines (pp. 59–63; pp. 61–66 pap.); gaining admission to Oak Ridge by lying (pp. 70–76; pp. 73–80 pap.); his adventure in Eugene (pp. 104–111; pp. 112–121 pap.); and meeting Cyclops for the first time (pp. 132–135; pp. 142–146 pap.).

Additional Selections

Big Brother watches in the futuristic society created by George Orwell in *1984* (Harcourt, 1949, $12.95).

The end of the world is chronicled by a seven-year-old Irish boy in Brian Cullan's *What Niall Saw* (St. Martin's, 1987, $11.95).

The crew of a U.S. Navy destroyer believes they are the only survivors of complete nuclear destruction in William Brinkley's involved novel *The Last Ship* (Viking, 1988, $19.95).

After a nuclear holocaust a young woman is being held by an alien race in Octavia Butler's *Dawn* (Warner, 1987, $15.95).

Residents of Australia face death after nuclear war in Nevil Shute's now classic *On the Beach* (Morrow, 1957, $12.95; pap., Ballantine, $2.95).

Philip K. Dick explores life in America had we lost World War II in *The Man in the High Castle* (pap., Berkley, $2.95).

In George R. Stewart's *Earth Abides* (Archive, 1974, $14.95; pap., Fawcett, $2.75) a catastrophe almost wipes out the earth's population.

Earth is on the brink of a nuclear war when a strange starship/asteroid appears in Greg Bear's *Eon* (Bluejay, 1985, $16.95; pap., Tor, $3.50).

The perils of a nuclear war are discussed in Jonathan Schell's *The Fate of the Earth* (Knopf, 1982, $11.95). Two other nonfiction titles on the subject are Laurence Pringle's *Nuclear War* (Enslow, 1985, $12.85) and Leon Wieseltier's *Nuclear War, Nuclear Peace* (pap., Henry Holt, $2.95).

About the Book
Booklist, September 15, 1985, p. 90.
Library Journal, October 15, 1985, p. 104.
VOYA, February 1986, p. 392.
See also *Book Review Index*, 1985, p. 97; 1986, p. 107.

About the Author
Locher, Francis C., ed. *Contemporary Authors*. Detroit: Gale, 1981. Vol. 102, p. 74.

Conroy, Pat. *The Prince of Tides*
Houghton, 1986, $19.95; pap., Bantam, $5.95

Pat Conroy has stated that each of his novels contains autobiographical elements and often their publication has caused strained relationships in his family. For example, *The Prince of Tides* caused problems with his sister. Conroy began his professional career as a schoolteacher in South Carolina where he believed he might alter the racism he encountered. Instead he lost his job within one year. This became the subject of his second novel, *The Water Is Wide* (Houghton, 1972, $9.95; pap., Bantam, $4.95), which was filmed as *Conrack* in 1974. *The Prince of Tides* contains many adult situations and is suitable for mature senior high students.

Plot Summary

Tom Wingo, a teacher and high school football coach, was born, raised, and lives in the lowcountry of South Carolina. As the story opens, both his career and his marriage are crumbling. On the day his wife, Sallie, tells him she has been having an affair, Tom also learns of the suicide attempt of his twin, Savannah, in New York City. Called one of the most gifted poets of her generation, Savannah, as Tom is all too painfully aware, has been sliding toward emotional disaster for a long, long time. More than any of the tortured Wingos, Savannah has been carrying the burden of the family's dark and violent past within her.

Self-deprecating, his humor often a mask to hide the depth of his hurt, Tom flies to Manhattan and to Savannah's psychiatrist, Susan Lowenstein, who enrolls him in the fight to bring Savannah back from her madness. And in trying to save his sister, Tom realizes a chance to save himself.

Settled in his sister's Greenwich Village apartment, his problems with Sallie put aside for the moment, Tom meets often with Susan Lowenstein—Savannah has refused to see him—and begins to tell her the story of the Wingos of the South, of the lowcountry, of a sea island off the Carolina coast where Tom and Savannah were born. Henry Wingo, their father, is a shrimper, one of the best, but a man given to dark and violent moods. With always a dream of wealth and glory around the corner, he is not above using his fists to gain at least submission from his wife and children when he cannot earn their respect. He is given to eccentricities, too, such as keeping a Bengal tiger, named Caesar, in the backyard.

Their mother, Lila Wingo, seems to inhabit a world of her own making. In Lila's world, the Wingos are above reproach, respected, honored, even when the truth is sometimes all too obvious to the children. And there is Luke, the older brother, perhaps not with the sharpness of mind given to Tom and Savannah, but with such a depth of love and loyalty to his land and his roots that it will ultimately cause his destruction.

Tom reveals his island world to Susan Lowenstein, trying to make her understand the events and the background that went into making Savannah the troubled, desperate woman who tried to take her life. He speaks of their growing-up years, of his growing hate for his father, of his longing for the day when he would be old enough to beat him back. But he also speaks with great love and passion of the beauty of the island, of the smells and sights and sounds of their small, unique haven.

And, finally, Tom shares with Susan the terrible tragedies of his life and of Savannah's and of all the Wingos. He tells of the unspeakable night when the stillness of their island is shattered, leaving them all damaged in a way they can never repair, the night when three escaped convicts find their way to the Wingo home, one to settle an old grudge. He tells of the rapes of his mother, his sister, and himself, of how Luke avenges their anguish by unleashing Caesar on the three men, and of how the Wingos dispose of their bodies and remove all traces of the crimes and, at their mother's insistence, do not seek medical treatment because Lila declares she has to "think of our family's position in this town."

"Mama's crazy, Luke," Tom tells his brother.

"No, she isn't," Luke replies. "She's just afraid. We just got to go along with her."

Then Tom tells Susan of the final tragedy, of how government officials declare that the beautiful and unique area that makes up the lowcountry is to be "off limits," "set aside" to preserve it, and in so doing they "erase" a county and its people from the map. When Luke discovers the underlying greed and dishonesty that has taken away the land he calls home, he heads a one-man army to stop them. And despite Tom's and Savannah's desperate attempts to save him, Luke dies defending the land he loves.

Tom's story of the Wingos of the lowcountry changes Susan's life, too, and involves the two of them in a way they never imagined. For these two unhappy people find a gift of love in each other.

But when Tom's story is done, and when the hurt that is within both Tom and Savannah begins to heal, Tom realizes he must return to his home, to the South that is his heritage, to the family that he loves, to a new life he must make for himself, even as he realizes that the woman who is Susan Lowenstein will never be far from his heart.

Thematic Material

This is a beautifully written story of a family's deep torment and pain, of the love of sibling for sibling, of love for the land and the sea, and for a way of life that is called southern. There is cruelty and sadness and laughter and dignity, and *The Prince of Tides* is peopled with characters one will not easily forget, nor want to. The author vividly portrays the deep bond of love and understanding that can exist between brother and brother, and brother and sister. Despite the sadness and tragedy that seem to follow the Wingos, this is not a sad book, for the author has a deep gift of humor and good nature about the people he obviously knows so well. One may despair for the Wingos and cry for them, but one must smile with them as well.

Book Talk Material

More arresting than all the turns of plot, depth of feelings, eccentricities of character, and flashes of warm humor are the deeply moving passages that describe some small moment of life in the southern lowcountry, obviously written by the author with great love and understanding. Readers will especially enjoy: in their youth, the Wingo children accompany their eccentric Grandmother Tolitha (the first Wingo feminist) to buy her own coffin (pp. 174–186; pp. 205–219 pap.); Grandfather Amos Wingo and the Good Friday ordeal (pp. 266–283; pp. 310–330 pap.); the town battles for the white porpoise (pp. 297–307; pp. 345–351 pap.); graduation night for the Wingos and a talk about life (pp. 400–406; pp. 462–472 pap.); Tom's one moment of college football glory (pp. 454–456; pp. 528–532 pap.); and Grandpa's extraordinary gesture (pp. 471–483; pp. 546–565 pap.).

Additional Selections

The gradual mental breakdown and suicide attempt of a brilliant young woman is the subject matter of Sylvia Plath's largely autobiographical novel *The Bell Jar* (Harper, 1963, $16.45; pap., Bantam, $4.50).

An isolated island off South Carolina where a community of black residents lives is the setting of Gloria Naylor's *Mama Day* (Ticknor, 1988, $18.95).

A mother believes a young boy is her lost son in a novel about the Holocaust's effects on survivors, *The Sunflower Effect* by Tony Hayden (Putnam, 1984, $15.95; pap., Avon, $3.95).

Allie Fox uproots his family taking them to a Honduran wilderness in the nightmare novel *The Mosquito Coast* (Houghton, 1982, $13.95; pap., Avon, $4.50) by Paul Theroux.

Twins Ben and Willie become involved with Claire Bishop after Ben is responsible for her paralysis in Nancy Willard's *Things Invisible to See* (Knopf, 1985, $14.95).

In Charles Carillo's tough, poignant novel *Shepherd Avenue* (Atlantic, 1985, $16.95), a 10-year-old boy is sent to live with his Italian grandparents.

The family saga of the Neumillers and the consequences of their mother's death are chronicled in Larry Woiwode's *Beyond the Bedroom Door* (Farrar, 1975, $12.50; pap., Avon, $2.95).

Life is brutal for Gertie Nevels and her husband when they move to Detroit from Kentucky to find work in Harriette Arnow's *The Dollmaker* (Univ. of Kentucky, 1984, $24.00; pap., Avon, $4.95).

A girl grows up full of responsibilities, guilt, and unable to love in Sheila Ballantyne's *Imaginary Crimes* (pap., Penguin, $6.95).

Caring becomes a burden for Dan Courser after he causes his wife's complete paralysis in Rosellen Brown's *Tender Mercies* (Knopf, 1978, $10).

About the Book
Booklist, July 1986, p. 1561.
Library Journal, October 15, 1986, p. 108.
New York Times Book Review, October 12, 1986, p. 14.
School Library Journal, April 1987, p. 117.
See also *Book Review Digest,* 1987, p. 375, and *Book Review Index,* 1986, p. 167; 1987, p. 160.

About the Author
Locher, Francis C., ed. *Contemporary Authors.* Detroit: Gale, 1980. Vols. 85–88, pp. 113–114.

Dickens, Charles. *Hard Times*
pap., NAL, $1.95

Hard Times was written in 1854, roughly midway through Dickens's career, and was published immediately after *Bleak House* but before *Little Dorrit*. It originally appeared as a serial in *Household Words*, a twopenny weekly that Dickens edited. Though not in the forefront of Dickens's works, it is nevertheless considered a minor masterpiece. For young readers, it has many appealing aspects. It is, for example, shorter and less formidable than many of his other novels and deals with such engrossing subjects as tyranny in the classroom, an overbearing father, a bank robbery, and framing of an innocent man. The action takes place in the 1850s in grimy, smoke-enshrouded Coketown, a dismal mill and mining city in the English midlands. Other paper editions include Bantam ($1.95) and Penguin ($2.25). It is enjoyed by better senior high school readers.

Plot Summary

Thomas Gradgrind, a retired successful industrialist and soon-to-be member of Parliament, has opened a model school devoted to the mastery of his favorite subject—facts. No room here for imagination and fantasy, only figures, science, and empirical knowledge. The pupils include Gradgrind's children, 15-year-old Louisa and slightly younger Thomas, Jr. In stern Mr. Choakumchild's classroom, there is a new temporary pupil, Cecilia "Sissy" Jupe, daughter of a failing clown with a circus operated by Mr. Sleary.

Gradgrind's best friend is Josiah Bounderby, a stuffy, pompous man in his late forties who owns a textile mill and bank in Coketown and takes exalted pride in his gutter origins and a mother who deserted him at birth, placing him in the care of a drunken grandmother. His meteoric rise to his present position of power and wealth is another source of inflated pride. Bounderby is a bachelor with intentions of eventually marrying Louisa, but at present he lives alone with his housekeeper, Mrs. Sparsit, a disagreeable woman who feigns humility while claiming a high-born status.

Gradgrind and Bounderby realize that Sissy, representing as she does the world of fantasy, must leave the school. They visit her at her lodgings in the Pegasus Arms and find Sissy completely shattered because her father has abandoned her, taking with him his trained dog, Merrylegs.

Gradgrind offers to adopt her, seeing in Sissy a suitable companion for his wife, a silly woman frail in both mind and body. The circus troupe, along with Sissy, convinced that this is only a temporary measure, consents.

In the midst of the poverty and squalor of the slums of Coketown lives Stephen Blackpool, an honest powerloom weaver in Bounderby's factory. Many years before, he married an unfortunate creature who became an alcoholic and is now making a living hell of his life. Stephen seeks advice from Bounderby concerning a divorce so that he can marry his true love, a factory hand named Rachel. Characteristically, Bounderby dismisses him coldly, but outside his mansion, Stephen meets a mysterious old lady who asks adoringly about Bounderby's health.

Under her father's strict regime, Louisa grows to be a somewhat distant but beautiful woman whose spiritual nature remains undeveloped. Her only interest and emotional attachment in life is her weakling brother, Tom. When she reaches 20, she allows herself to be given in a loveless marriage to Bounderby, seeing in this liaison an opportunity to forward her brother's position in Bounderby's bank. A joyless wedding takes place and a highly disgruntled Mrs. Sparsit is asked to move to new quarters above the bank where she is attended to by the porter, Bitzer. She plots revenge on an unsuspecting Louisa.

A stranger, James Harthouse, arrives in town with a letter of introduction to Bounderby. He is a suave, smooth-talking dilettante who, bored with life, has decided, on Gradgrind's advice, to leave London and enter politics in Coketown. He meets the Bounderbys, and being immediately attracted to Louisa, uses a feigned friendship with Tom to gain her favor. All this is carefully noted by Mrs. Sparsit. However, she does not know that Louisa has secretly exhausted her small reserve of cash and jewelry to help pay for her brother's gambling debts.

Because of a promise to Rachel, Stephen is the only worker not to join the labor union led by a rabble-rouser named Stackbridge. Called before Bounderby and in the presence of his family, Stephen receives not gratitude but a termination notice. Louisa, moved by pity, persuades Tom to accompany her to Stephen's lodgings, where she meets Rachel and offers Stephen money. Tom secretly also suggests that if Stephen will wait outside the bank every afternoon of the following week, he will try to get him further help.

Stephen does and one afternoon he is joined by the mysterious lady who once again inquires solicitously about Bounderby. All these events are carefully monitored by Mrs. Sparsit. At week's end, without hearing from Tom, Stephen leaves. That evening the bank is robbed of more than £150 and Stephen becomes the prime suspect, though inwardly Louisa believes her brother Tom is guilty.

While the search for Stephen progresses, so do Harthouse's attentions to Louisa, who for the first time feels attracted to a man but is petrified of the consequences. While Bounderby is absent on business, Harthouse visits Louisa and, overheard by a hidden Mrs. Sparsit, asks her to elope with him that evening. When Louisa later leaves the house, Mrs. Sparsit is convinced that she intends meeting with Harthouse and she boards a train to inform Bounderby of these events.

Actually Louisa, unable to cope with these feelings, flees to her father's home and there, in a state of turmoil, tells him that her stunted upbringing has made her unable to handle the situation. Gradgrind, saddened by his daughter's plight, realizes his philosophical shortcomings.

Led by Mrs. Sparsit, Bounderby returns. Although he discovers that Louisa is guiltless and upbraids Mrs. Sparsit as a result, he demands that Louisa return immediately to his house. Still confused and requiring time to sort out her feelings, she refuses. An insulted Bounderby effects a permanent separation and Louisa remains with her father, young sister, Jane, and Sissy, too, who has become a fine young lady.

Indefatigable Mrs. Sparsit locates the mysterious lady who watches Bounderby from afar and, hoping to regain his favor, publicly drags her before him. It is Mrs. Pegler, his own loving mother who years before he disowned to pursue his own interests. The myth of his deprived childhood is exploded, and furious at Mrs. Sparsit, he dismisses her forever.

Rachel knows of Stephen's whereabouts and sends for him to clear his name. When he doesn't arrive, she and Sissy set out to find him. They locate him at the bottom of a deserted mine shaft where he has accidentally fallen. A rescue operation is mounted, but it is too late. He dies after forgiving all for his misfortunes, including Tom, who he realizes had tried to incriminate him falsely. Sissy manages to spirit Tom away from the vengeful mob and hides him disguised as a clown in Sleary's circus. There Gradgrind and Louisa hear his confession, and are able to place him safely aboard an overseas steamer. The remains of the Gradgrind family return home to try to rebuild their shattered lives.

Thematic Material

In this novel Dickens assaults many of the ills of nineteenth-century Britain. First he attacks educational systems that emphasize only utilitarian goals and deny the growth of the spirit. He also attacks both the unfettered, callous greed that underlies the economic system, and the society that allows the living conditions created by industrialization to exist. In addition to a graphic portrait of workers' lives and values, he vividly portrays family relationships, the awesome responsibility of child rearing, the position of women, the sins of hypocrisy and pride, and the class structure of Victorian England.

Book Talk Material

A description of Gradgrind's school and a discussion of possible consequences of such an education could introduce this novel. Memorable passages are: life in Gradgrind's school (pp. 12–18); Bounderby is introduced (pp. 23–26); Sissy talks about her stupidity in school (pp. 62–65) and about her father's departure (pp. 66–68); Stephen and Rachel first appear (pp. 71–78); Stephen asks for Bounderby's help (pp. 77–82); and Gradgrind presents Bounderby's proposal of marriage to Louisa (pp. 101–107).

Additional Selections

A young boy remembers the hard life of miners and their families in Wales years ago in Richard Llewellyn's *How Green Was My Valley* (Macmillan, 1940, $17.95; pap., Dell, $4.95).

The trials of Norwegian pioneers in western America are well portrayed in O. E. Rolvaag's *Giants in the Earth* (pap., Harper, $3.95), and another novel of beginning farmers and their difficult life is Knut Hamsun's *Growth of the Soil* (Knopf, 1953, $16.95; pap., Random, $5.95).

Institutional child abuse in 1847 is the theme of Ann Schlee's *Ask Me No Questions* (Holt, 1982, $13.95).

The smug Victorian middle class and their oppressive educational practices are explored in Samuel Butler's classic novel of 1903 *The Way of All Flesh* (many editions are available).

A Lithuanian immigrant must work under filthy conditions in Chicago stockyards at the turn of the century in Upton Sinclair's *The Jungle* (many editions available).

In George Orwell's first novel, *Down and Out in Paris and London* (pap.,

Harcourt, $3.95), he describes life with the poor and unemployed during the Depression.

Augie, an illegitimate child, grows up in poverty in Chicago in *The Adventures of Augie March* by Saul Bellow (Viking, 1953, $12.95; pap., Avon, $3.95).

The Victorian era of the early twentieth century is evoked in John Galsworthy's monumental *The Forsyte Saga* (Scribner's, 1933, $25.00, pap., $2.95).

In Studs Terkel's nonfictional *Hard Times* (pap., Pantheon, $6.95) there is an oral history of life during America's Depression period.

About the Author
General encyclopedias and standard literary reference works contain information on Charles Dickens. One well-known biography is Edgar Johnson's *Charles Dickens: His Tragedy and Triumph* (Penguin 1983).
Kunitz, Stanley J., ed. *British Authors of the Nineteenth Century.* New York: Wilson, 1936, pp. 182–184.

Gordimer, Nadine. *July's People*
Viking, 1981, $10.95; pap., Penguin, $5.95 (same pagination)

Nadine Gordimer has been called the conscience of South Africa and, since the death of Alan Paton, is now regarded by many as the leading novelist exploring the complexities of apartheid and the most outspoken opponent of its injustices. Although this is a short novel it is powerful in its compactness. It is read by mature readers in the senior high school grades.

Plot Summary
The long-feared massive black uprising has come to South Africa. With help from the Russians and Cubans and utilizing army bases in neighboring countries like Mozambique, the downtrodden blacks are now successfully waging a full-scale war against their white oppressors. The government has toppled and the big cities are under siege and in flames.

The Smales family is fortunate in being rescued from their home in suburban Johannesburg, where they have lived in upper middle-class prosperity in an eight-room house. In their yellow "bakkie," a jeeplike truck, they are led to safety by their faithful, trusted black servant of 15 years, named only July. The family consists of fortyish Bam, short for Bamford, his wife, Maureen, and their three young children, Victor, Gina, and Royce. Bam is a successful architect. Both he and his wife are educated, sensitive, and liberal. Maureen, once a dancer, had grown up in the countryside where she fondly remembers that her best friend and companion was one of her family's servants, a black girl named Lydia.

These well-intentioned people were often sickened by racial conditions in their country and had thought many times of leaving South Africa and beginning again elsewhere. At one crisis point, they even withdrew most of their money from their banks, but procrastination and indecision caused them to stay. Now, with this money and what few personal possessions they could snatch at the last minute, they have fled their home.

Utilizing the trails he had known since childhood, July leads them on a three-day trek to the home of his family, who live in a group of thatched mud huts where they eke out a primitive existence from the land. In spite of the rudimentary nature of their new surroundings, the Smales feel fortunate to be alive and well, and are anxious to adjust to this new situation, where their roles and that of July have been reversed concerning dependency and power.

At first July feels obliged to treat them as honored guests in spite of his wife's and mother's resentment of the appearance of these whites in their midst. The Smales try to fit in. Bam helps them construct a water tank and mends some of their tools. At one point, armed with an eight-bore shotgun he brought with him, he goes hunting with July's friend, a former milkman named Daniel. Bam is able to bag two young warthogs and that night July's family and the Smales in their separate quarters dine on meat.

The children soon begin playing with their counterparts and adopting their ways. For example, Maureen notices with concern that the youngest, Royce, has begun using rocks instead of the precious toilet paper she has so carefully squirreled away.

One day, without consultation, July takes the keys to the bakkie and drives off. Maureen in particular is angry. When he returns with the groceries he bought at the local store, the confrontation between Maureen and July occurs. Unconsciously and in spite of her liberal background, she has assimilated some of the master-servant racial assumptions of the white culture she despises. July also inwardly feels tinges of resentment and distrust from his years of servitude. Loyalty and dignity prevail, however, and a major crisis is averted, but July retains the keys to the jeep.

As the days drag on and the news from the Smales' battery radio becomes more confused and discouraging, the final vestiges of their former life—like canned sausages and toilet paper—run out. Even their marital relationship, once shored up by everyday conventions, begins to wear thin, and Bam, no longer able to assert his authority, begins to crumble. Meantime, the hostility between Maureen and July increases.

During their third week in the bush, the Smales are summoned to appear before the tribal chief some miles away. They are fearful he will deny them continued refuge in July's compound. With the help of July and Daniel, the tense meeting is a success and the chief even offers to help oust the foreign invaders from the country to reinstate the former order.

Back in the village, a traveling entertainer with a gumba-gumba, a wind-up phonograph, arrives. Homemade beer is brought out and there is a family party. When the Smales return to their hut, they discover that their shotgun, the last symbol of their power, has disappeared.

Maureen is furious. She seeks out July and demands that he find and return their gun. July tells her that Daniel stole it before running off to join the revolution. A second confrontation occurs, and the scars produced by a culture based on oppression once more emerge.

A few days later, the sound of a helicopter is heard overhead and is seen landing nearby. Maureen is unable to decipher its markings and can't tell if it is friend or foe. Nevertheless, instinctively Maureen knows that for better or worse, this might be her only chance to leave a world where she now knows she doesn't belong—the world of July's people. She runs toward the spot where the plane landed.

Thematic Material

This novel has been called a parable. Its theme is a devastating one— that people no matter how well intentioned cannot escape from the conditioning of their culture or its consequences. It is about people trapped by their past to live a foreordained future. Maureen accepts the only alternative she has, which is to flee. The novel is also about power, its symbols, and conflicts involving white versus black, man versus woman, master versus servant, child versus parent. It also shows that no upheaval, regardless of how cataclysmic it may be, can ever make master and servant equal. Differences in cultures are explored as are the changes that occur when people are deprived of the superficial but often essential trappings of civilization. The difficulty of accepting role reversal is well depicted, as is the human need for dignity and respect even in servitude. The irony inherent in the title is also an interesting theme. Who are July's people? Only his black bush family or also those whites who have employed him and treated him well?

Book Talk Material

A brief description of the Smales family and their life before arriving in July's village, with a hint of the events to follow, should interest readers. Because of the frequent shifts in time and points of view, it is difficult to isolate specific passages for reading or relating. However, some possibilities are: Maureen's friendship with Lydia (pp. 30–33); July returns with the car (pp. 52–56); the hunt for warthogs (pp. 74–78); and meeting the tribal chief (pp. 108–121).

Additional Selections

Excerpts from Nadine Gordimer's fiction and 60 photographs by David Goldblatt are combined in *Lifetimes: Under Apartheid* (Knopf, 1986, $29.95) to create a moving document.

Stories that dramatize race relations in South Africa are found in Doris Lessing's *African Stories* (pap., Simon, $10.95).

The classic novel of the tragedy of prejudice is Alan Paton's *Cry, the Beloved Country* (Scribner's, 1961, $22.50, plus many paperback editions). Also use Paton's *Ah, but Your Land Is Beautiful* (Scribner's, 1983, $22.50, pap. $6.95).

A modern Nigerian girl rebels against tribal customs in Buchi Emecheta's tragic *The Bride Price* (Braziller, 1976, $6.95).

Various aspects of the horror of apartheid are explored in Ernst Havemann's *Bloodsong and Other Stories of South Africa* (Houghton, 1987, $12.95).

The roots of apartheid are explored in eight generations of Afrikaners in the nonfictional *White Tribe Dreaming* by Marq de Villiers (Viking, 1988, $19.95).

A play that dramatizes the corrosive conditioning of apartheid is Athol Fugard's *Master Harold and the Boys* (Knopf, 1982, $11.95).

Three novels that explore life in another troubled land, Northern Ireland, are Benedict Kiely's *Proxopera* (Godine, 1987, $12.95), in which terrorists hold a family hostage, *Cal* by Bernard MacLaverty (Braziller, 1983, $12.95), about an ill-fated Protestan/Catholic romance, and Leon Uris's pageant of Irish history from the 1840s to 1916 *Trinity* (Doubleday, 1976, $19.95; pap., Bantam, $4.95).

About the Book
Booklist, February 15, 1981, p. 774.
Library Journal, March 15, 1981, p. 680.
New York Times Book Review, June 7, 1981, p. 1.
See also *Book Review Digest*, 1981, pp. 559–560, and *Book Review Index*, 1981, p. 220.

About the Author
Evory, Ann, ed. *Contemporary Authors* (New Revision Series). Detroit: Gale, 1981. Vol. 3, pp. 239–242.
Harte, Barbara, and Riley, Carolyn, eds. *Contemporary Authors* (First Revision). Detroit: Gale, 1969. Vols. 5–8, p. 459.
Wakeman, John, ed. *World Authors 1950–1970*. New York: Wilson, 1975, pp. 577–579.

Hugo, Victor.   *The Hunchback of Notre Dame*
Dodd, 1947, $11.95

In translation, Victor Hugo is known chiefly as a novelist, but in France he is also renowned as both a fine poet and playwright. Like his fellow Frenchman Emile Zola, he was active politically, and in Hugo's case, this involved almost 20 years in exile, chiefly in the Channel Islands. Here he wrote some of his most important works including *Les Misérables* (1861) (various editions available). One of his early works was *Notre Dame de Paris*. Published in 1831, this has come down to us as *The Hunchback of Notre Dame*. Although it contains no great depth of characterization, it has an exciting story and evokes fifteenth-century Paris and the presence of the great cathedral. Three of the many paperback editions available are Airmont ($1.95), Bantam ($1.95), and NAL ($2.50). It is enjoyed by better readers in the senior high grades.

Plot Summary
This historical novel of fifteenth-century France evolves against a backdrop of the great Cathedral of Notre Dame in Paris.

In January 1482, King Louis XI is awaiting Flemish ambassadors to his court. Louis's son is to marry Margaret of Flanders. The day his ambassadors are to arrive is also the feast of Epiphany and of the Festival of Fools. Great crowds of Parisians are gathered, awaiting the production of a morality play and also to crown the so-called Prince of Fools in the festival's honor.

The crowd grows restless as it waits for the play to begin, and finally Gringoire, a somewhat dull-witted poet, loudly orders the play to start. However, the performance is soon interrupted by the royal procession, after which the crowd, no longer interested in the play, cries for the Prince of Fools to be crowned.

The Prince of Fools by tradition must be physically ugly, but since it is an honor of sorts, many of the misshapen folk of the city vie for the chance to be crowned. But this time the crowd has an easy decision, for Quasimodo, the bell ringer of Notre Dame, comes into view. Quasimodo is hideously deformed, with teethlike tusks, one eye hidden under an ugly skin fold, arms that hang like an ape's, and a great snout of a nose. Although Quasimodo is deaf, his eyesight is acute.

Quasimodo is given the honorary robes and paraded through the streets with great hilarity. But the procession stops at one point to watch a lovely gypsy dancer named Esmeralda, who performs with her trained goat. She is so captivating that some in the crowd think she must be a witch.

Later that night when the poet Gringoire is walking the deserted city streets because he has no home, he sees a black-hooded figure grab Esmeralda and begin to drag her away. He also sees the hooded figure's helper; it is Quasimodo, who hits Gringoire over the head. But before the hooded figure can carry Esmeralda away, a horseman rides up and chases him and Quasimodo.

Esmeralda's rescuer turns out to be Captain Phoebus de Chateaupers, and the gypsy dancer immediately falls in love.

The black-hooded figure who tried to kidnap the lovely Esmeralda was none other than the evil archdeacon of Notre Dame, Claude Frollo. A man whose only interest in life is garnering knowledge, Frollo shuns all human contact, and because he denies the human side of his nature, his attraction for Esmeralda turns into a lust that is very near madness. Knowing Esmeralda would have nothing to do with him, he decides to capture her and keep her for himself. Quasimodo aided him out of an animal-like loyalty and devotion, for the hunchback knows that Frollo was the only one to befriend and care for him when he was dumped on the steps of Notre Dame and abandoned.

Meantime, as Gringoire wanders through the dangerous parts of the city, he is captured by thugs and told he will be killed unless some woman will marry him. Esmeralda appears, and, to save his life, marries Gringoire, but there is no wedding night, for Esmeralda's heart now belongs to Phoebus.

Talk grows among the citizens of Paris that Esmeralda is a witch and Frollo a sorcerer, and Quasimodo is taken in court to be questioned about his relationship with Frollo. As a result, he is severely beaten in public, and the crowd in its frenzy begins to throw stones at him. Once again, Esmeralda comes to the rescue. This time, she climbs the scaffold where Quasimodo is being tortured and gives him water for his parched lips. Quasimodo sees that Frollo is also in the crowd but does nothing to help him.

Sometime later, Phoebus and Esmeralda meet again and arrange to spend the next evening together. Because Gringoire has told Frollo that Esmeralda, although technically his wife, is in love with Phoebus, the archdeacon confronts Phoebus with a plan. Saying that he merely wants to make sure that Esmeralda is who she says she is, he arranges to hide in the room where Phoebus and Esmeralda are to meet. Phoebus has no objections.

But during the romantic meeting, Frollo jumps out from his hiding place and stabs Phoebus. Esmeralda is sent to prison for the crime, and although Phoebus lives, he does not come forward and explain what happened for fear of getting involved with a charge of witchcraft.

Esmeralda is convicted of witchcraft; she is to do penance at the Cathedral of Notre Dame and then to be publicly hanged. Frollo goes to the prison and tells her that he will free her if she will consent to be his. Esmeralda refuses.

When Esmeralda is taken to the porch of the cathedral for her penance, Quasimodo carries her into the church and to his cell, where he lives. He locks the cell to keep her from harm and enters only to bring her food and water.

But Frollo has a key to the cell and enters, once more trying to take Esmeralda away. But Quasimodo arrives in time to save her again.

Days later a mob gathers outside Notre Dame demanding Esmeralda. Using construction materials left by the workers, Quasimodo becomes a one-man army as he throws stones and molten lead down on the crowd and pushes away the ladders they try to climb. All in all he manages to kill or injure hundreds of people in his attempt to keep Esmeralda safe.

When Quasimodo returns to the cell once more, Esmeralda is gone. Frollo has given a key to Gringoire, who stupidly leads Esmeralda into a trap. He takes her to a hidden boat where Frollo is waiting. Esmeralda manages to run away, but she is soon captured by the soldiers.

Quasimodo goes to the tower of Notre Dame where he finds Frollo laughing hysterically at the scene below. When the hunchback looks down from the great tower, he sees a figure clad in white. It is his beloved Esmeralda, on the gallows. She is dead. Finally understanding what the evil Frollo has done, Quasimodo picks up the archdeacon and throws him to his death from the tower of Notre Dame.

Then Quasimodo disappears and is seen no more.

During the reign of Charles VIII (1483–1498), son of Louis XI, a vault is opened that contained the remains of criminals. The body of a woman who had been clad in white is discovered in the arms of what appears to have been a deformed figure.

Thematic Material

Considered a classic romance novel, *The Hunchback of Notre Dame* illustrates Victor Hugo's conviction that the "sublime and grotesque" must coexist in literature and art just as they do in life. Each of the main characters has a personality that is centered on one main theme: Quasimodo illustrates devotion and loyalty; Esmeralda is purity; and Frollo is lust. Against the background of the great cathedral, which is so strongly presented in the story as to be almost a character itself, emerges Hugo's Christian belief that the imperfect image created by God can overcome its imperfections and attain spiritual greatness.

Book Talk Material

The descriptions of places and people in Paris of the fifteenth-century should give readers a good sense of time and location and can help to explain the actions of the central characters and of the mob. See: the crowd at the Great Hall of the Palace of Justice (pp. 11–23); Gringoire calls for the play (pp. 24–31); Quasimodo is crowned (pp. 46–51); Esmeralda is rescued by Phoebus (pp. 66–69); and a look at the Cathedral of Notre Dame (pp. 98–105) and at Claude Frollo (pp. 130–134).

Additional Selections

Mary W. Shelley's unique contribution to English literature is the story of a young German scientist's creation of a humanlike monster, *Frankenstein* (various editions available). In a continuation by Vonda N. McIntyre, *The Bride* (pap., Dell, $2.95), Viktor, the monster, falls in love with Eva, another of the doctor's creations.

Michael Shea, a master of horror and adventure, displays his skill in the seven stories collected in *Polyphemus* (Arkham, 1987, $16.95).

Another French novel of horror and suspense is Gaston Leroux's *Phantom of the Opera* (several editions available).

Two other classics of the macabre are Robert Louis Stevenson's *Doctor Jekyll and Mr. Hyde* and Bran Stoker's *Dracula* (several editions of each are available).

Two well-loved novels of the French Revolution are Baroness Orzy's *The Scarlet Pimpernel*, about a fop who is really a hero, and Charles Dickens's *A Tale of Two Cities* (several editions of both are available).

A badly deformed man tries to gain acceptance by his peers in the play *The Elephant Man* (pap., Grove, $4.25) by Bernard Pomerance.

Evelyn Waugh presents a distorted view of life and death in *The Loved One* (Little, 1977, $13.95, pap. $6.70).

Also use the classic French adventure novels by Alexander Dumas— *The Count of Monte Cristo* and *The Three Musketeers* (various editions are available).

About the Author

General encyclopedias and standard literary reference works contain information on Victor Hugo. One well-known biography is Andre Maurois's *Olympio: The Life of Victor Hugo* (Carroll & Graf, 1988).

Kunitz, Stanley J., and Colby, Vaneta, eds. *European Authors*. New York: Wilson, 1967, pp. 426–430.

Morrison, Toni. *Beloved*
Knopf, 1987, $18.95

In Toni Morrison's first book published in 1970, *The Bluest Eyes* (pap., Washington Square, $3.95), she tells the story of an 11-year-old black girl, Pecola Breedlove, who after being raped by her father becomes pregnant and retreats into insanity. Her other novels are *Tar Baby*

(Knopf, 1981, $14.95; pap., NAL, $3.95), the story of a successful black woman set in the Caribbean; *Song of Solomon* (Knopf, 1977, $14.95; pap., NAL, $3.95), whose central character is a young black male; and *Sula* (Knopf, 1974, $14.95; pap., NAL, $5.95). In *Beloved,* her Pulitzer Prize winner, she continues to explore the frequent tragedy and heartbreak of being born black. The epigraph of the novel is a verse from the Bible's Book of Romans, "I will call my people which were not my people, and her beloved which was not beloved." This message of rejection is transformed in the next verse, however, to one of hope when all of the unloved and unwanted of the world are nevertheless considered "children of a living god." *Beloved* is a historical novel that deals with the abomination of slavery and spans several years surrounding the American Civil War. Although it begins in a black community on the outskirts of Cincinnati in 1873, much of the action occurs before the war in the slave state of Kentucky. This and Morrison's earlier novels are suitable only for mature senior high school readers.

Plot Summary

The book's episodes are told through a series of flashbacks, but to simplify the plot retelling, a tighter chronological approach is used.

Sethe's childhood as a slave was one of unremitting horror and privation. She remembers being separated from her mother, a fieldworker, at an early age and being raised by a one-armed woman, Nan. At age six she is told her mother has been executed and sees her body hanging from a tree. Her luck changes in 1849 when at age 13 she is sold to the Garners to work on a small farm named Sweet Home in northern Kentucky close to the Ohio River. Sethe is to take the place of Mrs. Garner's former personal servant and housekeeper, the crippled Baby Suggs, whose son Halle, also a slave at Sweet Home, has purchased her freedom by earning money working extra hours off the farm.

Baby Suggs has been bought and sold many times in her life and had had eight children by six different fathers. She has lost all contact with these children except Halle, because they had been bought or bartered to other slaveowners. Through the help of an abolitionist couple in Cincinnati, the Bodwins, Baby Suggs now lives alone in a many-roomed house in a rural black community outside of town. Halle's fondest hope is that one day he will be able to join his mother in slave-free Ohio.

Unlike the other white people Sethe has known, the Garners behave somewhat humanely toward their slaves. In addition to Halle Suggs, there are four other male slaves: Sixo and three brothers, Paul F., Paul D., and Paul A. Garner. Although the institution of marriage is denied slaves, after one year on the farm Sethe takes Halle as her man. To bless the union, Mrs. Garner gives her a pair of earrings.

In time Sethe and Halle have three children—two boys named Howard and Buglar and a baby girl. Things change catastrophically at Sweet Home when, after Mr. Garner's sudden death, the schoolteacher, Mrs. Garner's sadistic brother-in-law, arrives with his two young nephews to manage the farm. Paul F. is sold to pay accumulated debts, and for the remaining slaves, life now becomes a series of humiliations, beatings, chained imprisonments, and unspeakable hardships.

A plan for escape is devised, but things go awry. Paul F. and Sixo, the first to leave, are caught and burned alive. On the eve of her planned flight, Sethe, now several months pregnant with her fourth child, is trapped in the barn by the two nephews who strip her and suck the milk from her swollen breasts. Halle witnesses this outrage helplessly from a hiding place inside the barn. The enormity of this horror drives him to insanity.

When Sethe tells Mrs. Garner of her attack, the schoolmaster retaliates by beating her so furiously with a cowhide whip that her back looks like a tree with limbs of blood. Unable to get help from Halle, she sends the three children ahead and with the help of two blacks, John and Ella, they make the trip safely to Baby Suggs. That night Sethe also leaves, though more dead than alive.

In the woods she meets a white indentured servant girl, Amy Denver, who is also escaping her life of privation. Amy dresses her wounds and helps Sethe with the painful premature childbirth of a baby girl. Out of gratitude the child is named Denver. Miraculously mother and daughter survive the rest of the journey and arrive at Baby Suggs.

Sethe heals rapidly, but only four weeks after her flight a posse of white slave hunters, led by the schoolmaster, appears to take her and her children back. Crazed with fear and unable to accept slavery for her children, she tries to kill the children with a hand saw. The baby is saved, but both boys are injured and the two-year-old girl dies of a slit throat.

The schoolmaster and his cronies retreat in confusion. Sethe, without money, sells her body to a gravestone maker to secure a marker for her dead child. Instead of "dearly beloved" being chiseled on the marker as she requested, only "beloved" is carved—her payment is not sufficient for both words.

Sethe is taken into custody by the police, but through the intervention of the Bodwins, is given only a prison sentence. After her release, she returns to the family and Baby Suggs, but suddenly the house becomes haunted by the spiteful angry ghost of her dead daughter. In time the ghost drives both Howard and Buglar, now young teenagers, from their home.

The following year Baby Suggs, weakened by failing health, dies, leaving only Sethe and Denver to cope.

In 1873, 18 years after Sethe's escape from Sweet Home, a stranger appears at their door. It is Paul D., whose life since being sold has been a continuous history of wretchedness, including a stretch in a Georgia chain gang. With his arrival the ghost is silenced and love returns to Sethe's life.

One day a mysterious 20-year-old waif appears who calls herself only Beloved. Sethe takes her in, convinced that she is the embodiment of her dead child. Soon Beloved becomes the center of the family's attention. She seduces Paul D., who after learning from a coworker at the slaughterhouse, Stamp Paid, about the murder years before, is so filled with revulsion for Sethe and shame for his affair with Beloved that he moves out.

Sethe now devotes her entire life to Beloved's welfare, trying to lessen her guilt and gain expiation for her transgression. She leaves her job and spends every day playing with Beloved. Without money for food, Denver finds that she must leave the security of the house and find work.

Through Denver, the town ladies learn about Beloved's presence and they appear at the door to exorcise the spirit. At the same time Mr. Bodwin comes to take Denver to her first job. Sethe, fearful of again losing Beloved, attacks them with an ice pick but is subdued before doing any harm. The women pray and just as mysteriously as she appeared, Beloved vanishes.

When everyone has left, Sethe is alone in the quiet, now peaceful house. Paul D. appears and, hoping to start life again with the woman he loves, gently takes Sethe into his arms.

Thematic Material

This is one of the most powerful indictments of slavery and its legacy ever written. In its description of the horror inflicted on the black race, it is reminiscent of Nazi death camps, although this took place in our own United States. The dehumanizing aspects of slavery are best described in

Sethe's words when she says (on p. 131) that "[the worst part is] that anybody white could take your whole self or anything that came to mind, not just work, kill, or maim you, but dirty you, dirty you so badly you couldn't like yourself anymore." Mere survival is not enough unless it is accompanied with honor and dignity. Besides the telling of the near destruction of a race, this novel deals with the deliberate shattering of family unity, the passion of motherhood, and the limits to which maternal feelings can extend. The burden that guilt produces, its eventual expiation, and the need for self-acceptance are explored. Even in torment, Sethe is in turn gallant, pathetic, courageous, and a universal earth mother.

Book Talk Material

Perhaps because the story is too horrifying to be narrated sequentially, the author has instead used jagged shards of memory too painful to be seen chronologically to tell her story. Some episodes of importance are: Paul D. arrives and after exposition about Sweet Home drives away the ghost (pp. 6–19); the meeting with Amy and the birth of Denver (pp. 31–35, 78–85); the arrival of Beloved (pp. 51–54); and Paul D. on the chain gang (pp. 106–113).

Additional Selections

A first-person account of being born a slave and living to participate in the twentieth-century civil rights movement is told in Ernest Gaines's novel *The Autobiography of Miss Jane Pitman* (Doubleday, 1971, $16.95; pap., Bantam, $3.50). In his *A Gathering of Old Men* (Knopf, 1983, $16.95; pap., Bantam, $3.95), each member of a group of elderly black men claims to have committed a murder to prevent racial conflict.

The story of the abortive slave revolt in 1831 and its courageous leader is told in the novel *The Confessions of Nat Turner* by William Styron (Random, 1967, $16.95; pap., Bantam, $4.50) and the biography by Terry Bisson *Nat Turner* (Chelsea House, 1988, $16.95).

Two black Americans who have traced their families back to the days of slavery are Alex Haley in *Roots* (Doubleday, 1976, $17.95; pap., Dell, $5.95) and Dorothy Redford in *Somerset Homecoming* (Doubleday, 1988, $18.95).

A young escaped slave faces trial in Virginia Hamilton's *Anthony Burns: The Defeat and Triumph of a Fugitive Slave* (Knopf, 1988, $11.95) for younger readers.

The story of a black woman's childhood in the rural South to a loveless marriage and her departure to the North are told in Sara Brooks's *You May Plow Here* (Norton, 1986, $12.95).

Julius Lester presents the horror of slavery and its aftermath in three stories in *This Strange New Feeling* (Dial, 1982, $10.95; pap., Scholastic, $2.25).

Dorothy Sterling in *We Are Your Sisters* (Norton, 1984, $14.95) gives portraits of nineteenth-century black women, some free, some slaves.

About the Book
Booklist, July 1987, p. 1627.
Library Journal, September 1, 1987, p. 201.
New York Times Book Review, September 13, 1987, p. 1.
See also *Book Review Digest*, 1987, pp. 1317–1318, and *Book Review Index*, 1987, p. 543.

About the Author
Colby, Veneta, ed. *World Authors 1975–1980*. New York: Wilson, 1985, pp. 537–539.
Kinsman, Clare D., and Tennenhouse, Mary Ann, eds. *Contemporary Authors*. Detroit: Gale, 1972. Vols. 29–32, p. 429.

Twain, Mark.   *Puddn'head Wilson*
pap., Bantam, $1.95

Most readers unfortunately stop reading Mark Twain after *Huckleberry Finn* and *Tom Sawyer*, leaving untouched some of his other fine works such as *A Connecticut Yankee in King Arthur's Court* and the present volume. *Puddn'head Wilson* uses as a key plot device role reversals, in this case by substitution of babies. This literary gimmick was used in ancient literature in such works as Plautus's *Menaechmi* or Shakespeare's *A Comedy of Errors* and in modern times with such Broadway musicals as *The Boys from Syracuse* and Hollywood comedies such as *Big Business*. Unlike the latter, *Puddn'head Wilson* is not a comedy but a bitter indictment of humanity in general and slavery in particular. There are several editions in paperback besides the Bantam edition listed above and cited in the Book Talk section. Others include: Airmont ($1.75), New American Library ($1.95), and Penguin ($2.50). The action begins in 1850 in Dawson's Landing, a Mississippi River town in Missouri slightly south of St.

Louis, and extends through a period of more than 20 years. At this time slavery was still widespread in the slave states and the term "nigger," although now derogatory, was then considered an acceptable form of address. This novel, though written for adults, can be enjoyed by better readers in the junior high grades and up.

Plot Summary

Two important events occur during February 1850 in Dawson's Landing. The first is the birth of two boys, one Thomas à Becket Driscoll, scion of the town's finest family, and the other Valet de Chambre, born to the Driscolls's 20-year-old servant and former slave, Roxanne, or Roxy for short. Mrs. Driscoll dies in childbirth and Roxy is given responsibility for raising both children. Though the unmarried Roxy is only one-sixteenth black and her son has an unnamed white father, both are nevertheless considered "niggers" and in spite of their completely caucasian features must bear all the humiliations and servitude that this entails.

The other event is the arrival in town of David Wilson, a newly graduated lawyer from the East who intends to set up a practice. Unfortunately, the townspeople misunderstand many of his witticisms and label him "Puddn'head," an appellation that destroys the possibility of a law practice and causes him to resort to accountancy for a living. His major hobby is collecting the fingerprints of the townspeople, including babies like the Driscolls's and Roxy's boys at various stages of their development, to show that fingerprints remain constant during one's lifetime.

Mr. Driscoll correctly suspects that some of his servants are thieves. When he threatens to sell all of them down the river, the culprits confess, but the innocent Roxy realizes how precarious her son's future is and therefore one evening, she switches the identities of the two young lookalikes by simply changing their clothes and cradles.

As the years pass, her son, now Tom Driscoll, grows into a spoiled sniveling weakling who uses his servant's son, Chambers, a docile, well-mannered boy, as both a whipping post and bodyguard. Mr. Driscoll dies when Tom and Chambers are 15. Both boys go to live with the father's neighboring elder brother, Percy Driscoll, a true gentleman originally from old Virginia who lives with his widowed sister, Rachael Pratt. Here Tom is given a place of honor and Chambers is sent to the servants' quarters. Roxy, now assured of her son's safety, leaves Dawson's Landing to become a chambermaid on a Mississippi steamer.

During the next few years, Tom drops out of Yale and returns home to engage in bouts of gambling and dissolution in St. Louis, where he amasses many gambling debts. Fearing that disclosure of his financial situation would cause his uncle to disown him, he begins at night disguising himself as an old woman and committing burglaries in the neighborhood. An opportunity for several good heists occurs when an important social event leaves many of the best houses in town unattended.

The widow Cooper, also known as Aunt Patsy, and her daughter Rowena have a reception to honor the arrival in town of their two new tenants, the charming Italian identical twins, Luigi and Angelo Capello. That night several citizens are robbed, including the twins, who are incensed at the loss of their valuable, jewel-encrusted dagger. They post a reward for its return and the capture of the thief. Tom is furious because he will now be unable to pawn it safely.

A discouraged Roxy returns to Dawson's Landing, having lost her savings in a bank closure. Through Chambers she learns of Tom's gambling. When she confronts him with this truth, his disdainful and insulting attitude toward her forces her to tell him the truth of his origins and threaten him with public disclosure unless he mends his ways.

A temporary reformation occurs, but soon Tom's repugnant nature returns. Without cause he publicly insults the twin Luigi, who responds by administering a kick in the pants. When old Mr. Driscoll hears of this insult to his family, he shames his cowardly nephew by challenging Luigi to a duel. Although it is a standoff, enmity between the twins and Mr. Driscoll is declared.

More gambling debts are amassed and to save her son, Roxy allows him to sell her as a slave. To make as much money as possible, Tom knowingly sells Roxy down the river to a cruel plantation owner. After a few weeks of brutality, a half-dead Roxy escapes and seeks out her infamous son in his lair in St. Louis. She demands that he borrow enough money from his uncle to buy her freedom.

Tom returns unnoticed to Dawson's Landing and finds his uncle in the parlor with his open cashbox. He has fallen asleep over his accounts. When Tom robs some bank notes, Mr. Driscoll stirs and cries for help. Tom fatally stabs him with the stolen bejeweled knife. He flees, but the twins, walking in the neighborhood and hearing Mr. Driscoll's cries, are the first to enter the house. Other neighbors arrive. Circumstantial evidence points to the twins, who are arrested for murder. They secure the services of one of their few friends in town, Puddn'head Wilson, to act as their lawyer.

Puddn'head is convinced of their innocence because the fingerprints on the dagger do not match theirs, but whose are they? One evening during the court case Tom visits Wilson, who is pouring over his collection of fingerprint slides. When Puddn'head examines a print accidentally left behind on a glass by Tom, he knows he has found his killer. He checks the other of Tom's prints dating back to his infancy and is able to unravel the even stranger mystery of his true parentage.

The next day in a dramatic court confrontation, Wilson presents his evidence. Roxy admits the deception she has perpetrated and the twins are freed. Roxy is heartbroken but eventually finds solace in her church and faith.

Ironically, Tom eventually suffers a fate that he had once wished on his own mother. Now legally part of the Driscoll estate, he is sold as a slave down the river to help pay creditors.

Thematic Material

In spite of melodramatic overtones, this novel contains a serious message. After learning that he is actually a black, Tom muses, "What crime did the uncreated first nigger commit that the curse of birth was decreed for him?" and "Why is this awful difference between white and black?" The novel portrays realistically the odious institution of slavery, its blot on U.S. history, and the injustices forced on people because of racial prejudice. Twain was also one of the few nineteenth-century writers to create believable flesh-and-blood black characters. The book is full of ironies: for example, Roxy's audacious scheme to ensure a bright future for her son actually causes his tragic end. Some other themes are the unfortunate consequences of child indulgence, the inevitable nature of fulfilling one's destiny, mother-son relationships, and the oneness of humankind. Puddn'head is a likable, self-effacing hero who shows great innate wisdom and who eventually gives living proof that the meek shall inherit the earth.

Book Talk Material

An introduction to Roxy and the baby-switching episode should interest readers. Some specific passages are: Puddn'head gets his nickname (pp. 4–5); Mr. Driscoll threatens his slaves and frightens Roxy (pp. 10–13); Roxy changes babies (pp. 13–17); and the boyhood of the two youngsters (pp. 19–23). Some of Puddn'head's pithy expressions that introduce each chapter should also be used.

Additional Selections

The Wit and Wisdom of Mark Twain, edited by Alex Ayres (Harper, 1987, $17.50), is an alphabetically arranged book of quotations that are fun to browse through.

After the Civil War, Roman Hasford moves to St. Louis to hunt buffalo in Douglas C. Jones's *Roman* (Holt, 1986, $14.45), a sequel to *Elkhorn Tavern* (pap., Holt, $5.95).

In the early 1800s a backwoods boy and a lawyer go in search of a murderer in Scott R. Sanders's *Bad Man's Ballad* (Bradbury, 1986, $13.95), and in Charles Portis's *True Grit* (pap., NAL, $2.95) a spunky teenager sets out to find her father's murderer.

An 11-year-old con artist and the man she thinks is her father team up in Joe D. Brown's hilarious *Paper Moon* (pap., NAL, $2.50).

Life in a small Ohio town at the beginning of the twentieth century is the subject of Sherwood Anderson's *Winesburg, Ohio* (pap., Penguin, $3.95).

In the late 1800s in Nevada a lynching party is responsible for a terrible miscarriage of justice in Walter Van Tilberg Clark's *The Ox Bow Incident* (Peter Smith, n.d., $9.50; pap., NAL, $2.95).

Two boys—one white and one black—set out to prove a black man innocent of murder in William Faulkner's *Intruder in the Dust* (Random, 1948, $13.95, pap. $4.95).

Parent-child relationships are also explored in the classic French novel *Old Goriot* by Honoré de Balzac (many editions available).

About the Author
General encyclopedias and standard literary reference works contain information on Mark Twain. Two well-known biographies are Justin Kaplan's *Mr. Clemens and Mark Twain* (Simon, 1966, pap. $10.95) and Dixon Wechter's *Sam Clemens of Hannibal* (AMS Pr., reprint of 1952 ed., $27.00).
Kunitz, Stanley J., and Haycraft, Howard, eds. *American Authors 1600–1900.* New York: Wilson, 1938, pp. 159–161 (under Clemens).

Tyler, Anne. *A Slipping-Down Life*
pap., Berkley, $3.95

Anne Tyler's first novel, *If Morning Ever Comes* (pap., Berkley, $3.95), was published in 1964. *A Slipping-Down Life,* her third, appeared in 1970.

It was first classified as a young adult novel and, therefore, was not as widely reviewed as her other works. Her novels usually deal with the consequences in everyday life of how people accept or reject their fates. Past and present merge and the action is often circular in nature ending where it began. In this regard she is often compared favorably with Eudora Welty, the writer she most admires. Her novels are suitable for better senior high school readers.

Plot Summary

Two more unlikely lovers would be hard to imagine anywhere, let alone in the small southern town that is their home. In the first place, Evie Decker isn't much to look at; well, perhaps she is too much to look at—too plump, too short, too heavy-footed, a drab-looking, sort of wilted girl with too-big breasts and a quiet, almost unobtrusive manner.

Evie is 17, going into her senior year of her boring life, which she shares mainly with her father, a pleasant enough man who hardly talks and never seems to notice her, although she isn't much of a conversationalist either, so she really doesn't care much. About the only other people she talks to are Clotelia, who comes to clean the house when the spirit moves her, and her brassy friend Violet, who is even heavier than Evie, and doesn't care at all.

Evie gets this idea about going out to the tavern called the Unicorn on Saturday nights to see Drumstrings Casey perform on the guitar. She'd heard him on a radio program, and although she can't actually explain why, she wants to see him.

Violet would agree to go anywhere, so the two of them start to hitch a ride on Saturday nights with Fay-Jean, who is the only one they know with a car.

Drumstrings (whose real name is Bertram) Casey isn't much either by most standards. He has long shiny black hair and wears high leather boots. With just his drummer named David to accompany him, he plays and sings songs of his own making, seemingly in his own world, because, as Evie notices, no one in the audience seems to pay him much attention. And when his songs are over, Drum Casey just shuffles off the stage as though none of the audience mattered anyway, which actually, as Evie finds out later, they don't. Drum and his music make up his world, and neither his friend David, nor his mother, with whom he lives after quitting school, can make him sit up and take notice of anything else.

Then one night Evie causes quite a stir at the Unicorn. When Violet goes to look for her in the ladies' room, she discovers a dazed-looking Evie with letters cut into her forehead with scissors. The letters, if you look straight at them, say "CASEY."

They take Evie to the hospital and call her father, but she never will say just why she cut Drum Casey's name on her forehead. The story does get around though, and before she leaves the hospital David arranges for Drum Casey to go see Evie, for the "publicity." Drum just looks uncomfortable and leaves.

After Evie heals somewhat (although the doctors say she will need plastic surgery to repair the damage, which she refuses), she goes back to school. Then she talks to Drum's friend, the drummer David, about going to the Unicorn again for more publicity for Drum, and they agree, although Drum isn't too hot on the idea. Evie makes him uncomfortable.

But week after week, there she is at a lone table where everyone can see. "He must be something to have a girl do that over him," they whisper, which is just what Evie figured they would do.

Finally, after a lot of coaxing and prompting on David's and Evie's part, Drum gets a "break," a chance to play his music somewhere else. But it doesn't last and he is fired, which prompts a huge fight with his mother, who says she wants to be proud of him.

Without a home to go to, Drum takes to staying part-time with David and his family and sleeping some nights on Evie's porch, of which Evie's father is unaware. And one night, when Evie figures that their strange relationship is going nowhere, he just asks her to marry him. He doesn't talk about love, but he likes her well enough, and after all he needs a home.

It isn't exactly as Evie had figured it, but she agrees, and with David and Violet as witnesses, the two are married, to the anger of his mother and the bewilderment of her father.

Evie and Drum move out to a shack on the edge of town and set up a home. Surprisingly enough, it seems to work. Drum seems happy with his new life, even if he still doesn't talk much, and Evie, who has returned to school, hopes for that break that will make him a star, a notion that Drum resists, as he resists all efforts of people around him to change him.

Then Evie gets another idea to further Drum's career. This time she has Violet, Fay-Jean, and Fay-Jean's sister come to the shack and "kidnap" Drum for a few hours. Evie and David agree that they should get some publicity out of that. Drum, however, is most resistant to the idea and to being actually tied up and taken off by the three girls. Evie assures him that she'll come and get him in a few hours.

But soon after the "kidnapping," Evie learns that her father is in the hospital. By the time she gets there, he has died of a heart attack.

Evie does not return to their shack until the next morning. She walks in to find Fay-Jean in bed with her husband. After throwing Fay-Jean out, Evie tells Drum that she is leaving. No, not because of Fay-Jean, but because she, Evie, is going to have a baby and she needs to lead a more organized life. She is going to move back into her father's house. Drum is welcome to come. But Drum says he can't live there. And Evie says she must.

Before she leaves, Evie tells Drum the truth about her forehead. She didn't cut his name on it at all. She'd had a fight about him with a redhead, and the girl and her friend had held her down and carved the letters. She just never told anyone.

Drum says she'll be back. Evie says she never goes back on things.

And, indeed, next Saturday when Drum is once more playing his lonesome songs, Evie isn't there to hear.

Thematic Material

An offbeat love story of two misfits, this is a strange tale of two loners who come together for better or worse. She has romantic dreams that don't fit into her narrow town life. He wants only to be left alone to perform his music. The book talks about love, loneliness, communication, and more often the lack of it between two people who need each other, but don't know how to hang on to what they have.

Book Talk Material

The Unicorn can be used to introduce the background for the relationship that develops between these two unlikely lovers; see the first night out (pp. 24–30) and Evie's forehead is cut (pp. 37–38). See also: Drum visits the hospital (pp. 51–55); Evie calls his home (pp. 68–75); and David talks to Evie about publicity (pp. 80–83).

Additional Selections

Angela finds love with the brilliant budding scientist Tycho in Margaret Mahy's *The Catalogue of the Universe* (Atheneum, 1986, $11.95; pap., Scholastic, $2.50).

Graduate student Brad falls in love with Susannah who is prone to play with the truth in Kate Wilhelm's *Oh, Susannah!* (Houghton, 1982, $12.95).

A sexual coming of age novel set in turbulent Argentina of the 1960s is *El Yanqui* by Douglas Ungar (Harper, 1985, $16.95).

Mermaids by Patty Dann (Ticknor, 1985, $13.95) is a bizarre adult novel about a 14-year-old girl with feet of clay who wants to be a saint.

In Annie Dillard's nonfictional *An American Childhood* (Harper, 1987, $17.95), she writes affectionately about her girlhood and family.

A Vietnam veteran loses touch with reality and believes he can fly in William Wharton's *Birdy* (Knopf, 1979, $18.95; pap., Avon, $3.50). A similar theme is explored in the young adult novel by John LeVert *The Flight of the Cassowary* (Atlantic, 1986, $14.95).

After her father's death, 30-year-old Isabel Moore feels alone in Mary Gordon's *Final Payments* (pap., Ballantine, $3.95).

A wealthy spinster falls in love with a beautiful retarded young man in Colleen McCullough's *Tim* (Harper, 1974, $15.45), and in Alice Munro's *Lives of Girls and Women* (pap., NAL, $7.95) two adolescent girls reach sexual maturity.

About the Book
New York Times Book Review, April 3, 1977, p. 53.
See also *Book Review Index*, 1977, p. 443.

About the Author
Commire, Anne, ed. *Something about the Author.* Detroit: Gale, 1975. Vol. 7, pp. 198–199.
Ethridge, James M., ed. *Contemporary Authors.* Detroit: Gale, 1964. Vols. 9–10, p. 455.
Evory, Ann, and Metzger, Linda, eds. *Contemporary Authors* (New Revision Series). Detroit: Gale, 1984. Vol. 11, pp. 511–513.
Wakeman, John, ed. *World Authors 1970–1975.* New York: Wilson, 1980, pp. 828–831.

Walker, Alice. *The Color Purple*
Harcourt, 1982, $12.95; pap., Pocket, $5.95 (same pagination)

The Color Purple is Alice Walker's third novel. It was preceded by *The Third Life of Grange Copeland* (pap., Harcourt, $4.95) and *Meridian* (Harcourt, 1976, $14.95; pap., Pocket, $3.95). All three have certain elements in common. Their central characters are black women who share pain and hardship at the hands of stupid and weak men. Racism and sexism are two important themes in these powerfully moving novels. They are suitable for mature senior high school readers.

Plot Summary

"Dear God, I am fourteen years old" begins the story of Celie. "Dear God. Dear stars, dear trees, dear sky, dear peoples. Dear Everything. Dear God" ends the story of Celie. Between beginning and end unfolds the unforgettable life of one black girl in the South of years ago. It is a rare and bittersweet tale of pain and abuse, of a seemingly hopeless sense of worthlessness struggling against an indomitable will to survive. It is also a story of human love and laughter and joy, as in letter after letter to God, a young girl, without help or hope, so beaten down by those who abuse her and by the depths of her own ignorance, ever so slowly begins to find the extraordinary person locked inside her.

As the story opens, Celie has just faced the birth of her second child, a process she barely understands, although she does tie it in some way to the fact that Pa has for some time been forcing her to have sex with him. Her mother is ill. Celie is too terrified of him to resist and too terrified to tell her mother. Pa gets rid of both children, one Celie suspects he killed and the other sold.

Celie's mother dies, and soon after Pa brings a young girl into the house as his new wife. Celie vows to care for her younger sister, Nettie, but she fears the man she calls Mr. who keeps coming and asking for Nettie's hand in marriage. He already has four children and needs someone to care for them. But Pa says no. He does, however, offer to give Celie to the man. She's the oldest anyway, he says, ugly but a hard worker, and dumb. Celie accepts that description.

But young Nettie does not. Nettie goes to school and teaches Celie from her books. Celie never lets on, but she learns.

Before long Mr. arrives to take Celie away from Nettie and her home. They are married and return to his farm, where she is immediately set to work tending his four children, his house, and his wants.

One day in town Celie sees a little girl with a couple and she knows it is her child. They have named the girl Pauline, but Celie just knows the child is her Olivia, now almost seven.

Not long afterward, Nettie arrives at the farm. She tells Celie she had to get away from Pa. Celie convinces Mr. to let Nettie stay with them, although she fears the looks that Mr. keeps giving the young girl.

But Nettie will not give in to Mr.'s demands. "You got to fight," she keeps telling her sister. "You got to fight." But Celie doesn't know how to fight; she only knows, dimly, how to survive.

When Mr. realizes Nettie will not give in, he tells Celie her sister will have to go. Brokenhearted, Celie watches her beloved Nettie leave the farm, promising to write. But Celie never hears from her.

Life goes on for Celie in its dreadful monotony and loneliness, punctuated with backbreakingly endless work and beatings from her husband. And then two women come into Celie's life, and they help to change it forever.

Harpo, Mr.'s oldest boy, marries Sophia. When he, following his father's example, hits his wife in a fit of rage, Sophia just hits him back. Their battles become notorious, and Celie is amazed. She is even more amazed when Sophia leaves Harpo. But later, the white folk of the town are able to accomplish what Harpo never could; they are able to break Sophia's will—at least outwardly. Accused of talking back to the mayor's wife, Sophia is jailed and savagely beaten, enough to blind her in one eye. Then she is sentenced to jail.

When Celie visits her, she asks how the feisty Sophia can manage to get along in prison. Sophia answers, "Everytime they ask me to do something, Miss Celie, I act like I'm you. I jump right up and do just what they say."

The other woman to enter Celie's life is Shug Avery, blues singer, the true love of Mr.'s life, and the most beautiful woman Celie has ever seen. When Shug returns to town for a spell and becomes ill, Celie cares for her, and to Celie's amazement, the glamorous Shug Avery takes a liking to her.

The years pass. Sophia gets out of jail, Shug marries and returns from time to time and provides Celie with the love and closeness she is not yet aware she desperately craves.

And then one day a letter arrives from long-lost Nettie. The letter tells Celie that Nettie has been writing to her all these years, so Celie knows that Mr. must have been keeping the letters from her. This prompts Celie to be courageous enough to search for Nettie's letters, which, with Shug's help, she finds in Mr.'s trunk. In the letters, Celie reads that Nettie went to Africa with missionaries and that she has found and is with both Celie's daughter, Olivia, and Celie's son. But perhaps even more shocking is Nettie's news about their Pa. He was not their father. And that means that Celie's children are not the product of her own father.

With this new knowledge and Nettie's continuing letters, Celie at last finds the courage to fight. She leaves Mr. and goes to Memphis with Shug. She continues to correspond with Nettie and hopes that one day soon she will be able to return.

Then Celie learns the news that the man she called Pa had died, but that the house and land she thought was his actually belonged to her real father. It is now Celie's. With great joy, Celie writes to Nettie to come home; now they all have a home of their own.

Although it seems a lifetime later to Celie, one day as she sits on the porch of the home to which she has returned, a car drives up the road. At first Celie thinks it is Sophia; instead it is Nettie and Celie's children, now grown.

It has been a long and difficult road for Celie. She is a grown woman now, with a house to tend, and people to care for. At last she has found a family, and love, and a sense of worth. As she says in her last letter to God, "Matter of fact, I think this the youngest us ever felt. Amen."

Thematic Material

Beyond the deceptively simple writing style of author Alice Walker is a wealth of human emotions. *The Color Purple* is by turns funny, blunt, vivid, and touching in its portrayal of blacks and whites in the South of its time. But most of all this is a story of the suffering and injustice brought about through bigotry and discrimination—whites against blacks, men against women, ignorance against dignity. There is poverty here, rape and incest, physical and mental abuses, but also friendship, the strength of hope, and the wonder of sweet love. Although this novel speaks of much degradation and despair, of great sadness and misery, it also speaks of how courage and the freeing of the human mind can change even the most desperate of worlds. For all its sadness, *The Color Purple* is remarkably uplifting.

Book Talk Material

At the core of this book is the strength and character of Celie, who perseveres even when she does not yet understand what she is searching for, who comprehends the evil that people can bring upon each other even though she cannot yet explain it. One of the many rewards of reading *The Color Purple* is sensing the growth and determination of this central character, which can be seen in the following passages, all taken from Celie's letters to God. Before she is married to Mr., she writes of the man she thinks is her Pa, "Sometime he still be looking at Nettie, but I always git in his light. Now I tell her to marry Mr. I don't tell her why" (p. 15). Celie writes about her education, "The way you know who discover America, Nettie say, is think bout cucumbers. That what Columbus sound like." But then she goes on to write that it is hard to concentrate on Nettie's schoolbooks when instead she must think about getting married to Mr. (pp. 19–20). Sophia tells a disbelieving Celie that she has got to fight (pp. 45–47). Shug sings Miss Celie's song, "first time somebody made something and name it after me" (pp. 73–75). Celie finally gets a letter from Nettie (pp. 112–113). Celie and Shug find Nettie's letters (p. 118).

Additional Selections

A Greek girl new to this country and her black neighbors encounter prejudice in a West Virginia coal mining town during World War I in Christopher G. Janus's *Miss Fourth of July* (Sheffield, 1986, $15.95).

A black man is unjustly accused of rape and Atticus Finch defends him in the novel *To Kill a Mockingbird* by Harper Lee (Harper, 1961, $17.45; pap., Warner, $3.50) set in the 1930s.

Virgil Tubbs, a black detective, faces bigotry when he tries to investigate a murder in John Ball's *In the Heat of the Night* (pap., Harper, $3.50).

A deaf-mute and four other lonely individuals form a circle of friends in Carson McCullers's *The Heart Is a Lonely Hunter* (Harcourt, 1940, $13.95; pap., Bantam, $3.50).

A group of misfits is bound together by love in Marjorie Kellogg's *Tell Me That You Love Me, Junie Moon* (Farrar, 1984, $14.95).

Life in a southern Indian village is well portrayed in Kamala Markandaya's *Nectar in a Sieve* (pap., NAL, $2.95).

Detroit from 1930 to 1967 is the backdrop for Joyce Carol Oates's novel of poverty and privation, *Them* (pap., Fawcett, $3.95).

In Margaret Atwood's *The Handmaid's Tale* (Houghton, 1985, $16.95) a near future world uses able women solely for procreation.

John Steinbeck in *The Grapes of Wrath* (Viking, 1939, $20.00; pap., Penguin, $3.95) writes movingly about a poor white family driven off their land during the depression.

A poor white family gathers to celebrate Granny's ninetieth birthday in Eudora Welty's *Losing Battles* (Random, 1978, $13.95, pap. $5.95).

About the Book
Booklist, April 15, 1982, p. 1042.
Library Journal, June 1, 1982, p. 1115.
New York Times Book Review, June 25, 1982, p. 7
See also *Book Review Digest*, 1982, p. 1397, and *Book Review Index*, 1982, p. 529; 1983, p. 552.

About the Author
Colby, Vaneta, ed. *World Authors 1975–1980*. New York: Wilson, 1985, pp. 772–775.
Evory, Ann, and Metzger, Linda, eds. *Contemporary Authors* (New Revision Series). Detroit: Gale, 1983. Vol. 9, pp. 514–517.
Kinsman, Clare D., and Tennenhouse, Mary Ann, eds. *Contemporary Authors*. Detroit: Gale, 1973. Vols. 37–40, p. 524.

Welty, Eudora. *The Optimist's Daughter*
Random, 1969, $13.95, pap. $3.95 (same pagination)

Eudora Welty is one of the most famous contemporary southern writers along with Robert Penn Warren, Katherine Anne Porter, and Flannery O'Connor. Although she has lived most of her life in Jackson, Mississippi, Miss Welty is far more than a regional writer—her works transcend time or place. She basically has a hopeful outlook in life and many of her works are richly comical. Two of her finest collections of short stories are *A Curtain of Green* (pap., Harcourt, $5.95) and *The Bride of Innisfallen* (pap., Harcourt, $4.95). *The Optimist's Daughter* won the Pulitzer Prize for fiction and is suitable for better readers in the senior high grades.

Plot Summary
Laurel McKelva Hand has come to a New Orleans hospital to be with her father, who is undergoing eye surgery. She has been away from the South for a long time, living and working in Chicago, where she attended the Art Institute and met her husband, Phil. Their marriage was

short-lived, as Phil has been dead many years, a naval officer killed in the war.

Judge McKelva is the last of Laurel's family; her mother died about a dozen years before and her father has remarried. Laurel finds his new young wife, Fay, to be somewhat stupid, but her father seems happy.

To the shock of both women and the doctor, Judge McKelva unexpectedly dies sometime after surgery. Fay causes a scene in the hospital room as she berates the dead man for leaving her.

With Fay and her father's body, Laurel returns to her hometown of Mount Salus, Mississippi. She will stay for a few days after the funeral to help where she can and to see old friends before returning home.

Laurel is met at the train in Mount Salus by the six bridesmaids from her long-ago wedding party. While Fay goes off with the undertaker and her father's body, Laurel and the bridesmaids return to the house she grew up in, where the Judge had recently lived with his second wife. The house now belongs to Fay.

When Fay returns from the funeral parlor, she is annoyed to find the house full of people bringing flowers and foodstuffs, and demands to know what they are doing in "her house." Laurel tries to tell her that they are there to help, but Fay declares that no one is there to help *her*.

Laurel hopes, in the few days back home, to come to terms with the death of her father. Back once more in the midst of old family friends, who still refer to her as "Laurel McKelva" and who obviously find it difficult to deal with Fay, she relives once again life in this small southern farm town from which she has so long been separated.

On the day of the funeral, Laurel is surprised when Fay's mother, Mrs. Chisom, and a large group of family members arrive from Madrid, Texas. She is surprised because at the hospital Fay had told her that she had no family. The Chisoms declare that they'll be heading right back to Madrid after the funeral.

But after the Judge is buried, Fay informs Laurel that she will be returning to Texas with her family for a few days. When Laurel tells her that she will be returning to Chicago on Monday at noon, Fay says she won't be back until right after that time.

Fay leaves and Laurel is left in the house of her childhood to sort through her thoughts and relive the memories of her parents and her youth. She remembers falling asleep hearing her parents reading aloud to each other from their bedroom. She looks through her father's old desk, expecting perhaps to find letters written by her mother, but the desk has been cleared of all the Judge's papers. And she thinks about the needs of her beloved father that would make him want to marry such a woman as Fay.

The day before her departure, Laurel comes upon her mother's old desk and there finds letters her mother had kept, letters and snapshots that bring back a flood of memories. She relives her mother's own death and remembers the woman's increasing years of torment until she did not always know what she said. It was then that her father had started being what he had called with a scowl "an optimist." Because he loved his wife, whatever she said and did was all right. But, of course, it was not all right. And because he did not see his wife's desperation, but merely accepted her actions because of his love, it was made all the worse. When a stroke worsened her mother's condition, she began to believe she had been left alone with strangers, and she died keeping everything to herself.

Laurel remembers that Fay had at least once to her face called her mother "her rival." But now Laurel realizes that the rivalry was not what Fay believes; it is not between the living and the dead but between too much love and too little.

And Laurel comes to understand that people like Fay never really know the meaning of what has happened to them or seem to care to understand their lives. And she realizes, too, that she herself has been isolated. She has lived her life without becoming really involved with those around her. Even the love she had felt for her husband, Phil, she had carefully sealed away in the perfect memory of their life together.

Laurel readies herself to leave the house on Monday morning; the "bridesmaids" are calling for her to take her to the airport. In one last "look through" the house that is no longer hers in any sense, she comes upon a small item—a breadboard.

It is then that Fay returns; as Laurel realizes, fate would have it that they should meet once more. In a rush of emotion, Laurel accuses Fay of ruining her mother's breadboard, gouging it and letting it decay into dirt and grime. Fay cannot understand her being upset. Laurel's husband, as Laurel tells Fay, had made the breadboard for her mother as a labor of love. Fay declares that it is hers now.

In her emotional state, Laurel comes close to striking Fay with the board. She wanted to hurt her and she knew she was capable of doing so. But she does not.

Laurel leaves the breadboard behind her as she leaves her childhood home to her father's widow. She realizes that neither Fay nor Laurel nor anyone else can do anything to the past. It is a memory, a memory that will come back to her, like the memory of Phil, and may demand tears or its rightful due. She does not need such things as a breadboard to link her to her memories; they are in her heart, which can be empty but will fill again.

The last thing Laurel sees of her small southern town are the first-graders waving in the school yard.

Thematic Material

Eudora Welty has written a compelling novel of emotions and human relationships. The story's simplicity belies the depth of its feelings and interactions. It deals with people who never question beyond the superficialities of their lives and who live out their days without really knowing or caring to know what is happening to them. It also deals with grief and the painfulness of accepting memories that become part of the pattern of one's existence. Laurel is presented as a modern, independent woman who comes to terms with her own aloofness after the death of her beloved father. The author also richly presents the humor and warmth of a small southern town.

Book Talk Material

Laurel's and Fay's interactions in the hospital before and after the Judge's death can serve as an introduction to these two main characters and their relationship (see pp. 8–10, 14–17, 25–30). Other scenes of interest are: Fay demands to know what the people are doing in her house (pp. 53–58); the Chisoms arrive (pp. 66–73); and Fay's reaction at the funeral (pp. 84–88).

Additional Selections

In Lowry Pei's *Family Resemblances* (Random, 1986, $16.95), Karen learns from an aunt about the pains and trials of adulthood.

A story of ill-fated love between an Irishman and his English cousin in the early 1900s is told in William Trevor's *Fools of Fortune* (Viking, 1983, $13.95; pap., Penguin, $6.95).

In an autobiographical short novel, Truman Capote tells about depression time in Alabama and young Buddy who is bullied by 12-year-old Odd Hendersen in *The Thanksgiving Visitor* (Random, 1968, $14.95). Also use Capote's *One Christmas* (Random, 1983, $12.95), a nonfictional account of his sixth Christmas, and the enchanting story of Holly Golightly, *Breakfast at Tiffany's* (Random, 1958, $13.95; pap., NAL, $3.95).

Harry Agstrom is 26 and bored with life and his pregnant wife in John Updike's first Rabbit book, *Rabbit Run* (Knopf, 1960, $15.95; pap., Fawcett, $3.95).

Julian English's comfortable life falls apart when his wife threatens to divorce him in John O'Hara's *Appointment in Samarra* (pap., Random, $3.95).

Sinclair Lewis writes about middle-class life in America during the 1920s. The tyranny of convention is explored in *Babbitt* (Harcourt, 1922, $14.95; pap., NAL, $3.95), and class differences and the medical profession in *Main Street* (Harcourt, 1920, $14.95; pap., NAL, $3.95).

Jane Austen also writes about everyday occurrences but of an earlier time. Try *Pride and Prejudice* or *Emma* (many editions of both are available). Another family saga is told in Booth Tarkington's *The Magnificent Ambersons* (Peter Smith, 1960, $11.25; pap., Avon, $1.50).

About the Book
Booklist, July 15, 1972, p. 975.
Library Journal, June 1, 1972, p. 2119.
New York Times Book Review, May 21, 1972, p. 1; June 4, 1972, p. 24.
See also *Book Review Digest,* 1972, pp. 1372–1373, and *Book Review Index,* 1972, p. 505.

About the Author
Ethridge, James M., and Kopala, Barbara, eds. *Contemporary Authors.* Detroit: Gale, 1965. Vols. 11–12, pp. 439–440.
Kunitz, Stanley J., ed. *Twentieth-Century Authors* (First Supplement). New York: Wilson, 1955, pp. 1063–1064.

4

Stories of Other Lands and Times

In this section readers are taken away from present-day America to periods and places that range from the time of the ancient Roman Empire to contemporary South Africa. In between we visit Arthurian England, colonial New England, America's Civil War South, Victorian London, a Russian prison camp, and Vietnam of the 1960s.

Bradshaw, Gillian. *The Beacon at Alexandria*
Houghton, 1986, $17.95

As an undergraduate at the University of Michigan, Gillian Bradshaw wrote her first historical novel, *Hawk of May* (o.p.), which was to become the first volume of a trilogy dealing with King Arthur and his knights. The material for *The Beacon at Alexandria* was gathered while she worked on a master's degree in classics at Cambridge. In it the time span is roughly a nine-year period beginning in 371 A.D. In a brief preface Bradshaw confesses to taking some liberties with the historical chronology. The locale is various parts of the eastern Roman Empire, beginning in Ephesus on the Aegean coast of present-day Turkey, shifting to Alexandria and then to various locations in Thrace, the largest diocese, roughly comparable to today's Balkan region, which extended from the Danube to the Black and Mediterranean seas. (Maps are included to help the reader.)

At the time of the novel the western or Latin half of the empire was ruled by Valentinian, the eastern section by Valens. Although the empire was officially Christian, within this group were many sects, mainly the Arians and the Nicenes. The emperor professed adherence to the former, but in many parts of the empire, including Egypt, the latter had

131

more followers. Alongside these sects were those who still secretly believed in the pagan mysteries of the earlier cults plus followers of other religions such as the Jews.

Charis, later known as Chariton (when she dons a male disguise), is the heroine and narrator of this novel. Although it is written for adults, it is suitable for perceptive readers in grade 10 and up.

Plot Summary

Charis, now approaching age 16, is the daughter of a wealthy nobleman of consular rank, Theodorus of Ephesus. Her mother is dead and she has a brother, also named Theodorus, or Thorian for short, two years older than herself, as well as a faithful mother substitute, the maid Maia. Charis longs to be a doctor, a profession denied women in ancient times, and in her spare moments reads Hippocrates and Galen and practices her healing arts on injured animals and birds.

One day their household is invaded by the new governor, the cruel, unscrupulous Festinus and his troops, who accuse Charis's father of being involved in a plot against the emperor. Unfortunately, several of the servants, including Maia, are taken into custody and tortured before it is discovered to be a case of mistaken identity.

Festinus, a widower, however, spotted Charis and asks, rather demands, that she become his bride. The father, fearful of his life and fortune, acquiesces and a marriage is arranged for the spring, several months off. Charis refuses to accept this fate and with the help of Maia and her brother plans to disguise herself as a eunuch and voyage to Alexandria to study at the famed medical college there. Plans are made, and when the first boat leaves Ephesus in the spring, Charis is aboard, now shorn of her lovely hair, wearing a man's tunic, and carrying for her expenses the precious jewelry her mother had left her.

In Alexandria, Charis, now known as Chariton, finds it difficult to locate a sponsor to enter the university because she is of a despised group, eunuchs, and is without proper qualifications. Finally, Philon, an esteemed doctor who is also something of an outcast because he is a Jew, is so impressed with her knowledge that he accepts her as an apprentice, enabling her to attend classes conducted by such distinguished professors as Adamantios. She moves into Philon's house and grows to love this kindly man of great integrity, his wife, Deborah, and daughter, Theophila. As well, she slowly is accepted by the students, particularly a young Jew, Theogenes, who is courting Theophila.

Alexandria is seething with unrest and on the verge of religious riots. The Nicenes, of which the ruling aged Archbishop Athanasius is a member, are fearful that Valens will appoint the Arian Lucius to take Athanasius's place. Inadvertently, Charis becomes part of the conflict. A group of monks who operate a hospital where she wishes to place an indigent patient accuses her of being an Arian spy and drags her before Athanasius. The kindly man excuses her and after questioning her in a private interview, reveals that he senses that she is a girl in disguise. Some months later when he is deathly sick of pneumonia, he sends for her. Charis effects a remarkable cure and soon her fame spreads throughout Alexandria. Under Philon's urging, she takes her examinations and becomes a doctor of the medical faculty of the Museum of Alexandria.

An agent of the emperor, a handsome Goth named Athanaric, is assigned to the archbishop's palace. He tries to buy information from Charis about the archbishop, but she cannot be bribed. In spite of her dislike of this man, she tends him during his dangerous illness and restores him to health. When she in turn falls ill, Philon becomes her doctor. While treating her illness, he discovers she is a woman, but he agrees to guard her secret.

Theogenes and Theophila marry, but the joy Charis feels is spoiled by the death of Athanasius. Before his death he names an old monk, Peter, to be his successor and the much younger Theophilos to be his second in command. Valens sends Lucius to be the new archbishop. Riots break out. Peter is taken prisoner, but when he escapes shortly after Charis has visited him, she is accused of conspiracy and thrown into prison. Faced with torture and certain exposure, Charis is saved by the intervention of Athanaric, who persuades Lucius that she is innocent and suggests that she be allowed to leave and become an army doctor under contract to Thrace.

All parties agree. Three years after her arrival in Alexandria, a reluctant Charis leaves her adopted city and friends.

Sebastianus, duke of Scythia, a northern province that borders on the Black Sea and to the north the land of Theruingi, a Gothic nation, posts Charis, still known as Chariton, as director of the army hospital in Novidunum, only a few miles from the Danube River and the Goths. The assignment is a challenging one, particularly because the two doctors already there, Xanthos and Diokles, are totally incompetent.

Charis's only pleasure comes with brief visits from Athanaric, who has been transferred to Thrace and for whom Charis feels the pangs of first love. He helps secure needed drugs for the hospital and takes her on a medical mission across the Danube to the palace of Lord Fritigern of Theruingi, where Charis cures his wife, Amalberga, who is very ill.

Xanthos, Charis's inept and jealous coworker, quickly accuses her of sorcery. The trial takes place in Tomis, the provincial capital, with the new governor as judge. When he appears, Charis is astonished to see Thorian, her older brother. The case is dismissed and a joyful reunion takes place in private so that her identity remains a secret.

Back in Novidunum, a revengeful Xanthos attacks Charis with a knife while she is taking a bath. Seeing that she is really a woman, he tries to rape her. In a fierce battle, she kills him with his own knife.

Festinus, formerly of Ephesus, becomes governor of Moesia, another border province, and he with the Roman army commander Lupicinus begins an inhuman oppression of the Goths, who are now fleeing the invading Huns and seeking entry into the empire. The Goths organize a massive revolt. Charis is taken prisoner by Lord Fritigern's men and forced to work in one of the barbarian's hospitals. Here her true identity is revealed and she begins dressing as a woman and living in their quarters.

Months, indeed years pass, but escape is impossible. Finally, Athanaric in disguise is able to infiltrate their army ranks, reach Charis, and smuggle her out to freedom. They now realize the great love they feel for each other and make plans for marriage. Afterward Athanaric will continue in the service of the empire and Charis will open her own hospital for civilians.

Thematic Material

This novel colorfully reconstructs the drama and turmoil of life during the death throes of the Roman Empire. History becomes brilliantly alive with meaning. It is also a novel that explores the evil of injustice and oppression in a culture where individual rights are meaningless and slavery is accepted. Charis is a most appealing central character, gracious, determined, dedicated, but often filled with self-doubts. Her struggle for self-fulfillment is an inspiring one as is her overriding devotion to her profession and her insistence on equality in dealing with men. The novel also is a tender love story that supplies fascinating details on the practice of medicine in ancient times.

Book Talk Material

A brief introduction to the Mediterranean world of the fourth-century A.D. will set the stage for understanding Charis and her situation. Some important passages: Charis's father is accused of treason (pp. 14–25); Festinus courts Charis (pp. 34–37); she decides to go to Alexandria (pp. 44–48); the departure (pp. 51–55); and meeting the esteemed doctors in Alexandria (pp. 63–67).

Additional Selections

Mary Renault has recaptured ancient history stunningly in such novels as *The King Must Die* (Pantheon, 1958, $15.45; pap., Bantam, $4.95), a retelling of the Theseus story and his struggle with the Minotaur, and the excellent Alexander trilogy that begins with *Fire from Heaven* (Pantheon, 1968, $15.45; pap., Random, $5.95).

In Pamela Kaufman's *Shield of Three Lions* (pap., Warner, $3.95), a girl disguised as a page falls in love on a crusade to Jerusalem.

The Beekeeper's Daughter (Houghton, 1987, $18.95) by Gillian Bradshaw, a story about Empress Theodora's illegitimate son, takes place in sixth-century Constantinople.

Greek mythology comes alive with facts on sources and hidden meanings in Ellen Switzer's *Greek Myths* (Atheneum, 1988, $16.95), and a Cro-Magnon orphan learns how she can survive in Jean Auel's *Clan of the Cave Bear* (Crown, 1980, $18.95; pap., Bantam, $4.25).

Johnny Cash fictionalizes St. Paul's life to his conversion in *Man in White* (Harper, 1986, $13.95).

For younger readers, Barbara Cohen and Bahija Lovejoy retell an Arabic folktale in which a poor girl disguises herself as a boy in *Seven Daughters and Seven Sons* (Atheneum, 1982, $10.95).

In Tim Severin's *The Ulysses Voyage* (Dutton, 1987, $21.95), he and his crew retrace the route taken by Ulysses from Troy.

Post-Trojan War events are the substance of S. P. Somtow's *The Shattered Horse* (St. Martin's, 1986, $16.95).

About the Book
Booklist, September 1, 1986, p. 30.
Library Journal, September 1, 1986, p. 212.
See also *Book Review Index*, 1986, p. 101; 1987, p. 91.

About the Author
Locher, Francis C., ed. *Contemporary Authors*. Detroit: Gale, 1982. Vol. 103, p. 54.

Gordon, Sheila. *Waiting for the Rain: A Novel of South Africa*
Watts, 1987, $12.95

Although she now makes her home in New York City, Sheila Gordon
was born and educated in Johannesburg, South Africa. This firsthand
knowledge of conditions in the land of apartheid brings credibility to this
tragic account of friendships torn apart by society's prejudices and artificial barriers. It is suitable for readers in grade 8 and up.

Plot Summary
Tengo and Frikkie of South Africa have been friends since they were
small children. But their lives are very different. Frikkie is white, the
nephew of Oom Koos, whose farm he will one day inherit and where he
spends all his holidays and vacations from school. Tengo is black, and he
lives on the farm of Oom Koos, also. However, Tengo and Frikkie do not
share the same worlds. Tengo's mother and father work in servitude on
the farm.

Tengo envies Frikkie, not because he is white or because his uncle
owns the farm. He envies Frikkie because he desperately wants the education that Frikkie scorns. The only school Tengo can attend is far away,
and Tengo's mother, who has already lost two children to sickness and
whose daughter has tuberculosis, is afraid to let Tengo go off the farm to
school lest he, too, become ill. She has taught Tengo to read and write
and to do his numbers, but the young boy, who is bright and curious,
constantly longs for more.

One day Tengo's cousin Joseph visits from the city and Tengo for the
first time begins to learn a little about the world outside the sheltered
farm. Joseph tells him about the passbooks that all blacks must carry
when they reach age 16. The passbook contains a person's name, address, work, and family history. To be caught without it is to risk jail.
Even Tengo's father has a passbook, says Joseph, but on the farm no one
ever asks for it. Tengo is surprised to hear all this, but it is something he
has never really thought about.

When Joseph returns to the city, Tengo's mother sends along a note to
her sister, Joseph's mother, asking that she send some old textbooks to
Tengo, if she can get them from the kindly liberal white couple for

whom Joseph's mother works. Soon Tengo is delighted to receive a package of textbooks and he sets about getting an education.

As the boys grow into their teen years, the system of apartheid, about which Tengo has thought little, more and more intrudes into his life. On the day of Oom Koos's birthday party, one of Frikkie's young cousins demands that an old and respected member of Tengo's tribe clean up a mess the children have caused. In doing so, she calls him "boy." Almost without realizing it, Tengo flies into a rage and tells her never to use such an address again. Later Frikkie must bribe his cousin and sister to keep them from telling Oom Koos what Tengo has done.

When Frikkie finishes his indifferent education, he must go into the army for two years; then he will be free to return to manage his uncle's beloved farm. In the meantime, Tengo persuades his mother at last to let him go to the city for his education. He lives with Joseph's family and studies hard in order to take exams so that he might be able to go to one of the black colleges in South Africa and become a teacher.

As Tengo studies he is aware of the worsening of relations between South African blacks and the police. His friends and relatives urge him to join in the protests and boycotts, but Tengo is desperately afraid that he will lose his precious chance at an education. Finally, Joseph admits that he is a member of the underground movement working to overthrow the government and the dreaded system of apartheid. Joseph wants to smuggle Tengo over the border to be trained as a freedom fighter. Joseph also tells Tengo that some of those who cross the border are allowed to continue their education so that they might be of help to their country when apartheid is abolished.

Before Tengo has a chance to make a decision, he is swept up in a riot that breaks out between the blacks and the police. Tengo flees to an abandoned shed where he is pursued by a soldier. Thinking the soldier is about to kill him, Tengo hits him on the head with a bar. Then he realizes that it is Frikkie.

Tengo tries to help his friend and the two confront each other and their feelings about their country. Frikkie cannot understand why Tengo hates him after all their years together; Tengo cries out that Frikkie does not want to see how blacks must live in South Africa; he does not want to know the truth.

Knowing they cannot come to terms with their anger and bewilderment, these two young men of South Africa part. Tengo knows Frikkie will not betray his whereabouts. As he waits for his escape, Tengo decides that he will cross the border, but he will not be a part of the violence to come. He must continue his education; that will be the way he will fight.

Thematic Material

Although the characterizations of the two boys are perhaps a little too pat—the doltish young white man who scorns education and yearns only to work the land he loves, and the intelligent black youngster who longs to learn and only dimly understands what apartheid has done to his country—this is a believable story of how friendship and loyalty to one's country are distorted and ruined by the bigotry and prejudice of apartheid. It is also an interesting depiction of the feelings of blacks and whites, about South Africa and about each other.

Book Talk Material

The subtle ways in which apartheid shapes the minds and hearts of the people of South Africa may serve as a springboard to a discussion of that system and how it differs from the kinds of prejudice experienced in the United States and other countries. See: Tengo is served his tea outside (pp. 13–16); Joseph's visit (pp. 23–26); Tengo is "caught" in Frikkie's bedroom (pp. 57–59); and the incident at Oom Koos's party (pp. 59–65).

Additional Selections

A friendship between Becky, a privileged white, and a Zulu girl creates problems in Toeckey Jones's young adult novel *Go Well, Stay Well* (Harper, 1980, $12.89).

The 1948 novel *Mine Boy* (Heinemann, 1963, $5.50) by Peter Abrahams describes the fate of a country native who comes to Johannesburg to find work.

Mark Mathabane's *Kaffir Boy* (Macmillan, 1986, $18.95) is the autobiography of a black boy reaching maturity in apartheid South Africa.

Though white, Harry Moto has dark skin and therefore no identification card in Christopher Hope's novel *A Separate Development* (Scribner's, 1981, $10.95, pap. $4.95).

Elaine Pascoe gives good background information in *South Africa: Troubled Land* (Watts, 1987, $11.90).

Jason Laure's photographs highlight interviews with eight young South Afrikaners in *South Africa: Coming of Age under Apartheid* (Farrar, 1980, $15.95).

Also use Roger Omond's *The Apartheid Handbook* (Penguin, 1986, $5.95) and Joseph Lelyveld's Pulitzer-Prize-winning *Move Your Shadow: South Africa, Black and White* (Times, 1985, $18.95; pap., Penguin, $7.95). Three adult fiction works about South Africa are J. M. Coetzee's *Life and Times of Michael K.* (Viking, 1984, $13.95; pap., Penguin, $5.95); Ernst Havemann's *Bloodsong* (Houghton, 1987, $13.95); and Andre Brink's *Rumors of Rain* (pap., Penguin, $6.95).

About the Book
Booklist, August 1987, p. 1734.
Bulletin of the Center for Children's Books, July/August 1987, p. 207.
Horn Book, September 1987, p. 616.
New York Times Book Review, December 20, 1987, p. 21.
School Library Journal, August 1987, p. 95.
VOYA, December 1987, p. 234.
See also *Book Review Digest*, 1988, and *Book Review Index*, 1987, p. 296; 1988.

Miller, Arthur. *The Crucible*
pap., Penguin, $3.50

Arthur Miller is considered one of the giants of contemporary American drama. His first big success occurred with his second play, *All My Sons*, in 1947. *Death of a Salesman* (pap., Penguin, $2.95) was produced in 1949 and won many awards, including the Pulitzer Prize. Four years later *The Crucible* opened on Broadway. Although it is about Salem witch hunting, it is also about other kinds of witch hunts, specifically those of the McCarthy era. Whenever people are denied freedom of conscience and wrongly persecuted this play has relevance. It is suitable for senior high students.

Plot Summary
The Crucible, a play in four acts, tells of a dark and seemingly incredible period in American history—the witchcraft trials in Salem, Massachusetts, in the year 1692. The plot basically concerns the accusations by several young girls in the village of Salem—out of fear, hysteria, and certain other motives—that some of the townsfolk were possessed of the devil. The elders were "tried in court," found guilty, and put to death. To understand the atmosphere in which the play unfolds, it is neces-

sary to be aware of life in the Salem community in the year 1692. The village of Salem had been settled in the New World only about 40 years. Europeans regarded this new English territory as barbaric, and indeed the villagers lived in some fear of Indian attack. Ironically, the townsfolk, whose parents had known persecution in England, were of an intolerable bent themselves. Fearful that their beliefs and way of life would be corrupted by outside influences, they denied freedom to other sects and to other ideas. What started for a good purpose—keeping the community together by combining state and religious powers—eventually would reach the point in New England where the restrictions necessary to hold everything in order began to seem unnecessarily harsh when compared to the actual threats to the community that "different ideas" could cause. The witch trials in Salem illustrate perhaps the "high point" of the panic that gripped the people as the community balance began slowly to turn toward more individual freedom and expression of ideas.

When the play opens, the Reverend Parris, who believes himself persecuted wherever he goes and not wholly appreciated by his community, is distraught because his daughter, Betty, age 10, lies inert on her bed. He tells his niece, 17-year-old Abigail Williams, a beautiful orphan whom Parris had taken into his home, that there is talk of witchcraft in the village, of possession by the devil. Abigail denies any such notion, and says only that she and Betty and some other girls were merely dancing in the woods before Betty was so strangely afflicted.

Parris is upset to learn that the townsfolk have sent for Reverend Hale of Beverly, who has had some experience with witchcraft, to come to Salem to find out what has afflicted Betty, as well as other youngsters. As Hale and other citizens arrive at the Parris home, tensions mount as more tales of strange behavior and illnesses are told.

When John Proctor arrives, a farmer in his middle thirties whose wife, Elizabeth, has been ill for some time, we learn that months before John had succumbed to the lovely Abigail. Although he repents his mistake and will have nothing more to do with her, Abigail seems determined to have him.

When the talk grows more agitated, Tituba, Parris's slave from Barbados, is brought in for questioning about her part in the dancing of the young girls the night before. Tituba denies any wrongdoing, but when the questioning becomes too intense and she grows fearful for her life, she admits to seeing the devil, and what's more she has seen the devil come to others in the village. When the good citizens demand the names of those with whom the devil has visited, Abigail and the other young girls, caught up in the frenzy, now begin to scream out names of women in the village who have knowledge of the devil.

Within little more than a week, 39 women are arrested on the charge of witchcraft. It now seems merely enough for a child, or adult, to mention the name of a disliked neighbor, or perhaps someone against whom a grudge is held, and that person is hauled to jail to await trial.

There is great fear in the Proctor home when Elizabeth and John learn that her name has been suggested along with others so accused. Elizabeth knows of John's infidelity, and indeed it has been the cause of much discord between them, and both suspect that Abigail Williams is behind this accusation. But when Mary Warren, a young girl who has worked for the Proctors during Elizabeth's illness, returns from the trials with a "poppet" (a doll figure) and a needle is found inside it, the citizens in their frenzy accuse Elizabeth of witchcraft and she is taken to jail.

John Proctor does get Mary Warren to confess to those who are running the trials that the whole thing has been a hoax, that the girls, out of fear of punishment, are caught up in false accusations. But when she is confronted with the adamant and strong Abigail, Mary backs down.

From accusations that Mary makes against John when she breaks down, he is charged with being anti-Christ. Finally, given promises that his confession will save his wife, he confesses that he has seen the devil. But he will not implicate anyone else. And in the end, although he confesses, John Proctor cannot sign the document that the villagers demand. I have given you my soul, he tells them, but you will not have my name.

Proctor is marched outside to his death.

Thematic Material

The Crucible is a story of fear and of the dreadful harm that people can do to one another when freedom of ideas is suppressed. In their anxiety to keep their small community and their beliefs intact and in their own insecurity, the people of Salem could allow no deviation from their way of life. It also points up some of the baser qualities of the human condition: the eagerness with which some of the villagers accused their neighbors of witchcraft, perhaps to "get back" at an imagined or real wrong. It also says that to some people honor is more important than the prospect of death.

Book Talk Material

The buildup of tension, of panic and accusations, which culminates in the deaths of so many townspeople, is the key to this powerful play. See: Abigail denies any wrongdoing (pp. 10–12); a townswoman suspects Tituba (pp. 15–16); Abigail taunts John (pp. 21–24); Tituba confesses (pp. 44–47); and the girls start their accusations (p. 48).

Additional Selections

The hunted and wrongfully persecuted are no strangers to literature. Here are some examples. In Franz Kafka's *The Trial* (Knopf, 1917, $16.95; pap., Random, $4.95), Joseph K. is accused of crimes of which he has no knowledge. Major Scobie is the victim of blackmail in Graham Greene's *The Heart of the Matter* (Viking, 1948, $14.95; pap., Penguin, $3.95), and in Albert Camus's *The Plague* (Knopf, 1948, $14.95; pap., Random, $2.95) a whole town in Algeria is threatened by a senseless epidemic. Gypo Nolan squeals on a comrade and pays a terrible price in Lian O'Flaherty's *The Informer* (pap., Harcourt, $4.95), and in Joan Samson's *The Auctioneer* (pap., Avon, $2.75) a mysterious man has a strange power over the inhabitants of a New England town.

Three plays that deal with outsiders are Tennessee Williams's *The Glass Menagerie* (pap., New Directions, $3.95; pap., NAL, $3.50); Mark Medoff's *Children of a Lesser God* (pap., Gibbs M. Smith, $5.95); and Paul Zindel's *The Effects of Gamma Rays on Man-in-the-Moon Marigolds* (Harper, 1971, $12.70; pap., Bantam, $2.95).

For younger readers use Patricia Clapp's *Witch's Children: A Story of Salem* (Lothrop, 1982, $11.75; pap., Penguin, $3.95), a frightening story told by one of the 10 possessed girls; Ann Petry's *Tituba of Salem Village* (Harper, 1964, $14.70), about a Caribbean slave girl's involvement in the Salem witchcraft scandal; and Elizabeth Speare's story of Kit and her friend who is accused of witchcraft in *The Witch of Blackbird Pond* (Houghton, 1951, $12.95; pap., Dell, $3.50).

About the Book
Booklist, May 15, 1953, p. 299.
Library Journal, May 15, 1953, p. 920.
See also *Book Review Digest,* 1953, p. 647.

About the Author

Ethridge, James M., and Kopala, Barbara, eds. *Contemporary Authors* (First Revision). Detroit: Gale, 1967. Vols. 1–4, pp. 665–666.
Evory, Ann, ed. *Contemporary Authors* (New Revision Series). Detroit: Gale, 1981. Vol. 2, pp. 475–477.
Kunitz, Stanley J., ed. *Twentieth-Century Authors* (First Supplement). New York: Wilson, 1955, pp. 669–670.

Myers, Walter Dean. *Fallen Angels*
Scholastic, 1988, $12.95

Walter Dean Myers has become best known in young adult novels through his re-creation of coming of age in Harlem. His books include one about corruption in sports, *Hoops* (Delacorte, 1981, $13.95; pap., Dell, $2.50; condensed in *Juniorplots 3*, Bowker, 1987, pp. 249–253). Its sequel is *The Outside Shot* (Delacorte, 1984, $14.95). Now, for a slightly older audience, he has switched locales and subjects and writes stunningly about a conflict many wish to forget—the Vietnam War, an area long neglected in young adult literature. If any young readers still regard this war as a series of Rambo-like adventures, this novel will certainly disabuse them of these feelings. Its portrayal of warfare is often sickeningly real in detail and description. The language is adult and graphic, recapturing the conversation of men at war. It also contains scenes of gripping suspense and, particularly through the character of Peewee Gates, wonderful flashes of humor. It is told in the first person by Richie Perry, a most likable and sensitive hero who, though sickened by the brutality and death he sees around him, remains a loyal soldier and faithful friend. The novel is not for the squeamish; it is read in grades 9 through 12.

Plot Summary

It is September 15, 1967, and 17-year-old Richie Perry, a private in the U.S. Army, is on a flight bound for Vietnam. On the trip he meets Judy Duncan, a nurse from Texas, and another black grunt, the sardonic, wise-cracking Harry (Peewee) Gates, who originally hailed from Chicago. Richie was born and raised in Harlem by a mother whose husband has now left her. Partly because he had no other real alternative and partly to secure an income to help his mother and younger brother,

Kenny, Richie has joined the army. He has a trick knee that supposedly exempts him from combat duty. However, through some army foul-up he has been assigned to Vietnam, and the rest of his company to Germany. Richie is confident that he will be reassigned back to his company once his medical profile is forwarded to Vietnam.

Richie, Peewee, and a scared innocent named Jenkins are assigned to an outfit in the deep boonies, close to Chu Lai. In their squad are another black from Georgia, named Johnson, an Italian kid, Monaco, the soft-spoken Lobel from Hollywood, a pimply faced Polish kid, Walowick, a religious youngster named Brewster, or Brew for short, and also the unpopular, crude Corporal Brunner. The squad leader is Sergeant Simpson, a longtime veteran of the war, soon to be sent back to the States, or as the soldiers call any place outside the hell of 'Nam, he will be going to "the World." The platoon leader is decent, well-liked Lieutenant Carroll, whose superior is ambitious Captain Stewart.

Richie's first taste of real war occurs when, after a routine patrol operation, Jenkins steps on a mine planted in a field between the chopper landing zone and camp. Richie witnesses Jenkins's death and is sickened and frightened by the experience. At the brief service for Jenkins, Lieutenant Carroll says, "Let us feel pity for Private Jenkins and sorrow for ourselves and all the angel warriors that fall."

When the squad visits a neighboring village to distribute medical supplies and food, Richie is moved by seeing a doll-like lonely waif seven or eight years of age named An Linh.

In an engagement accompanying a television crew into an area where some VietCong have been spotted, Richie witnesses the death of a VietCong youngster who, on close inspection, reminds him of his brother, Kenny.

Although the squad becomes unified by the terrible conditions under which they live, sometimes tempers flare because of the constant tension and stress, such as the time Walowick and Johnson fight over a supposed racial slur. Lieutenant Carroll's gentle demeanor is a persuasive mediator.

While on a temporary assignment with another company, more than a dozen Americans are killed in a skirmish when, through a gross technical error, their comrades in another platoon open fire on them. Richie is sickened and despairing. In another operation Lieutenant Carroll is killed and Monaco recites the prayer that had been spoken by Carroll at Jenkins's death. Lieutenant Gearhart takes Carroll's place.

Life becomes a series of deadly encounters with the VietCong, punctuated by a few days in camp. On one patrol Gearhart sets off a flare accidentally at night, exposing his men to Cong cross fire and causing two to be wounded.

In a return to An Linh's village, Richie is cornered in a native hut by a VietCong. The guerrilla's gun fortunately jams and Richie blows away his face with a clip from his M16. When he examines the body, Richie vomits. That night in his bunk he begins sobbing uncontrollably until Peewee puts his arms around him and cradles him until sleep comes.

During another operation the gentle religious Brew is killed and Richie, wounded in the legs, sees the shattered corpse of his friend placed in a body bag.

After a two-week hospital stay during which he again meets Judy Duncan, he returns to his outfit, fearing and dreading the fighting still to come. In a native village Richie sees a mother give her booby-trapped child to a soldier; both are blown to bits in the explosion and the woman is gunned down before she can escape. Simpson's replacement, Sergeant Dongan, dies after both his legs are blown off in another operation.

On a raid into enemy territory, Peewee and Richie are separated from the rest of the squad. Surrounded by enemy forces, they take refuge in a hole on the side of a ridge. All night they cower in their hiding place, certain that every minute could be their last. In the morning the Cong begin to depart, but one of the last finds the hole and begins probing it with his rifle. Peewee pulls the soldier and Richie kills him before he can alert his comrades. When the rescue chopper finally appears, both Richie and Peewee are wounded by enemy gunfire, but they manage to board and be flown to safety. Peewee's wounds are so severe that he must be sent back permanently to the States, and Richie, though less severely injured, will also be sent home because his medical records have finally arrived.

After some investigation, Richie learns that nurse Duncan was killed when her field hospital was bombed. As Richie and Peewee board the C47 that will take them back to "the World," they see lines of silver caskets being loaded into the plane's tail end and think of the buddies they left behind in the boonies and of the dead comrades they will never see again.

Thematic Material

This novel gives the cliché "war is hell" a new meaning and dimension. The terrible waste in lost and shattered lives, the inhumanity and barbarism that war produces, and the endless carnage that it brings are graphically portrayed. This book also vividly creates the paralyzing fear of facing near-certain death, the submerged questions concerning the righteousness of waging war, and the inner strength and courage that even the most ordinary soldier must possess. Richie writes to Kenny (on pages 269–270), "I had thought that this war was right, but it was only right from a distance . . . but when this killing started there was no right or wrong except in the way you did your job, except in the way you were part of the killing." It also depicts well the comradery of war buddies and shows that in crises where one must rely on one's friends, the really important values surface and differences concerning race and religion become superfluous.

Book Talk Material
Some of the interesting passages: Richie meets Peewee and Judy Duncan (pp. 3–7); the death of Jenkins and the angel warrior speech (pp. 40–44); the pacification project and meeting An Linh (pp. 50–53); Lobel and Richie talk about home (pp. 70–77); the episode with the television crew (pp. 77–80); the death of Lieutenant Carroll (pp. 124–128); and Richie kills his first VietCong (pp. 176–181).

Additional Selections
A survival novel about the Vietnam War and a soldier that goes AWOL is Tim O'Brien's *Going after Cacciato* (pap., Dell, $2.50).

In an effort to find out about his father who was killed in Vietnam, Sam tries to find out about the war in Bobbie Ann Mason's *In Country* (Harper, 1985, $15.45, pap. $6.95).

A Vietnam War novel about friendship, death, and the scars caused by that war that never heal is Jack Fuller's *Fragments* (Morrow, 1984, $12.95; pap., Dell, $3.50).

The hell of World War I is re-created in the now-classic novel by Erich Maria Remarque *All Quiet on the Western Front* (Little, 1929, $15.45; pap., Fawcett, $3.95). Another classic novel of World War I is Ernest Hemingway's *A Farewell to Arms* (Scribner's, 1929, $10.95; pap. $4.95), a tender love story told against the background of the war in Italy.

A 15-year-old Australian boy bluffs his way into the army during World War II and sees action in the Pacific in Michael Noonan's *McKenzie's Boots* (Watts, 1988, $13.95). Some other World War II novels of importance: Thomas Heggen's *Mister Roberts* (Buccaneer, n.d., $16.95), a seriocomic novel of an undeclared war aboard the *Reluctant,* a supply ship; John Hersey's tragic story of life in the Warsaw ghetto, *The Wall* (Knopf, 1961, $25.00); and Irwin Shaw's *The Young Lions* (Modern Library, 1958, $7.95; pap., Dell, $4.95), about the fate of three soldiers, one a Nazi, and two Americans. Also use: *The Caine Mutiny* (pap., Pocket, $5.95) by Herman Wouk and Norman Mailer's *The Naked and the Dead* (Holt, 1976, $16.95, pap. $8.95).

About the Book
Booklist, April 15, 1988, p. 1419.
Bulletin of the Center for Children's Books, April 1988, p. 163.
Horn Book, July/August 1988, pp. 503–504.
School Library Journal, June/July 1988, p. 118.
VOYA, August 1988, p. 133.

About the Author
Commire, Anne, ed. *Something about the Author.* Detroit: Gale, 1982. Vol. 27, p. 153; updated 1985. Vol. 41, pp. 152–155.
Evory, Ann, ed. *Contemporary Authors* (First Revision Series). Detroit: Gale, 1978. Vols. 33–36, pp. 592–593.
Holtze, Sally Holmes, ed. *Fifth Book of Junior Authors and Illustrators.* New York: Wilson, 1983, pp. 225–226.
Kinsman, Clare D., ed. *Contemporary Authors.* Detroit: Gale, 1973. Vols. 33–36, p. 638.
Metzger, Linda, and Straub, Deborah A., eds. *Contemporary Authors* (New Revision Series). Detroit: Gale, 1987. Vol. 20, pp. 325–330.
Sarkissian, Adele, ed. *Something about the Author: Autobiography Series.* Detroit: Gale, 1986. Vol. 2, pp. 143–156.
Senick, Gerard J., ed. *Children's Literature Review.* Detroit: Gale, 1982. Vol. 4, pp. 155–160.

Pullman, Philip. *The Ruby in the Smoke*
Knopf, 1987, $11.95

On the first page of this novel set in nineteenth-century London, Pullman introduces his plucky heroine with the words "She was a person of sixteen or so, alone and uncommonly pretty. Her name was Sally Lockhart, and within fifteen minutes she would have killed a man." With this most readers are hooked into completing one of the best adventure mysteries in years, complete with bloody murders, cliff-hanging chapter endings, seedy Victorian flophouses and opium dens, and the search for a fabulous ruby that people would and do kill to possess.

The Ruby in the Smoke is the first volume of a trilogy about Sally. The second is *The Shadow in the North* (Knopf, 1988, $12.95), in which the heroine, now 22 and Cambridge educated, has become a business consultant. She, her lover, the photographer of *Ruby*, Fred Garland, and their colorful friends, challenge the sinister evil of the richest man in Europe, Mr. Bellmann, who is not above selling his own daughter in marriage to make money. Again, the action is rip-roaring, suspenseful, and at times gory. These novels are intended for an audience in grades 8 through 12, but are also enjoyed by adults who like a good, well-plotted thriller.

Plot Summary

It is early October 1872 and to the office of Lockhart and Selby, shipping agents in Cheapside, London, Sally has come to inquire about a mysterious message received in the post from her deceased father, but written by a second, almost illiterate person. It warns her to beware of the "Seven Blessings" and to seek help from a certain Marchbanks. Her father, Matthew Lockhart, had served as a British officer in the Indian mutiny some 15 years before, during which time Sally believes her mother was murdered. The violence and horror of these incidents have left Sally with a recurring unfinished nightmare she is unable to explain.

On his return to England, Lockhart had become a shipping agent with his partner, Selby. Hearing stories from the Far East of smuggling and mismanagement and interference by a Mr. van Eiden involving their shipments, Lockhart went to investigate. Scarcely three months ago Sally learned that her beloved father drowned when the schooner *Lavinia* sank in the South China Sea. Since then she has been living in London like an outcast with an unfeeling distant relative, Aunt Caroline Rees. Now this strange note has arrived and she is anxious to learn its meaning.

Selby is absent and Sally is taken by the saucy cockney office boy Jim Taylor to see Mr. Higgs, the company secretary. When Sally mentions the Seven Blessings, Higgs falls dead of a heart attack. Shocked and shaken, Sally explains her mission to Jim and gives him her address should he be able to help.

Meanwhile in the slums of the East End, a wicked crone named Mrs. Holland, proprietress of a squalid combination rooming house and opium den, is plotting with her lawyer to gain possession of a precious ruby from a man named Marchbanks. To her lodging house comes Matthew Bedwell, an opium-addicted sailor newly returned from the South Seas and seeking a floor to sleep on and a drug fix. He is escorted to a filthy room by Mrs. Holland's pathetic young girl servant, an orphaned slave named Adelaide. Here in his opium-induced delirium, Bedwell raves about the Seven Blessings, the firm of Lockhart and Selby, and the sinking of the *Lavinia*. At each session Mrs. Holland listens and soon realizes that this information can be used to blackmail Selby. During his lucid moments when alone with Adelaide, Bedwell tells her that he has a twin brother, Nicholas, a respected clergyman, and also that she must secretly contact Sally Lockhart through her father's firm and tell her the story.

With great fear and trepidation, Adelaide visits the company office and meets Jim who promises to arrange a meeting with Sally.

Via the newspaper account of Higgs's autopsy, Major George Marchbanks learns of Sally's whereabouts and writes a letter urgently inviting her to visit him at his coastal home on the outskirts of Swaleness. On the walk from the train to his house, Sally encounters a young photographer named Fred Garland who is busy taking pictures of the landscape.

Marchbanks hurriedly gives Sally a handwritten document and tells her that he has another visitor, an evil lady named Mrs. Holland, awaiting him. He bids Sally goodbye and warns her that she is in great danger.

On her way back to the station, Sally realizes that she is being followed by Mrs. Holland. She eludes her by hiding in the photographer's tent. Inside the train carriage, she begins reading the document that deals with the fate of the famed ruby of Agrupur and how it fell into the hands of Marchbanks. Before finishing it, Sally falls asleep. She awakens to find that the document has been stolen except for the last page, which had fallen on the floor. It contains a series of cryptic clues that deal with the present whereabouts of the ruby.

Mrs. Holland, who engineered the robbery, is furious at her loss. She sends her henchman to steal the page from Sally's room at Mrs. Rees's. The robbery is successful, but fortunately not before Sally had copied the contents into her diary and shared them with her friend Jim.

Life with Mrs. Rees becomes increasingly intolerable, so Sally moves out, collects a few pounds owed to her from her father's lawyer (the bulk of her inheritance has mysteriously disappeared), and sets out on her own. She calls on the young photographer who lives in spacious quarters behind his studios with his young assistant, a failed pickpocket named Trembler, and Fred's sister, a struggling young actress, Rosa Garland. Not only is Sally made welcome, but also she is hired as their business manager.

Sally tells them her story. News reaches them that Marchbanks has been murdered, and after Sally learns Bedwell's story from Adelaide, and about his virtual imprisonment by Mrs. Holland, the group decides to contact his twin brother. With the reverend's help, an exciting rescue is carried out that frees both Bedwell and a terrified Adelaide. Upon recovery, Bedwell tells his story. He had been mate on the *Lavinia* on which Mr. Lockhart had sailed, convinced that his partner, Selby, was part of an international conspiracy involving an insurance racket that included both the ship and its cargo. He was right. The day of sailing, the ship was boarded by a group of pirates known as the Seven Blessings under their leader, the villainous Ah Ling. Mr. Lockhart was murdered, the cargo transferred to the pirates' junk, and the ship was sunk.

Fortunately, Bedwell and Lockhart's native servant, Perak, escaped. It was Perak who had copied down Lockhart's dying words and sent them to Sally.

In another part of London, a stranger checks into the fashionable Warwick Hotel under the name Mr. Reynolds. Within the next days both Selby and Matthew Bedwell are murdered and an advertisement appears in the *Times* from Reynolds requesting a meeting with Sally. She ignores it and takes the precaution of purchasing a revolver. Jim is convinced that Reynolds is involved with the Seven Blessings.

In the interim, Mrs. Holland has been busy. By using her cunning, she has solved the riddle of the whereabouts of the ruby. She follows each direction only to discover that someone has preceded her—the hiding place is empty. It was Jim. When Sally gets the ruby, she decides that she must confront Mrs. Holland to determine the truth behind the half-revealed horror of her nightmare.

At midnight they meet on London Bridge. Sally places the gem on the parapet between them. To secure the ruby, Mrs. Holland talks. In India many years back, Mrs. Holland, then Polly Andrews, was the mistress of the maharajah, who once promised her the ruby. Instead he gave it to Lockhart to ensure protection during the mutiny. Unfortunately, because of Marchbanks's opium habit, the maharajah was betrayed and murdered. Marchbanks and Lockhart quarreled violently—this was

Sally's recurring nightmare. Marchbanks, a widower, begged Lockhart for the ruby to repay his growing drug debts. In exchange he offered his daughter. Filled with disgust, Lockhart agreed, and in that instant Sally Marchbanks became Sally Lockhart.

Sally throws the cursed ruby into the water and the half-crazed Mrs. Holland jumps after it, only to be killed on the pilings below. Within minutes a cab drives up and a voice invites Sally in. The stranger identifies himself as Reynolds, alias van Eiden alias Ah Ling, leader of the Seven Blessings. He threatens her with either immediate death or enslavement in the Far East. His ship is about to sail. Sally remembers the gun in her purse. She shoots and amid the sight of gushing blood, she escapes from the cab.

Although no body is found by the police, Sally and company are convinced that van Eiden could not survive such a serious wound. Within a few days there is a final surprise, this time a pleasant one. It comes in a letter from Nicholas Bedwell. Shortly before his murder, his brother had remembered one last message to Sally from Mr. Lockhart. It was "tell her to look under the clock."

Sally returns to their former home in the country and following directions, finds in large bills her inheritance plus a final note from Matthew Lockhart begging her forgiveness for not telling her the truth of her origins.

At last Sally's future is bright. The missing inheritance ensures financial security for herself and her new-found friends, and soon perhaps a new business, Garland and Lockhart.

Thematic Material

This is essentially a tense, intricately plotted, very entertaining thriller, but it also effectively evokes the atmosphere and living conditions in the London of Dickens. Surface prosperity and gentility contrast with invasive inner squalor and violence. The author also supplies horrifying details on the conduct and effects of the government-sponsored opium trade in the nineteenth century. Sally is portrayed as an intrepid, resourceful heroine, at times unsure of herself but usually mature beyond her years. Several other characters, like Jim and Mrs. Holland, could have stepped out of Dickens, but basically this is a story in which in spite of fantastic odds, right triumphs over might.

Book Talk Material

After a brief introduction to the time and locale of the novel, the first few pages (pp. 3–7) introduce Sally and the Seven Blessings and conclude with the sudden death of Mr. Higgs, which should grab the attention of most readers. Other interesting passages are: the story of Sally's background and the nightmare (pp. 12–15); Mrs. Holland and the ruby are introduced by a conversation with her lawyer (pp. 20–25); Matthew Bedwell finds shelter at Mrs. Holland's lodgings (pp. 25–27); Sally visits Mr. Marchbanks and meets both Fred Garland and Mrs. Holland (pp. 30–38); and she reads from the manuscript before it is stolen (pp. 39–43).

Additional Selections

Leon Garfield has written several young adult mysteries set in Victorian England. One of the latest is *The Wedding Ghost* (Oxford, 1987, $11.95). He has also done a masterful job of completing Charles Dickens's novel of murder and opium dens *The Mystery of Edwin Drood* (Pantheon, 1981, $12.75). In the adult mystery *The Great Train Robbery* (Knopf, 1975, $13.95) author Michael Crichton uses a similar locale.

Laurel fears she will face a similar fate as Roc's other wives in the historical thriller *Bride of Pendorric* (pap., Fawcett, $2.95) by Victoria Holt. Also use her other novels including *Mistress of Mellyn* (pap., Fawcett, $2.75).

At the time of the American Revolution a 15-year-old girl matures through her father's death and her brother's dedication in Ann Rinaldi's *Time Enough for Drums* (Holiday, 1986, $12.95).

Two waifs find themselves penniless and homeless in the England of 1843 in Joan Aiken's *Midnight Is a Place* (pap., Dell, $3.50; condensed in *More Juniorplots*, Bowker, 1977, pp. 75–79).

Sir Arthur Conan Doyle's Sherlock Holmes could be introduced. Start with *The Hound of the Baskervilles* (various editions available). Sherlock and others are introduced in Ron Gowlart's short story collection *The Great British Detective* (pap., NAL, $4.95).

Two modern writers of Sherlock Holmes stories are Lloyd Biggle, Jr., in his *The Quallsford Inheritance* (pap., Penguin, $3.95) and Nicholas E. Meyer, who wrote *The West End Horror* (pap., Ballantine, $2.50).

About the Book
Book Report, November 1987, p. 28.
Booklist, March 1, 1987, p. 1009.

Bulletin of the Center for Children's Books, May 1987, p. 176.
Horn Book, May/June 1987, p. 347.
New York Times Book Review, June 14, 1987, p. 26.
School Library Journal, April 1987, p. 112.
VOYA, October 1987, p. 206.
See also *Book Review Digest,* 1988, and *Book Review Index,* 1987, p. 624; 1988.

Solzhenitsyn, Alexandr. *One Day in the Life of Ivan Denisovich*
pap., NAL, $2.95

On February 9, 1945, Alexandr Solzhenitsyn, then a commander of an artillery battery in the Russian army, was arrested because some of his letters were critical of Stalin. He was sentenced to eight years' detention, which he spent in various prisons. Ironically, his release date was the day of Stalin's death. When his account about prison life, *The Gulag Archipelago* (in 3 vols.; pap., Harper, $4.95, $4.95, and $3.95), was published in the West in 1973, Solzhenitsyn was charged with treason and exiled. He now lives on a farm in Vermont. *One Day* originally appeared in Russia in 1962. Another paperback edition is available from Bantam ($2.95). It is suitable for readers in the senior high grades.

Plot Summary

Ivan Denisovich Shukhov is a Russian carpenter by trade. But he does not practice his trade, because he is in a concentration camp in his own country. His sentence is 3,653 days—the 3 extra days being for leap years.

For the record, Shukhov is sentenced for treason. He surrendered to the Germans with the idea of betraying his country and then returned to Russia with specific orders from his captors, so says the record. Although Shukhov knows well that he had no intention of betraying his country, he also knows that if he hadn't agreed with the charge of treason, he would have been killed anyway. And so he signed.

In truth, the Russian army of which Shukhov was a part was trapped on the northwestern front by the Germans in 1942. They were without ammunition, supplies, or food. Before the Germans captured them, they had cut off the hooves of their horses and eaten them. After a few days in a POW camp, Shukhov and four others escaped, but only two of them made it. Perhaps if all of them had lived, the authorities would have believed their story. As it was, Shukhov was charged with treason . . . and now he spends his days in a Russian concentration camp.

Life for Ivan Denisovich is made up of small things. He is one tiny cog in the endless human machine that accounts for the material progress of the Soviet Union.

On this one day in his monotonous life, Ivan Denisovich awakens to the 5:00 A.M. sound of reveille. Usually he rises immediately in order to have extra time for perhaps a chore or two—sweeping out a supply room, sewing someone's mittens—that would gain him extra food. But on this particular morning, Shukhov isn't feeling too well. He wasn't able to get warm all night, and now he is aching and shivery.

Shukhov heads first for the mess hall where he eats his cold gruel with the spoon he always carries in his boot. He has carried it since 1944, and he made it himself. It is very precious to him.

From the mess hall, he goes to the hospital block. But, alas, his temperature is only slightly elevated. If it had been more than 100 degrees, he might have had a chance to be sick. But not today. . . .

Shukhov gets in line for roll call; it is not yet light. In the cold air the prisoners are frisked; perhaps the guards are looking for knives or other weapons of escape. Shukhov doesn't care; he has nothing to hide.

And so continues the long day of Ivan Denisovich Shukhov, Russian carpenter, imprisoned for treason. With resolution, acceptance, knowledge, and a smattering of humor, he marches through the minutes and hours of his endless day.

And at the end of this one day in his life, Shukhov has cause to be grateful after all. It has been a pretty good day for him. He wasn't thrown in the "cooler." He'd managed to get an extra bowl of mush at the noon meal. He'd been able to get some tobacco. And he doesn't feel so sick now, as he had in the morning. All in all, not a bad day. . . .

When he hears a fellow prisoner talk about freedom, Ivan Denisovich wonders to himself: Do I want freedom? He really doesn't know anymore. He used to, that he knows. He would add up the days until he would be free, but then he became tired of that and there didn't seem to be much point in it. Besides, even when his sentence is up, they won't let him go home anyway. . . .

Thematic Material

Written by the former Russian physicist and mathematician, himself an inmate of his country's concentration camps, this is a stark and powerful account of the evils of totalitarianism. It is also a tribute to the human spirit in its depiction of one man's unceasing attempt to preserve some shred of dignity in the endless misery and despair of his surroundings. It is a morality play of the twentieth century.

Book Talk Material

The small indignities suffered by the prisoners may begin a talk on the far more painful ways in which freedom is taken away than merely being put behind bars. See: Shukhov goes to the warders' room to work (pp. 9–12); he visits the mess hall (pp. 15–17); the trip to the hospital (pp. 21–26); and the line up for roll call (pp. 30–40).

Additional Selections

A Russian is imprisoned for treason in the novel *Darkness at Noon* by Arthur Koestler (Macmillan, 1941, $15.95; pap., Bantam, $3.95) based on the Moscow trials of the 1930s.

In Boris Pasternak's *Doctor Zhivago* (Pantheon, 1958, $17.45; pap., Ballantine, $3.50) a turbulent love affair is enacted with a backdrop of the Russian Revolution. Another respected novel of the Revolution deals with a group of Cossacks, Mikhail Sholokhov's *And Quiet Flows the Don* (pap., Random, $8.95), followed by *The Don Flows Home to the Sea* (pap., Random, $6.95).

In Robert K. Massie's nonfictional *Nicholas and Alexandra* (Atheneum, 1967, $29.95; pap., Dell, $4.95) good background information is given on the Revolution.

In pre-revolutionary China a touching family saga is chronicled amid great poverty in Pearl Buck's *The Good Earth* (Crowell, 1931, $16.30; pap., Pocket, $3.95).

A young anti-Fascist returns to Fascist Italy in the days before World War II in Ignazio Silone's *Bread and Wine* (pap., NAL, $2.95).

In David Kherdian's *The Road from Home: The Story of an Armenian Girl* (Greenwillow, 1979, $13.00), he tells of his mother's life during the Turkish persecutions.

Diane Pearson's *Summer of the Barshinskeys* (Crown, 1984, $16.95; pap., Fawcett, $4.50) is a sweeping novel that moves from the English country-side to revolutionary Russia.

During World War II, some teenage soldiers try tragically to establish contact with some German counterparts in William Wharton's *A Midnight Clear* (Knopf, 1982, $12.95; pap., Ballantine, $3.50).

A Jewish guerrilla in British-controlled Palestine faces a moral decision in Elie Wiesel's *Dawn* (pap., Bantam, $2.95). Wiesel's *Night* (pap., Bantam, $2.95) is the harrowing account of life in Nazi death camps.

About the Book
Library Journal, February 1, 1963, p. 576.
New York Times Book Review, April 7, 1963, p. 4.
See also *Book Review Digest*, 1963, pp. 947–948.

About the Author
Bowden, Jane A., ed. *Contemporary Authors*. Detroit: Gale, 1978. Vols. 69–72, pp. 543–550.
Wakeman, John, ed. *World Authors 1950–1970*. New York: Wilson, 1975, pp. 1343–1348.

Stewart, Mary. *The Wicked Day*
Morrow, 1983, $15.95; pap., Fawcett, $4.50

Since the appearance of her first novel, *Madame Will You Talk?* (Morrow, 1955, $8.95; pap., Fawcett, $2.50), the British writer Mary Stewart has produced a series of excellent Gothics, each combining romance and suspense in an exotic locale. Right always triumphs without involving complicated issues. In 1970 she changed to writing historical fiction with a retelling of the Arthurian legends of fifth-century England as seen chiefly through the eyes of Merlin. In order they are: *The Crystal Cave* (pap., Fawcett, $3.95); *The Hollow Hills* (Morrow, 1973, $9.95; pap., Fawcett, $3.95); *The Last Enchantment* (pap., Fawcett, $3.95); and *The Wicked Day*.

Plot Summary
"The wicked day" of Mary Stewart's tale is the day of King Arthur's last battle. The legendary sixth-century king of the Britons fought and died at Camlann, as did his illegitimate son, Mordred, who is at the center of this gripping Arthurian novel.

As a peasant boy growing up on one of the lonely Orkney islands, young Mordred is unaware of his parentage until the day that he comes to the aid of Prince Gawain, eldest son of Queen Morgause, who rules the Orkneys. Summoned to the castle, Mordred is told by the queen that he is, in fact, the illegitimate son of her late husband, King Lot. Now that he knows the truth, the queen tells him, he will come and join the life of the castle.

Mordred does join Queen Morgause and her four sons: Gawain, the twins, Agravain and Gaheris, and Gareth, the youngest. Shortly afterward, he is horrified to discover that his foster parents have died in a fire that burned their hovel to the ground.

As Mordred is growing into young manhood, Queen Morgause receives what amounts to a summons from King Arthur, who is her half-brother. She is to travel to Camelot for an audience with Arthur, and Mordred and the four young princes are to accompany her.

Mordred is fascinated by the grandeur of King Arthur's court, although he and the princes are upset to learn that Arthur has plans for his half-sister to be put away in comfortable isolation. Morgause is accused of poisoning Merlin the Enchanter; Merlin did not die, but the poison left him with a sickness that will eventually cause his death. Then Mordred chances to come upon the man who killed his foster parents (on the queen's orders) and he kills him.

Taken before King Arthur, young Mordred finally learns the truth of his birth. He is not the son of King Lot; he is the illegitimate son of King Arthur himself. What is more, Mordred's mother is none other than Queen Morgause, who had enticed her half-brother to her bed when the young Arthur was still unaware of their blood relationship. The queen had the boy raised in secret against the day when he would make Merlin's prophecy come true. For Merlin has said that Mordred will be the doom of King Arthur, whom Morgause hates.

Mordred now enters into the life of King Arthur's court, not openly acknowledged as Arthur's son but treated as a special favorite, even by the lovely Guinevere; Arthur and his queen have no children.

Mordred is dismayed when he is told of Merlin's prophecy, and he swears that he will never bring harm to the man who is his father.

More and more, King Arthur depends on the loyalty and strength of his son. Then comes the day when Arthur must leave Camelot to face the warring factions that threaten his confederation of Britain. In his place, he leaves Mordred to guard Camelot and the life of Queen Guinevere.

Vowing his loyalty to king and queen, Mordred cannot help but think of the day when he might take over the land as his father's successor, the High King. And he cannot help but think of the lovely Guinevere by his side as well.

The news from the Burgundian battlefront is grim; a courier shouts that Arthur is dead. Yet, when Mordred presses him further, he learns that although the king was seen to fall, his body has not been found.

With the king's fate in doubt, Mordred assumes command and convenes the Council, stating that the people must be assured that there is still a central power in control in Britain. With Guinevere's approval, the Council accepts Mordred's leadership.

Meanwhile, Arthur, who is recovering from wounds and unable to return to Camelot, receives a letter carried by ship from Duke Constantine. The letter says that Mordred has assumed the kingship and is rallying the heads of neighboring lands under his command. The letter also says that, with Arthur gone, Mordred plans to make Guinevere his wife.

Although the facts of the letter are mainly true, who can tell what is in Mordred's heart? Each day his feeling of power grows; each day his longing for Guinevere becomes stronger. Perhaps he truly means no harm to his father the king; perhaps it is no longer possible for him to turn from the course he has set.

And so Arthur sails for home, but a stormy sea drives him ashore in Saxon territory, the land of the enemy. Before Arthur goes against his foes, he spends a few moments at the side of Prince Gawain, Morgause's eldest son, who is dying from wounds he received on the battlefield. Gawain tells Arthur that he will need help "to kill . . . the traitor . . . Mordred."

Back in Camelot, Mordred hears of the fighting and the news that Arthur still lives. Although the Saxons are his allies, Mordred swears he will not fight against Arthur. Yet, when he goes to the battlefield, Arthur's troops scream the word "traitor!"

And even though neither man wishes it, it seems inevitable that they must battle: Mordred, swearing allegiance to his father but filled with his own power, and Arthur, remembering the prophecy of Merlin.

"This was the wicked day of destiny." The two armies meet, as do father and son. Arthur and Mordred stand on the battlefield, face to face. There are no words to be said. Arthur is the first to strike. His spear enters Mordred's body below the rib cage. As he falls, Mordred strikes a deadly blow to the king's head. The blood of father and son join on the ground.

Thematic Material

This book shows how strong can be the pull of power even when confronted with loyalty. And it demonstrates how events can sometimes gain such momentum that, once begun, they cannot be stopped. The conflict within Mordred, the pull between his love for Arthur and his own craving for power are powerful themes. Was Mordred actually a traitor, or the victim of an unshakable prophecy? The age of knights and intrigues in sixth-century Britain is well portrayed in this stirring adventure.

Book Talk Material

King Arthur—real or legendary—has been a fascinating figure throughout the ages. Readers interested in history or tales of the Knights of the Round Table will enjoy the characterization of this hero by author Mary Stewart. See; Mordred first sees his father (pp. 156–164; pp. 137–143 pap.); King Arthur tells Mordred of his true parentage (pp. 176–190; pp. 140–151 pap.); Arthur calls a council (pp. 236–242; pp. 209–214 pap.); the king grows angry at vicious talk against his friend (pp. 303–305; pp. 289–292 pap.).

Additional Selections

In Persia Wooley's *Child of the Northern Spring* (Poseidon, 1987, $17.95), the first book of an Arthurian trilogy, a lively teenaged Guinevere is introduced.

Anna and her brother flee the ravages of the plague during the Middle Ages in Malcolm Bosse's *Captives of Time* (Delacorte, 1987, $14.95).

Medieval England is the setting for Sharon Kay Penman's *Falls the Shadow* (Henry Holt, 1988, $19.95), the story of the Baron's War during Henry III's reign.

Details on the lives and ways of the men and women that inhabit the Arthurian legends are given in John Matthews's and Bob Stewart's *Warriors of Arthur* (Sterling, 1988, $24.95).

Many Arthurian legends are retold in Neil Phillip's *The Tale of Sir Gawain* (Philomel, 1987, $11.95), but the classic retelling of the Arthurian legend is T. H. White's *The Once and Future King* (pap., Berkley, $4.95).

The Tristan and Iseult story is retold in Dee Morrison Meaney's *Iseult* (pap., Berkley, $2.95).

A pirate queen challenges the might of Elizabeth I in Morgan Llywelyn's *Grania: She-King of the Irish Seas* (Crow, 1985, $17.95; pap., Ballantine, $4.50).

Thomas Berger in *Arthur Rex* (Delacorte, 1978, $11.95; pap., Dell, $4.95) re-creates the world of Arthur and the Round Table knights. Also use the source of many of the Arthurian tales, Sir Thomas Malory's *Tales of King Arthur* (pap., Schocken, $14.95), and the script of the stage musical *Camelot* by Alan Jay Lerner (Random, 1961, $10.95).

About the Book
Booklist, September 1, 1983, p. 4.
Library Journal, September 15, 1983, p. 1809.
New York Times Book Review, January 1, 1984, p. 20.
School Library Journal, March 1984, p. 178.
See also *Book Review Digest*, 1984, p. 1490, and *Book Review Index*, 1983, p. 512.

About the Author
Commire, Anne, ed. *Something about the Author*. Detroit: Gale, 1977, Vol. 12, pp. 217–219.
Ethridge, James M., and Kapola, Barbara, eds. *Contemporary Authors* (First Revision). Detroit: Gale, 1967. Vols. 1–4, p. 910.
Evory, Ann, ed. *Contemporary Authors* (New Revision Series), Detroit: Gale, 1981. Vol. 1, pp. 636–638.

Walker, Margaret. *Jubilee*
pap., Bantam, $4.50

This panoramic novel traces the lives of some blacks, poor whites, and landowners on a Georgia plantation from the 1840s through the Civil War and Reconstruction. Each chapter begins with a line from a song or spiritual of the time. In addition to being a novelist, Margaret Walker has been a professor of English at Jackson State College and a published poet. So popular was *Jubilee* that with coauthor Nikki Giovanni, Walker wrote *How I Wrote "Jubilee"* (Third World, 1972, o.p.). This novel, which originally appeared in 1966, is popular with senior high school readers.

Plot Summary
In the years before the Civil War, Vyry is born a slave on the plantation of John Morris Dutton in rural Georgia. Dutton is her father. Her mother, a black slave, dies when Vyry is two years old.

When Vyry is seven, she is delighted to learn that she is to be a "house slave." She will live at the Big House of Marster Dutton and his wife, Big Missy, and attend to young Missy Lillian, who is Vyry's age. What Vyry does not know is that Big Missy hates her. The reason is obvious, if Vyry only had a mirror to look into. For with their light skin, gray-blue eyes, and sandy hair, Vyry and Lillian are often mistaken for sisters.

Life in the Big House is not what Vyry expected, and it turns into terror when she displeases Big Missy and is "hung" in a closet as punishment, saved by her father when he returns from a trip.

But at least there is always enough to eat in the Big House, and Aunt Sally, who is the cook and in charge of the kitchen, loves her and cares for her. Until comes the darkest day of Vyry's life when without warning Aunt Sally is sold.

Big Missy tries out a number of slave cooks after that but nobody suits her and so, reluctantly, she allows Vyry to take over the kitchen, even though she is only a teenager.

Soon after, Randall Ware, a blacksmith, appears on the plantation. Randall is black, but he is a free man and was never a slave. He takes a liking to Vyry, who will have nothing to do with him. But when he hints that he might be able to buy her freedom, she becomes intrigued.

In June Miss Lillian marries Kevin MacDougall. Soon after, two events send Vyry into deep despair. Two black female slaves are accused of murdering their master and are publicly hanged. And one of Dutton's female slaves, Lucy, after running away, is caught and branded with an R on her forehead.

Although by now Vyry hears rumors of impending war between the states, she is no closer to her own freedom. With Randall promising to buy her if he can find a white person to do it for him (although Randall has the money to pay, he cannot buy her outright), Vyry, who by now has grown to care for him, gives in to his wishes and they are "married" by a black preacher.

Finally, Vyry gets the courage to approach the Marster, asking for permission to marry because she is about to have a child. When Dutton hears that she wants to marry a free man, which, of course, would mean her freedom, he explodes in rage, and Vyry realizes that she will never be free. True enough, when Randall is able to arrange with a white man to buy Vyry, the sale is abruptly stopped.

Vyry and Randall have two children, Jim and Minna. As the war grows closer, Randall tells Vyry that he must leave the area, where his life is in danger for his work in helping slaves. He persuades her to meet him and leave with the children. But Vyry is caught by the plantation overseer and savagely whipped. The scars on her back will never go away.

Randall has disappeared, and Vyry can do nothing but wait and pray that he will return to her. It is 1861 and Lincoln is now president of the United States. War comes to the country and to the plantation in rural Georgia.

Dutton dies without granting Vyry her freedom as he had promised. His son, Johnny, goes off to war and is killed. Miss Lillian's husband, Kevin, returns to the plantation mortally wounded. Then it is 1864 and Sherman is marching through Georgia, burning and destroying as he goes. Big Missy dies of a stroke. Finally, the Yankee troops reach the plantation and destroy it, an act from which Miss Lillian never recovers emotionally.

The war is over, and Vyry, along with all the other slaves, is now free. But where is she to go? Illiterate and penniless with two children to care for and never having heard again from Randall Ware, she can only stay on the ruined plantation that is her home.

But Innis Brown comes into Vyry's life and changes it. A slave all his life like Vyry, he wanders to the plantation looking for work. But Innis wants a farm of his own. He persuades Vyry to marry him "legally" and with the children to go in search of a new life that the Emancipation Proclamation has promised to all former slaves.

In 1866 Vyry and Innis and the children start out in search of their own land. As they wander through Georgia and Alabama, they see the devastation that the long years of the Civil War have brought to the South. They see the hatred and bigotry that have not been wiped out by the law. They see the ugliness of the Klan in operation, and in fear for their lives and the lives of their children, they seem forever on the run. Innis is in search of his own farm, and Vyry longs for her own home and, more than anything, an education for her children. She vows they will not grow up ignorant, as she has done.

And, finally, Vyry and Innis do find a home in southern Alabama, in the midst of white people who help them build a house in return for Vyry's services as a midwife. When it seems as though the family may actually be settled, Randall Ware appears. He has been looking for Vyry all these years, returning to the Dutton plantation when he could only to find it destroyed and Vyry and his children gone.

Randall wants Vyry to go to Selma with him, where he lives, now a fairly wealthy man. But Vyry decides that her future and her love belong to Innis Brown, who has been a father to Randall's two children, and to Harry, the child born to him and Vyry. And so Randall returns to Selma, taking the oldest child, Jim, now a young man, and promising Vyry that he will get the education she has always wanted. He also promises to send money so that Minna can go to school.

After seeing Randall and Jim off on the train, Vyry and Innis return to the farm with the two children, and for the first time in her life, she feels an inner peace she cannot express.

Thematic Material

This is a sweeping, historical saga of life just before, during, and after the Civil War, told through the eyes of a courageous slave woman. Vyry is portrayed as an uneducated but intelligent woman who dreams of freedom and education, who endures the indignities and harshness of slave life with courage and resolution, but who never condemns all whites as evil. She is a survivor, and the story of her survival is uplifting and inspiring, even while the details of slave life and treatment are unbearably harsh. History told with emotion and vividness.

Book Talk Material

The treatment of slaves on the plantation of Marster Dutton, who prides himself on how well he treats his chattel, can serve as an introduction to a discussion of slavery, how it was viewed by those who were masters, how it was endured by those who were chattel. See: Marster Dutton visits Vyry's dying mother (pp. 6–9); Vyry goes to the Big House (pp. 15–18); Grandpa Tom is beaten to death (pp. 57–59); Aunt Sally is sold (pp. 70–71); and the thought of freedom comes to Vyry (pp. 77–80).

Additional Selections

The classic novel of the American Civil War that involves Scarlett and Rhett is Margaret Mitchell's *Gone with the Wind* (Macmillan, 1936, $16.95; pap., Avon, $5.95).

Gore Vidal has written a number of fine historical novels dealing with American history. One is *Lincoln* (Random, 1984, $19.45; pap., Ballantine, $4.95); another is *Burr* (Random, 1973, $19.45; pap., Ballantine, $4.95).

An entertaining offbeat Civil War novel is Dee Brown's *Conspiracy of Knaves* (Holt, 1987, $17.95). Also use his *Kildeer Mountain* (pap., Pocket, $3.95), about a mysterious Civil War hero (or coward?) named Rawley.

The battle of Second Bull Run (Second Manassas) is brilliantly re-created in fiction in Tom Wicker's *Unto This Hour* (pap., Berkley, $4.95).

First-person accounts of escapes to freedom have been collected by Charles Blockson in *The Underground Railroad* (Prentice, 1987, $18.95).

A Civil War novel for young teenagers is Belinda Hurmence's *Tancy* (Clarion, 1984, $11.95), about a freed young slave finding her identity.

The harrowing story of life in a southern Civil War prison camp is told in MacKinlay Kantor's *Andersonville* (pap., NAL, $3.95).

After the Civil War, a white veteran forms a friendship with Comanche Chief Kwahadi in Douglas Jones's *Gone the Dreams and Dancing* (Holt, 1984, $15.95; pap., Tor, $3.95).

The story of three marriages among black families in Florida is told in Zora Neale Hurston's 1937 novel *Their Eyes Were Watching God* (Greenwood, 1937, $29.75; Univ. of Illinois, 1978, $6.95).

About the Book
Booklist, September 1, 1966, p. 35.
Library Journal, October 15, 1966, p. 4978.
New York Times Book Review, September 25, 1966, p. 52.
See also *Book Review Digest*, 1966, p. 1255, and *Book Review Index*, 1966, n.p.

About the Author
Locher, Francis C., ed. *Contemporary Authors*. Detroit: Gale, 1978. Vols. 73–76, p. 626.

5

Possible Worlds

ONE of the fastest growing genres in popularity with teenagers is science fiction. Here we have three of the all-time classics by Asimov, Clarke, and Heinlein, respectively, one by the creator of the world of Pern, Anne McCaffrey, and two for a slightly younger but no less quality conscious audience—one by the continually amazing William Sleator and another by the veteran writing team Annabel and Edgar Johnson.

Asimov, Isaac. *Foundation*
pap., Ballantine, $3.95

Isaac Asimov was born in 1920 in Russia but moved at an early age to the United States. Although he is a biochemist, he is best known as one of the most prolific authors and editors in the English language with more than 200 books to his credit. Most of these are in the areas of science and science fiction. He is a great popularizer of science subjects with such titles as *The Collapsing Universe* (Walker, 1977, $14.95; pap., Pocket, $3.95) and *The Realm of Numbers* (pap., Fawcett, $2.50). In the area of science fiction, he is perhaps best known for his Foundation series and Empire books. The former consists of a basic trilogy, *Foundation, Foundation and Empire,* and *Second Foundation* (pap., Ballantine, $2.75 each; single volume, Doubleday, 1983, $19.95), plus additional titles. Recently Asimov has been trying to bridge these two series with such titles as *Prelude to Foundation* (Doubleday, 1988, $18.95). This title also contains a helpful chronology of events in each of the novels. These books are read by science fiction fans in senior high schools.

Plot Summary

Gaal Dornick, from the faraway world of Synnax at the edges of the Blue Drift, has come to Trantor to work with the legendary mathematician Hari Seldon, born in the 11,988th year of the Galactic Era. Trantor has been the center of the Imperial Government for hundreds of generations. It is the most densely populated and industrially advanced world of the Galactic Empire. But Dornick discovers that Hari Seldon is much out of favor with the authorities, for Seldon has declared that the total destruction of Trantor will come about and cannot be prevented.

The Commission of Public Safety brings Seldon to trial. Seldon declares that the coming destruction of Trantor is only part of the total destruction that is forthcoming—the developing decline and fall of the Galactic Empire. The fall cannot be prevented, declares Seldon. However, by saving the knowledge of the human race, Seldon also declares that he can prevent thousands of years of suffering for human history. He can do this by the completion of his project—the *Encyclopedia Galactica*—which the 30,000 men in his employ are now working on. The encyclopedia will be a giant summary of knowledge, and by the time Trantor falls, it will be complete, says Seldon, and will be in every major library in the galaxy. The human race will not have to start over to pick up the pieces of civilization.

The commission's response to Seldon is to banish him and his entire project staff to Terminus, at the edge of the galaxy, where they can be left in peace to "complete their work."

And so it is done. Fifty years pass, and the first volume of the encyclopedia is now due in five years.

But Salvor Hardin, the mayor of Terminus City, is now faced with trouble from other planets, such as Anacreon, whose royal governor has just assumed the title of king. Terminus is small and defenseless.

To the astonishment of Hardin, the figure of Hari Seldon appears, now confined to a wheelchair and declaring that he is "not really there." Seldon tells Hardin and members of the Board of Trustees that the entire encyclopedia project has been a fraud, part of a grand scheme. Seldon wanted his project to be banished to Terminus. The years that followed, Seldon says, have brought the inhabitants of Terminus inevitably to this path, a path worked out by Seldon for a reason. The Galactic civilization is in decline; the fall of the Galactic Empire has begun. In its place, the Foundation on Terminus and a companion foundation at the other end of the empire are the seeds of a new beginning—the start of the Second Galactic Empire.

Then Seldon declares that the Galactic Empire, though dying, is still mighty, and must be overcome; there are still 920 years of his plan left to go.

And so through the coming years emerge the Traders, who seek to establish economic fingerholds for the new Foundation on the edges of space. And Traders become Master Traders, and then Merchant Princes, bringing money power to the fledgling Foundation as it begins to rise to power and domination of the kingdoms on the outskirts of the Galaxy.

Thematic Material

This is a science fiction classic, the first of three in the series, followed by *Foundation and Empire,* which tells the story of how the Foundation becomes strong enough to finally defeat the First Empire, and *Second Foundation,* which tells of the time after the defeat of the First Empire and the growth of a dangerous mutant. The 1,000-year period covered in these three volumes deals with the building of an ideal universal ruling corporation. Good reading for all devotees of science fiction.

Book Talk Material

Some of the details of life in the worlds of the galaxy will be of special interest to science fiction readers; see the landing on Trantor (pp. 4–6) and the elevator ride (pp. 10–14). To gain an understanding of what Asimov has in mind for the basis of the Foundation, the reader should pay close attention to the speeches of Hari Seldon (see pp. 14–17, 22–29, 72–75).

Additional Selections

In his Eden trilogy, Harry Harrison has created a fantastic alternative world threatened by the reptilian female-dominated Yilane. Start with *West of Eden* (pap., Bantam, $4.50).

Janet Asimov, wife of Isaac, has written a novel about an alliance between robots and humans in *Mind Transfer* (Walker, 1988, $17.95).

In his six challenging Dune novels, Frank Herbert has created an amazing family, the Astreides, banished to the planet Dune. Two of the earliest are *Dune* (Putnam, 1984, $17.95; pap., Ace, $4.50) and *Children of Dune* (pap., Berkley, $3.95).

Ray Bradbury's collections of stories combine science fiction and fantasy. Two examples are *The Toynbee Convector* (Knopf, 1988, $17.95) and *The Stories of Ray Bradbury* (Knopf, 1980, $20.00).

A Canticle for Leibowitz by Walter M. Millis (pap., Harper, $6.95; pap., Bantam, $3.95) poses the question "Is history always going to repeat itself?"

Residents of Dayworld are kept in suspended animation for six days of the week in Philip J. Farmer's *Dayworld* (Putnam, 1985, $16.95; pap. Berkley, $3.50).

Metals begin to disappear mysteriously from a small planet colony in Timothy Zahn's *Spinneret* (Bluejay, 1985, $15.95; pap., Baen, $3.50).

Harlan Ellison encouraged 33 top science fiction writers to write daring stories. The result: *Dangerous Visions* (pap., Berkley, $8.95). Its continuation is *More Dangerous Visions* (pap., Berkley, $10.95).

About the Author
de Montreville, Doris, and Hill, Donna, eds. *Third Book of Junior Authors.* New York: Wilson, 1972, pp. 21–25.

Ethridge, James M., and Kopala, Barbara, eds. *Contemporary American Authors* (First Revision). Detroit: Gale, 1967. Vols. 1–4, pp. 34–35.

Evory, Ann, ed. *Contemporary Authors* (New Revision Series). Detroit: Gale, 1981. Vol. 2, pp. 27–32.

Wakeman, John, ed. *World Authors 1950–1970.* New York: Wilson, 1975, pp. 89–90.

Clarke, Arthur C.   *Rendezvous with Rama*
pap., Ballantine, $3.50

The English writer Arthur C. Clarke was born in 1917. A scientist by education and profession, he began his writing career with nonfiction works in some of which he predicts future scientific developments. For example, in a magazine article in 1945 he predicted the use of communication satellites. He began writing science fiction in 1951 and now moves comfortably from one genre to another with more than 50 books to his credit. Perhaps his most famous work is the screenplay for *2001: A Space Odyssey*, which he wrote with director Stanley Kubrick. Later he novelized it (pap., NAL, $3.50) and produced a sequel, *2010: Odyssey Two* (Ballantine, 1982, $14.95). Like *Rendezvous with Rama*, which was first published in 1973, many of his novels deal with the exploration of other worlds and the search for a superior intelligence. These novels are popular with science fiction enthusiasts in grade 9 and up.

Plot Summary

In the year 2130 a large spinning asteroid is detected outside the orbit of Jupiter. At first it is cataloged simply as 31/439, but as its presence becomes more fascinating, it is eventually named Rama. (Scientists have long since exhausted the names in Western mythology and are now using Hindu gods.) It is observed to be cylindrical in shape, about 40 kilometers (30 miles) long, 20 kilometers (12 miles) across, and rotating on its axis once every 4 minutes while whirling through space.

The spacecraft *Endeavour* under command of William Norton is dispatched to explore Rama. His ship, navigated by Joe Calvert, lands close to three pillboxlike structures, each about 10 meters in diameter, near Rama's polar axis. Norton and Lieutenant Commander Karl Mercer enter the UFO by unscrewing the top of one of the pillboxes and find themselves in a world of complete darkness. By using flares they are able to detect three ladders that lead to a massive plain below. In the distance surrounding it is an oceanlike frozen expanse they dub the "Cylindrical Sea," and beyond this are six groups of tall skyscraperlike structures they name after cities on the earth, such as London and New York.

All of the ship's activities are being monitored and directed by the Rama Committee of the United Planets, a group of seven statesmen and scientists consisting of the chairman, Dr. Bose, and a representative from each of the six cooperating planets.

With extreme caution many entries are made into Rama, each probing deeper into its interior. Each crew member seems to have a different theory concerning Rama's purpose. For example, Lieutenant Boris Rodrigo, a communications officer, is a religious man who believes it to be a cosmic ark sent out by a dying civilization. All realize that regardless of whether their exploration is complete, at perihelion, the point where Rama is too close to the sun for their safety, they must leave the artificial planet.

A base camp, Alpha, is established and a group led by Surgeon Commander Laura Ernst travels to the edge of the frozen Cylindrical Sea when suddenly spring comes to Rama. The ice melts and dazzling light appears revealing the wonders and immensity of this magical new world. From other observed changes, including the appearance of oxygen in the atmosphere, it seems that within a brief time period Rama is undergoing a process of evolution that took millions of years on earth.

By raft, the "city of New York" is explored and they find a vast series of mysterious factorylike structures without windows. Further southern exploration seems impossible when they confront a 50-meter-high cliff that bars their way.

A young crewman, Jimmy Pak, however, has a solution. He has smuggled on board a skybike, which he uses to fly over the cliff. He sees one gigantic, sharply pointed spire and six smaller ones around it. When massive electrical charges begin emanating from these spikes, the buffeting causes his bike to crash. Suddenly three-legged robotlike creatures appear (Ramans seem to be governed by the power of three) and clear up the debris.

Using his shirt as a parachute, Jimmy is able to jump unharmed into the Cylindrical Sea and is rescued. At base camp other harmless, three-legged beings, like huge variations on a daddy long-legs, begin infesting the plain. Laura dissects the brain of one of them and discovers that only a giant battery is used as the source of energy.

A missile containing a bomb is sighted heading for Rama. At a meeting of the general assembly of the United Planets, the ambassador from Mercury admits that his people, the Hermians, are responsible for this violation of space laws. They are fearful that because Rama appears headed for Mercury, its cosmic purpose is to destroy their planet. Therefore, this giant missile has been launched. They will not be dissuaded from this paranoid course of action.

On the *Endeavour* Norton and his crew are convinced that Rama's intentions are not warlike. Boris Rodrigo volunteers to intercept and disable the bomb via his space scooter to allow Rama to complete its mysterious mission.

After much deliberation Norton consents and Rama is saved.

The exploration of Rama continues. In "London" the crew breaks into one of the city's glass columns and finds holographic images of all sorts of tools and implements, again all adhering to the principle of three. Perhaps Boris's ark theory has validity.

Slowly the light fades in Rama and after furious last minute activity by the biots (the name given to the robots), they disappear and night descends as though one phase in the evolution of this planet has been completed.

The *Endeavour* flies off. From afar the crew sees Rama pass dangerously close to the sun and suddenly the purpose of this intrusion into the solar system becomes clear. This is simply a refueling stop. Its source of energy renewed, Rama heads again into the universe, leaving behind many questions and few answers.

Norton is now vindicated for preventing the destruction of Rama, and it appears that the rendezvous with Rama is complete. But is it? After all, Ramans do everything in threes.

Thematic Material

Clarke affords the reader the opportunity to explore a new world as the English adventurer Captain Cook did centuries earlier on his ship the *Endeavour*. The possibility that a superior intelligence exists in the universe and could visit our solar system is an intriguing idea, and Clarke explores the various reactions from excitement and wonder to suspicion and hostility that could accompany this event. That this intelligence is indifferent to humans and their accomplishments adds an ironic twist. Politics, religion, teamwork, and human relationships are additional subjects explored. The wealth of astrological information given by the author adds authenticity and excitement.

Book Talk Material

An introduction to UFOs in general and Rama in particular plus the discussion of possible reasons for their visits should fascinate prospective readers. Important passages are: Rama is first sighted (pp. 4–9); data are collected concerning its size (pp. 10–12); the landing on Rama (pp. 19–22); the interior is described (pp. 38–40); the descent into Rama (pp. 48–56); and dawn comes to Rama (pp. 101–107).

Additional Selections

On Jupiter's moon, Granymede, a young boy joins an expedition to find primordial monsters in Gregory Bentford's *Against Infinity* (Ultramarine, 1983, $15.00, pap., Pocket, $3.50). Also use his Nebula Award winner *Timescape* (pap., Pocket, $3.95).

A third space odyssey novel by Arthur C. Clarke is the recent *2061: Odyssey Three* (Ballantine, 1988, $17.95), in which Heywood Floyd attempts a landing on Halley's comet.

In *Lord Valentine's Castle* by Robert Silverberg (pap., Bantam, $3.95), the planet Majipoor is ruled by an impostor. Also use the sequel, *Majipoor Chronicles* (Arbor, 1982, $12.95; pap. $5.95).

On a lighter note, use Douglas Adams's hitchhiker series, which begins with *The Hitchhiker's Guide to the Galaxy* (Harmony, 1980, $9.95; pap., Pocket, $3.95), and his later *Dirk Gently's Holistic Detective Agency* (Simon, 1987, $14.95).

Five beings—only one of them human—are sent to explore the planet Enigma in Hal Clement's *Still River* (Ballantine, 1986, $16.95).

Frederick Pohl's Hecchee books begin with *Gateway* (pap., Ballantine, $3.50), a prize-winning novel that introduces Rob Broadhead and his career on Gateway, an asteroid.

Intelligent amoeba-like inhabitants are living on a neutron star in Robert L. Forward's *Dragon's Egg* (Ballantine, 1980, $9.95, pap. $2.95). Its sequel is *Starquake* (pap., Ballantine, $3.95).

Aliens, time travelers, and other assorted strangers unburden themselves at Spider Robinson's *Callahan's Crosstime Saloon* (Enslow, 1977, $13.95; pap., Berkley, $2.95).

About the Book
Library Journal, August 1973, p. 2339; November 15, 1973, p. 3474.
New York Times Book Review, September 23, 1973, p. 38.
See also *Book Review Digest*, 1973, pp. 228–229, and *Book Review Index*, 1973, p. 92.

About the Author
Commire, Anne, ed. *Something about the Author*. Detroit: Gale, 1978. Vol. 13, pp. 22–24.
de Montreville, Doris, and Crawford, Elizabeth D., eds. *Fourth Book of Junior Authors and Illustrators*. New York: Wilson, 1978, pp. 82–84.
Ethridge, James M., and Kopala, Barbara, eds. *Contemporary Authors* (First Revision). Detroit: Gale, 1967. Vols. 1–4, pp. 179–180.
Evory, Ann, ed. *Contemporary Authors* (New Revision Series). Detroit: Gale, 1981. Vol. 2, pp. 118–119.
Kunitz, Stanley J. *Twentieth-Century Authors* (First Supplement). New York: Wilson, 1955, pp. 205–206.

Heinlein, Robert A. *Stranger in a Strange Land*
Putnam, 1973, $11.95; pap., Ace, $4.50

When Robert Heinlein died in May 1988 at age 80, he was generally recognized as one of the three greatest science fiction writers of our time, along with Arthur C. Clarke and Isaac Asimov. His output was unusually large; at the time of his death 64 of his books were listed in *Books in Print*. They range in scope from many titles written for teenagers, such as *Citizen of the Galaxy* (Scribner's, 1957, $15.00; pap., Ballantine, $2.25;

condensed in *Juniorplots*, Bowker, 1967, pp. 160–162), to many books like the present volume written for adults. The prophetic nature of his writing is sometimes uncanny. For example, this novel, though first published in 1961, anticipated the philosophy and life-style of the flower children of some years later. It also introduced a new verb into our vocabulary—"to grok"—which means approximately to comprehend fully and assimilate inwardly the essence of an idea, situation, or person, as in "science fiction fans grok Heinlein." This novel is popular with senior high school students.

Plot Summary

The spaceship *Envoy* with four couples aboard was the first to attempt to colonize Mars from our planet, Terra. This expedition failed with no survivors, and so 25 years later (World War III having intervened), a second landing is completed by the spacecraft *Champion* under the leadership of Captain Willem van Tromp. The expedition not only studies the Martian culture and civilization but also returns to Terra with Valentine Michael Smith, son of two of the original colonists. He was born on Mars, and after the death of his parents and the other colonists, was raised by the natives as a true Martian.

Mike, aka the Man from Mars, is indeed a stranger in a strange land. He knows little English and has never seen a woman or been exposed to the concept of sex. (Martians are three-legged unisexuals.) Like other Martians, he is, however, endowed with unusual mental powers, such as teleportation (the ability to move the mind from place to place while the boy remains stationary), telekinesis (the ability to move objects), and telepathy (the ability to enter another's mind). As well, he is able to make objects or people disappear at will and can control his own metabolism so that he can enter periods of hibernation when he wishes.

At present he is being held incognito for observation and gradual conditioning to Terra's gravity at Bethesda Medical Center. Ace newspaperman Ben Caxton realizes that the Man from Mars might be in a politically dangerous situation. As sole survivor of the first expedition, he not only is heir to the accumulated wealth of the participants, but also by international laws adopted by the Federation, could claim ownership of Mars. The Federation, a political union of many states including the United States, would certainly find this awkward, and therefore Ben correctly surmises that its leader, Secretary General Joseph Douglas, would like to dispose of Mike.

Ben contacts his fiancée, Gillian "Jill" Boardman, on the hospital floor where Mike is held under tight security. She is able to bug Mike's room and from the collected tapes, Ben and Jill overhear a conversation in which Douglas unsuccessfully tries to coerce Mike into signing away his rights.

When Douglas introduces for international television a more cooperative, articulate impostor who claims to be the Man from Mars, the situation becomes critical. Ben tries to contact the expedition's physician, Dr. Nelson, to confirm his fears of duplicity, but his conversations are tapped and, to silence him, he is kidnapped by members of the Special Service, the Federation's secret police.

Jill disguises Mike as a nurse and they escape from the hospital to the country mansion of Jubal Harshan, a friend of Ben who is both a successful writer and an accomplished doctor and lawyer. Jubal is a lovable cynic who has in his employ a personal servant and diamond-in-the-rough, Duke, and three delightful, attractive secretaries, Dorcus, a brunette, Miriam, a redhead, and Anne, a blond. Under Jubal's tutelage, Mike begins to grok Terran concepts and culture, and in turn Jubal and his friends are amazed at Mike's powers and marvel at his angelic innocence, although Duke has difficulty groking the Martian ritual of eating their dead.

In time Jubal is able to contact Douglas through a mutual friend, the famed astrologer Madame Becky Vesant, adviser to Douglas's wife, Agnes. An agreement is reached. Ben is released, Mike relinquishes his rights to Mars, and Douglas becomes Mike's financial adviser and guardian of his immense fortune.

Jill and Mike remain at Jubal's where the Man from Mars is introduced to such Terran institutions as the joy of sex and an evangelical temple, the Archangel Foster Tabernacle of the Church of the New Revelation, where he meets a reformed stripper named Dawn Ardent. Mike introduces his friends to the Martian ritual of sharing water, the uniting of lives and brotherhood through drinking from the same glass of water.

When Mike decides to enter the world, Jill, now his lover, accompanies him. At first he becomes a magician, Dr. Apollo, with a circus that also employs Patty Paiwonski, a tattooed lady who performs nude using her pet boa constrictor, Honey Bun, to cover her modesty. Mike's circus career fizzles, as do several other jobs he tries. Finally, he realizes that his mission on Earth is to guide humans into the sharing and caring ways of the Martians. He forms a large commune where people progress through stages of study and meditation called circles, until they reach the ninth circle, where liberated from earthly vices and selfish concerns, they live governed by universal love. Their greeting is "thou art god" and their lives beatific. Mike calls his inner circle "the Nest" and here he gradually gathers together his loved ones—some like Jill, Dawn, Duke, and Patti become permanent members; others like Ben, Jubal, and his three secretaries make short visits, but all fall under the spell of the messianic Michael.

The general public, however, is outraged when they learn of this cult that practices nudity and free love. A gang burns their temple, and Michael with other members of the Nest takes refuge in a hotel he owns in St. Petersburg. Once again an angry mob assembles, and now Michael, although able to use his powers to make them all disappear, knows he must fulfill his destiny by providing his group with a lasting inspirational act. Alone he confronts the mob members, who kill him with their rocks and fists. His last words are "thou art god."

Knowing that Michael's soul will continue to guide them from above, the members of the Nest disperse to spread the teachings of Michael and the Martians to the far corners of the Federation.

Thematic Material

In his life and death Michael represents a Christ-like figure passing on a modern message of love and unselfishness, but derided and scorned and eventually martyred for his beliefs. His fate is that of many contemporary great people who have died for humanity. By using the purity of Mike together with the cynicism of Jubal, the author presents a sardonic and disturbing picture of such modern institutions as organized religion, marriage, and power politics. It is also an inspiring story of faith, honor, and friendship that explores the depth and variety of human love. The author has also created a fascinating and believable picture of the alien but morally advanced culture of the Martians and contrasts this tellingly with our own.

Book Talk Material

An introduction to the Man from Mars and his arrival on Earth should interest readers. Some good passages are: Jill first visits Mike in the hospital (pp. 21–24; pp. 14–17 pap.); Mike's parentage and possible future (pp. 30–33; pp. 24–27 pap.); Ben contemplates Mike's possible murder (pp. 33–38; pp. 27–32 pap.); Ben interviews Mike and is kidnapped (pp. 49–56; pp. 44–51 pap.); and Mike's escape from the hospital (pp. 60–63; pp. 56–58 pap.). In Chapter 23 Mike, Jill, and Jubal visit the Foster Tabernacle.

Additional Selections

Earth is about to be invaded by two alien races in Greg Bear's *The Forge of God* (Tor, 1987, $17.95). Also use his *The Infinity Concerto* (pap., Berkley, $2.95).

A similar theme, with alien visits on earth, is found in Alan Dean Foster's *Starman* (pap., Warner, $2.95). Also by Foster is *To the Vanishing Point* (Warner, 1988, $15.95), in which a female hitchhiker is actually an alien trying to prevent the end of the world.

An 18-year-old and his girlfriend are marooned on Mars in James Blish's *Welcome to Mars* (pap., Avon, $1.95).

Some evil force is preventing Alvin's growth in Orson Scott Card's *Seventh Son* (Tor, 1987, $17.95), the first book in the Tales of Alvin Maker series.

In Philip K. Dick's *Blade Runner* (pap., Ballantine, $1.95) Rick Deckard is searching for six rogue androids who have escaped from Mars.

Dorsai! (pap., Ace, $3.50) is Gordon R. Dickson's distant world where the inhabitants are mercenaries.

The Deryni are a race of people with special mental powers invented by Katherine Kurtz. They are featured in many novels including *Deryni Rising* (pap., Ballantine, $3.50) and *Deryni Checkmate* (pap., Ballantine, $3.50).

Larry Niven has given a sweeping view of a future world in his Ringworld books. Two are *Ringworld* (pap., Ballantine, $3.50) and *Ringworld Engineers* (pap., Ballantine, $2.50).

About the Book
Booklist, July 15, 1961, p. 695.
Library Journal, August 1961, p. 2680.
See also *Book Review Digest*, 1962, pp. 533–534.

About the Author
Commire, Anne, ed. *Something about the Author*. Detroit: Gale, 1976. Vol. 9, pp. 102–103.
Ethridge, James M., and Kopala, Barbara, eds. *Contemporary Authors* (First Revision). Detroit: Gale, 1967. Vols. 1–4, p. 440.

Evory, Ann, ed. *Contemporary Authors* (New Revision Series). Detroit: Gale, 1981. Vol. 1, pp. 259–260.

Fuller, Muriel, ed. *More Junior Authors*. New York: Wilson, 1963, pp. 109–110.

Kirkpatrick, D. L., ed. *Twentieth-Century Children's Writers* (2nd edition). New York: St. Martin's, 1983, pp. 365–367.

Kunitz, Stanley J., ed. *Twentieth-Century Authors* (First Supplement). New York: Wilson, 1955, p. 432.

Johnson, Annabel, and Johnson, Edgar. *The Danger Quotient* Harper, 1984, $13.70, pap. $2.95

In a writing career that spans more than 30 years, the Johnsons have written a series of young adult titles that utilize various settings and time periods including the future. Most of their titles, like *Alien Music* (Four Winds, 1982, $9.95) and *Prisoner of Psi* (Macmillan, 1985, $12.95), are intended for a slightly younger audience than *The Danger Quotient*. This novel is somewhat more complex than their other works, but it contains their usual stamp of tight plot constructions and interesting, believable characterizations. It is read and enjoyed by science fiction fans in grades 8 through 12.

Plot Summary

The year is 2127 and what remains of the human species after the total nuclear holocaust of 1996 now lives guided by advanced technology in a gigantic underground world situated near what was once Denver, Colorado. Radioactivity has doomed them to a highly computerized, well-regulated subterranean life in a complex that had been built more than 130 years ago before World War III by a mysterious visionary named Midas Forsythe. His uncanny foretelling of the catastrophe to come led him to build an underground community equipped with the latest technology, where he, his family, and world prominent scientists were able to escape the total destruction of the world and preserve the human species.

Through genetic intervention, five individuals equipped with super brains have now been cloned by the complex's leading scientist, Helmut Eddinger. Unfortunately, each of the first three has died in their teens and the life expectancy of the next, known as K/C-4 (Sci)6229/E by the tattoo on his right buttock, has been predicted by the computer Pinocchio, Pokey for short, as only a few more months. Fiver, the pesky, precocious last one, is only seven and therefore not in imminent danger.

Number four has just perfected a refractor, also worked on by number three before her death. This allows individuals to travel back in time as well. Knowing she was doomed, number three did copious historical research for her friend number four to try to save him. He believes that the research was to uncover the mysterious danger quotient that is killing them, but somehow enabled humans before the war to live much longer lives.

During a computer search, K/C-4 discovers his physical description—age: 18; height: 5 foot 11 inches; hair: light blond; eyes: one blue, one green; plus a tattoo identical to that of a young man who was booked by police in a Denver suburb on June 20, 1981.

K/C-4 time travels to that date and finds himself naked (clothes don't refract) in a public park where he is soon nabbed by police and charged with indecent exposure. In the holding pen he helps save a wino named Max Hunter from being brutalized by two other inmates. Max, believing that his new friend is suffering from amnesia, invents a new identity for him: He is Casey (from the K/C in the tattoo) Anderson, a UCLA student who had been robbed and beaten by a hitchhiker he had picked up. Max also gives him an address in Denver, the home of his grandmother, Lisa Kent, where he can get help. It works and Casey, sporting cast-off clothes, is sprung from jail.

At the Kent home, Casey is admitted by a hoydenish 11-year-old girl named Gil, who is Max's niece and is interested only in getting her uncle, a burned-out Vietnam vet, who is now an alcoholic, out of jail. She has only a few dollars, not nearly enough for bail, but Casey, who has done his historical homework, chooses (miraculously to Gil) the winning daily double at the local racetrack and garners $3,985 from a $10 bet.

Beneath Gil's tough, wise-cracking exterior is a pathetically unhappy young girl. She tells Casey that her great-grandfather, Lisa's husband, died in an insane asylum and that her grandfather was acquitted in a bizarre murder trial where the body was never found. Her father, Howard, had waited out the Vietnam War in Canada for chiefly cowardly reasons. (He and her mother, both successful business people, are usually absent from the household.) Gil is convinced that she is the bearer of bad genes and that she, too, is destined to live a tragic, useless life.

In Lisa Kent's bedroom Casey discovers an ancient photograph of himself. Under his questioning, Lisa, now in her eighties and forgetful, states that this man saved her life back in 1918.

Casey time travels to the last days of World War I and enters the life of the Hessler family, poor Colorado farmers who are being persecuted by their neighbors because of their German background. Casey becomes their farmhand and grows to love the family, including young Betsy who in later life was to become known as Lisa. Unknown to the rest of the family, Betsy is pregnant by their former helper Billy MacDonald, who after joining the army became a victim of a severe influenza epidemic now ravaging the country. Betsy herself succumbs and is saved only by Casey's giving her a massive transfusion of his own blood. To legitimatize the baby who was to be Gil's grandmother Grace, Betsy marries a local eccentric, Al Kent. Casey miraculously misses death by influenza by returning to the complex in time for medical attention.

After further investigation, Casey discovers that the man supposedly murdered in 1945 by Grace's husband, Clint Hunter, wore a strange tattoo on his right buttock. He time travels to the Hunter home a few days before the killing and finds Clint, a much-decorated army hero, home for a few days before being reassigned to Okinawa. (With his powers of hindsight, Casey knows that Clint's outfit was later wiped out in combat at that location.) Casey must find an honorable way of detaining Clint in the United States. Subtly, Casey convinces Clint that he is a Russian spy programmed to reveal secrets involving America's atomic bomb. When Clint tries to take him captive, Casey feigns an escape during which he is shot. He reaches the complex in time to have his wounds dressed, but luckily has left behind a trail of blood sufficient to have Clint accused of murder.

Casey returns to 1981 and Gil. He explains his origins to her, how he has determined that her family is an honorable one, and that she should be proud of her great-grandfather Billy and grandfather Clint. Gradually she accepts Casey's explanation as the truth.

Back at the complex Casey somehow feels the story is incomplete. Surely number three had some broader purpose in mind concerning his interventions in the history of Gil's family. Further investigation reveals that Gil later married Midas Forsythe, so named because of the fabulous wealth he amassed by his uncanny ability to forecast stock market activities and later known more importantly as the builder of the underground complex that would save humankind. Who is this man who mysteriously appeared in Denver seemingly from nowhere in the late 1980s? Casey now knows the destiny for which number three has prepared him. He sets the gauges on his time refractor at 1988 and bequeaths to Fiver the remainder of the search for the danger quotient.

Thematic Material

This is a taut, complex futuristic novel that is also a cautionary tale because it gives the reader a glimpse of each of the major twentieth-century wars in which the United States has been involved and of the waste and tragedy that each produced, plus a horrifying picture of life after the ultimate holocaust. Everyday life in the United States during these historical periods is vividly recreated as reflected in the saga of one family. The fragility and preciousness of human life is stressed. Time travel, inner space life in the twenty-second century, and the ultimate fate of a gutsy hero are also important themes in this story.

Book Talk Material

K/C-4's problem concerning his predicted life span is outlined in the opening pages of the novel (pp. 3–6, both eds.). Other passages of interest: number three's last message (pp. 13–16; pp. 12–16 pap.); Casey's first time travel and his bout with the police (pp. 27–33; pp. 26–31 pap.); he meets Max and establishes an identity (pp. 33–39; pp. 32–38 pap.); and Gil and Casey attend the racetrack (pp. 43–49; pp. 41–47 pap.).

Additional Selections

A street smart 15-year-old girl flees her planet aboard a tramp starship in John Maddox Roberts's *Spacer: Window of the Mind* (pap., Ace, $2.95).

Nita, who has been raised in complete isolation by a furry alien, discovers another human in her institution in Pamela Sargent's *Alien Child* (Harper, 1988, $11.89, pap. $2.95).

Keill Randor sets out to avenge the destruction of his home planet in Douglas Hill's *Galactic Warlord* (pap., Aladdin, $3.95; pap., Dell, $2.50). There are many sequels including *Planet of the Warlord* (pap., Dell, $2.50) and *Day of the Starwind* (pap., Dell, $2.50).

In Jack L. Chalker's *Web of the Chosen* (pap., Ballantine, $2.50) Bar Holliday finds he is changing into a subhuman.

A slum orphan named Cat becomes involved in a strange psychic experiment in Joan D. Vinge's *Psion* (Delacorte, 1982, $12.95; pap., Dell, $2.95; condensed in *Juniorplots 3*, Bowker, 1987, pp. 202–205).

Eighteen-year-old Robin attempts to rescue his father who has been kidnapped by aliens in Laurence Yep's *Monster Makers, Inc.* (Arbor, 1986, $15.95; pap., NAL, $2.95).

H. M. Hoover has written some fine novels for young teenage science fiction enthusiasts including the story of an alien race that controls the earth, *The Delikon* (pap., Penguin, $3.50; pap., Avon, $1.50), and a story that takes place on the planet Blathor, *The Lost Star* (pap., Avon, $1.50).

About the Book
Book Report, September 1984, p. 34.
Booklist, 1984, p. 1392.
Bulletin of the Center for Children's Books, July 1984, p. 206.
School Library Journal, August 1984, p. 84.
VOYA, October 1984, p. 206.
See also *Book Review Index,* 1984, p. 370.

About the Authors
Commire, Anne, ed. *Something about the Author.* Detroit: Gale, 1971. Vol. 2, pp. 156–158.
de Montreville, Doris, and Hill, Donna, eds. *Third Book of Junior Authors.* New York: Wilson, 1972, pp. 150–152.
Kirkpatrick, D. L., ed. *Twentieth-Century Children's Writers* (2nd edition). New York: St. Martin's, 1983, pp. 410–411.
Kinsman, Clare D., and Tennenhouse, Mary Ann, eds. *Contemporary Authors* (First Revision). Detroit: Gale, 1974. Vols. 9–12, pp. 435–436.

McCaffrey, Anne. *Moreta: Dragonlady of Pern*
Ballantine, 1983, $14.95, pap. $3.50 (same pagination)

Pern is a planet circling the star Rukbat created by Anne McCaffrey where telepathic dragons and their riders live a communal existence. There are two series of books about Pern. One is aimed at a young adult audience and begins with *Dragonsong* (Atheneum, 1976, $14.95; pap., Bantam, $2.95; condensed in *Juniorplots 3,* Bowker, 1987, pp. 178–181); the other, for adults, now numbers five titles starting with *Dragonflight* (Ballantine, 1981, $8.95, pap. $3.95) and ending with *Nerilka's Story* (Ballantine, 1987, $12.95, pap. $3.95). *Moreta* is the fourth in the series in which the ongoing war against the Thread continues. The series is enjoyed by senior high school students.

Plot Summary

When humans settle the planet Pern, the third world of Rukbat in the Sagittarian Sector, they pay little attention to the so-called Red Star, a stray planet that circles Pern in an erratic orbit. But after about two generations of colonization have passed, the Pern inhabitants realize that the erratic orbit of the Red Star will bring it, at one point, very close to their own new world. When it does approach, the erratic planet drops silver Threads onto Pern; the Threads destroy everything they touch.

Although the losses on Pern are dreadful after the first attack of Threads, the colonists survive and begin to devise a plan. They realize that the orbit of the Red Star will bring back the Thread menace on a regular, if long-term basis. When the Red Star is at the far end of its orbit, for about 200 turns of Pern, there is no threat of Thread. But when the Red Star returns, the Thread attack will go on for an interval of about 50 years. And so they devise a plan to fight the Threads and survive.

The key to the plan is the development of a new life form, a type of fire-lizard, or dragon. The flying dragons travel from one place to another in an instant and they emit a type of gas flame that burns up the Threads before they reach the ground of Pern and destroy whatever they touch.

The second phase of the counterattack against Thread is more complicated. Once Thread, a kind of spore, hits the ground, it burrows beneath it with great speed. To kill Thread beneath the ground, the people of Pern develop their own spore, a grub that is placed into the soil. It kills what Thread the dragons miss.

Naturally, the people who ride the dragons become very important in the Pern society. When what is called a Fall of Thread is about to occur, the riders take their dragons into the Pern sky to protect the people and the planet.

At the time of this story, the Red Star is nearing the end of its sixth passing over Pern, about 1,400 turns of the planet Pern since it was first inhabited. Six so-called Weyrs are pledged to protect the planet, each in a different geographic location. The rest of the people of Pern pay taxes to support the Weyrs, as the dragonriders cannot spend time making their own living.

The dragons are distinguishable by color. Gold and green are female; blue, bronze, and brown are male. Only the gold are fertile; therefore, the rider of the senior queen dragon, the Weyrwoman, has great responsibility for the entire Weyr during and after an attack of Thread. It is her job to preserve the dragons and to her falls the responsibility of the safety of the Weyr.

Moreta is a Weyrwoman and her golden dragon is Orlith, who is heavy with egg and soon about to clutch. As Moreta prepares herself for the festivities of a Gather, she reflects that this Fall of Thread will be completed in another eight turns of the planet Pern, and then the fighting will be over for a long while.

After arriving at the Gather on the back of Orlith, Moreta meets and is attracted to the new Lord Holder of Ruatha, Alessan. The settlements on Pern are divided into Holds, usually developed around natural caves as protection. Each Hold is self-sufficient, and the Lord Holder is responsible for administration, population control, and the safety of the people during the dreaded Fall of Thread.

Moreta enjoys herself at the Gather. But soon after, without warning, Holders, craftspeople, and dragonriders begin to fall ill. Some die. What is this terrible and mysterious ailment? Campian, a Masterhealer, explains the symptoms as fever, cough, headache, and no appetite. It is not long before the strange fever is threatening to turn into an epidemic. This spells doom for the planet Pern, for if the dragonriders cannot take to the sky to combat the Fall of Thread, everything and everyone will be destroyed.

Even though she is able to take part in an attack on Thread, Moreta falls ill to the strange virus. However, she recovers. And now Campian, who also contracted the disease, comes up with the idea of a blood serum to combat the virus. All those who have had the virus and survived must give blood to make the serum.

Some good news comes to Pern in that Moreta's golden dragon, Orlith, has a clutch of 25 eggs, although that is not a generous amount.

When it seems as though the vaccine will stop the epidemic, more panic occurs when Campian decides that the plague is transmitted to animals by people, and therefore it may break out a second time. What is needed is for both animal and humans to be vaccinated, and the vaccine—which Lord Alessan has concocted—must be delivered to all distribution points, preferably on the same day. Only the dragonriders can accomplish this, Campian tells Moreta. If the plague is not stopped within the next few days, they will be hit by a second wave and there will not be enough dragonriders to take to the sky against Thread.

Although the vaccine is ready, Alessan informs Moreta that there are not enough needlethorns in any of the Holds to vaccinate all animals and people; the needlethorns cannot be reused. The only way that Moreta and other dragonriders can harvest enough needlethorns in time is through the use of dangerous time travel.

Despite the danger, Moreta successfully returns with the needlethorns and she and other dragonriders take to the skies to deliver the necessary vaccine in time. As Orlith cannot fly yet, Moreta takes the old queen dragon, Holth. And though Holth is valiant, she wearies from the flying. With just one last jump to make, Moreta urges her on . . . but they go *between* . . .

It is Moreta's dragon, Orlith, who first realizes what has happened when Moreta does not return. They were too tired; the old dragon could not jump so far . . . they went *between, to nothing*.

Moreta, the brave Weyrwoman of Pern, gave her life for her planet. The epidemic is over; Pern lives on.

Thematic Material

This science fiction tale has alien planets and marvelous flying dragons, but it also has very Earth-like people with the same needs and fears and devotions to each other and to the animal creatures that share their world. Entertaining, imaginative reading for admirers of the sci-fi genre.

Book Talk Material

The dragons themselves are especially entertaining features of this book and may serve as an excellent introduction to the strange planet of Pern. See: Moreta communicates with Orlith (pp. 2–3); they fly to the Gather (pp. 6–8); Moreta and Alessan discuss dragon racing (pp. 16–19); at the races (pp. 20–30); and Orlith enjoys the festivities and takes Moreta home (pp. 40–45).

Additional Selections

The stellar musician known as the Queen of Hearts conceals a strange secret behind her mask in Patricia A. McKillip's *Fool's Run* (Warner, 1987, $15.95).

An intricate adventure begins when a 17-year-old girl saves a man on a distant planet in C. J. Cherryh's *Angel with the Sword* (pap., DAW, $3.50). A warrior hero journeys to the land of Ealdwood in Cherryh's *The Dreamstone* (pap., DAW, $2.95). Its sequel is *The Tree of Swords and Jewels* (pap., DAW, $2.95).

Ursula K. LeGuin is another leading science fiction writer. Two of her best are: *The Dispossessed* (pap., Avon, $2.25), which contrasts two imperfect utopians, and *The Lathe of Heaven* (Bentley, 1971, $12.50; pap., Avon, $3.50), in which a twenty-first century young man's dreams foretell the future.

Glen Cook writes about the Darkwar. In one, *Doomstalker* (pap., Warner, $2.95), a young female warrior survives a nomad raid on her tribe.

A Welsh teenager falls in love with an astral spirit in Louise Lawrence's *Moonwind* (Harper, 1986, $12.50, pap. $2.95).

A healer searches for a serpent whose venom will heal the terminally ill in Vonda N. McIntyre's *Dreamsnake* (pap., Dell, $2.25). Also use her *Superluminal* (Houghton, 1983, $12.95; pap., Pocket, $3.50).

Empires clash but our hero has a hidden goddess to help him in Tanith Lee's *The Storm Land* (pap., DAW, $2.95).

A girl defies the social conventions of her world in George R. Martin and Lisa Tuttle's *Wildhaven* (Ultramarine, 1980, $17.50; pap., Pocket, $3.95).

About the Book
Book Report, March 1984, p. 34.
Booklist, September 15, 1984, p. 114.
New York Times Book Review, January 8, 1984, p. 18.
School Library Journal, February 1984, p. 87.
VOYA, April 1984, p. 38.
See also *Book Review Index,* 1984, p. 449.

About the Author
Commire, Anne, ed. *Something about the Author.* Detroit: Gale, 1976. Vol. 8, p. 127.
Holtze, Sally Holmes, ed. *Fifth Book of Junior Authors and Illustrators.* New York: Wilson, 1983, pp. 206–207.
Metzger, Linda, ed. *Contemporary Authors* (New Revision Series). Detroit: Gale, 1985. Vol. 15, p. 309.
Nasso, Christine, ed. *Contemporary Authors* (First Revision Series). Detroit: Gale, 1977. Vols. 25–28, pp. 470–471.
Riley, Carolyn, ed. *Contemporary Authors.* Detroit: Gale, 1971. Vols. 25–28, pp. 489–490.

Sleator, William.   *Singularity*
Dutton, 1985, $12.95; pap., Bantam, $2.95

Like many fine science fiction writers, Sleator likes to speculate on the consequences of applying established scientific facts and theories in unusual or extreme situations. For example, in *House of Stairs* (Dutton, 1974, $12.95; pap., Scholastic, $1.95; condensed in *More Juniorplots*, Bowker, 1977, pp. 43–46), the possible limits of human conditioning experiments are explored, and in *The Duplicate* (Dutton, 1988, $12.95), a young boy discovers a machine that enables him to clone himself. A "singularity," as explained in the text of the hardcover edition (on pages 63–65), is a collapsed star or black hole that has sufficient gravitational pull that the speed of time on either side of the singularity can be quite different. Bearing this in mind the action of the novel takes place in a period slightly over a week, or a year, depending on one's point of view. This novel, like most of Sleator's other science fiction stories, is popular with grades 7 through 10 and useful with older reluctant readers.

Plot Summary

Although Barry and Harry Krasner, age 16, are identical twins, they possess very different personalities. Barry is aggressive, impulsive, and domineering, whereas Harry, the narrator, is more introspective, cautious, and timid. News comes to the Krasners at their home in Boston that Mom has inherited her eccentric Uncle Ambrose Kittery's house near the town of Sushon, Illinois. Because Mr. and Mrs. Krasner have immediate plans to attend a two-week conference in San Francisco, Barry prevails on them to allow him and reluctant Harry to precede them to the house, investigate it, and protect it from burglars.

Accompanied by their dog, Fred, the twins make the trip to rural Illinois. They are met by the probate lawyer, Mr. Crane, who takes them to the isolated, many gabled home owned by their great-uncle. Now alone, the boys enter this strange, forbidding house. Inside they find a large accumulation of dilapidated Victorian furniture, dozens of skeletons of grotesque animals not of this world, such as a catlike creature with six legs. On the property behind the house, the boys discover a 12-by-6-foot recently built structure they call the playhouse. It has a single door with no windows. Their explorations are interrupted by the arrival of a neighbor about their age, Lucy Coolidge. She gives them some background on quirky Uncle Ambrose. Some years ago several of her grandfather's farm animals disappeared after wandering onto Kittery's property. One evening her relatives trailed a recently strayed milk cow and found it emaciated and gaunt as though it had aged 20 years. However, after Kittery built his playhouse, the animals stopped disappearing.

Their curiosity aroused, the boys find the keys to the playhouse and all three enter. On the surface it appears to be an above-ground bomb shelter equipped with a toilet, a bed, a large supply of food, and a door lock that operates immediately on closing.

The next day, however, they discover a more sinister function. While the boys are cleaning the playhouse, Harry leaves for scarcely a minute. When he reopens the door he finds an irate Barry who claims to have been closed in overnight. He even has a beard stubble to prove it. Later that day they discover that their dog, Fred, had been accidentally left behind in the playhouse. When they open the door they find only a skeleton.

Perusal of Uncle Ambrose's papers confirm their outlandish suspicion that the playhouse was built on the entrance to another universe—a singularity where time proceeds much faster than on earth. This unknown universe begins disgorging material, each item being reflected in the washbasin as it travels through space on what is known as an event horizon. The first is a glowing pebblelike glass object that Harry thinks is some kind of cosmic clock. The next day a green bit of material arrives that reminds Lucy of an extraterrestrial hair ball. When the reflection of the next slated visitor appears, the three are terrified. It is a gigantic monster equipped with rows of teeth. The boys now know the origin of Uncle Ambrose's bizarre skeleton collection.

Harry wants to throw away the keys to the playhouse and notify the police. The long pent-up animosity that Barry has felt toward his brother due to resentment at being a twin now erupts. He vehemently refuses Harry's suggestions and takes possession of the keys.

Harry, hurt and resentful, devises a daring plan of action. He decides to spend a night, or the equivalent of one year, in the playhouse, end the condition of being an identical twin, and thus develop a different relationship with his brother.

That night he steals the keys and after gathering extra clothes, books, and provisions, enters the playhouse where each earth minute becomes a day. The stay seems endless, but each day he undergoes a rigid regime of exercise, meditation, and recreation. Twice, at several-month intervals, he allows himself recesses of 15 minutes each in the outside world. He notices many boggling changes; his physique matures and his height increases by three inches. He also notices that the monster reflected in the washbasin is getting closer.

In the morning Harry emerges to a startled and uncomprehending Barry. During the reconciliation there is a loud explosion. The monster has broken through. It is as terrifying as expected with a teeth-lined mouth the size of a stepladder.

Fortunately the monster begins devouring its own tail with such ferocity that it consumes itself. In its violent entry to this world it has cracked open and released the time change power that had been concentrated in that location. Two kinds of singularity have ended, one involving the cosmos and the other a pair of identical twins.

Thematic Material

Although this book is essentially a fascinating science fiction thriller and builds to a stunning climax, there are also other subjects touched on, including the problem of being identical twins. Sibling rivalry is explored and the misunderstandings and unhappiness it can bring, as well as the differences between dominant and submissive brothers. The solutions to these conflicts, albeit externally motivated, are interesting. Harry's growth to both physical and spiritual maturity is well portrayed.

Book Talk Material

The title as it applies to the universe and to the Krasner twins should interest readers. Specific passages are: Barry talks his parents into allowing the trip (pp. 3–6; pp. 4–7 pap.); the boys enter the house and see the playhouse (pp. 18–22; pp. 16–19 pap.); Lucy tells about the missing livestock (pp. 30–33; pp. 35–39 pap.); and Barry spends a night in the playhouse (pp. 39–45; pp. 46–53 pap.).

Additional Selections

The famous science fiction trilogy about three boys and the Tripods by John Christopher consists of *The White Mountain* (pap., Collier, $3.95), *City of Gold and Lead* (pap., Collier, $3.95), and *Pool of Fire* (pap., Collier, $2.75).

In William Sleator's *The Boy Who Reversed Himself* (Dutton, 1986, $12.95) Omar and teenage Laura travel into the fourth dimension, and in *Interstellar Pig* (Dutton, 1984, $11.95; pap., Bantam, $2.95; condensed in *Juniorplots 3*, Bowker, 1987, pp. 198–202) Barney plays a deadly game with outerspace aliens for control of the universe.

Two young people question the highly organized British society of the twenty-first century in Robert Westall's *Futuretrack 5* (Greenwillow, 1984, $10.25).

A courageous teenage girl gives up her life to save humanity in James Tiptree's *The Starry Rift* (Tor, 1986, $14.95).

Young readers enjoy the classic science fiction of H. G. Wells. Some examples: *The Invisible Man, The Time Machine,* and *The Island of Dr. Moreau* (several editions available). A good omnibus edition is *Seven Science Fiction Novels* (Dover, 1951, $15).

Sixteen-year-old Olwin Pendensis is the only human on planet Isis and is charged with maintaining the galactic lighthouse in Monica Hughes's *The Keeper of the Isis Light* (Atheneum, 1981, $11.95; pap., Bantam, $2.25).

After a dreadful war, children find thought control is being introduced into their school in James Clavell's *Children's Story* (Delacorte, 1981, $7.95; pap., Dell, $2.50).

Six teenagers defy oppression in a future United States in John Neufeld's *Sleep, Two, Three, Four* (pap., Avon, 75¢).

About the Book
Booklist, April 1, 1985, p. 1114.
Bulletin of the Center for Children's Books, June 1985, p. 195.
Horn Book, May 1985, p. 320.
School Library Journal, August 1985, p. 82.
VOYA, October 1985, p. 270.
See also *Book Review Digest*, 1986, p. 1489, and *Book Review Index*, 1985, pp. 569–570.

About the Author
Commire, Anne, ed. *Something about the Author*. Detroit: Gale, 1972. Vol. 3, p. 207–208.
Evory, Ann, ed. *Contemporary Authors* (First Revision Series). Detroit: Gale, 1978. Vols. 29–32, p. 645.
Holtze, Sally Holmes, ed. *Fifth Book of Junior Authors and Illustrators*. New York: Wilson, 1983, pp. 295–296.
Kinsman, Clare D., ed. *Contemporary Authors*. Detroit: Gale, 1972. Vols. 29–32, p. 585.

6

Fantasy

Pure fantasy usually involves such standard elements as the quest, as in Dungeons and Dragons. The Terry Brooks and Shirley Rousseau Murphy novels in this section typify this genre, but the others fall outside this pattern to varying degrees. The Vonnegut and Hilton books give up two contrasting pictures of a future world, and the Mahy novel, though about a girl's journey to maturity, is also about three intriguing ghosts.

Brooks, Terry. *Magic Kingdom for Sale—Sold!*
Ballantine, 1986, $16.95, pap., $4.50

Terry Brooks originally gained prominence in the world of fantasy with his Shannara trilogy involving three generations of Ohmsfords and their battle against evil. It begins with *The Sword of Shannara* (pap., Ballantine, $9.95), continues with *The Elfstones of Shannara* (pap., Ballantine, $3.95), and concludes with *The Wishsong of Shannara* (Ballantine, 1985, $18.95).

In the first sequel to *Magic Kingdom, The Black Unicorn* (Ballantine, 1987, $16.95), Brooks continues this humorous fantasy series. In it Ben Holiday loses the royal medallion that can summon Paladin, is betrayed by his wizard, and loses Lady Willow on a search for the mysterious Black Unicorn. All of these volumes are enjoyed by fantasy fans in the senior high grades.

Plot Summary

Ben Holiday, a wealthy Chicago lawyer, cannot get over the death of his pregnant wife, Annie, some two years before. Except for his work, he has no interest in living. Then, in a Christmas catalog from Rosen's, Ltd. addressed to Annie, he chances to see a strange ad: "Magic Kingdom for Sale." The ad explains that the Kingdom of Landover is for sale for

$1 million. The purchaser will rule over a land of enchantment and adventure as king and high lord.

Preposterous as it seems, the ad haunts Ben, so much so that he flies to New York City and Rosen's, Ltd. to inquire of a Mr. Meeks, as the ad instructs. Mr. Meeks tells him that if he decides to purchase Landover, he will be given ten days to examine his new kingdom and decide if he wants to stay. If he does not, the purchase price will be refunded. If he decides to stay, the purchaser must agree to spend at least a year in Landover; if not, he will lose the $1 million.

The hard-nosed lawyer in Ben rejects this whole proposition as ridiculous, but the emptiness of his life makes him reach out to a dream of a world of enchantment, full of dragons and damsels and fairy folk, all waiting for his benevolent rule. With no ties to keep him at home, Ben purchases Landover for $1 million.

Ben flies to Virginia, where he is given instructions to drive into the Blue Ridge Mountains, leave his rented car, and walk into the woods for some distance. He is also given a medallion, which the note says is his key in and out of the magic kingdom. "Wear it," says the note, "and you will be recognized as the rightful heir to the throne. Only you can remove it. No one can take it from you."

Following instructions, Ben finds a tunnel, which he enters, and is transported to Landover, where he is promptly almost frightened to death by a black, winged thing and its rider and nearly run down by a knight. Just as he is regretting his decision, he meets Questor Thews, wizard of the court and chief adviser to the throne of Landover. Questor shows Ben around what is obviously a very dilapidated kingdom and castle. He also explains that the black thing and its rider is the Iron Mark, a demon lord who strays into Landover now and again, and the knight—although Questor refuses to believe that Ben actually saw him—is Paladin, legendary champion of the Landover kings.

Ben also learns much about his kingdom in the next few days. For one thing, there have been many kings to come and go, but none has lasted since the original king died many years back. And the knights and nobles of the kingdom have lost faith in rulers and now refuse allegiance to anyone. The kingdom is divided and is slowly falling to ruin; the castle is tarnished; the magic is disappearing.

Despite all this, Ben lets the 10 days go by and is committed to his kingdom for at least a year. He meets his staff, which consists of a dog named Abernathy, who is also the court scribe as well as Ben's personal attendant (naturally, Abernathy talks), and two large-eared monkeylike creatures called "kobolds."

Questor tells his new king of how Landover came to such a state of dilapidation, how the original king's son cared nothing for the kingdom, how the treasury emptied, and the farmlands withered, and the castle tarnished, and the people grew despondent and gave up. But law can be restored, assures Questor, especially by a man like Ben, a man of vision and courage. Questor also tells Ben of Paladin, once the protector of the kingdom. No one could stand against Paladin; but when the old king was gone and the kingdom fell to ruin, Paladin disappeared, too, and no one has seen him—although Ben claims to have done so when he entered Landover.

Questor saves the worst news for last. Each midwinter, the Iron Mark, the demon, comes out of Abaddon into Landover to challenge the king. No one has ever accepted the challenge, as well Ben can understand, and so there is no peace in the kingdom. But no one can ever hope to defeat the great Mark, especially without the aid of Paladin.

Ben wrestles with his own feelings. If he stays in Landover, he must surely face the Mark. But if he returns to his world, only emptiness is there. Ben makes up his mind. He will stay and fight the demon Mark.

King Ben tries to gather the nobles and knights of Landover around him, but as Questor has told him, they will not join to back the new king in whom they have no faith. Ben also meets the lovely Willow, a sylph, the child of a sprite become human. She tells Ben that she belongs to him, but Ben, whose heart is still filled with the loss of Annie, cannot accept her love.

In trying to gain backing and strength for his test with the Mark, Ben speaks to the witch called Nightshade. She consents to tell him where he can retrieve the magic that will help him, a magic called Io Dust that can be found only in the fairy world. Although Willow and the others beg him not to enter the fairy world alone, Ben does so.

But as Ben walks off into the mist, he finds himself back in Chicago! Ten years have passed, his astonished law partner tells him. Ben is but a memory to everyone. He doesn't exist in his own world any longer. And then Ben sees his beloved Annie, who tells him she is only a ghost. She admonishes him for leaving this world, telling him that they are separated forever.

And just as suddenly Ben is back in Landover. But this time the kingdom and his friends have withered into hideous shapes and are dying because their king has abandoned them.

Now Ben is fully determined. He does enter the fairy world for the Io Dust with which he tames the dragon Strabo. The dragon will take him to Abaddon to face the Mark.

Meeting the Iron Mark is the most terrifying moment of Ben Holiday's life. For the Mark is at least eight feet tall with black armor and he sits astride a wolf-serpent. Ben realizes in despair that he can never defeat this formidable enemy. Then he remembers the words of Mr. Meeks when he bought Landover; Meeks said that no one could ever take the medallion from him. And Ben realizes that all he has to do is use the medallion to free himself from this magic kingdom, and he will live.

But in the next second Ben realizes that the Mark is waiting for him to do just that, to use the medallion to free himself from this terrible danger, to leave Landover forever, to leave it to the Iron Mark.

Instead of ripping off the medallion, Ben places it outside of his tunic for all to see. This is his home, this is his commitment, his world.

As the Iron Mark charges with his terrible sword, Ben stands fast. And suddenly, out of the light comes Paladin!

In a mighty battle, the Iron Mark is defeated, and the legendary Paladin disappears once more. Who is he?, the people ask. But Ben now knows the answer; he himself is Paladin. He brought forth the courage and strength of the legendary hero when he decided to commit himself once and for all to this new life and this kingdom. He had become Paladin and truly king of Landover.

With the defeat of the demon, the knights and nobles and all of Landover are united under the new king. Ben has committed himself to a new life in this magic land, with Willow at his side.

Thematic Material

This fantasy mixes the real world against the enchantment and magic of a fairy-tale place. It shows how the pressures and sometimes sorrows of life can make individuals lose all interest in people and things around them. But it also says that a commitment to what one believes in, backed by determination and strength and the willingness to reach out to others, can bring rewards that surpass even one's most fantastic dreams.

Book Talk Material
Descriptions of this magical kingdom are a good introduction to this fantasy. See: Ben arrives in Landover (pp. 44–52; pp. 51–58 pap.); the meeting with Questor (pp. 53–55; pp. 62–66 pap.); Ben first sees his castle and staff (pp. 71–77; pp. 78–86 pap.); Ben's coronation (pp. 87–104; pp. 109–117 pap.); and Ben meets Willow (pp. 153–157; pp. 174–177 pap.).

Additional Selections
In Diana Wynne Jones's charming fantasy *Howl's Moving Castle* (Greenwillow, 1986, $10.25; condensed in *Juniorplots 3*, Bowker, 1987, pp. 170–174), a witch's curse turns Sophie into an old woman.

A misfit named Talia is rescued by a telepathic steed in Mercedes Lackey's *Arrows of the Queen* (pap., DAW, $2.95).

Stephen R. Donaldson has produced two series of epic fantasies about Thomas Covenant the Unbeliever. Begin with *Lord Foul's Bane* (pap., Ballantine, $3.95).

Becky walks through a fog and finds herself in a land of centaurs in Robert Siegel's *Alpha Centauri* (pap., Crossway, $5.95).

Two fantasies about the godson of Merlin are H. Warner Munn's *Merlin's Godson* (pap., Ballantine, $2.95) and *Merlin's Ring* (pap., Ballantine, $2.95).

Marion Zimmer Bradley is the author of a series of Darkover novels. One of the most popular is *Hawkmistress!* (pap., NAL, $3.50), about a teenager who learns to communicate with hawks.

One of the most enduring fantasies of all time is Antoine de Saint-Exupery's *The Little Prince* (Harcourt, 1961, $2.95), about a young prince and the knowledge he gains about life on earth.

William Goldman has produced a hardy spoof of fantasies in *The Princess Bride* (pap., Ballantine, $3.50).

Terri Windling and Mark Alan Arnold have edited some excellent anthologies of fantasy. One of their later ones is *Elsewhere, Volume 3* (pap., Ace, $3.95).

About the Book
Booklist, March 1, 1986, p. 913.
Library Journal, April 15, 1986, p. 97.
See also *Book Review Index*, 1986 volume, p. 110.

About the Author
Locher, Frances Carol, ed. *Contemporary Authors.* Detroit: Gale, 1979. Vols. 77–80, p. 64.
Metzger, Linda, ed. *Contemporary Authors* (New Revision Series). Detroit: Gale, 1985. Vol. 14, pp. 72–73.

Hilton, James. *Lost Horizon*
Morrow, 1933, $13.45; pap., Pocket, $3.50

During his relatively short life (from 1900 to 1954), James Hilton, the British writer, contributed greatly to popular literature. It is difficult to remember a time when there was no Mr. Chips or a Shangri-La, but both came into being in the 1930s, the former in 1934 in the novelette *Good-bye, Mr. Chips* (Little, 1935, $14.45; pap., Bantam, $2.75), a warm tribute to the teaching career of Mr. Chipping, and the latter in 1933 when Hugh Conway finds himself in a utopian community in *Lost Horizon.* Although much of his writing is now unfortunately out of print, one more of his very popular novels, *Random Harvest* (Buccaneer, 1982, $18.95; pap., Carroll & Graf, $4.50), is still available. It is the story of love gained, lost, and regained because of amnesia caused by a wound received by the hero during World War I. All three of these novels can be read and enjoyed by good readers in the junior high grades and up.

Plot Summary
Like Alice's "Wonderland" and Gulliver's "Lilliput," Shangri-La is one of the most famous of imaginary places. And *Lost Horizon* is its story.
At the outset, the narrator tells the strange tale of Hugh Conway, British consul in India, and three companions: Roberta Brinklow, a missionary, young Charles Mallinson, a vice-consul and Conway's friend, and the American, Henry D. Barnard. All white residents being ordered to leave the Baskul area in light of local unrest, the four regard themselves as extraordinarily lucky to gain transport on a small airplane.
Yet the flight is but a few hours old before they sense that something is amiss. The pilot, whom they do not know, is not flying in the direction of Peshawar, their supposed destination. And, in fact, after a quick stop for refueling in a remote area, where the passengers are kept in the plane by threat of force, they are airborne again for a flight of many long hours.

Only Conway has a vague idea of where they are when eventually they land, and their unknown pilot almost immediately dies.

The four have been transported to a remote Tibetan lamasery—Shangri-La. Although their hosts are gracious and polite, it is soon evident that they cannot leave the lamasery, despite vague promises of "porters" arriving from the outside, perhaps in a few months' time.

Only Conway among them is relatively undisturbed by this strange happening. The remote beauty and tranquility of Shangri-La begin to capture him, as does the lovely young Chinese girl Lo-Tsen.

Not long after their arrival, young Mallinson discovers that the American, Barnard, is actually Chalmers Bryant, wanted for questionable dealings concerning great sums of money lost on Wall Street. But of more immediate concern to Conway is the news that the High Lama wishes to have an audience with him.

Conway discovers that the High Lama is a little old man in Chinese dress, who tells him the almost unbelievable story of Shangri-La.

This most remote of places—called the valley of Blue Moon—was accidentally discovered by a Capuchin friar in the 1700s. He was never physically able to leave the valley, and though he sent messages to tell his superiors of his find, there is no record that they were ever received. In time another stranger wandered into the valley, an Austrian named Henschell. It was he who devised the system for bringing comforts and supplies to the lamasery, but forever keeping it hidden from the world. His system was surprisingly simple; strangers would not be allowed to leave. Conway and his three companions had been deliberately taken to Shangri-La because the presence of new people was, of course, needed from time to time, and as Conway eventually learns, because the High Lama has designated him as his successor.

But perhaps the most surprising secret of all is that to live in the valley of the Blue Moon is to have almost eternal youth. The aging process is incredibly slow. However, once at Shangri-La for only a short time, to leave the valley might mean swift death, and certainly would mean instant aging.

Conway is not entirely dismayed by his news, for the contemplation of a life in Shangri-La is not repugnant to him, nor, as it turns out, is it repugnant for his missionary companion and the American who is wanted by the authorities. But that is not the case with Conway's young friend, Mallinson.

Mallinson informs Conway that the promised porters are nearing the lamasery and they must go. Then Conway tells Mallinson the story of Shangri-La. The young man is not only aghast at the prospect of remaining there, for he finds the place hellish and evil, but scoffs at Conway for believing such a story, suggesting that he is losing his mind. Mallinson also tells him that the lovely young Chinese girl wishes to leave, too. Conway, who believes that in reality the girl is an old, old woman, cannot believe that she wishes to go.

Mallinson and the girl leave, but are soon back. The young man cannot manage the escape through the valley alone. He implores Conway to go with them. They are young, he says, with their whole lives ahead of them. Conway wonders whether he had been mad and was now sane, or whether he had been sane for a time and now was mad again. He agrees to help them leave the valley.

No one knows what happens to Mallinson. Conway turns up at a hospital in dreadful shape. He is brought in by a woman who dies soon after. Reportedly, she is Chinese, and very, very old.

After Conway recovers and leaves the hospital, no one knows what happens to him. Is he wandering about, wonders the narrator, looking still for the valley of Blue Moon?

Thematic Material

Lost Horizon has been a classic almost from its publication. Readers find many compelling characteristics in this strange and absorbing tale of the mythical Shangri-La: fantasy, a serenity of mind and spirit, eeriness, mysticism, and adventure. It is a story with a timeless quality, and a must for all those who savor tales of escapism.

Book Talk Material

For adventure, readers will enjoy the strange flight to the valley of Blue Moon (see pp. 22–26, 31–36, 39–46; pp. 35–39, 41–43, 49–53 pap.). For beauty, there is the description of the valley and Shangri-La (see pp. 46–50, 85–87; pp. 56–60, 101–104 pap.). See also Conway's first meeting with the High Lama (pp. 119–135; pp. 129–149 pap.).

Additional Selections

Aeriel falls in love with a vampire and tries to free him from an evil spell in Meredith Ann Pierce's *The Darkangel* (Little, 1982, $14.45) and its sequel, *A Gathering of Gargoyles* (Little, 1984, $13.45; pap., Tor, $2.95).

A view of a very different world, one in which science reigns, is depicted in Aldous Huxley's *Brave New World* (Harper, 1932, $12.45; pap. $2.95).

Jennie, a waif, mysteriously ages rapidly in Robert Nathan's unusual love story *Portrait of Jennie* (Knopf, 1949, $14.95).

Grendel tells his side of the story in a variation on the Beowulf story, John Gardner's *Grendel* (Knopf, 1971, $12.95; pap., Ballantine, $2.25).

Edward Bellamy wrote the classic tale of utopian society in *Looking Backward* (pap., NAL, $1.95).

Various elements of Irish history are woven together in Andrew M. Greeley's fantasy *The Magic Cup* (McGraw, 1979, $10.95; pap., Warner, $4.95).

The jungle world of Rima still interests readers in W. H. Hudson's *Green Mansions* (various editions available).

An allegory about totalitarianism in a colony of talking wild cats is the subject of Clare Bell's *Ratha's Creature* (Atheneum, 1983, $12.95).

Such writers as Dickens, Doyle, and Wilde are represented in *Isaac Asimov Presents the Best Fantasy of the 19th Century* (Beaufort, 1982, $14.95). Another fine collection is Isaac Asimov's *100 Great Fantasy Short Stories* (Doubleday, 1984, $15.95; pap., Avon, $2.95).

About the Book
Booklist, November 1933, p. 79.
New York Times Book Review, October 1933, p. 15.
See also *Book Review Digest*, 1933, pp. 435–436.

About the Author
Commire, Anne, ed. *Something about the Author*. Detroit: Gale, 1984, Vol. 34, pp. 114–122.
Kunitz, Stanley J., and Haycraft, Howard, eds. *Twentieth-Century Authors*. New York: Wilson, 1942, pp. 652–653.
May, Hal, ed. *Contemporary Authors*. Detroit: Gale, 1983. Vol. 108, p. 221.

Mahy, Margaret. *The Tricksters*
McElderry, 1986, $12.95

The New Zealand writer Margaret Mahy has been awarded the Carnegie Medal twice, in 1982 for *The Haunting* (Atheneum, 1982, $10.95; pap., Scholastic, $1.95) and in 1984 for *The Changeover* (Atheneum,

1984, $12.95; pap., Scholastic, $2.25; condensed in *Juniorplots 3*, Bowker, 1987, pp. 132–137). The latter tells how a teenage girl must be transformed into a witch in order to save her young brother from death. *The Tricksters* also deals with the occult and tells how a group of holidayers, including a sensitive, imaginative 17-year-old girl, falls under the spell of three sinister young men. The entire action takes place in present-day New Zealand during the Christmas/New Year period. Those readers used to snow and ice at this time of year will have to be reminded that December and January "down under" is a time for warm summer weather. This book is enjoyed by readers in grades 9 through 12.

Plot Summary

Jack and Naomi Hamilton have five children; the oldest son is Charlie, next is 21-year-old Christo, or Christobel, the two other daughters are 17-year-old Harry (real name Ariadne) and Serena, and the youngest is 7-year-old Benny. Harry, Serena, and Benny arrive first at their vacation home, Carnival's Hide, a large beach house, to spend the Christmas holidays. The 90-year-old house is supposedly haunted by the ghost of Teddy Carnival, son of the builder, Edward. Teddy was drowned at age 20, and after his death, widower Edward with older daughter Minerva left the Hide for England, never to return. With the Hamiltons is a guest, an English forester named Anthony Heskett, who has come to study Carnival's ancient forestry pamphlets.

Harry's room is an atticlike loft where she often retreats secretly to write her fantasy novel about a romantic villain, Belen, the pure Prince Valery, and fair lady Jessica.

Charlie and friend Robert Huxley arrive via Charlie's boat, the *Sunburst*. Robert and Christo have been off-on partners, but Christo's capricious nature has prevented Robert from pursuing a more permanent attachment.

While swimming at the cove, Serena and Benny, who often speak in a secret language, evoke the spirit of Teddy Carnival. When Harry enters an underwater cave, a chilling hand takes hold of her. She escapes, but on a rock she sees an apparition of a young man with a bloody gash on his forehead.

Naomi, with family cat Crumb, next arrives. Lastly Christo appears; she is attractive, spoiled, and so disarming that everyone succumbs to her blandishments. With her is a dear friend, the orphaned Emma Forbes, whom the Hamiltons consider another daughter. Though unmarried,

Emma has a two-year-old daughter, Tibby, whose father has never been identified.

Family conversation centers about the spate of wife-swapping that occurred three years ago in the beach community and also the possible appearance of Teddy's ghost.

The following morning Harry encounters three men on the beach. Two are identical twins, and the third, their spokesman, has a long scar at his hairline. They claim to be three brothers, distant members of the Carnival clan, newly arrived from England and intent on exploring the old family house. When they enter they already seem familiar with the layout and contents. The leader who is something of a magician introduces himself as Ovid and the twins as Hadfield and Felix. Later Harry notices in the bookcase close to where they were standing a copy of Ovid's *Metamorphoses,* edited by John Hadfield, and next to it, *Felix Holt* by George Eliot. She wonders who these mysterious strangers really are—visions evoked by her from Belen's fantasy world or perhaps manifestations of Teddy Carnival.

The three get permission to stay in the boat house. Harry is intrigued by all three but is attracted to Felix, the gentle one, whom she notices also has a scar at his hairline. Her feelings are reciprocated.

One evening when she goes to the beach to retrieve one of Tibby's toys, she is accosted by one of the twins who claims to be Felix. She fights him off by striking him on the head with the toy. The next morning it is Hadfield who appears sporting a facial bruise.

In the evening the family scatters to attend various functions, leaving Harry to babysit with Tibby. Felix returns early and the two talk. Even though much of his conversation is in half-understood riddles, Felix shows great affection toward Harry and the two kiss tenderly.

The next morning the family discovers that both furniture and wall coverings of the hallway have been completely changed to their former state before the Hamiltons redecorated. While Harry and Felix walk alone on the beach, Ovid and Hadfield confess that they were responsible for the room's transformation. Naomi is upset, but in the spirit of Christmas keeps quiet.

Later that day Ovid visits Harry in her loft. He tells her that Felix belongs to him and she must let him go or risk destructive consequences for her family.

At the evening's fancy dress party on the beach, Harry defies Ovid and continues to spend time with Felix. From Felix's remarks she begins to realize that all three brothers are really various aspects of Teddy Carnival. Ovid is the complete person and the twins are spin-offs. Hadfield represents the cruel, heartless side, and Felix the gentle, loving alter ego.

Hadfield deliberately provokes a savage fight with Felix that is ended only when, in an unusual commanding tone, Anthony Heskett orders them to stop. While Felix and Harry wander away from the group, the rest return home to sing carols. In the kitchen Anthony reveals to Naomi that he is really the great-grandson of Minerva Carnival, who before her death had confessed that her father, a martinet, had killed his wild, licentious son during a violent quarrel by a blow on the forehead with a garden spade. The drowning story was pure fabrication.

When these two return to the living room, they hear Christo reading aloud in a mocking fashion from a romantically naive, handwritten manuscript about villains and fair ladies that Ovid has found.

Felix and Harry make love on the crest of a hill; they return and on entering the living room, Harry hears her own secret writing being read derisively by Christo and sees in Ovid's eye a look of triumph.

Furious, Harry seizes the book and informs them that she is the author. Then she tells Christo that for all her smugness, Harry knows something that she doesn't—that her own father, Jack, is also the father of Emma's child, Tibby. This revelation, though previously known by Naomi, tears the family apart. During the violent argument that follows, Felix, knowing that this is the work of Ovid, throws his arms around his brothers, causing all three to disappear.

Harry returns to the beach and burns her book. In the flames she again sees the apparition of the man with the head wound and in his face those of Ovid, Hadfield, and Felix, now once again united.

Many members of the family disperse, leaving Harry to care for Serena and Benny. Gradually, strengthened and renewed by the ordeal caused by the tricksters, they all reassemble for the New Year, including Emma and Tibby. In a gesture of reconciliation, Christobel gives Harry a blank book, and Harry begins again, "Once upon a time. . . ."

Thematic Material

This is a ghost story in which the real and the supernatural become intertwined by the evocative power of Harry and her writing. It is also the story of the magical awakening of teenage sexuality and of its power to change those affected by it. In passing from child to woman, Harry becomes aware of the depth and complexity of human feelings. It also deals with the multilevels of human personality and complex family relations involving interactions among father, mother, and children, particularly those involving Harry and her older, domineering sister. Stresses that can affect family solidarity are portrayed as well as the unifying forces of love, forgiveness, and compassion.

Book Talk Material

The retelling of the history of Carnival's Hide should interest readers. Some important passages are: Harry's book is introduced (pp. 12–15); she sees the ghost of Teddy Carnival (pp. 24–28); Christobel and Emma arrive (pp. 35–40); Harry first meets the tricksters (pp. 52–56); and the three brothers introduce themselves to the family (pp. 61–71).

Additional Selections

Teenager Bobbi Yandro's life changes abruptly when she receives a mysterious black stallion, actually Shane, the Dark Rider, in Nancy Springer's *The Hex Witch of Seldom* (Baen, 1988, $15.95).

An earthling is pitted against his changeling in a magical world in *Changeling* (pap., Ace, $2.95) by Roger Zelazny, who also wrote *The Last Defender of Camelot* (pap., Timescape, $3.50).

Australian aborigine legends form the basis of the Wirrun the Hero trilogy, which begins with *The Dark Bright Water* by Patricia Wrightson (Atheneum, 1979, $7.95; pap., Ballantine, $2.95).

Creep, an abused child, escapes to the nineteenth century in *A Chance Child* (pap., Avon, $1.95) by Jill P. Walsh.

A confused teenager gets his values straightened out with the help of a most unusual girl in Ursula LeGuin's *Very Far Away from Anywhere Else* (Macmillan, 1976, $10.95; pap., Bantam, $2.50).

A mother and an unusual male friend search for her daughter in San Francisco in R. A. MacIvoy's *Tea with the Black Dragon* (pap., Bantam, $2.75).

Fearing that she is the last unicorn on earth, a unicorn sets out with a magician to prove this is wrong in Peter S. Beagle's *The Last Unicorn* (pap., Ballantine, $2.25). Also use Beagle's story of an old man who lives in a graveyard and talks with ghosts, *A Fine and Private Place* (pap., Ballantine, $2.25).

Robin McKinley's *Beauty* (Harper, 1978, $11.70; pap., Pocket, $2.95) is an excellent retelling of the *Beauty and the Beast* story.

About the Book
Booklist, March 1, 1987, p. 1008.
Bulletin of the Center for Children's Books, March 1987, p. 131.
Horn Book, July 1987, p. 471.
New York Times Book Review, May 17, 1987, p. 31.
School Library Journal, March 1987, p. 172.
VOYA, June 1987, p. 80.
See also *Book Review Digest*, 1987, p. 1183, and *Book Review Index*, 1987, p. 488.

About the Author
Bowden, Jane A., ed. *Contemporary Authors*. Detroit: Gale, 1978. Vols. 69–72, pp. 391–392.
Commire, Anne, ed. *Something about the Author*. Detroit: Gale, 1978. Vol. 14, pp. 129–131.
de Montreville, Doris, and Crawford, Elizabeth D., eds. *Fourth Book of Junior Authors and Illustrators*. New York: Wilson, 1978, pp. 248–250.
Kirkpatrick, D. L., ed. *Twentieth-Century Children's Writers* (2nd edition). New York: St. Martin's, 1983, pp. 504–506.
Metzger, Linda, ed. *Contemporary Authors* (New Revision Series). Detroit: Gale, 1984. Vol. 13, p. 342.
Senick, Gerard J., ed. *Children's Literature Review*. Detroit: Gale, 1984. Vol. 7, pp. 176–188.

Murphy, Shirley Rousseau. *Nightpool*
Harper, 1985, $11.70, pap. $2.95 (same pagination)

Shirley Murphy is a well-known writer of fantasy. The five-part saga of the children of Ynell, written before *Nightpool*, deals with a race that possesses a fearful and mighty power, the ability to foretell the future, and their quest to join together sections of a runestone that will help conquer the evil forces on earth. It begins with *The Ring of Fire* (pap., Avon, $1.75) and ends with *The Joining of the Stone* (pap., Avon, $2.25).

Nightpool is the first volume of the Dragonbards trilogy. In the second, *The Ivory Lyre* (Harper, 1987, $12.70), Teb, with his dragon, Seastrider, and her three siblings, venture into the land of Dacia to continue the fight against Quazelzeg and the power of the dark. Dacia, under the unscrupulous King Sardira, has remained unconquered and is now used by the armed forces of the dark as a base from which to attack other countries. The four dragons change shape to become four magnificent white horses and together with Teb, disguised as a merchant, enter

Dacia. Inside the king's palace Teb becomes friendly with Kiri, a young page who is actually an informer for the underground movement, of which Garit, Teb's former friend and savior, is a member. Through a series of adventures, Teb routs the evil forces, gains possession of a magic lyre, and is reunited with his missing sister, Camery. The last volume, *The Dragonbards* (Harper, 1988, $12.20), contains the final confrontation between Teb and Quazelzeg, in which the prince emerges victorious and the devoted wise otter, Thakkur, dies. Queen Meriden rejoins her children, and Kiri, now a Dragonbard herself, finds her own dragon. This series is suitable reading for young people in grades 7 through 12.

Plot Summary

Much of the story of *Nightpool* is told as flashback after Teb leaves the island of the otters. For clarity, the plot summary is given chronologically.

When Teb, short for Tebriel, was only seven, his beloved mother, Queen Meriden, wife of King Everard of Auric, mysteriously left their palace and some months later was reported drowned, although no body was found. Teb and his sister, nine-year-old Camery, did not know that their mother was a Dragonbard and was left a strange mystical power that, when united in song with a magical white dragon, could produce music that freed humans and animals from an enslaving spell used by the power of the dark, led by evil Quazelzeg. Many years later Teb was to discover that his mother had actually left on a quest to find her dragon in order to help combat this wicked force. Teb was born with an unusual birthmark on his arm. Unknown to him, this mark signifies that he, too, is a Dragonbard.

One year after the queen's disappearance, a rebellion occurs in Auric, led by villainous Sivich, supposedly a trusted lieutenant but actually a traitor in the service of the forces of the dark. The king is brutally murdered and Teb and his sister are separated and kept prisoners in different parts of the palace.

Four years pass. Teb, now 12, has become a kitchen drudge in the palace while still imprisoned at night in a filthy dungeon guarded by the swinish Blaggen and a group of ravenous winged jackals. It is reported to Sivich that the gigantic white dragon, long thought extinct in the entire continent of Tirror, has been spotted in the land of Baylentha, several days' journey away.

Sivich decides to trap the dragon and, aware of Teb's secret power, uses him as bait. As the armed party leaves the castle, Teb sees his sister, Camery, gaze mournfully down from her prison tower.

Several members of the group, including the horsemaster, Garit, however, are still loyal to the former king and plot a daring escape for Teb. That night a sleeping potion is placed in the food, and with the help of his friends, Teb escapes to the ruins of a deserted city, Nison-Serth, now a cavernous maze of caves and tunnels. There he is helped by a group of talking foxes, led by Piven and his mate, Kenata, who send a message to Ebis the Black, the honorable king of neighboring Ratsisbon, asking for his assistance.

Unfortunately Sivich's men recapture Teb and he is placed in fetters on a large wooden platform constructed to trap the dragon. On several occasions the dragon, who had emerged from years of hibernation to find a mate, visits Teb secretly at night. Finally sensing that this is a trap and that Teb is a potential Dragonbard, she melts his chains with her hot breath. At the same moment Ebis the Black attacks. In the ensuing battle Teb's leg is crushed by a falling horse, and he crawls, more dead than alive, to a marsh inland. There two mischievous talking otters, Mikki and Charkky, find him and, after constructing a raft of greens, float him first to an otter colony at Rushmarsh and then on to their own home on the island of Nightpool, where he is nursed by maternal Mitta and the wise guru of the colony, a white otter named Thakkur.

Months pass. Teb, suffering from amnesia, slowly recovers physically, but Thakkur realizes that Teb must have cooked food and organizes a party to return to the battlefield to search for flints and knives. On the return voyage they are attacked by a gargantuan sea monster, the three-headed hydrus, who is also in the power of the dark. Teb wounds it but it escapes back into the sea.

Teb continues to stay with his loving otters in spite of opposition by a small group led by Ekkthurian, who does not wish a human on their island. Thakkur and Teb engineer a daring raid of Sivich and steal weapons for defense should Nightpool be invaded, while on a faroff island the white dragon, whose name is Dawncloud, has mated and is in the process of hatching five eggs.

One night after a harrowing troubled sleep, Teb's memory returns. He now realizes that although he is only 16, he must leave to begin his struggle against Quazelzeg. The hydrus attacks again, several otters are killed, and Teb knows that the target is really himself. He bids farewell to his mentor, Thakkur, and his many otter friends.

Within days the hydrus captures him in an unguarded moment and transports him to a half-submerged deserted city where he is kept prisoner as slowly the power of the dark tries to control his brain. He discovers a ruin that contains some of his mother's clothes. She had lived there after leaving the palace. The songs she had taught him as a child return to his memory. Their effect is so powerful that many miles away they stir Dawncloud and her brood, who fly off to save Teb.

In a fierce conflict the hydrus and a young dragon are killed. A survivor, the beautiful Seastrider, becomes Teb's bonded dragon. Together they set out to challenge the power of the dark.

Thematic Material

This is a thrilling tale of good versus evil with all the trappings of superior fantasy writing, enhanced in this case by noble dragons, engaging talking animals, and a courageous, sympathetic hero. The action is fast-moving, the setting vivid, and the characterization interesting.

Book Talk Material

Displaying one or all of the dust jackets of the trilogy, giving brief background information, should evoke interest. Specific passages are: the sighting of the dragon and plans to catch her (pp. 16–17, 20–22); Garit tells Teb of his escape plans (pp. 46–50); in the caves of Nison-Serth Teb meets the foxes (pp. 63–69); and he sees Dawncloud while in the trap (pp. 83–84).

Additional Selections

In Patricia C. Wrede's *The Harp of Imach Thyssel* (pap., Ace, $2.95), a young minstrel protects a magic harp from thieves. This is a sequel to *Daughter of Witches* (pap., Ace, $2.95).

Jane Yolen's Pit Dragon trilogy begins with *Dragon's Blood* (Delacorte, 1982, $14.95; pap., Dell, $2.75; condensed in *Juniorplots 3*, Bowker, 1987, pp. 205–208), in which Jakkin raises and trains his own dragon.

A graduate student is transported to a wizard's world in Alan Dean Foster's *Spellsinger* (pap., Warner, $2.95).

Fantasy readers interested in the classics will gravitate to J. R. R. Tolkien's *Lord of the Rings* trilogy (Houghton, 1974, $13.95), beginning with *The Fellowship of the Ring* (pap., Ballantine, $2.95).

Lovers of dragons and quests will enjoy Robin McKinley's story of Aerin in her land of Damar in *The Hero and the Crown* (Greenwillow,

1984, $11.25; pap., Berkley, $2.95; condensed in *Juniorplots 3*, Bowker, 1987, pp. 182–186) and its continuation *The Blue Sword* (Greenwillow, 1982, $13.00; pap., Berkley, $2.95).

Peter Dickinson's *The Gift* (Atlantic, 1974, $12.45) is about the ability to read other people's thoughts.

Orphan Maggie Turner finds a magical family in dolls she locates by strange voices she hears in Sylvia Cassedy's *Behind the Attic Wall* (Crowell, 1983, $12.95).

The possession of an ancient stone links three stories in Alan Garner's *Red Shift* (pap., Ballantine, $1.95).

About the Book
Book Report, March 1986, p. 30.
School Library Journal, December 1985, p. 104.
VOYA, December 1985, p. 326.
See also *Book Review Index*, 1986, p. 524.

About the Author
Commire, Anne, ed. *Something about the Author*. Detroit: Gale, 1984. Vol. 36, pp. 142–145.
Metzger, Linda, ed. *Contemporary Authors* (New Revision Series). Detroit: Gale, 1984. Vol. 13, pp. 382–383.
Nasso, Christine, ed. *Contemporary Authors* (First Revision). Detroit: Gale, 1977. Vols. 21–24, p. 626.

Vonnegut, Kurt, Jr.   *Cat's Cradle*
pap., Dell, $3.95

While a prisoner of the Germans during World War II, Kurt Vonnegut, Jr. witnessed in 1945 one of the most horrifying scenes of the war, the fire bombing of Dresden by British and American aircraft. This event not only figures prominently in his *Slaughterhouse 5* (pap., Dell, $4.50), but also helped to formulate the author's philosophy of the absurdity and meaninglessness of life. These attitudes couched in prose relieved somewhat with brilliant flashes of black humor form much of the thematic background of *Cat's Cradle*. The title comes from an ancient game played with a loop of string that produces interesting geometric arrangements but is, like life, really a cheat because it produces neither a real cat nor a cradle. The time of the novel is the early 1960s. It begins with shades of *Moby Dick* in the line "Call me Jonah," although we later learn the narrator's real name is John. It is divided into 127 brief, often parable-like chapters, each bearing a title sardonically related to its contents. The novel was first published in 1963 and is suitable for better readers in senior high school.

Plot Summary

Jonah, or John, an author, once a Christian and now a convert to Bokononism, founded by a humanistic skeptic named Bokonon (a corruption of Johnson), begins his narrative with events surrounding research he did for a nonfiction book tentatively titled *The Day the World Ended*, which was intended to chronicle happenings in the lives of important Americans on August 5, 1945, the day the atomic bomb was dropped on Hiroshima. He begins with contacting by letter a midget named Newt Hoenikker, the youngest of three children of deceased Dr. Felix Hoenikker, the acknowledged father of the atomic bomb. Newt was only 6 at the time; he is now 20. He remembers that day being frightened by a cat's cradle constructed by his eccentric, absent-minded father, and being later comforted by his 12-year-old brother, Frank, and 22-year-old sister, Angela, who since their mother's death had managed the household.

Jonah's search next takes him to the small town of Ilium, New York, where in a small laboratory of the General Forge and Foundry Company, Dr. Hoenikker did his research. Here he meets Dr. Asa Breed, in charge of research, who tells him more about the eccentric scientist and that his last project involved developing ice-nine, a substance able to solidify water instantly. Jonah is convinced that Dr. Hoenikker had developed ice-nine before his death and that each of his children was given slivers of this lethal substance.

In a newspaper Jonah sees a supplement on the Caribbean island of San Lorenzo with pictures of a beautiful native girl, Mona Aamons Monzano, the adopted daughter of the island's dictator, Papa Monzano, and the minister of science and progress, Major General Frank Hoenikker. He decides to visit.

On the plane he meets Newt and Angela, who are going to see their brother, H. Lowe Crosby and his wife, Hazel, all-American hoosiers intent on building a bicycle factory on the island, and the new American ambassador, Horlick Minton, and Claire, his wife. During the flight he reads a history of the island by Philip Castle, son of Julian Castle, an altruistic, Albert Schweitzer-like millionaire who has constructed a free hospital for the natives of the island. The account tells how shortly after World War I, two sailors, a black man named Lionel Boyd Johnson and his white friend, Earl McCabe, were shipwrecked on San Lorenzo and assumed power over the natives. To unify the inhabitants and consolidate their power, they decided that Johnson should construct a new religion, Bokononism, convert the natives, and then McCabe would assume political power, outlaw it, and banish Johnson to the interior. It has worked. After McCabe's death, Papa Monzano became dictator but the same pseudo-war against Bokononists, now the religion of the entire island population, is still being waged. The struggle between politics and religion has brought a form of stability to the island. Bokononists believe that all religions, like their own, are nothing but lies, that there is a oneness of humanity not based on birth and affiliations, and that human love is experienced best by a ritualistic foot-touching ceremony called Boko-maru.

Jonah soon becomes a part of the island's affairs. He meets all of the prominent residents including father and son Castle, the fatally ill Papa Monzano, the luscious Mona, and Frank Hoenikker, who suggests that at Monzano's death Jonah marry Mona and become the island's new dictator.

Jonah consents. He later learns from the Hoenikkers that they owned slivers of ice-nine, but through misunderstandings each has given away a part of the cache—Newt to the Russians, Angela to the U.S. government, and Frank to Papa Monzano.

All the island notables gather at Monzano's fortress castle to witness an air show. In his chambers far from his guests, Monzano decides to end the pain of his disease by an ice-nine suicide. He consumes his particle and immediately becomes frozen in death. Unfortunately a fighter plane crashes into the castle and dislodges the contaminated body. It falls into the sea and immediately the destruction of the world begins. The sea begins to freeze and giant tornadoes encompass the earth.

Jonah and Mona find refuge in the castle's bomb shelter. In four days they emerge and while wandering in the countryside encounter a massive valley filled with the bodies of islanders, many in the attitude of Boko-maru. Under instructions from Bokonon, they believed god no longer needed them and committed suicide by placing some of the contaminated earth into their mouths. Before Jonah can intercede, Mona joins her people in a similar death.

Jonah is found by the only other survivors, little Newt, Frank, and the

Crosbys. Like pioneers, they start over and Jonah begins writing his book. One day Newt and Jonah come upon Bokonon sitting on a rock by the side of the road. He has just finished the final sentence of his scripture and with that, takes some ice-nine, thumbs his nose heavenward, and dies.

Thematic Material

The shortest book in Bokonon gospels is entitled "What can a thoughtful man hope for mankind on earth given the experience of the past million years?" The text reads "nothing." This admission that life is absurd, meaningless, and uncontrollable is paramount in Bokonon's (and thus Vonnegut's) thinking. Even the cat's cradle is a delusion, and human goodness seems always thwarted by thoughtlessness and cruelty. The book contains a warning that both spiritual and physical deaths face our planet unless we become more responsible for assuming moral choices. In this novel Vonnegut satirizes formalized institutions like religion and patriotism that obscure true values. He also shows that scientific solutions cannot help world problems and that indeed because of human weakness they can produce the ultimate apocalypse. The book asks that people be responsible for their own righteousness and destiny. At one point Jonah says, "Each one of us has to be what he or she is," and at another Ambassador Minton says, "Think of what paradise this earth would be if man were kind and wise."

Book Talk Material

An introduction to the Hoenikker family and ice-nine will interest readers. Some particular incidents are: Jonah's letter to Newt and its answer (pp. 14–21); ice-nine is explained (pp. 36–39); the newspaper introduction to San Lorenzo (pp. 59–60); and Jonah meets the Crosbys (pp. 86–88). Minton's speech against war is on pp. 169–171.

Additional Selections

In Michael Swanwick's *In the Drift* (pap., Ace, $2.95), a meltdown at a nuclear reactor causes a death zone in the United States.

Survivors of a nuclear attack display the best and worst in human nature in Pat Frank's novel *Alas, Babylon* (pap., Bantam, $3.50).

The far from ideal future we face is the subject of John Brunner's complex novel *Stand on Zanzibar* (Bentley, 1968, $16.50).

An excellent allegory set in a time when animals could speak is Walter

Wangerin, Jr.'s *The Book of the Dunn Cow* (Harper, 1978, $12.70; pap., Timescape, $2.50), as is George Orwell's novel about the political future of the world, *Animal Farm* (Harcourt, 1954, $10.95; pap., NAL, $2.95).

Men are brutes and the animals intelligent in Pierre Boulle's futuristic *Planet of the Apes* (Vanguard, 1963, $14.95; pap., NAL, $2.50).

In *A Clockwork Orange* (Norton, 1987, $14.95; pap., Ballantine, $2.25), Anthony Burgess creates a future world that violent teenagers dominate. Also use *The Clockwork Testament* (McGraw, 1984, $12.95, pap. $5.95).

Lovers of Vonnegut's black humor will also enjoy Joseph Heller's World War II novel *Catch 22* (Simon, 1961, $17.95; pap., Dell, $4.95) and John Irving's *The World According to Garp* (pap., Pocket, $4.95).

About the Book
Library Journal, March 15, 1963, p. 1180.

About the Author
Ethridge, James M., and Kopala, Barbara, eds. *Contemporary Authors* (First Revision). Detroit: Gale, 1967. Vols. 1–4, pp. 970–971.
Evory, Ann, ed. *Contemporary Authors* (New Revision Series). Detroit: Gale, 1981. Vol. 1, pp. 678–684.
Wakeman, John, ed. *World Authors 1950–1970.* New York: Wilson, 1975, pp. 1494–1496.

7

Adventure Stories

IN SHAKESPEARE'S *Othello,* Desdemona confesses that it was her husband's stories of his adventures and escapes that won her heart. Good suspenseful cliff-hangers are still potent ways of capturing readers. Here are examples by three old pros in the adult market—Crichton, Forsyth, and Higgins—plus two quality novels written specifically for young adults, one by Alexander and the other by Paulsen.

Alexander, Lloyd. *The El Dorado Adventure*
Dutton, 1987, $12.95

Readers first met the intrepid teenager Vesper Holly in *The Illyrian Adventure* (Dutton, 1986, $12.95; pap., Dell, $2.50), where, with her bumbling loyal guardian, the narrator Brinton Garrett, nicknamed Brinnie, she travels from her home in Philadelphia to Illyria, a tiny kingdom on the Adriatic, to continue an archaeological investigation begun by her deceased father, Dr. Benjamin Rittenhouse Holly. Instead Vesper and Brinton become involved in a revolutionary plot to murder the king, plus an exciting search for treasure. *The El Dorado Adventure* is the second in the series, and in the third, *The Drackenberg Adventure* (Dutton, 1988, $12.95), while attending the diamond jubilee of the grand duchess of Drackenberg, Brinnie's wife, Mary, is kidnapped, Vesper lives with a gypsy band, and a hitherto unknown DaVinci painting is rescued. These novels take place in the mid- to late 1870s, and in each Vesper and Brinton eventually confront their nemesis, the archvillain Dr. Helvitius. In addition to breathless adventure, each bubbles with sly humor, usually caused by the contrast between Vesper's straightforward, honest approach to situations and Brinnie's very proper convention-bound attitudes, which invariably lead to incorrect assumptions and conclusions. His formalized circumlocutions—he refers to a "cuspador" as "a

212

hygienic conconvience"—also add to the fun. These books are enjoyed by readers in grades 7 through 10.

Plot Summary

Seventeen-year-old Vesper Holly has inherited from her father a tract of land in the tiny Central American republic of El Dorado. Her land includes Ocotalpa, a supposedly extinct volcano, and a lake of tar. A mysterious telegram arrives at her house in Philadelphia signed by Alain de Rochefort urgently requesting that Vesper and her guardian Brinnie sail to El Dorado to tend to this real estate. Included is the fare for two ship tickets. Vesper notes with some apprehension that they are only for one-way passages.

After arriving in the capital city, Puerto Palmas, the two explore their environs. In a seedy waterfront cantina, they meet identical twins, Slider, a ship pilot, and Smiler, an engineer, who both work on the *Libertador*, a decrepit riverboat that plies the inland waters of Rio Culebra, El Dorado's main river. Soon they are joined by the ship captain and owner, Blazer O'Hara, and his raucous parrot Adelita. Blazer tells them that de Rochefort is a thorough scoundrel, a former engineer for de Lesseps at Suez, who now wants Vesper's land to build a similar canal in El Dorado. But this will destroy great stretches of arable land, driving the few remaining Indians, the Chiricas, from their homes into dispersal and probably annihilation, which means nothing to him.

When Vesper and Brinnie meet de Rochefort later that day, he appears, however, to be completely charming and honorable. This impression is unfortunately short-lived. On a rail trip to visit de Rochefort's jungle work camp, the two realize they are being kidnapped. Vesper breaks the carriage window and they escape into the jungle where they are eventually found by the crew of the *Libertador*. They travel upstream to deliver cargo to the only remaining Chirican village. Vesper is horrified to see that this involves a large shipment of guns and ammunition, which the Indians intend to use to protect their land against de Rochefort.

Vesper meets the Indian chief Acharro, a handsome, Cambridge-educated man in his midtwenties who also happens to be Blazer's son by a marriage to a native woman. ("Acharro" is the native's version of "O'Hara.") At the village she and Brinnie meet several of the Indian women, including Suncha and Ita, and learn about their customs and handicrafts. Vesper devises a plan to avoid the proposed battle which would only lead to a slaughter of the Indians. She suggests throwing enough tar-soaked torches down the volcano's crater to simulate an eminent eruption and force de Rochefort to abandon his construction site.

Vesper persuades Acharro to let her attend a meeting of the all-male council to unveil her scheme. Unfortunately the members shout her down, but she does convince Acharro to let her and Brinnie visit the volcano and test the feasibility of the plot. During this expedition they are once more captured by de Rochefort, who presents them to his boss and the real power behind the canal plot, the evil Dr. Helvitius, who has been able to blackmail de Rochefort into service by unearthing evidence of embezzlement to pay gambling debts. Now he plans to kill Vesper and to purchase her lands after her death to ensure the success of his canal project. However, Helvitius plans a cat-and-mouse game with his captives; Vesper is able to outwit him by setting fire to their prison, an ancient abandoned opera house in the jungle.

Brinnie and Vesper make a daring escape. They once again seek safety aboard the *Libertador,* but Helvitius and his gang of ruffians pursue them on their appropriately named yacht, the *Midas.* O'Hara's ship is boarded, and Helvitius, now out of patience, orders de Rochefort to shoot Brinnie and Vesper. He refuses, and though it might mean his own death, casts his lot with our heroine.

At that tense moment the Chirican women, who have witnessed the boarding from their canoes, silently creep up on Helvitius's men and attack them from behind with their paddles. The villains are forced back onto the *Midas,* and the *Libertador* gets under steam. The *Midas* gives chase and an earthquake hits, causing a tidal wave that swallows it but leaves the *Libertador* unharmed.

Back at the Indian village, there is general rejoicing. As a reward for her efforts, Vesper requests and receives permanent places on the council for the gallant women who effected their rescue. De Rochefort will stay behind to make a new life, and Vesper, her mission completed, gives her lands to the Indians. She and Brinnie return to Philadelphia where more adventures await her.

Thematic Material

This is basically a rollicking, high adventure novel of good versus evil, but it does have some serious underlying themes. The heroine, a women's libber before her time, continually refuses to compromise her beliefs in sexual equality, and fights to rectify the injustices that this form of discrimination brings. The novel also deals with the disgraceful Western exploitation of native populations for wealth. When most adventure novels feature males as central characters, it is refreshing to meet Vesper—intelligent, courageous, independent, and totally appealing.

Book Talk Material

Introduce the central characters, Vesper and Brinnie, to readers and then use one or more of these passages to develop the plot elements: they journey to El Dorado (pp. 3–9); Captain O'Hara talks about de Rochefort (pp. 22–28); the escape from the railroad car (pp. 36–41); the reunion with Dr. Helvitius (pp. 96–103); and two futile escape attempts from him (pp. 113–118, 121–126).

Additional Selections

In a Latin American dictatorship, Marta's family is placed in house arrest in *The Honorable Prison* by Lyll Becerra de Jenkins (Dutton, 1988, $14.95).

Fiction becomes reality when Sarah finds she is writing about marathons and also running for her life in Barbara Abercrombie's *Run for Your Life* (pap., Fawcett, $2.95).

Tracy and her punk boyfriend, while in Holland, get involved in drug smuggling in Lynne Reid Banks's *The Writing on the Wall* (Harper, 1984, $11.70).

For younger high school readers, Diana Shaw has written a series of mystery novels featuring a teenage girl, Carter Colburn, who is an amateur detective. Two in the series are *Gone Hollywood* (Little, 1988, $12.95) and *Lessons in Fear* (Little, 1987, $12.95).

Four teenagers try to cover up a hit and run accident in Lois Duncan's *I Know What You Did Last Summer* (Little, 1973, $12.45; pap., Archway, $2.75). Another excellent title by this popular writer is a thriller about a girl trapped by a family who has found the secret of eternal life in *Locked in Time* (Little, 1985, $12.95; pap., Dell, $2.95; condensed in *Juniorplots 3*, Bowker, 1987, pp. 125–129).

Two boys of different backgrounds become friends when they join forces to find a gang of dognappers in Thomas Baird's *Finding Fever* (Harper, 1982, $12.70).

In a takeoff on Sherlock Holmes, Inspector Mantis and his grasshopper helper solve entomological mysteries in William Kotzwinkle's *Trouble in Bugland* (pap., Godine, $9.95).

Sixteen-year-old Lucinda is isolated by her father when a young archaeologist arrives on their island in Scott O'Dell's *The Spanish Smile* (Houghton, 1982, $12.95; pap., Fawcett, $2.25). With the same heroine, use *The Castle in the Sea* (Houghton, 1982, $12.95; pap., Fawcett, $2.25).

About the Book
Booklist, April 1, 1987, p. 1202.
Bulletin of the Center for Children's Books, April 1987, p. 141.
Horn Book, May 1987, p. 369.
New York Times Book Review, June 7, 1987, p. 29.
School Library Journal, May 1987, p. 105.
See also *Book Review Digest*, 1987, pp. 24, 26, and *Book Review Index*, 1987, p. 13.

About the Author
Block, Ann, and Riley, Carolyn, eds. *Children's Literature Review*. Detroit: Gale, 1976. Vol. 2, pp. 11–18.
Commire, Anne, ed. *Something about the Author*. Detroit: Gale, 1972. Vol. 3, pp. 7–9.
de Montreville, Doris, and Hill, Donna, eds. *Third Book of Junior Authors*. New York: Wilson, 1972, pp. 6–7.
Ethridge, James M. *Contemporary Authors* (First Revision). Detroit: Gale, 1967. Vols. 1–4, p. 17.

Crichton, Michael. *Sphere*
Knopf, 1987, $17.95; pap., Ballantine, $4.95

Michael Crichton has successfully combined a fertile imagination with his scientific background (he is a medical doctor) to produce a series of thrillers that are often considered science fiction because, like *Sphere*, they may rely on a scientific background and application of scientific principles in the development of the plots. His first major success was with *The Andromeda Strain* (Knopf, 1969, $15.95; pap., Dell, $3.95), in which a contaminated capsule falls from space and kills the inhabitants of a Nevada town. Four scientists frantically adjourn to an underground laboratory in a race against time to find an antidote before the world's population is extinguished. In his second most popular book, a psychological thriller, *The Terminal Man* (Knopf, 1972, $13.50; pap., Avon, $3.50), the reader meets Harry Benson, computer expert and murder-minded sufferer of extreme paranoia who is subjected to a mind-controlling experiment in which a computer controls his behavior through wires in his brain. These novels are enjoyed by senior high students.

Plot Summary

When psychologist Norman Johnson receives a call from the U.S. Navy, he thinks he is once again being taken to the scene of an air disaster to help the survivors get over shock and feelings of guilt about living when others died. But this time he is taken in great secrecy to a spot in the South Pacific. There he learns of the Navy's amazing discovery; a spaceship has been found deep in the ocean, and the Navy believes that it may be from another civilization out in space.

An investigation team, which includes the Navy commander Harold Barnes, astrophysicist Ted Fielding, biochemist Beth Halpern, mathematician Harry Adams, Norman, and other Navy personnel, is sent to the ocean floor to spend a few days in the undersea quarters the Navy has erected near the spacecraft. The team is requested to enter the craft and find out what it is and where it is from.

Norman and the others almost immediately receive two surprises. First, when they approach what appears to be the entrance to the "alien" craft, not only does it look remarkably like the doorway of an "earth" airplane, but the instructions for opening it are written in English! Not long after entering the spaceship, they come upon their second surprise. The craft was built in 2043! The team theorizes that the spaceship was sent on a mission and entered a "black hole" and perhaps another universe in space, but on its return, the ship "overshot" itself and went too far into the past.

And yet another surprise is in store. The craft obviously found and picked up something in space, something alien. It is a perfect silver sphere, about 30 feet in diameter, with no features of any kind, just an intricate pattern cut into its surface. There is no entrance to the sphere.

Harry Adams, the mathematician, thinks the sphere is hollow and that something is inside. But despite their efforts, no one can find a way to open it . . . until Norman, watching television monitors in another part of the ship, sees the sphere open and close, and soon after sees Harry enter the sphere and the sphere closing behind him.

Harry reappears after three hours, saying he is fine but cannot remember what went on inside the sphere except that it was beautiful. Norman is skeptical, and worried.

In the meantime, what started out to be a short stay deep on the ocean floor has become a mission of several days. A fierce tropical storm has developed topside; the Navy has had to remove all surface craft from the area until it clears. Norman and the investigation team, plus a few Navy personnel, are left alone in their undersea home, although with adequate air and supplies for the next several days.

Norman's uneasiness about their situation slowly turns to real fear as strange things begin to happen. Where before the ocean floor surrounding the craft had been strangely free of all sea creatures, it is now suddenly teeming with thousands of foot-long squid. The squid are soon followed by thousands of shrimp, and then jellyfish. When one of the Navy personnel leaves their undersea lab to photograph the jellyfish, they attack and kill her.

Now the television monitor in their undersea quarters suddenly fills with numbers. From where?

The team decides that something or someone is trying to contact them. They "decode" the numbers and are able to contact this "thing," which communicates with them on the television screen, and says his name is "Jerry"!

Norman alone of the team thinks that "Jerry" might actually be a hostile alien. And he is proven all too right as member after member of the team and Navy personnel are killed in frightening ways. Until, with the storm still raging above them and no chance to escape, there are only three left: Beth, Harry, and Norman.

The alien tries to attack their undersea craft and threatens them in increasingly frightening ways. Finally, Beth and Norman conclude that the bizarre happenings are actually being caused by Harry, who alone of them had entered the sphere. They figure that after being in the sphere, Harry is now able to cause things to happen merely by willing them to occur or thinking of them, even though he is unaware of this power.

Beth and Norman keep Harry under sedation in order to prevent his "thoughts" from causing their deaths until they can rise to the surface. But the bizarre events go on, and Norman finds out that Beth, too, had entered the sphere. She now has this strange alien power as well.

To save his own life, Norman must find out what happens inside the sphere. He wills the sphere to open; it does and he enters an alien world that seems to be filled with dancing, luminous foam. It is beautiful and peaceful, and he is able to communicate with a presence; he asks whether the presence is God, to which he receives the reply "God is a word." Norman leaves the sphere, and he, too, now has the "power."

The storm above has cleared and Norman enters the escape sub to rise to the surface, intending to save his own life. But his conscience overcomes him and he returns for both Beth and Harry.

After a harrowing trip to the surface, the three must spend time in a decompression chamber before they will be required to tell of their ordeal. During that period, Beth, Harry, and Norman decide that the world is not ready for the kind of power that they possess, and so they decide that they must "will themselves" to forget this power. They do will themselves to forget the sphere; and it is forgotten.

By the time the three survivors are interviewed, all thoughts of the sphere and the magic power they had possessed are driven forever from their minds.

Thematic Material

A fine, "scary" thriller that is both undersea adventure and space fiction, *Sphere* is also a good study of people under pressure in strange environments and how they learn to work together for a common cause. Norman Johnson is portrayed as an intelligent, educated man who reacts with perfectly understandable fear and a sense of self-preservation when his life is threatened, but who also displays the admirable human quality of helping another in trouble when the need arises. The author includes some interesting, simplified explanations of such phenomena as "black holes" and theories of time travel.

Book Talk Material

Readers who enjoy space travel stories will be interested in the author's descriptions of the spaceship from 2043 and its possible mission. See: the team enters the spacecraft (pp. 65–75; pp. 73–80 pap.); Ted explains the space and time relationship to Norman (pp. 85–92; pp. 82–89 pap.); the team looks at "another universe" (pp. 103–105; pp. 100–102 pap.); they discover the sphere (pp. 106–108; pp. 102–104 pap.); the Anthropomorphic Problem (pp. 115–119; pp. 110–117 pap.); and the team makes contact with the alien (pp. 177–178, 189–191; pp. 180–182, 193–197 pap.).

Additional Selections

In William Katz's thriller *Face Maker* (McGraw, 1988, $16.95) a reporter discovers that her newly shaped plastic-surgeon face belongs to someone else.

In Michael Bishop's Nebula Award winner *No Enemy but Time* (pap., Pocket, $3.95) the hero, Joshua Kampa, spends time in the present and in prehistoric times with a band of hominoids.

In present-day New Mexico, contact is made with aliens on the star Vegas, which stirs a conflict between science and religion in Carl Sagan's *Contact* (Simon, 1985, $18.95; pap., Pocket, $4.95).

A woman on the run must establish a new identity in Brian Garfield's *Necessity* (St. Martin's, 1984, $13.95).

What originally is thought to be a killing epidemic is actually a fiendish plot in Robin Cook's thriller *Mortal Fear* (Putnam, 1988, $17.95). Also use his *Coma* (pap., NAL, $3.50), about a plot to kill hospital patients.

A group of Russians discovers a deadly virus and plans on spreading it in the United States in Elleston Trevor's *Death Watch* (Beaufort, 1984, $15.95; pap., Jove, $3.50).

Cartoon characters and live humans coexist in the humorous detective story *Who Censored Roger Rabbit?* (movie title, *Who Framed Roger Rabbit?*) by Gary Wolf (pap., Ballantine, $2.50).

In a particularly gory novel, James Herbert's *The Fog* (pap., NAL, $3.50), mysterious murders and suicides occur in London when a yellowish-green fog descends.

Vampire bats bring death and horror to Hopi Indians in Martin Cruz Smith's *Nightwing* (Hill, 1987, $9.95; pap., Jove, $3.95).

About the Book
Booklist, May 15, 1987, p. 1384.
Library Journal, July 1987, p. 93.
New York Times Book Review, July 12, 1987, p. 18.
See also *Book Review Digest*, 1987, pp. 401–402, and *Book Review Index*, 1987, p. 172.

About the Author
Metzger, Linda, ed. *Contemporary Authors* (New Revised Series.) Detroit: Gale, 1984. Vol. 13, pp. 127–133.
Riley, Carolyn, ed. *Contemporary Authors*. Detroit: Gale, 1971. Vols. 25–28, pp. 183–184.

Forsyth, Frederick.   *The Day of the Jackal*
pap., Bantam, $4.95

The Day of the Jackal, first published in 1971 and detailing a complicated assassination plot, was one of Forsyth's great successes. It has been
followed by a series of quality thrillers. One is *The Devil's Alternative*
(Viking, 1980, $12.95; pap., Bantam, $4.95), which weaves such threads
together as the assassination of the KGB chairman, a Russian security
agent spying for the British, a highjacked Swedish tanker, and a mysterious man found in the ocean off the coast of Turkey. Another is *The
Odessa File* (pap., Bantam, $4.50), in which a young German reporter
infiltrates an organization of former Nazi S.S. members in his pursuit of
the Butcher of Riga, the infamous Commandant Roschmann. These
novels are enjoyed by senior high school readers.

Plot Summary

It is 1963, and Charles de Gaulle has taken France out of Algeria.
Although many of the French are displeased with the general's decision
to withdraw, none is so enraged as the fanatical right-wing Secret Army
Organization, sworn to a man to kill de Gaulle and bring down his
government. In their eyes, the withdrawal of their beloved country from
what they consider their territory has brought disgrace and dishonor to
France. De Gaulle must be assassinated.

However, in six attempts, the organization has not been able to accomplish their objective. Now they seek outside help. They contact a professional killer-for-hire, who is unknown to the French police. When the
blond, gray-eyed Englishman meets three of their leaders in Vienna, his
creed is contained in these words: "A professional does not act out of
fervour and is therefore more calm and less likely to make elementary
errors."

The code name of the killer is Jackal. For $500,000, he demands total
secrecy, even from his employers, and gives them a promise that their
objective will be met.

And so begins the hair-raising, step-by-step anatomy of an assassination, made not one whit less exciting by the reader's knowledge that
President Charles de Gaulle died later of natural causes, not an assassin's
bullet.

Part of the excitement, and almost admiration, comes from the exacting methods of the killer-for-hire. His plan is meticulous and excruciating in its detail. The reader is swept along as the Jackal methodically goes about his business of forging identification papers, falsifying passports, giving himself alternate identities, and most important, perhaps, building for himself a collapsible, powerful, incredibly accurate rifle, with its specially made bullet. Finally, the Jackal plans his approach to the time and place where he knows the general will be, and will be assassinated. No one stands in the Jackal's way; without regard for life and totally without compassion, he leaves no trace of person or thing as he prepares for his work.

What can stand in the way of this finely tuned professional? Almost laughably, his only opposition seems to be a rather short, rumpled French policeman, Deputy Commissaire Claude Lebel. He is given police assistance from as far away as the United States and from all over Europe, and much support from within his own country where he is highly regarded.

And yet how can even the best of detectives track down a killer about whom he knows absolutely nothing? In fact, what has he to go on? There is no crime—not yet; only the word that an attempt will be made on the general's life. There are no clues, no witnesses—to what? He has nothing, just a code name.

But in his own way, Lebel is as professional as the Jackal, and certainly as methodical. After he reasons that the attempt on the president's life will be made by a foreigner rather than a Frenchman, he begins his hunt by contacting all the top crime officials in the United States and Europe, swearing them to secrecy and asking them to search their files for a political assassin with several successful kills. And from this flimsy beginning follows one of the most fascinating hunts—by both hired killer and dogged detective—in modern-day fiction.

As the assassin completes his plans and nears his destination, the French detective ever so slowly amasses clues. The offhand thought of a young inspector at Scotland Yard that perhaps so professional a killer, if English, would operate only outside the country leads to England's Foreign Office. And that leads to the remembrance of an extraordinary assassination by a killer rumored to have been English . . . and so it goes.

Through painstaking sifting of the smallest clues, Lebel tracks the unknown killer until he learns his code name and that he is inside France. The Jackal himself realizes how much the authorities know of him as well; perhaps it just makes the task more exciting.

Eventually the chase comes down to Sunday, August 25, 1963. The Jackal stands before a window on the sixth floor of a house that looks down onto a square where President Charles de Gaulle is about to bestow medals on deserving veterans. As the Jackal squints down the telescopic sight and slowly pulls the trigger, the French president does something that no Englishman—even the Jackal—would first think of; de Gaulle stoops to kiss the veteran on both cheeks. The bullet barely misses; but it does miss.

The Jackal is astonished at his error. But the few seconds it takes to reload the rifle gives Lebel the time he needs to break into the room. The two men acknowledge each other by name. But this time the detective is faster.

The next day the body of an unknown man is buried in a Paris cemetery. The death certificate states that a foreign tourist was the victim of a hit-and-run accident.

"The day of the Jackal was over."

Thematic Material

Frederick Forsyth has written an edge-of-your-seat thriller with all the elements of good detective/spy fiction. It has great adventure, fascinating details of deception and master planning, believable characterizations, a background of history to add the authenticity that is needed to build its suspense, and a breath-stopping ending that makes the reader want to tell President de Gaulle to "watch out" or detective Lebel to "hurry up!"

Book Talk Material

The Jackal's beginning preparations and the detective's beginning search are good introductions to this work; see the Englishman sets the terms (pp. 39–50) and Lebel begins his seemingly hopeless manhunt (pp. 190–196, 211–219). Readers who enjoy knowing the details behind an intricate plot will especially be interested in how the Jackal goes about obtaining a weapon and a disguise (see pp. 54–63, 64–80).

Additional Selections

In Geoffrey Household's *Rogue Male* (pap., Penguin, $3.95) a well-bred Englishman hunts a European dictator but in time he becomes the hunted. Also use: *Rogue Justice* (pap., Penguin, $3.95) and *Watcher in the Shadows* (Ian Henry, 1985, $20.00).

Since the death of Ian Fleming, John Gardner has continued the

James Bond series. Two of the later ones are *No Deals, Mr. Bond* (Putnam, 1987, $12.95) and *Scorpius* (Putnam, 1988, $12.95).

In *The Charm School* (Warner, 1988, $17.95), Nelson DeMille has written a first-rate thriller about Russian spies infiltrating the United States.

During World War II, prisoner of war Colonel Joseph Ryan plans on hijacking a train to escape in David Westheimer's *Von Ryan's Express* (pap., NAL, $3.50).

A top-ranking KGB official tells his true story in Stanislav Levchenko's *On the Wrong Side* (Pergamon, 1988, $18.95).

Eric Ambler is an old-time master of the novel of suspense. Two of his classics are *A Coffin for Dimitrios* (Amereon, 1937, $15.95; pap., Berkley, $2.95) and *Journey into Fear* (pap., Berkley, $2.95).

In *Eye of the Needle* by Ken Follett (Arbor, 1978, $17.95; pap., NAL, $4.50), a Nazi spy threatens a young couple on an isolated Scottish island. Also use Follett's *The Key to Rebecca* (Morrow, 1980, $12.95; pap., NAL, $4.50).

About the Book
Booklist, September 15, 1971, p. 82.
Library Journal, September 1, 1971, p. 2669.
New York Times Book Review, August 15, 1971, p. 3.
See also *Book Review Digest*, 1971, pp. 441–442, and *Book Review Index*, 1971, p. 163.

About the Author
Colby, Vineta, ed. *World Authors 1975–1980.* New York: Wilson, 1985, pp. 242–244.
Locher, Frances Carol, ed. *Contemporary Authors.* Detroit: Gale, 1980. Vols. 85–88, pp. 180–181.

Higgins, Jack. *Solo*
pap., Dell, $3.50

Solo, first published in 1980, uses contemporary settings and is a suspenseful cat-and-mouse yarn about a hired assassin, the "man from Crete," aka John Mikali, a brilliant concert pianist, and his nemesis, the tough Welshman and terrorist hunter Morgan. Several of Jack Higgins's successful works have a World War II background. One of these is *The Eagle Has Landed* (pap., Bantam, $3.95), in which a small force of crack

German paratroopers lands on the coast of England in November 1943; their assignment is to kidnap Winston Churchill, who is weekending in a country house nearby. These novels are enjoyed by senior high readers.

Plot Summary

John Mikali is a famed concert pianist; his talents on occasion almost reach perfection. He is also nearly perfect in his other profession; Mikali is an assassin, a fact known only to a lawyer named DeVille. But when Mikali takes on the assassination of a wealthy Londoner, he writes the beginning of his own destruction. For in fleeing the police, Mikali accidentally runs down and kills a young girl on a bicycle. The girl is the daughter of Colonel Asa Morgan, the soldier's soldier, the ultimate military man, a man so enraptured with the thrill of the fight that his wife, feeling she could not compete, left him years before and took their daughter with him.

Morgan vows to find the assassin, known as the Cretan lover for his attraction to women and for his accent. (Mikali is actually from the Greek island of Crete and at the time of the assassination deliberately spoke in the accent of his long-ago homeland to send the police on a merry chase.)

Against the warnings of the British intelligence agencies, Morgan sets out to track down the mysterious Cretan lover. He has few clues to the murderer's identity, but his pursuit is relentless, bringing him in contact with terrorists of all kinds. He also meets Dr. Katherine Riley, an American in London and an expert on terrorism. They are attracted to each other, although Katherine deplores his relentless pursuit of the man who ran down his daughter.

In a strange twist of fate, and unbeknownst to Morgan, Katherine Riley also has another admirer, John Mikali. She finds herself attracted to both men. Unwittingly, as Morgan confides more and more of the details of his pursuit to Katherine, she makes Mikali aware that he is being pursued and by whom.

Putting clues and circumstances together, Morgan at last has reason to suspect that the killer he seeks is the renowned pianist. Eluding the British agents in hot pursuit, Morgan goes to the Greek island of Hydra, Mikali's hideaway home. There he discovers the true nature of the relationship between Katherine and the man he seeks. He also comes face to face with Mikali and is shot by the assassin, who believes he has killed Morgan.

Instead, Morgan's wounds are tended by an old Greek couple on the island, and when Katherine discovers he is there, she begins to believe that the quarry he seeks may actually be one of the men she loves.

Safe in his belief that Morgan is dead, Mikali returns to London for a special concert. And, against Morgan's wishes, Katherine informs the British intelligence community that Morgan is planning to confront the assassin at the concert hall. When Morgan returns to London, the British put him in "protective custody" until after the performance and surround the concert hall, planning to take Mikali when his concert is over. But Morgan escapes and waits in the wings, where he is seen by a shocked Mikali during the performance.

At the end of his repertoire, Mikali realizes there is no escape, not from the British, who have all exits guarded, nor from Morgan. He goes to a deserted concert room and begins to play, his gun in full view on the piano. Katherine enters, followed shortly by Morgan. When Mikali picks up the gun, Morgan kills him instantly, only to discover that the Cretan lover's gun was empty. He had chosen that way to die.

Morgan runs after Katherine, but she has disappeared in the darkness of a London park.

Thematic Material

This is a nonstop, roller-coaster adventure story, with all the exciting elements of the daring killer being tracked by the relentless pursuer, set against the backdrop of the wealthy in the famed cities of Europe and the beauty of the Greek isles. It is both a fast-paced action thriller and a look into the precarious life of the assassin for hire.

Book Talk Material

Mikali's "hit" in London is a good introduction to the action pace in this book (see pp. 12–14). The reader might also like to contrast the "other side" of this elegant artist and paid killer. See: after the hit, Mikali prepares for his concert (pp. 14–16); he "romances" a young maid just before a killing (pp. 58–61); and Mikali's relationship with Katherine (pp. 109–111).

Additional Selections

Another master of the thriller is Robert Ludlum. Arab terrorists and a handsome fearless hero are components of *The Icarus Agenda* (Random, 1988, $19.95). Two others are *The Rhineman Exchange* (pap., Dell, $4.95) and *The Bourne Identity* (pap., Bantam, $4.95).

A sunken Russian submarine, kidnapped diplomats, and a Roman treasure are ingredients in Clive Cussler's thriller *Treasure* (Simon, 1988, $18.95). Cussler's *Raise the Titanic* (pap., Bantam, $4.50) is a thriller about recovering the riches of the sunken liner.

A five-man British army team is chosen to silence *The Guns of Navarone* (pap., Fawcett, $2.95) by Alistair MacLean. MacLean has more than 20 other adventure stories in print. Two others are *Ice Station Zebra* (pap., Fawcett, $2.95) and *Force 10 from Navarone* (pap., Fawcett, $2.95).

Friendship and courage are themes in Len Deighton's novel about World War II fighter pilots, *Goodbye Mickey Mouse* (Knopf, 1982, $14.95; pap., Ballantine, $3.95). Two of his other best-sellers are *The Ipcress File* (pap., Ballantine, $3.95) and *The Berlin Game* (Knopf, 1984, $15.95; pap., Ballantine, $4.50).

For better readers, Graham Greene's novel *The Human Factor* (Viking, 1983, $20.95; pap., Avon, $2.95) tells about a mysterious lack of information in the British Secret Service, and in *The Little Drummer Girl* by John Le Carré (Knopf, 1983, $15.95; pap., Bantam, $4.95) we are introduced to terrorism in Israel and an illicit Palestinian organization.

About the Book
Booklist, June 15, 1980, p. 1491.
Library Journal, June 1, 1980, p. 1331.
See also *Book Review Index,* 1980, p. 395 (under Patterson, Henry).

About the Author
Kinsman, Clare D., ed. *Contemporary Authors* (First Revision). Detroit: Gale, 1975.
   Vols. 13–16, pp. 624–625 (under Patterson, Henry).

Paulsen, Gary. *Hatchet*
   Bradbury, 1987, $12.95

In his many books for young people and adults, Gary Paulsen's love of nature and the outdoors is often apparent. This love is also demonstrated in his favorite hobby, raising and training sled dogs. His 1985 title *Dogsong* (Bradbury, 1985, $11.95; pap., Penguin, $3.95), like *Hatchet,* is also a survival story and tells of a 14-year-old Eskimo boy and his 1,400 mile journey across the plains. In *Tracker* (Bradbury, 1984, $10.95; pap., Penguin, $3.95) a solitary deer hunt through the Minnesota wilderness helps

13-year-old John to accept the news of his beloved grandfather's approaching death. *The Island* (Watts, 1988, $13.95), in which a 15-year-old boy finds his own private island, is a quiet evocation of the beauty of the wilderness. *Hatchet* is suitable for readers in both junior and senior high school grades.

Plot Summary

Brian Robeson, age 13, thinks the hatchet his mother gives him for his scout belt is a little hokey, but he doesn't say so. He doesn't say much of anything to her, as he gets ready to leave to stay with his father for the summer in the Canadian north woods.

Brian's mother and father have just divorced—at his mother's insistence—and Brian is to spend summers with his father, a mechanical engineer who is working in the oil fields. Besides the heartache of the divorce, Brian is angry with his mother because he has found out The Secret. Unbeknownst to her, Brian saw his mother and a man (not his father) kissing in a station wagon. So he knows why she wanted the divorce; he knows The Secret. And he can't wait to tell his father.

Brian is flying north to his father from a small airport in New York State. He is the only passenger in the Cessna, and the pilot is taking Brian and some equipment his father needs into the north woods.

Despite the hurt and anger of the divorce, Brian is looking forward to seeing his father and is excited about his first ride in a plane. The pilot even tells him something about the controls and lets him "fly" for a few minutes.

Then, to Brian's horror and disbelief, the unthinkable happens. The pilot suddenly has a heart attack, and apparently dies. Brian is left alone, thousands of feet in the air, without any idea of where he is or how to fly the plane.

The plane crashes in a lake, and Brian survives. But the plane sinks, and with it the survival gear. Brian is left with nothing but the clothes he is wearing, and his hatchet.

So begins the struggle of Brian's 54 days in the wilderness. At first, this unskilled, panic-stricken city boy has no idea how to begin to survive. Initially, he can think only that a rescue party will soon come for him. It is only later that he remembers that when the pilot had the heart attack, the plane lurched off course, and Brian has no idea how far they strayed from the original flight plan.

But slowly the will to live begins to surface in the young boy. With drinking water from the lake, he now starts to search for food, at first finding only berries, which make him sick, and eventually learning how to catch fish from the lake, and much later, birds in the woods.

Brian fashions a shelter for himself under a rock ledge, which one night is invaded by a porcupine that injures Brian's leg. Finally, he learns how to fashion a campfire for himself, which keeps away the animals, and cooks his food.

When one day Brian hears the drone of a plane engine, he thinks he is about to be rescued. But when the plane flies off without seeing him, he plunges into great despair, to the point where one night he tries to cut himself with his hatchet, hoping he will die.

Brian regards that night as the time of his rebirth into the new Brian. No matter what it takes, no matter what happens, he will not give in. Brian will survive.

But disaster strikes again, this time in the form of a tornado, which whips across the lake, ruining his shelter and scattering his meager possessions. He very nearly knows once again the panic he felt earlier.

But the next morning, Brian sees that the heavy winds have dislodged the plane somewhat so that the tail is now sticking up out of the water. Trying to put the body of the pilot, still lodged in the plane, out of his mind, Brian remembers the survival kit stored somewhere in the tail of the plane. He must get it.

This is easier said than done, for he must build a raft to reach the plane, and when he does he can find no way to get inside. Using his hatchet, he chops away at the flimsy covering and eventually is able to get inside and locate the survival kit . . . trying all the while not to see what the fish have done to the head of the pilot.

The survival kit is like Christmas Day to Brian—a sleeping bag, freeze-dried food, pots and pans, a lighter, even a transmitter!

In his thrill at finding food, Brian only momentarily fiddles with the transmitter, but cannot seem to make it work. Thinking it has been damaged in the crash, he puts it aside.

Just as Brian is settling down to his first "home cooked" meal in 54 days, he is astonished to see a plane appearing. It lands on the lake; a pilot jumps out and says he heard the emergency transmitter. Brian is rescued.

After Brian's ordeal, he is a celebrity for a few days, and in their joy at having him alive, his parents almost seem as though they will get back together . . . almost. But things soon return to normal, except that Brian is forever changed. Not just that his body has become lean and wiry, not just that all kinds of food are still a wonder to him, not just that he becomes more thoughtful, or that he has quiet reflective times about his period of survival, but Brian knows that he has come of age; he is tough now, tough where it counts—in the head.

And although he thinks about it, Brian never tells his father about The Secret.

Thematic Material

This is a realistic story of strength, toughness, survival, and a boy's growing up in almost impossible conditions. Brian is a likable boy who, when faced with true terror and almost insurmountable odds, finds strength and courage within himself, although he at times almost gives in to despair. It is also an exciting picture of survival in the wilderness and how the small, seemingly inconsequential lessons learned in some almost forgotten classroom can make the difference between survival and death.

Book Talk Material

The ways in which Brian tries to reason out his problems and struggles to remember techniques of survival are a good introduction to this tale. See: Brian tries to land the plane (pp. 13–25); should he drink the lake water? (pp. 43–45); the search for berries (pp. 60–66); building a fire (pp. 84–86); and the first plane brings despair (pp. 115–118).

Additional Selections

A now-classic story of survival is Jean Craighead George's *Julie of the Wolves* (Harper, 1972, $12.70, pap. $2.50; condensed in *More Juniorplots*, Bowker, 1977, pp. 213–217), which tells of Miyox's lonely trek across 300 miles of Alaskan wilderness.

Theo and two unlikely companions share an adventure-filled trip to Tibet in Peter Dickinson's *Tulku* (pap., Ace, $2.25).

Howie and Laura must struggle to survive when their fellow campers leave them naked and alone on an island in Brock Cole's *The Goats* (Farrar, 1987, $11.95).

Jack McCaskill's fourteenth summer is enlivened by a forest fire in Montana's wilderness, an alcoholic ex-forest ranger, and an older brother with personal problems in Ivan Doig's *English Creek* (Atheneum, 1984, $15.95; pap., Penguin, $6.95).

Three motorcycles threaten 18-year-old Laura and a group of backpackers in P. J. Petersen's *Nobody Else Can Walk It for You* (Delacorte, 1982, $13.95; pap., Dell, $2.95).

After a prank causes the death of a fellow student, four students try to hide their guilt in Jim Murphy's *Death Run* (Clarion, 1982, $11.95).

In Farley Mowat's *Lost in the Barrens* (Little, 1956, $14.45; pap., Bantam, $2.95), two boys are lost in Canada's barren northlands.

Two very different boys set out for help after a plane crash in Arthur Roth's *Two for Survival* (pap., Avon, $1.95).

A writer of adult adventures is Ernest K. Gans, whose *The Aviator* (Arbor, 1981, $12.95; pap., Ballantine, $2.95) is a tale of flying and survival set in the United States of 1929. Also use his *Fate Is the Hunter* (pap., Simon, $9.95).

About the Book
Booklist, November 15, 1987, p. 572.
Bulletin of the Center for Children's Books, December 1987, p. 73.
Horn Book, March 1988, p. 210.
School Library Journal, December 1987, p. 103.
VOYA, February 1988, p. 283.
See also *Book Review Digest*, 1988, and *Book Review Index*, 1988.

About the Author
Commire, Anne, ed. *Something about the Author*. Detroit: Gale, 1981. Vol. 22, pp. 192–193.
Locher, Frances Carol, ed. *Contemporary Authors*. Detroit: Gale, 1978. Vols. 73–76, pp. 489–490.

8

Suspense and Mystery

TEENAGERS, like their parents, enjoy a good scare and a puzzler. Here are one classic in the field by Daphne du Maurier and two by relative newcomers Mary Higgins Clark and Ruth Rendell. Dick Francis, as usual, competently combines sports and murder, and Avi supplies a more easily read novel written directly for young adults.

Avi. *Wolf Rider: A Tale of Terror*
Bradbury, 1986, $12.95

Avi's first books for young people began appearing in the mid-1970s. Since then he has had a string of successes including such novels as *Sometimes I Think I Hear My Name* (Pantheon, 1982, $9.95; pap., NAL, $3.50), in which 13-year-old Conrad runs away from his home in St. Louis to track down his divorced parents in New York City, and *A Place Called Ugly* (Pantheon, 1981, $8.99; pap., Scholastic, $1.95), a novel on environmental conservation in which 14-year-old Owen refuses to leave his family's beach cabin. *Wolf Rider* is popular with readers in grades 7 through 10.

Plot Summary

Fifteen-year-old Andy Zadinski and his father, who teaches at the local college, have just moved into a new apartment, about a year following the death of Andy's mother. On the evening of the day their new phone is installed, Andy takes a call as he is on the way out with his friend Paul. A voice on the other end says, "I just killed someone."

While Andy gets Paul to go out to alert the police so that they may be able to trace the call, the stranger tells Andy that his name is Zeke and that he has just killed a student at the college, a girl named Nina Klemmer. He also says that he just happened to dial Andy's number because he needed someone to talk to.

Andy thinks the phone call is serious, but the police, although praising Andy for his alert thinking, regard it as a crank call or as one of Andy's friends pulling a prank. And when Andy tells his father about the incident the next day, Dr. Zadinski agrees with the police and tells Andy to forget about it.

But Andy can't forget. Annoyed that no one takes this seriously, he decides to go out to the college to see if a student named Nina Klemmer exists and if she is alive.

Nina Klemmer does exist and she is very much alive. Again, Andy informs the police and says that he believes the strange man named Zeke means to kill her. The police politely but firmly tell him to forget about it. So does Andy's father.

But Andy cannot let go. This time he goes out to the college and confronts Nina, telling her of the strange call. Instead of believing him, she threatens to call the police if he does not stop harassing her.

The police and Andy's father find out what he has done, and Andy finds himself in the office of the school counselor, Mrs. Baskin. She wants him to meet with her regularly. Mrs. Baskin believes, as does Andy's father, that his emotional involvement in this strange incident is the result of the turmoil he still feels after the death of his mother, which followed other deaths of close relatives in the family. Mrs. Baskin reminds Andy of the story of the young sheepherder who cried wolf when no wolf was about, and then when a wolf did threaten the flock, no one would come to his rescue.

But Andy is absolutely convinced that he is right about Zeke. Then he gets the idea that perhaps Zeke is a member of his father's department at the college. He remembers that his father took their new phone number to work with him that morning to give to the department secretary. However, he forgot about it until he was at a school meeting that evening—the evening of the phone call from Zeke. Right after the meeting, Dr. Zadinski dropped the phone number on the secretary's desk. Someone from the department might very well have seen it and made the phone call, Andy reasons.

Andy phones all the department members until he gets Dr. Lucas, his father's colleague and long-time friend, on the line. From the moment Lucas says hello, Andy recognizes him as Zeke.

When Andy tells his father what he has learned, his father is furious. Declaring that Andy is far more disturbed emotionally than he suspected, his father decides that Andy will leave school early—it is near the end of the term—and spend the summer in the South with his aunt for a change of scene. He is to leave in a few days.

Andy realizes that he must prove that Dr. Lucas is Zeke before he leaves or no one will ever believe him. So he begins to make calls to Lucas, saying that he knows his identity and telling Lucas that Nina wants to meet him. Andy thinks that if Lucas confronts her, she will believe that Andy was telling the truth and vindicate him.

Andy tells Lucas that Nina wants to meet him after an evening class. But he reckons without Zeke's cleverness. While Andy is waiting in the bushes, Lucas sneaks up on him and sticks a knife in his back, ordering him into the car.

Lucas drives up into the mountains, telling Andy that he fully intends to murder Nina because she will not go out with him; he also says that he is thinking of killing Andy.

When the car stops, Andy tries to get away, breaking Lucas's glasses as he dives out of the car. The car rolls forward and crashes. As Andy runs away he picks up something glittering on the ground. It is Lucas's cufflink, which Andy unthinkingly puts in his pocket.

Later, when Andy's father takes him to the airport, after going back into the apartment to get his son's baseball glove, Dr. Zadinski tells him that Lucas is dead, and from the elaborate steps he took to disguise his whereabouts on the night he died, the police believe it to be suicide. But Andy realizes that Lucas was protecting himself because he intended to murder Andy.

As Andy leaves his father for the summer, he decides not to tell him the story of what happened. He reasons that his father would be too hurt if he found out the truth; better that he think his friend has committed suicide.

As Dr. Zadinski leaves the airport, he takes the cufflink he found in his son's room from his pocket and drops it in the trash. It is wet with his tears.

Thematic Material

This is a fast-paced thriller. Andy is presented as an average, likable teenager who is, perhaps, a little more sensitive to people's emotions due to the fairly recent death of his mother and others in his family. His relationship with his father is warm and true, and both characters are believable as they struggle to deal with Andy's growing obsession. However, the true sadness in the tale is that both father and son decide not to communicate fully, for now each will bear a secret forever and the closeness between the two will never be the same.

Book Talk Material

How Andy reacts to the phone call and how he struggles to vindicate himself and convince others that he is telling the truth are good beginnings to a discussion of how such a situation could best be handled. Did Andy overreact? How else could he have convinced others that he was right? What would you have done? See: the phone call (pp. 1–9); Andy tells his father (pp. 15–21); Andy finds Nina (pp. 24–26); Andy talks to the police (pp. 41–46); and Andy discovers Lucas (pp. 91–93).

Additional Selections

Jay Bennett has written many excellent junior mysteries. In *The Dangling Witness* (pap., Dell, $1.95) an organized crime ring threatens a 17-year-old after he witnesses a murder.

The Outsider, an evil monster, stalks Travis's dog, a golden retriever, in Dean R. Koontz's *Watchers* (Putnam, 1987, $17.95).

Strange deadly happenings occur to Mary Elizabeth Rafferty at the health club where she works in Joan Lowery Nixon's *The Dark and Deadly Pool* (Delacorte, 1987, $17.95).

A boy genius meets himself at various other ages, and together "they" solve a puzzling mystery in Jane Louise Curry's *Me, Myself and I* (McElderry, 1987, $12.95).

Ready or Not: Here Come 14 Frightening Stories (Greenwillow, 1987, $11.75) is a bone-chilling anthology edited by Joan Kahn.

Hillary witnesses a kidnapping but no one will believe her in Nina Bowden's *Devil By the Sea* (Lippincott, 1976, $12.70; pap., Avon, $1.95), and high school junior Sean Prince finds himself in a similar position in Laurence Yep's *Liar, Liar* (Morrow, 1983, $10.25; pap., Avon, $2.50; condensed in *Juniorplots 3*, Bowker 1987, pp. 156–160).

What starts as a harmless excursion into the occult becomes a case of multiple murders for a group of girls in Joan Lowery Nixon's *The Séance* (Harcourt, 1982, $12.95; pap., Dell, $2.75; condensed in *Juniorplots 3*, Bowker, 1987, pp. 141–145).

Judith St. George's *Do You See What I See?* (Putnam, 1982, $9.95; pap., NAL, $1.95) is a murder mystery set on Cape Cod with a teenager as sleuth.

For older readers, two boys find friendship through learning magic, but this soon becomes a frightening experience in Peter Strand's *Shadowland* (pap., Berkley, $4.95).

About the Book
Book Report, May 1987, p. 35.
Bulletin of the Center for Children's Books, December 1986, p. 61.
School Library Journal, December 1986, p. 111; March 1987, p. 120.
VOYA, October 1987, p. 165.
See also *Book Review Index,* 1987, p. 38.

About the Author
Bowden, Jane, ed. *Contemporary Authors.* Detroit: Gale, 1978. Vols. 69–72, pp. 621–622.
Commire, Anne, ed. *Something about the Author.* Detroit: Gale, 1978. Vol. 14, pp. 269–270 (under Wortis, Avi).
Holtze, Sally Holmes, ed. *Fifth Book of Junior Authors and Illustrators.* New York: Wilson, 1982, pp. 15, 16.
Metzger, Linda, ed. *Contemporary Authors* (New Revision Series). Detroit: Gale, 1984. Vol. 12, pp. 517–518 (under Wortis, Avi).

Clark, Mary Higgins. *Weep No More, My Lady*
Simon, 1987, $17.95; pap., Dell, $4.95

One of Mary Higgins Clark's earliest mysteries first appeared in 1975 and was entitled *Where Are the Children?* (pap., Dell, $3.95). In it Nancy Eldridge was almost convicted of the deaths of her two children some years before. Now she has remarried and again has two children. When they vanish mysteriously the finger of guilt again points to her and in the course of unraveling the plot the author reveals solutions to both crimes. This situation is typical of Clark's work, where in taut, suspenseful stories, the present is often used to solve mysteries of the past. In another example, *Stillwatch* (Simon, 1984, $14.95; pap., Dell, $4.50), television reporter Patricia Traymore finds herself in deadly danger as her investigations of a possible vice-presidential candidate uncover secrets involving the shooting of her parents years before. All of the novels are enjoyed by good senior high school readers.

Plot Summary

The beautiful Leila LaSalle, famous stage and screen star and beloved sister of Elizabeth Lange, herself an actress, is dead. And charged with her murder is Ted Winters, handsome, wealthy, and Leila's lover. Elizabeth, subconsciously herself in love with Ted, will be the star witness for the prosecution. Leila's body, claims the state, was thrown from the balcony of her New York penthouse apartment. It is Elizabeth, via a phone call at the time of her sister's death, who can place Ted Winters in the apartment. Although Ted denies he killed Leila, he admits to being drunk and cannot remember the events of that tragic evening.

Hiding her personal feelings for Ted, Elizabeth is determined to make him pay for the death of her beloved sister. But several days before the trial is to begin, Elizabeth receives a call from her and Leila's old friend, Baroness Minna von Schreiber, who with her husband, Baron Helmut von Schreiber, own and operate the luxurious Cypress Point Spa, a health resort situated on the beautiful California coast that caters to the rich and famous. Min persuades Elizabeth to fly out to the spa to spend a few days relaxing before she must endure the tensions of the trial.

Against the prosecuting attorney's wishes, Elizabeth flies to California and almost immediately regrets her decision. For Min did not tell her that many of Leila's old "friends and acquaintances" would also be there, among them Ted Winters himself, who with his longtime friend and business associate Craig Babcock and Henry Bartlett, Ted's lawyer, are spending a few days at the spa trying to come up with the best possible defense for Ted.

Much to Elizabeth's distress, the other guests include Cheryl Manning, the beautiful actress who kept losing parts to Leila and who should benefit from her death, and Leila's former agent, Syd Melnick, a man Leila once humiliated and fired and who now sees Cheryl Manning as a last chance at the big time. He would have wanted Leila dead, too.

Also at the spa is someone who had no connection with Leila's death. She is Alvirah Meehan from the borough of Queens in New York City, winner of millions in the state lottery, who has come to the famous spa to spend some time in the lap of luxury. Unbeknownst to Elizabeth and the other guests, and to the baron and baroness, Alvirah is an avid and knowledgeable movie fan who is "bugged" to record conversations of the rich and famous in order to write an article for a magazine once she returns home.

Furious at being tricked into going to the spa and having to see these people, Elizabeth intends to return immediately to New York. However, she decides to wait for the return of Sammy, the elderly woman she has known for years and who works for Min and Helmut. Sammy sent Elizabeth a message that she must see her, and she is due back to the spa the next day.

Sammy does return, but before Elizabeth has a chance to talk to her, Sammy is murdered. Elizabeth learns that Sammy had discovered the poison pen letters that were being sent to Leila, who, largely due to her childhood, had very little faith and trust in men during her lifetime. The letters indicated that Ted Winters was in love with someone else, a fact Ted vehemently denies. Ted does, however, admit to himself that his affair with Leila was at its end before her death, that he could no longer live with her constant accusations and tantrums. Did he truly murder her? He cannot remember.

After Sammy's death and with the help of Scott, the sheriff, Elizabeth tries to piece together the facts relating to Leila's murder. Little by little she allows herself to admit that Ted might not be guilty, even though she is absolutely certain she talked to him on the phone in Leila's apartment and heard them quarreling shortly before her death. But the others at the spa have motives, too, even the baron and baroness, who Elizabeth discovers are in financial trouble with their multimillion-dollar operation.

Elizabeth, who nightly takes a swim in the spa pool for relaxation, feels she is being watched. She is about to return to New York when another tragedy occurs. Alvirah Meehan is nearly murdered, from what seems like an injection of insulin, and lies in a coma. Elizabeth finds Alvirah's tapes and realizes what she has been doing.

Against Scott's wishes, Elizabeth decides to set a trap for her sister's murderer, who she now believes is not Ted. And, indeed, as she swims alone in the darkness, Elizabeth is attacked by someone at the bottom of the pool wearing scuba equipment. At the last possible moment she is rescued by the sheriff and Ted, and the real killer is uncovered as Craig Babcock. This longtime devoted friend, who knew Leila before she met Ted, was jealous of Ted's relationship with the beautiful star. It was Craig who was in Leila's apartment the night of her death and it was Craig who knew that if Ted went to prison, he would become the top man in the Winter financial empire.

But it was none other than Alvirah Meehan, the housewife from Queens, who started Elizabeth thinking in the right direction. For Alvirah, with her avid reading of fan magazines and close scrutiny of the lives of the rich and famous, once reminded Craig at the spa that long ago, according to stories, he used to imitate his friend Ted's voice to keep unwanted people from bothering him. Elizabeth then realized that she had not heard Ted's voice the night of her sister's death; she had heard Craig's voice imitating Ted.

With her sister's murder solved, Elizabeth and Ted look toward a future together.

Thematic Material

Mary Higgins Clark has written an intriguing mystery set against the backdrop of luxury and wealth on the beautiful coast of California. The suspense gradually builds toward its final climax as more and more of the characters come under the umbrella labeled "suspect."

Book Talk Material

An introduction to the characters in this mystery is a good orientation to this novel. See: Leila's and Elizabeth's childhood (pp. 13–17; pp. 33–40 pap.); Elizabeth meets Alvirah (pp. 44–46; pp. 61–65 pap.); the baron and baroness (pp. 53–57; pp. 71–73 pap.); and Ted, Craig, and the lawyer arrive at the spa (pp. 61–65; pp. 80–84 pap.).

Additional Selections

Murder and espionage combine in Margaret Truman's *Murder in the CIA* (Random, 1987, $17.95), one of her many mysteries set in Washington that include murder in such institutions as the Supreme Court, FBI, and the White House.

Phyllis A. Whitney is a master of romantic mysteries. In *Feather on the Moon* (Doubleday, 1988, $17.95) the search for the kidnapped daughter leads Jennifer Blake to British Columbia. Two other Whitney novels are *Spindrift* (pap., Fawcett, $2.95) and *Rainsong* (Doubleday, 1984, $14.95; pap., Fawcett, $3.95).

Elizabeth Peters has written a delightful series of mysteries featuring Victorian archaeologist Amelia Peabody. Two titles are *The Mummy Case* (pap., Tor, $3.50) and *The Deeds of the Disturber* (Atheneum, 1988, $16.95).

Emily Polifax is the grandmotherly CIA agent in Dorothy Gilman's amusing adventure series that includes *Mrs. Polifax and the Golden Triangle* (Doubleday, 1988, $15.95) and *The Amazing Mrs. Polifax* (pap., Fawcett, $2.95).

In *The Ariadne Clue* by Carol Clemeau (pap., Ballantine, $2.50), a female classics professor investigates the disappearance of valuable artifacts and a graduate student.

A psychopathic killer is loose in a London rooming house at Christmas season in Marion Babson's *The Twelve Deaths of Christmas* (pap., Walker, $2.95).

When a girl falls in love with a mysterious stranger, she brings danger to an entire town in John Farris's *The Uninvited* (pap., Tor, $3.95).

About the Book
Booklist, May 1987, p. 1314.
Library Journal, July 1987, p. 101.
New York Times Book Review, June 28, 1987, p. 24.
See also *Book Review Index*, 1987, p. 145.

About the Author
Commire, Anne, ed. *Something about the Author*. Detroit: Gale, 1987. Vol. 46, pp. 53–54.
Locher, Frances Carol, ed. *Contemporary Authors*. Detroit: Gale, 1979. Vols. 81–84, p. 91.
Metzger, Linda, and Straub, Deborah A., eds. *Contemporary Authors* (New Revision Series). Detroit: Gale, 1986. Vol. 16, pp. 63–64.

---

du Maurier, Daphne. *Rebecca*
Doubleday, 1938, $15.95; pap., Avon, $3.95.

Manderley, Maxim de Winter, and Mrs. Danvers are three names that conjure up the suspense-filled world of Rebecca and the birth of the modern gothic novel. This story has survived many incarnations since it first appeared in 1938, including a fine film directed by Alfred Hitchcock and a successful television series. In another of her best-sellers and a good companion volume, *My Cousin Rachel* (Bentley, 1971, $15.95; pap., Dell, $3.95), Philip Ashley falls under the spell of his deceased uncle's widow, Rachel, but events point to the fact that she may have poisoned his beloved relative. Du Maurier has written many such novels suitable for senior high school readers and has also written extensively about her own family including an autobiography, *Myself When Young: The Shaping of a Writer* (pap., Avon, $1.95).

Plot Summary

Maxim de Winter returns to the grand English country estate of Manderley after a long absence. He brings with him the second Mrs. de Winter, painfully shy, naive, and many years his junior. In Monte Carlo where the young woman was in the employ of the obnoxious Mrs. Van Hopper, the two had formed an acquaintance, which led to a proposal of marriage and a hasty wedding and honeymoon in Venice.

The new bride adores her handsome, aristocratic husband, but life at Manderley is far from the happiness she had envisioned. Each room she enters, each time-worn custom she is expected to perform, and the scent of each flower brought in from the expanse of gardens are reminders of Rebecca, her husband's first wife. That Rebecca was breathtakingly beautiful, her portrait leaves no doubt, but the new Mrs. de Winter is also reminded in countless ways of the sophistication, the charm, the many talents, the warmth, and the wit of the former mistress of Manderley, all traits that the new mistress sees as woefully lacking in herself.

At the time of their homecoming to Manderley, Rebecca has been dead about a year, and it is some time after their arrival that the young mistress learns the truth of her death. Rebecca, an expert sailor, was drowned not far from the estate in her own boat. It was some months before her body was recovered and identified by her husband. Soon after, he left Manderley to travel in what his new wife sees as an effort to forget his great grief. And now the second Mrs. de Winter wants desperately to blot out the tragedy of his past.

But her task is not easy, for often she catches Maxim in moments of brooding sadness, his dark, handsome face etched with lines of despair, which she fears will never be erased. And in her attempts to make him forget, she often blunders into reminding him of Rebecca in many ways. This is complicated by her own shyness, which prevents her from assuming command of the vast household estate, especially from standing up to the stern Mrs. Danvers, who adored Rebecca and makes no secret of her displeasure with the newcomer.

Befriended only by Maxim's sister, Beatrice, his business agent, Frank Crawley, and a cocker spaniel named Jasper, the young woman gradually begins to feel that in some sinister way, Rebecca, although dead, will never die, that she lives on in Manderley, that she will forever be the only mistress there.

Then one day Maxim is urged to reinstitute the "great ball" that was the social event of the year for the people in the surrounding country-side. Although she is frightened by the prospect of hosting, with her husband, such an affair, the new Mrs. de Winter is determined to make Maxim proud of her; this may be her chance to erase Rebecca's memory from his mind. With growing excitement and with the surprising aid of Mrs. Danvers, she plans her ball gown. Mrs. Danvers suggests a copy of a white dress in a portrait of a de Winter ancestor. Keeping the surprise from Maxim, she has the gown made in a London shop. When the night arrives and her husband and guests are downstairs, she dresses in her new finery, complete with dark wig to hide her mousey hair, and descends the staircase . . . to a horrified and furious Maxim de Winter. Too late she learns she has been tricked by Mrs. Danvers, for the white gown is exactly what Rebecca had worn at the last Manderley ball before her death.

Believing that his young wife has deliberately attempted to embarrass him, Maxim de Winter rushes from the house before she can explain. When he returns, she attempts to tell him of her innocence, but a new crisis has occurred, a crisis that prompts Maxim de Winter to tell his wife the truth of his past.

Sometime during the night a ship has run aground in the waters off Manderley. Rescue attempts have turned up a small boat, which appears to be the one lost at sea when Rebecca de Winter died. However, this boat contains a body; it is Rebecca's!

How is this possible, the new Mrs. de Winter asks? Her husband then recounts his unbelievable story. Far from loving the beautiful Rebecca, Maxim de Winter despised her. Their marriage was a sham, he tells his young wife. Rebecca flaunted her constant affairs, dangling the possibility of scandel in front of him unless he kept the facade she desired. For Rebecca de Winter loved no one but herself and used her beauty and wit for her own pleasure and whims. On the night of her death, Maxim confronted her once again down at the boat house. She taunted him with the likelihood of her pregnancy, saying he had no choice but to accept the child, although he was not the father. Maxim killed Rebecca and put her body in her boat, which he sent out on the waters.

As Maxim seems to disintegrate with what has happened, his young wife seems to grow. They will tell the authorities that the year before when he identified the body that had washed ashore as his wife's (although he knew it was not), he was distraught and could not be held accountable for his actions at the time. And, indeed, Rebecca's death is ruled a suicide.

Now enters Favell, Rebecca's cousin and one of her many lovers. He accuses Maxim of murder and produces a letter sent to him from Rebecca on the day of her death; it speaks of something urgent she must tell Favell and asks him to meet her. Would someone planning suicide write such a note, Favell accuses?

With the help of Mrs. Danvers, Colonel Julyan, who is called in to investigate this new turn, finds out that Rebecca had an appointment on the afternoon of her death with a Dr. Baker. Along with Maxim and his wife, Crawley, and Favell, Julyan goes to see Baker. Both Maxim and young Mrs. de Winter are certain that the doctor will reveal Rebecca's pregnancy, and so point the finger of suspicion at Maxim. Instead, Dr. Baker reveals the fact that Rebecca de Winter was suffering from cancer and had little time to live. She had merely taunted her husband with her pregnancy.

Favell is furious and vows revenge. Maxim and his wife leave to make the journey by car back to Manderley. Before reaching home they learn that Mrs. Danvers has packed and left. As they approach Manderley in the early morning hours, they see the red streaks of crimson that are not made by the approaching dawn. Manderley is no more.

Maxim and the second Mrs. de Winter now spend their days in quiet, simple contentments, far from their beloved English countryside, traveling from inn to inn, somewhat homeless perhaps and sometimes a bit bored, but together with their past, their memories, and their love.

Thematic Material

Here is a classic romantic Gothic novel, long considered a masterpiece of the genre. It contains all the elements for true Gothic romance and suspense: the brooding, slightly mysterious but handsome hero, the naive, pure heroine, a sinister air that pervades the atmosphere concerning the death of a major character, and, of course, a labyrinth of an estate, beautiful but somehow frightening in its endless rooms and corridors and great expanses of too-lush gardens, its very vastness giving it an air of desolation. True to its calling, *Rebecca* contains suspense, mystery, murder, and romance. The use of the second Mrs. de Winter, whose name is never given, as the narrator adds a haunting realism to the story. The author has skillfully captured an earlier time in the lives of the

English higher society, when people dressed for tea and lived their lives according to certain rules of honor, no matter what the consequences. It is also a sympathetic portrait of a young woman coming of age.

Book Talk Material

Readers will be most fascinated and sympathetic as the painfully shy and anxious-to-please new mistress of Manderley tries to fit in but keeps bumping into the ever-present ghost of Rebecca de Winter. See: the second Mrs. de Winter discusses the subject of a personal maid with Mrs. Danvers (pp. 70–75; pp. 71–73 pap.); she is told that the first Mrs. de Winter always used the morning room (pp. 80–83; pp. 81–82 pap.); Frank Crawley tells her about Rebecca's death (pp. 122–129; pp. 128–134 pap.); Maxim's grandmother cries for Rebecca (pp. 171–177; pp. 183–187 pap.); and the disaster at the ball (pp. 200–203; pp. 210–214 pap.).

Additional Selections

Daphne du Maurier's Classics of the Macabre (Doubleday, 1987, $18.95) is a handsome new edition of six stories including "The Birds."

Another mistress of the romantic Gothic is Victoria Holt. Among her many recommended novels are *The Time of the Hunter's Moon* (Doubleday, 1983, $14.95; pap., Fawcett, $3.95), in which a young schoolteacher is involved in a mystery in nineteenth-century England, and the more recent *The India Fan* (Doubleday, 1988, $18.95), in which the friendship and adventures of two English girls involve India and a fan that is an omen of disaster.

Young Sara Causely encounters murder when she becomes a governess in pre-World War II England in Robert Barnard's thrilling *The Skeleton in the Grass* (Scribner's, 1988, $15.95).

Mignon G. Eberhart is another veteran writer of romantic mysteries. Two of her titles are *Three Days for Emeralds* (Random, 1988, $14.95) and *Postmark Murder* (pap., Warner, $2.50).

The classic governess romantic Gothic is still Charlotte Bronte's *Jane Eyre* (available in many editions).

A British heroine escapes from slavery in Afghanistan to claim her birthright in Madeleine Brent's *Stormswift* (Doubleday, 1985, $15.95; pap., Fawcett, $3.50).

In Helen MacInnes's *Cloak of Darkness* (pap., Fawcett, $3.95), terrorist hunter Robert Benwich discovers he is a target for assassination. Two others by this master thriller writer are *Above Suspicion* (pap., Fawcett, $3.50) and *Message from Malaga* (pap., Fawcett, $3.25).

About the Book
Booklist, October 15, 1938, p. 65.
New York Times Book Review, September 25, 1938, p. 7.
See also *Book Review Digest*, 1938, p. 276.

About the Author
Commire, Anne, ed. *Something about the Author*. Detroit: Gale, 1982. Vol. 27, pp. 74–83.
Evory, Ann, ed. *Contemporary Authors* (New Revision Series). Detroit: Gale, 1982. Vol. 6, pp. 144–146.
Harte, Barbara, and Riley, Carolyn, eds. *Contemporary Authors* (First Revision). Detroit: Gale, 1969. Vols. 5–8, pp. 321–322.
Kunitz, Stanley J., and Haycraft, Howard, eds. *Twentieth-Century Authors*. Wilson, 1942, pp. 405–406.

Francis, Dick. *Bolt*
Putnam, 1987, $17.95; pap., Fawcett, $4.95

Dick Francis was born in 1920 and as a young man took up horseback riding as a jockey. He was a champion steeplechase rider of the 1953 to 1954 season. He retired in 1957 and took up "racing" journalism, which in turn led to writing a number of top-flight mysteries like *Bolt* that combine a horse racing setting with fast-paced suspense stories. Two others are *Break In* (Putnam, 1986, $17.95; pap., Fawcett, $4.95), in which a smear campaign directed at a millionaire gradually involves Kit Fielding, a championship steeplechase jockey, and the story of how a crippled ex-jockey solves the mystery of the deaths of four thoroughbred horses, *Whip Hand* (pap., Pocket, $3.50). Dick Francis's novels are read and enjoyed by sports and mystery fans in the senior high school grades.

Plot Summary
Christmas (Kit) Fielding is the tallest English jockey in steeplechase racing. He also is a fair hand at solving crimes, as he proved in *Break In*, when he saved lives as well as his family's honor and got himself engaged

to the lovely Danielle de Brescou, niece of Princess Casilia's husband. The princess owns a number of the horses that Kit rides, generally with much success, and his relationship with her is one of admiration and respect.

At this point, Kit Fielding should be a very happy, as well as a successful, man. But he is not. His distress stems mainly from the coolness that Danielle is suddenly showing toward him and their engagement, a distress that is not allievated by the fact that she goes off on a "fifteenth-century junket" weekend with the princess's nephew, the aristocratic Count Litsi, whom despite himself Kit likes.

But Kit soon pushes his own distress into the background when the princess asks him not only to accompany her to her elegant home, but to stay there for a time as well. She is frightened for the safety of her husband and family members. Kit learns that her husband, the wheelchair-bound French aristocrat Roland de Brescou, has been threatened by Henri Nanterre, descendant of the man who was de Brescou's business partner. Nanterre, thoroughly without scruples, has demanded that de Brescou sign papers that will allow their company in France to make arms. For both the honor of his family name and for his own principles, de Brescou cannot and will not consent. Nanterre threatens the ailing man and his family.

Kit cannot believe that Nanterre will actually carry out such threats. But he changes his mind when he is called to the racing stables to discover that two of the princess's top horses, one of them in the running for the Grand National, have been killed by a "bolt," a so-called humane killer for animals in which the killing agent is shot from a gun into the exact spot in the horse's head, killing the animal instantly.

Convinced now that Nanterre is a desperate man who will stop at nothing, Kit orders dog patrols around the racing stables to protect the other animals. But trouble continues. A third horse is killed, and while watching Kit ride one day, Count Litsi is nearly killed from a fall. Kit saves his life and then discovers that Litsi had been lured to the unsafe spot by a man who claimed that "Danielle wanted to meet him there."

Kit tracks down the messenger and finds that the man who initiated the message was Nanterre. Cousin Beatrice, who has arrived for a prolonged stay with the princess and who has met and adores Nanterre, informs Kit that the man has threatened to kill him and to disfigure Danielle!

As he tries to protect her, Kit also learns the cause of Danielle's coolness. She is unsure whether she can live a life of fearing for his safety every time he goes out on the track. Kit can do nothing to ease her fears, but he feels that his life would be nothing without her.

Faced with the ever-increasing danger and sensing that Nanterre will not be stopped, Kit comes up with a plan. By giving the unwitting Beatrice information on his whereabouts, Kit ensures that Nanterre will have the opportunity to harm him. Indeed, Nanterre is caught planting a bomb in his car. Faced with witnesses to his act, Nanterre signs a contract that Kit had drawn up by de Brescou's lawyers. It changes the name of the firm and requires that both partners sell their interests. This crisis over, it looks as though Kit can once again turn his full attention to Danielle.

Then Kit inadvertently learns, through a photograph, that Nanterre could not have been at the stables on the night one of the horses was killed. Nanterre may have been responsible for all else, but he was not the killer of the horses!

Kit arrives at the stables too late to save another horse, but he learns the horse-killer's identity—Maynard Allardeck, who had long carried on a feud with Kit's family and who begrudged him any kind of success. Allardeck is dead.

With the mystery solved and the princess's family no longer in danger, Kit can fully resume his life because Danielle tells him that if she must live in fear for his safety, that it is better than living without him at all.

Thematic Material

This is a fast-paced mystery with the added action of steeplechase racing. Kit Fielding is presented as an intelligent, dedicated, and above all honorable man. It also nicely portrays the sense of honor that often governs the lives of people. And for readers who enjoy a look into the lives of the wealthy, in this case the "in England" aristocracy, the scenes of home life with the Princess are especially interesting.

Book Talk Material

Readers who like sports and action will be especially interested in descriptions of the races and racing stables; see the details of racing (pp. 10–15, 66–69, 137–142; pp. 9–13, 58–66, 130–137 pap.). See also the description of the "bolt" (pp. 77–90; pp. 74–85 pap.).

Additional Selections

Humor and skulduggery are combined in the story of a hapless CIA agent, Walter Peabody, assigned to a Polynesian kingdom in Alex Alben's *Our Man in Mongoa* (Scribner's, 1987, $15.95).

A paraplegic church business manager is found murdered and there is a host of suspects in Isabelle Holland's *A Death at St. Anselm's* (pap., Fawcett, $2.95).

In Terence Hughes's *The Day They Stole the Queen Mary* (pap., Jove, $3.50), a Nazi plot is developed to kidnap Winston Churchill.

Ngaio Marsh wrote many stylish murder mysteries; her last was *Light Thickens* (pap., Jove, $2.95).

Two popular clerical detectives are Harry Kemelman's Rabbi Small who solves murders by the day of the week, for example, *Friday the Rabbi Slept Late* (pap., Fawcett, $3.50), and Ralph McInerny's Father Roger Dowling, star of such quiet mysteries as *The Basket Case* (St. Martin's, 1987, $14.95).

A tough New York detective becomes a murder target while investigating the death of an Israeli politician in E. V. Cunningham's *The Wabash Factor* (Delacorte, 1986, $14.95).

Martin Beck, a Swedish police detective, solves a case of mass murder on a bus in *The Laughing Policeman* by Maj Sjowall and Per Wahloo (pap., Random, $3.95).

A losing race horse is brought to race in Calcutta, India, in the suspenseful and humorous *The Dark Horse* by Rumer Godden (Viking, 1981, $11.95).

A former jockey ace tells his true story in *Shoemaker* by Bill Shoemaker (Doubleday, 1988, $17.95).

About the Book
Booklist, December 1, 1986, p. 529.
Library Journal, March 1, 1987, p. 95.
New York Times Book Review, March 29, 1987, p. 22.
See also *Book Review Digest*, 1987, p. 618, and *Book Review Index*, 1987, p. 260.

About the Author
Evory, Ann, and Metzger, Linda, eds. *Contemporary Authors* (New Revision Series). Detroit: Gale, 1983. Vol. 9, pp. 174–178.
Harte, Barbara, and Riley, Carolyn, eds. *Contemporary Authors* (First Revision). Detroit: Gale, 1969. Vols. 5–8, pp. 399–400.

Wakeman, John, ed. *World Authors 1970–1975.* New York: Wilson, 1980, pp. 271–273.

Rendell, Ruth. *Heartstones*
Harper, 1987, $10.95; pap., Ballantine, $3.50

Since her first crime novel, *From Doon with Death* (pap., Ballantine, $3.95) appeared in 1964, Ruth Rendell has published nearly 40 books, many of them featuring Chief Inspector Wexford. She has been called the best living mystery author writing in the English language and is often compared favorably to Agatha Christie, a comparison that seems unfair; whereas Christie is slick and superficial, Rendell probes deeply into the dark psychological recesses of her characters' minds and eschews such standard clichés as a denouement where all the suspects are gathered and the culprit unmasked.

Heartstones is a very short novel (only 80 pages); nevertheless it is full of power and suspense, and though sparse, combines these elements with an unexpectedly chilling ending. It is written in the form of a journal kept sporadically over a three-year period by the central character, Elvira Zoffany. Although written for adults, the book can serve as a good introduction to the author's work for readers in grade 10 and up.

Plot Summary
Shortly before Elvira's sixteenth birthday, her mother, Anne, dies of cancer, leaving behind a husband, Luke, a theologian who teaches at the local university, St. Leofric's, and two daughters, Elvira, and 13-year-old Spinny, short for Despina; Anne had a weakness for Mozart operas.

Until the funeral, the girls stay with their maternal grandmother, but immediately afterward they move back to their fifteenth-century home across the square from a Gothic cathedral in the center of town. At the time of construction of the house, a cat belonging to a local presumed witch, Green Margery, was buried in the walls. Since then many claim that the house is haunted, and after her mother's death, Spinny claims to see the ghost of the cat who visits her nightly in her bedroom.

The sisters are a study in contrasts. Spinny is sweet, bovine, and given to earthy pleasures like boyfriends, television, and always gorging herself on sweets and desserts. Elvira is precocious, spiritual, and almost other-worldly in her aestheticisms. She scorns food to the point of starvation and sublimates all worldly needs to learning and to the grand passion of her life—her father. She worships Luke obsessively and he, still feeling the loss of his wife, encourages his daughter's attentions.

Some months after Anne's death, Luke announces that he will have a dinner party for some locals and faculty members. The cook, Sheila, and maid Rosemary spend much time in preparations. One of the guests not known to the girls is Dr. Mary Leonard, an attractive medievalist from the faculty. She and Luke are obviously in love and a few weeks later they announce wedding plans. Elvira is seething with rage and jealousy and tells Spinny that she will do anything to prevent the marriage.

Mary moves into the guest bedroom immediately below Elvira's and at night Elvira spies on her through a crack in the floorboards. Elvira's fasting, combined with her preoccupation with terminating the engagement, lead to bouts of dizziness and fainting. She steals a spoonful of cyanide from the van of a wasp exterminator and, while Spinny watches, hides it in her bedroom.

To clean the western front of the cathedral, scaffolding is built. Mary suggests that this would afford an excellent opportunity to get a close look at the church's many stone carvings. A climbing party is planned including the girls.

On the uppermost catwalk, the guide rope mysteriously snaps and Mary plunges to her death below onto the heart-shaped flagstones. Later that night Elvira finds a pocket knife with rope fibers on one of its blades. Could she in her near delirium be responsible for Mary's death?

Months pass. Grandma has moved in to care for the girls. Elvira is so weakened and ill that she cannot attend school, but Spinny continues to over-eat horrendously, and her disturbing nocturnal visitations by the ghost cat increase. Luke, burdened with inconsolable sorrow because of Mary's death, sinks into severe bouts of depression. One evening he shows Elvira a suicide note he keeps in his desk in the event that his grief becomes unbearable. Elvira shares this information with Spinny.

Sometime later—weeks? days? (time has become meaningless to Elvira)—she is awakened by a distraught Spinny who has seen blood oozing from underneath Luke's bedroom door. They enter and find him dead in bed, his wrists slashed, and the suicide note beside him. The coroner determines that he had taken a heavy sleeping potion and somehow before the drug took effect, he cut himself with a pearl-handled razor that had been a family heirloom.

At her father's death, Elvira collapses and is taken to the hospital where she is diagnosed as having a severe case of anorexia. After several months of physical and psychological treatment, she emerges a changed person. She eats normally, has a healthy attitude toward herself and other people, and is even anxious to meet and date boys. Spinny, on the other hand, is growing worse. She is eating uncontrollably and now claims to have visits from the witch woman Green Margery.

Two other events distress Elvira. The stolen cyanide has disappeared and large jagged holes are found in the plaster of several rooms. One weekend Gram goes to London and the girls are alone. On Saturday evening, Elvira is awakened from a nap by strange scraping sounds. She investigates and finds Spinny digging into a wall with hammer and chisel. She is looking for the bones of Green Margery's cat to exorcise the house.

This aberrant behavior suddenly makes Elvira face the truth. It was Spinny's penknife she had found in her room. Spinny also knew about the suicide note and the whereabouts of the razor. Elvira vows that on Monday she must get Spinny to a psychiatrist. She also realizes that in the meantime nothing can be done; after all what is a mere 24 hours?

Spinny enters the room to give her a comforting cup of coffee.

Thematic Material

This is a suspenseful thriller that probes the tormented psyche of one troubled girl and leaves the reader to do the same for the other protagonist. Elvira is a pathetically disturbed girl who is unaware of either the cause or the seriousness of her condition. Anorexia and other eating disorders are convincingly explored as well as unusual family relationships, particularly those involving a daughter's unhealthy attachment to her father.

Book Talk Material

An introduction to the Zoffany family, the arrival of Mary Leonard, and Elvira's reactions should produce interest. The hardcover edition includes some excellent illustrations that could be used, including the cover and the picture of the ghost cat (p. 33). Some brief passages of interest are: the family home and Spinny's first encounters with the ghost cat (pp. 12–14; pp. 5–7 pap.); Luke tells the history of the house (pp. 23–34; pp. 19–20 pap.), and Elvira meets Mary Leonard and vows she will never marry Luke (pp. 28–32; pp. 25–29 pap.).

Additional Selections

In a recent Ruth Rendell novel, *The Veiled One* (Pantheon, 1988, $16.95), Inspector Wexford investigates a murder in an underground parking lot.

Better readers will enjoy Peter James's English horror novel *Possession* (Doubleday, 1988, $17.95), the story of a mother haunted by the ghost of her only son killed in a car crash.

When a beautiful woman falls to her death a murder investigation reveals her unsavory past in Dorothy Simpson's *Element of Doubt* (Scribner's, 1988, $14.95).

In Gloria Murphy's *Blood Ties* (Fine, 1987, $16.95), a disturbed teenager who had been kidnapped, sexually molested, and used by a pornographer as a child, returns disguised to his family.

P. D. James is another master of the English mystery novel. One of her popular titles is *The Black Tower* (pap., Warner, $3.95).

Two excellent collections of crime short stories in paperback are *Prime Suspects* (pap., Ballantine, $2.95) and *Suspicious Characters* (pap., Ballantine, $2.95), both edited by Bill Pronzini and Martin Greenberg.

Constance Blackwood was acquitted of murdering her family and is now living with Sister Mary Catherine, but who is guilty? Shirley Jackson explores this situation in *We Have Always Lived in the Castle* (Rivercity, 1962, $17.95). Also use Jackson's *The Haunting of Hill House* (Rivercity, 1959, $17.95; pap., Penguin, $5.95).

Lovers of horror stories will enjoy the novels of Stephen King, particularly *Carrie* (Doubleday, 1974, $15.95; pap., NAL, $3.50), about a teenager's telekinetic revenge on classmates, and *Christine* (Viking, 1983, $16.95; pap., NAL, $4.50), about a most unusual automobile.

About the Book
Booklist, June 1, 1987, p. 1493.
Library Journal, June 15, 1987, p. 86.
New York Times Book Review, August 30, 1987, p. 20.
See also *Book Review Digest,* 1988, and *Book Review Index,* 1987, p. 639.

About the Author
May, Hal, ed. *Contemporary Authors.* Detroit: Gale, 1983. Vol. 109, pp. 394–395.

9

Sports in Fact and Fiction

SPORTS form a strong interest for teenagers—both as spectators and participants—and many extend this interest to the printed page. Here are five titles—two of which are nonfiction—that cover baseball, track, and hockey. Other sports and aspects of the sporting life are covered under "Additional Selections."

Allen, Maury. *Jackie Robinson: A Life Remembered*
  Watts, 1987, $16.95

Jackie Robinson will be remembered not only as the black who broke the color barrier in major league baseball but also as a remarkable man who was a credit to both his sport and his race. *Jackie Robinson: A Life Remembered* is a frank, interesting biography that reveals many sides of the subject's personality and life. It is an adult biography and, therefore, recommended for readers in grade 9 and up. For a simpler, shorter treatment of the same subject use Harvey Frommer's *Jackie Robinson* (Watts, 1984, $10.90).

Plot Summary
America has lots of baseball heroes; some of the best get into the Baseball Hall of Fame in Cooperstown, New York. Jack Roosevelt Robinson, who first became a Brooklyn Dodger in 1947, joined that select group on July 23, 1962. These are his credentials:

1947　Led the National League in stolen bases (also in 1949)
1949　Most Valuable Player
　　　　Leading National League batter
　　　　Led second basemen in double plays (also in 1950, 1951, 1952)
1951　Joint record holder, most double plays by second baseman
Lifetime batting average: 311
Best fielding mark for second baseman playing in 150 or more games: .992

253

The figures don't lie; Jackie Robinson was a genuine sports hero, but not only because of his statistics, for it fell on Robinson's shoulders to become the first black man to join the major leagues in baseball, and he bore the responsibility with courage and dignity. It was not an easy task, for up until 1947 America's national pastime was also America's "white" national pastime.

Organized baseball in America, as we know it today, dates from 1869. Although a few black players did play with the league that formed after the Civil War, racism was rife in the country and it wasn't long before blacks were banned altogether. Near the middle of the twentieth century, young black players understood that their chances for a professional career in baseball were relegated to the "colored" leagues, which in fact produced many outstanding players, whom most of the country never heard of. It wasn't "written down" anywhere that blacks couldn't play in the major leagues, but no one fought it either. Baseball was a white man's sport.

After World War II ended in the mid-1940s, cries were heard to give blacks a chance in the major leagues. Branch Rickey, boss of the Brooklyn Dodgers, was looking around for new talent to spark his club. He decided to sign a black. Why did he choose Robinson? The reasons were probably many and complex. Rickey knew that this first signing of a black into the major leagues would be a momentous happening in the sports world and that his name would be forever linked with this act. So Rickey chose wisely and well.

Jackie Robinson came from a hard-working, respected family and he was a well-known California college athlete. He had been born in Georgia in 1919, the baby of the Robinsons' five children. In 1920, after Jackie's father left the household saying he was looking for a new job and never returned, Jackie's mother, Mallie, took her family to Pasadena, California, where her brother lived. Life was hard and the family endured much prejudice, but Jackie and his brothers grew up to be recognized athletes. He went to Pasadena Junior College where he starred in football, basketball, baseball, and track, then on to UCLA where he was the first winner of four varsity letters for sports in one year.

Robinson was drafted into the army in 1942 where he became involved in an attempt to open up the army PX (post exchange) on the post to more black soldiers. This later gave Robinson the reputation of being a troublemaker, but to Rickey it indicated that Robinson would fight for his rights, which Rickey knew the young black player would have to do when he became the first in the major leagues.

After the army Robinson signed with the black Kansas City Monarchs. They needed a shortstop, but the scouting reports said that Robinson couldn't play at short; he should be tried at second base.

So this was the young man Branch Rickey met in 1945 and signed to a contract with the Dodger organization on October 23; he was sent to the Montreal Royals. On April 10, 1947, came this announcement from the Dodgers' front office: "The Brooklyn Dodgers today purchased the contract of Jack Roosevelt Robinson from the Montreal Royals. He will report immediately."

In the midst of cries of outrage, petitions to stop his playing, outright prejudice from fellow ballplayers, threats of violence, and shock from the public, Jackie Robinson was given number 42 and became a Brooklyn Dodger.

Although the rest, as they say, is history, as far as Robinson's baseball career is concerned, much less well known are the slurs and racial epithets he quietly endured either at bat, in the field, or in the cities where the Dodgers played. He was accused of everything imaginable by other team players; he was threatened and vilified. He was tough, he was a fighter, he loved the game, and he endured.

By the end of the 1947 season Robinson was still there. The prejudice still swirled around him, the threats and the name-calling kept on, but Robinson had proved he was a baseball player, and anyone who cared about baseball knew it. The unofficial color ban in professional baseball was over, and Jackie Robinson was named Rookie of the Year.

Robinson died October 24, 1972, after some years of failing health, but for sports fans anywhere his name will never be forgotten. For black players, he paved the way for their careers; for sports fans he gave the joy of watching a gifted athlete doing his best; for all Americans he epitomizes courage and dignity against bigotry and the worst in the human character.

Thematic Material

This is a straightforward biography of a gifted baseball player and an admirable man. It is filled with warm remembrances by family, friends, and other players giving a complete and sensitive picture of Robinson and helping the reader to understand the times in which he played and what the situation was like for a black man in baseball in 1947. It also shows how Robinson's personal character helped him to endure and to survive the bad times with dignity. In addition, it is filled with facts and anecdotes about the baseball world during Robinson's time, which all baseball fans will enjoy.

Book Talk Material

To understand the true significance of Robinson's contribution to the baseball world, one must understand the situation in the major leagues in the 1940s; see, for example, the white man's game (pp. 47–50); agitation to admit blacks (pp. 53–60); Branch Rickey and his decision to sign Robinson (pp. 69–80); the crowds in Montreal (pp. 81–84); and Jackie goes to Brooklyn (pp. 107–123).

Additional Selections

Alison Gordon tells about her five years as a reporter covering the Toronto Blue Jays in *Foul Ball!* (Dodd, 1985, $14.95).

Willie Mays, another famous black baseball player, recalls his life in *Say Hey* (Simon, 1988, $17.95).

The 1987 Red Sox season is re-created brilliantly in John Hough's *A Player for a Moment* (Harcourt, 1988, $17.95).

Robert Wood rates both major league ballparks and their fans in *Dodger Dogs to Fenway Franks* (McGraw, 1988, $16.95).

A superior collection of color photographs captures the essence of baseball in John Thorn's *The Game for All America* (Sporting News, 1988, $35.00).

Ron Luciano, a former major league umpire, has three books about his career: *The Umpire Strikes Back* (pap., Bantam, $3.95), *Strike Two* (pap., Bantam, $3.95), and *The Fall of the Roman Umpire* (Bantam, 1986, $15.95; pap., Bantam, $3.95).

A history of the game plus statistics are given in Bill James's *The Bill James Historical Baseball Abstract* (Villard, 1986, $24.95).

In another sport, tennis, Martina Navratilova speaks frankly about her life in *Martina* (Knopf, 1985, $16.95).

In the nonfictional *Who Goes Out in the Midday Sun?* (Viking, 1986, $18.95), Benedict Allen sets out on a 1,000-mile trek in the South American jungle.

About the Book
Book Report, March, 1987, p. 8.
Booklist, March 15, 1987, p. 1080.
Library Journal, April 15, 1987, p. 94.
School Library Journal, September 1987, p. 208.
VOYA, October 1987, p. 182.
See also *Book Review Digest,* 1988, and *Book Review Index,* 1987, p. 15; 1988.

About the Author
Evory, Ann, and Metzger, Linda, eds. *Contemporary Authors* (New Revision Series). Detroit: Gale, 1984. Vol. 11, p. 19.
Kinsman, Clare D., ed. *Contemporary Authors* (First Revision). Detroit: Gale, 1976. Vols. 17–20, p. 19.

Kinsella, W. P.   *Shoeless Joe*
pap., Ballantine, $5.50

You will not find Shoeless Joe Jackson in the Baseball Hall of Fame, because although he was a star batter for the Chicago White Sox, he and his teammates succumbed to bribes to lose the 1919 World Series. He is, however, one of the deceased baseball heroes that Ray, an Iowa farmer, hopes will rise from the dead to play on a baseball diamond he has constructed in a cornfield in W. P. Kinsella's whimsical but touching novel. This author is a Canadian who now lives close to Vancouver, British Columbia. *Shoeless Joe* originally appeared in 1982 and is recommended for senior high readers.

Plot Summary
    As Iowa farmer and avid baseball fan Ray Kinsella gazes out over his farmland one dusky spring evening, a voice comes to him. The voice is that of a ballpark announcer, who says, "If you build it, he will come."
    Ray knows that "it" means a baseball diamond, and "he" is Shoeless Joe—Joseph Jefferson Jackson, born 1887, died 1951, called by Ty Cobb the best left fielder of all time, and one of eight whose career was ruined when the Chicago White Sox were accused of throwing the 1919 World Series. Shoeless Joe was said to have gained his nickname in the minor leagues when, during the sixth inning of a game, he took off his new spikes because they hurt his feet, and he played the rest of the game in his socks.

The dream is born, and Ray decides to build a ballpark—actually he is really interested only in left field—right in his cornfield. This is not easy. For three seasons Ray seeds, waters, and fusses over his project, while the townsfolk think he has gone slightly daft. But his remarkably understanding wife, Annie, and his daughter, Karin, seem to tolerate his passion for the great god baseball, and do not find his antics strange.

So it is not too surprising when Annie herself tells Ray one evening that a man in a baseball uniform is standing on their lawn. Sure enough, Ray knows it is Shoeless Joe, who has come to play just as the announcer predicted. Ray is proud when Shoeless Joe tells him that the ball bounces true on his cornfield ballpark.

Shoeless Joe promises to return and says he might even bring along some others who would enjoy playing on Ray's Iowa ballpark, guys long gone from the game now, but always remembered.

With Joe's promise in mind, Ray sets about improving the ballpark. And, remarkably, one day there they all are. Ray, Annie, and Karin take their places in the bleachers to watch the pros at their game.

And then it happens; Ray hears the announcer's voice again. Annie is afraid that this time Ray will be told to build a football stadium. But, no, the announcer gives Ray another mission. This time Ray Kinsella is to "ease the pain" of writer J. D. Salinger of *Catcher in the Rye* fame, who as everyone knows has been holed up on a mountaintop in New Hampshire for about 25 years. What this has to do with baseball, Annie doesn't know, but she tells Ray that if that's what he has to do, then he'd better get on with it.

So, Ray Kinsella hops in his car and drives off to ease the pain of one J. D. Salinger, who, on Ray's arrival, does not want his pain eased. Ray has to practically kidnap the writer to get him to a baseball game in Boston. For Salinger has dropped out of life, and through the baseball game, Ray wants to help him back to the living.

Not only does Salinger enjoy the baseball game, but he, too, hears Ray's ballpark announcer, and soon the two men are off on a journey to Minnesota, this time to find out about another baseball player, Moonlight Graham, a man who played one inning of baseball for the New York Giants in 1905. He never even came to bat.

On their journey, Ray and Salinger mix memories and history and love and imagination, meeting the great people of the game and those who knew them. And, finally, as Ray knows he will, Salinger insists on going with Ray to his Iowa farm, to see if the magic that Ray insists comes to that ballpark is really true.

Back in the Iowa baseball field, the magic is truly still there. Salinger, Annie, and Ray watch the greats at their game. But it is spoiled for Ray when he overhears Shoeless Joe and some of the others ask Salinger if he wants to go out with them after the game is over. "Why not me?" Ray asks. "I built the field!"

But when Salinger explains, of course Ray understands. For J. D. Salinger says that he will write about this—"a man able to touch the perfect dream."

Ray Kinsella, with Annie and Karin beside him, watches as Salinger, Shoeless Joe, and the others slowly leave the Iowa cornfield that is his dream baseball field.

Thematic Material

This is a sports story a little off the beaten track. It combines stories of some of the old-time great baseball heroes with fantasy, imagination, humor, and the stuff of which dreams are made. Those who enjoy baseball stories will especially like its rich folklore; those who like to see dreams come true will enjoy "a good read."

Book Talk Material

Highlights of the book are the sights and sounds of baseball. See, for instance, Ray first talks to Shoeless Joe (pp. 11–13); the Cubs of Wrigley Field (pp. 37–38); the game in Boston (pp. 59–80); and the stop at the Hall of Fame in Cooperstown (pp. 93–96). Baseball fans will also enjoy Ray's description of building his ballpark (see pp. 7–9, 21–23).

Additional Selections

A literary anthology of many writers including Kinsella, edited by Mike Shannon, is *The Best of Spitball* (pap., Pocket, $5.95). W. P. Kinsella's novel *The Iowa Baseball Confederacy* (Houghton, 1986, $16.95; pap., Ballantine, $3.95) is a funny time-warp baseball story.

A commentator for a basketball team is mysteriously murdered in Michael Katz's *Murder Off the Glass* (Walker, 1987, $14.95), and a retired athlete investigates the disappearance of the Celtics' star forward in Richard Rosen's *Fadeaway* (Harper, 1986, $15.45).

For those interested in a career in baseball, Al Goldis and Rick Wolff have written *Breaking into the Big Leagues* (Leisure Press, 1988, $10.95). Donald Honig has written two excellent, attractive nonfiction baseball books: *The American League: An Illustrated History* (Crown, 1987, $22.50) and *The National League: An Illustrated History* (Crown, 1987, $22.50). Three excellent junior sports novels are: Bruce Stone's *Half Nelson, Full Nelson* (Harper, 1985, $12.25, pap. $2.95), about a boy and his wrestler father; Robert Lipsyte's *The Contender* (Harper, 1967, $11.89; pap., Bantam, $2.50; condensed in *More Juniorplots*, Bowker, 1977, pp. 66–69), a boxing story about a black slum kid; and Rosemary Wells's *When No One Was Looking* (Dial, 1980, $14.95; pap., Fawcett, $1.95; condensed in *Juniorplots 3*, Bowker, 1987, pp. 253–257), about an obsessively driven tennis star and the death by drowning of her rival.

About the Book
Booklist, March 15, 1982, p. 941.
Library Journal, April 1, 1982, p. 745.
New York Times Book Review, July 25, 1982, p. 10.
School Library Journal, August 1982, p. 131; December 1982, p. 29.
See also *Book Review Digest*, 1982, p. 732, and *Book Review Index*, 1982, p. 287; 1983, p. 299.

About the Author
Kinsman, Clare D., ed. *Contemporary Authors* (First Revision) Detroit: Gale, 1976. Vols. 17–20, p. 407.
Straub, Deborah A., ed. *Contemporary Authors* (New Revision Series). Detroit: Gale, 1987. Vol. 21, pp. 217–223.

Malamud, Bernard.   *The Natural*
pap., Avon, $3.50

Bernard Malamud was one of the leading Jewish American writers who grew up after World War II. Before his death in 1986 he had won two National Book Awards and a Pulitzer Prize. Two of his other popular novels are *The Assistant* (pap., Farrar, $4.95; pap., Avon, $3.95), about a Jewish grocer and his gentile Italian helper, and *The Fixer* (Farrar, 1966, $17.50, pap. $7.95), the story of a Jew, Yakov Bok, a handyman wrongly accused of murdering a Christian boy in czarist Russia. *The Natural*, which originally appeared in 1952, is a baseball allegory about the perversion of natural talent by society. It is recommended for better readers in the senior high grades. It is also available in paperback from Farrar, $8.95.

Plot Summary

All his life Roy Hobbs has wanted only one thing—to be the best baseball player there ever was. And he has all the natural talents to reach that goal, but not all the luck.

As a young man Roy is on his way to a tryout with a professional baseball team. He has no experience, but his high school years are legendary. He is a natural. And he wants to play ball so badly that it consumes his life. He has even made himself a special bat out of special wood, which he calls Wonderboy. On the train going to his tryout, the talk turns to stories of a mysterious woman who has been in the papers lately for shooting professional athletes. During the trip Roy is attracted to a beautiful woman. In Chicago she invites him to her room, where she shoots him in the stomach. In the early part of the twentieth century, this is a scandal.

Roy recovers, but confused and embittered he drops out of baseball before he has a chance to enter it. Then, at the age of 34, Roy signs with the last place New York Knights for $3,000. Manager Pop Fisher is skeptical, and Roy, along with Wonderboy, sits on the bench.

Roy gets his chance to play and prove himself when the regular left fielder, Bump Bailey, dies after a crash into the outfield wall. As his talent is recognized, Roy also attracts the attention of Bump's girl, Memo, and Roy falls for her—hard. But Memo does not seem overly impressed with Roy until his fame begins to grow, as he becomes a hero to fans, and as his teammates, buoyed by his presence and great talent, respond by better play and a boosting of the team's standings.

Roy becomes such a hero that the Knights hold Roy Hobbs Day and he is given a Mercedes-Benz, which Memo consents to ride in. She tells Roy that she could not consider settling down with any man unless they could live a decent life. And what can Roy Hobbs offer? Nearly 35, how many years does he have left to play? How could they live a "decent life" on $3,000?

Roy goes to the owner of the Knights, Judge Goodwill Banner, and asks for a raise. He is refused.

Roy goes into a batting slump, and the rest of the team suffers as well. Now the fans who had been so adoring a few days before turn on their hero; he has become a bum. Roy himself is bewildered by his sudden loss of control and bitter at the fans' reaction.

As the Knights pull into Chicago for a game, a truck driver stops Roy and asks him to hit one for his little boy who is in the hospital and doing poorly after an operation. He is a big fan of Roy Hobbs's. Roy replies that he couldn't hit the side of a barn, but he'll do the best he can.

That night as Roy looks up into the stands, he sees a dark-haired woman in a red dress standing up in the grandstand. She is wearing a white flower and staring into the Knights dugout. Roy gets the feeling that she is staring at him. He sits on the bench, because Pop Fisher told him to use another bat besides Wonderboy to break out of his slump and Roy refused. Now, with one Knight on base and the team one run behind, Pop gives Roy the nod, Wonderboy and all. He walks up to the plate and sees the lady in the red dress. Roy knows she is smiling just for him. The pitch streaks toward him; Roy hits it out of the park. The slump is over; the sick little boy gets his hit.

Through a picture in the paper, Roy learns the identity of the lady in red. They meet and have a brief romantic interlude. He learns that Iris became interested in him, his career, and his batting slump. She says that there are so few heroes, she hates to see them fail. She thought that if he knew that someone believed in him, he would regain confidence in himself. That was why she went to the game and stood up in the grandstand so he would see her.

Although Roy cares for Iris, he cannot get Memo out of his mind or heart. She wants him to get enough money out of baseball to buy into a business "for the future." When she visits Roy in the hospital after he has had an emergency appendectomy, she tells him that there is a way he can earn a good deal of money. The rejuvenated Knights are in the playoffs. The Judge wants him to "drop" the playoff game, to make sure the Knights do not win. The betting odds will have a field day, and Roy will be well compensated. After all, how much longer does he have in baseball anyway?

Because he cannot face a life without Memo, Roy agrees. But in the seventh inning of the playoff game against the Pirates, with two Knights on base and the crowd screaming for him to come through, he suddenly feels anguish at what he has agreed to do. He swings and misses. Then he hits a ball foul, and another. He chops a third foul, which slams into the crowd and hits a woman spectator. Even without looking, Roy knows who she is. He runs into the stands to find Iris, unconscious. He carries her into the trainer's room where the doctor sends for an ambulance. She has contusions and lacerations, but she will live. Iris revives and tells him to go back to the game. She also tells him that she is pregnant with his child.

"Win for us," Iris says, "you were meant to."

Roy goes back into the game with a count of 0 and 2. After three more pitches it is three balls and two strikes. The pitcher streaks the ball in toward home plate and Roy swings from his heels and from his heart. With a resounding crack, Wonderboy splits in half, and the ball goes foul. Roy Hobbs fails to lift his bat on the next pitch. It is a perfect strike.

Now it is the ninth inning. The Pirates are one run ahead. Roy has saved another run by his catch for the third out. The Knights come to bat.

Now there are two outs and a man on third. Once more Roy comes to bat, and the crowd roars. He knows what he must do.

With a two-strike count, the pitcher throws, and with the crowd's roar in his ears, Roy Hobbs strikes out.

Later Roy goes to the Judge's office, where he finds Memo and the Judge's bookie. He throws down the money the Judge has had delivered to him in disgust, and when Memo tries to shoot him, he takes the gun from her. As he leaves he tells himself that he never did learn anything from his past; now he must suffer again.

Out on the street the headlines are already screaming about a suspicion that Hobbs threw the game. As Roy thrusts the newspaper back at the paperboy, the kid says, "Say it ain't true, Roy." In response Roy Hobbs, who only wanted to be the best there ever was, lifts his hands to his face and weeps.

Thematic Material

Set against a detailed background of professional baseball in its earlier years, this is a powerful story of ambition, desire, greed, human frailty, and courage. Roy Hobbs is presented as a man of enormous talent and confidence who finds great difficulty in adjusting to the loss of his early years after the shooting incident and the loss of his dream to become the best there ever was. Unable to face the loneliness of a life without Memo and too devoid of cunning to see what she really wants and needs, he sells out, though he realizes that it dishonors the game he loves. And although he cannot carry it through, Roy Hobbs knows his guilt, and weeps.

Book Talk Material

The colorful details of baseball serve as an excellent introduction to this novel. See: Roy joins the Knights (pp. 39–41); he talks about Wonderboy (pp. 59–61); Roy takes Bump's place (pp. 72–75); and he wins the big one for the kid and sees Iris (pp. 127–134). Readers will also be interested in the shooting in the hotel room (pp. 32–34) and the fans grow to love Roy Hobbs but Memo disdains him (pp. 78–84).

Additional Selections

In a frank novel of the sixties, John Hough's *The Conduct of the Game* (Harcourt, 1985, $14.95; pap., Warner, $3.95), a young man joins the ranks of professional umpires.

1933 Was a Bad Year by John Fante (Black Sparrow, 1986, $14.00, pap. $3.50) is a funny, touching novel about a high school senior coming of age and dreaming of pitching in the major leagues.

Mark Harris's novel *Bang the Drum Slowly* (pap., Univ. of Nebraska, $6.50) is about baseball, friendship and a player suffering from Hodgkin's disease.

A reform school teenager uses his running ability to get even with the System in Alan Sillitoe's *The Loneliness of the Long Distance Runner* (Knopf, 1960, $10.95; pap., NAL, $2.50).

The friendship of two Jewish boys is tested when their baseball teams play each other in Chaim Potok's *The Chosen* (pap., Fawcett, $3.50).

Three very different men—an East German, a Japanese man, and an American—compete in the Boston Marathon in Mark Kram's novel *Miles to Go* (Morrow, 1982, $11.50).

Thomas Boswell analyzes America's love of baseball in the nonfiction *How Life Imitates the World Series* (pap., Penguin, $6.95).

For young readers, Thomas J. Dygard presents an unflattering picture of professional baseball in *The Rookie Arrives* (Morrow, 1988, $11.95). Two other fine junior sports novels are Barbara Stratton's *You Never Lose* (Knopf, 1982, $14.95), about a high school senior's football coach father who has cancer, and Michael French's *The Throwing Season* (Delacorte, 1980, $8.95; pap., Dell, $2.50), the story of a young athlete's conflict over a bribery offer.

About the Book

Library Journal, September 1, 1952, p. 1408.

New York Times Book Review, August 24, 1952, p. 3.
See also *Book Review Digest,* 1952, p. 595.

About the Author
Harte, Barbara, and Riley, Carolyn, eds. *Contemporary Authors* (First Revision).
    Detroit: Gale, 1969. Vols. 5–7, pp. 723–725.
May, Hal, ed. *Contemporary Authors.* Detroit: Gale, 1986. Vol. 118, pp. 306–307.
Wakeman, John, ed. *World Authors 1950–1970.* New York: Wilson, 1975, pp.
    917–920.

Plimpton, George.   *The Open Net*
    Norton, 1985, $16.95

George Plimpton has been called the professional amateur of sports,
sort of a Walter Mitty who really lives his fantasies. In well-observed,
exuberant accounts, this writer-not-athlete has turned his hand to baseball in *Out of My League* (pap., Penguin, $4.95), football in *Paper Lion*
(Holtzman, 1965, $19.95), and golf in *Bogey Man* (o.p.). Behind this
dilettante exterior, however, is a man seriously interested in the course
of literature. He is, for example, the principal editor and publisher of
the *Paris Review. The Open Net,* on his career in hockey, and his other
sports books are enjoyed by readers in the senior high grades.

Plot Summary
    George Plimpton, the professional amateur, regarded ice hockey as
one sport he would not attempt to investigate. For one thing he has a
tendency to skate on his ankles, so much so that someone told him he is
the same height with or without ice skates. But when the Boston Bruins
professional team says he can train with them for part of the summer of
1977 "to get a feel for the game," which he can then describe in a book,
Plimpton decides to give it a try. He is to be the goalie, and he will get to
play for five minutes in an actual game against the famed bullies, the
Philadelphia Flyers.
    Plimpton almost reconsiders. Besides trying his best to stand up on the
ice, Plimpton is concerned about the reliability of his face mask. Strange
as it seems, face masks in ice hockey have been around only since 1959;
before that goaltenders went out on the ice "barefaced," which probably

accounts for the numerous missing teeth and facial scars of so many ex-goalies. But in 1959 Jacques Plante of the Montreal Canadiens took the ice at Madison Square Garden in New York City against the Rangers wearing a mask over his face. Both fans and fellow players thought he'd gone "soft." As Plante explained, he wanted to wear the mask because he had already had a broken jaw, about 200 stitches in his head, two broken cheekbones, and four broken noses. Today all goalies in the professional league wear face masks.

Next, Plimpton finds that just getting dressed for a practice game of ice hockey is an ordeal, and takes him about half an hour. Over a long white union suit (before putting on their outside top uniforms, hockey players in the locker room tend to look like a meeting of huge rabbits) goes a pair of thick socks, then a protective cup made of hard plastic, and then a garter belt that holds up the heavy wool stockings (in the Bruins' case colored yellow and black). Next come the hockey pants, which Plimpton describes as being so stiff that it is like pulling up a pair of barrels. Now come the skates, designed with toe and ankle protectors for the goalie and a comparatively dull blade so that the goaltender will not be stopped short by the sharp edges. After the skates come the leg pads, as thick as a mattress and cumbersome. And after all that come knee pads, a chest protector, arm protectors, and a small device worn around the neck to keep the Adam's apple from getting caved in! Finally, the gloves go on, then the mask, and Plimpton is ready.

Interspersed with these details of the violent world of professional hockey are interesting insights into the players themselves—the stars, the rookies, those who have been around for a long while, and those who won't last a season. Plimpton tells of life in the training season, grueling two-a-day practices, the unbelievably loud craaaack of the puck as it whistles across the ice and slams into the boards, the comradery of teammates, and the beer rounds at a local bar with the players at the end of the day.

And then comes Plimpton's big day; he will take the ice against Philadelphia. He is given his game jersey—with two zeroes on it. He suspects it is a judgment of his talent.

The locker room is tense after the Bruins' warm-up. Plimpton is more so. Just the sight of the fearsome Flyers in their orange and white has brought the reality of it all home to him.

Plimpton takes the ice and stands somewhat wobbly in front of the goalie cage. During the "Star Spangled Banner" he wonders if he should remove his face mask, but he is afraid to do so in case he can't get it back on straight. Then the game is on and the Flyers are tearing down the ice, right toward him. The first shot of the Flyers goes right in. Plimpton barely has a chance to see the puck, let alone stop it.

The next five minutes seem an eternity, and when viewed later on film show that Plimpton spends a rather amazing part of the time sprawled on the ice. He does, however, stop a score from that position by clapping his big glove over the puck as it whizzes by.

But before Plimpton's eternity is over he hears that Philadelphia has been granted a penalty shot, a not-too-frequent occurrence. This means that one Flyer will come barreling down the ice and attempt to put the puck in the net against the Bruins's goalie—Plimpton. Down the ice the Flyer thunders toward a nearly paralyzed rookie goalie, and then, miracle of miracles, the puck hits the edge of Plimpton's blade and misses the net! Later the Bruins tell him that the Flyer who missed the shot may never play again, just from the pure shame of missing a goal against Plimpton.

Plimpton retires from ice hockey after that one moment of glory. In 1985, however, he comes back to Edmonton for a look at the Oilers and their legend, the great Wayne Gretsky.

Thematic Material

This is a humorous, colorful look at the often-violent world of professional ice hockey. Plimpton fills in the small details that are of interest to the sports fan and gives the reader a sense of life in the big leagues, as well as a feeling of "being there" as he describes the sights and sounds of the ice arena as they swirl about a somewhat timid and seemingly defenseless goalie.

Book Talk Material

Plimpton's description of dressing for the game and his feelings and observations out on the ice are a good introduction to this rough but fascinating sport. See: preparing for the ice (pp. 41–46); Plimpton's entrance (pp. 47–48); controlling the puck (pp. 61–63); and Plimpton talks about hockey violence (pp. 126–130, 153–170).

Additional Selections

David Halberstam gives an in-depth look at an Olympic rowing team in *The Amateurs* (Morrow, 1985, $14.95; pap., Penguin, $6.95).

Michael Barnberger's *The Green Road Home* (Contemporary, 1986, $16.95) is subtitled "A Caddie's Journal of Life on the Pro Golf Tour."

Cyra McFadden's *Rain or Shine: A Family Memoir* (Knopf, 1986, $16.95) is her story of growing up on the rodeo circuit with a difficult father.

Pam Shriver in her first-person diary, *Passing Shots* (McGraw, 1986, $16.95), recalls a year on the tennis circuit.

An excellent collection of poems covering a variety of sports is *American Sports Poems* (Watts, 1988, $14.95) edited by R. R. Knudson and May Swenson.

Biographies of a gold-medal gymnast and her coach combine in *Mary Lou: Creating an Olympic Champion* (McGraw, 1984, $16.95) by Mary Lou Retton and Bela Karoly.

Bonnie Tiburzi tells of her experiences as the first woman pilot for a major airline in *Takeoff!* (Crown, 1984, $15.95).

The role that such sciences as physics, aerodynamics, and physiology play in a variety of sports is explored in *Newton at the Bat* (pap., Scribner's, $6.95) by Eric W. Schrier and William F. Allman.

For readers interested in ice hockey, Zander Hollander compiles annually *The Complete Handbook of Pro Hockey* (pap., NAL, $4.95), and Frank Polnasznek has some brain teasers in *505 Hockey Questions Your Friends Can't Answer* (pap., Walker, $3.95).

James A. Michener has an interesting overview in *Sports in America* (Random, 1976, $15.95; pap., Fawcett, $3.50).

About the Book
Booklist, November 1, 1985, p. 703.
Library Journal, December 1985, p. 124.
New York Times Book Review, November 24, 1975, p. 16.
See also *Book Review Digest*, 1986, p. 1289, and *Book Review Index*, 1985, p. 491; 1986, p. 581.

About the Author
Commire, Anne, ed. *Something about the Author*. Detroit: Gale, 1976. Vol. 10, pp. 121–122.
Nasso, Christine, ed. *Contemporary Authors* (First Revision). Detroit: Gale, 1977. Vols. 21–24, pp. 682–683.

Voigt, Cynthia. *The Runner*
Atheneum, 1985, $11.95; pap., Fawcett, $2.50

The Tillerman family was first introduced in the novel *Homecoming* (Atheneum, 1981, $13.95; pap., Fawcett, $2.25; condensed in *Juniorplots 3*, Bowker, 1987, pp. 110–113). In it, a distraught and unbalanced Liza Tillerman abandons her four fatherless young children in a Connecticut shopping mall. The oldest, 13-year-old Dicey, takes charge. She leads her sister and two brothers on an amazing odyssey that takes them to Crisfield, a small town on the eastern shore of Maryland where they are grudgingly allowed to stay by their maternal grandmother, Abigail Tillerman, a bitter, ill-tempered recluse. Dicey later learns why Abigail has become so sour and remote. Her deceased husband, a despotic, heartless man, had driven her children one by one from home. The oldest, Dicey's mother, left to join a shiftless sailor named Frank Verriker in New England; the next, Johnny, left for college on a scholarship and never returned; the youngest, Samuel, nicknamed Bullet, joined the army at age 18 and was killed in Vietnam. Although other novels by Voigt continue the story of Dicey and her brood, *The Runner* is Bullet's story. It begins in September 1967, some 12 years before the events of *Homecoming*, and ends in March of the following year with Bullet joining the army. A brief coda is dated December 1969, when Abigail learns of her son's death. Written for a slightly older audience than the other Tillerman books, it is suitable for readers in grades 8 through 12.

Plot Summary

Bullet is 17 and beginning his junior year in high school, one year behind his age-mates because he flunked the fifth grade. Since his sister and brother left home, he has been alone in his parents' farmhouse with a cruel, dictatorial father and a mother so terrorized and demoralized by her husband's behavior and the jolt of her children's departure that she has become practically a nonperson. They are poor farmers who live a bleak existence.

Faced with this dismal home life and the seeming desertion of his brother and sister, Bullet has retreated into himself. He is a loner, taciturn, independent, proud, but so emotionally wounded that he is unable either to give or receive feelings and affection. His only friend is a fisherman named Patrice for whom he works, crabbing in the summer, hauling oysters in the winter, and at present helping to rebuild the wreck of a boat that Patrice has salvaged from the marshes. Patrice, who is also a loner, understands instinctively the boy's silences and antisocial behavior.

Bullet sleeps through most of his school classes, but has one passion and outlet in his life—cross-country running. Every night he tackles a 10-mile course close to home. The exhilaration and dizzying exhaustion that the run produces help him cope with the grinding confinement of his existence. At school he is the one shining light on the lackluster track team. Although he is a fine athlete, he participates in the school meets totally without team spirit or a desire to win, but only for the joy of running.

One evening at the usually silent dinner table, Bullet's father demands that the boy get his hair cut because long hair, he says, is effeminate. Bullet remains quite but inwardly seethes under this latest edict. The next day, to spite his father, he has his head shaved. In retaliation that evening Mr. Tillerman orders him from the table with instructions not to eat with them again until his hair has grown back. After that Bullet faithfully shaves his head.

Bullet sometimes eats his lunch of peanut butter sandwiches with some seniors, acquaintances from years ago. They are Tommy Leeds, the outspoken, liberal editor of the school newspaper; his assistant, Jackson; and their girlfriends, Lou and Cheryl. When their conversation is not on school affairs like the new practice teacher in history, Mr. Walker, it often reveals their confused and conflicting attitudes about the Vietnam War and the draft. As usual, Bullet remains silent.

A new black student named Tamer Shipp joins the track team. He is 19, married, and trying to complete high school while working part-time jobs. Tamer also actively opposes the tacit Jim Crowism that exists in the high school. Because he violates the unspoken rule that no blacks use the student lounge, Tamer is cruelly beaten off the school property by a gang of students. The school officials do nothing, but when the same group of whites is about to jump Tamer again in the school cafeteria, Bullet tackles the leader and takes away his knife. He characteristically ignores the gestures of appreciation.

After a track meet against a neighboring school in which only Bullet won his race, the coach asks him to help Tamer improve his cross-country performance. Bullet, who doesn't wish to mix with "coloreds," whom he has been taught to believe are different and inferior, stubbornly refuses. The coach, who also can be stubborn, orders him off the Crisfield team for disobedience.

Bullet now hangs out more with Patrice, who through intuition and some adroit questions determines why Bullet is not staying after school for track. He begins telling Bullet about himself. At age 15 during the German occupation of his country, France, he acted as a courier for the Resistance. Caught by the Germans, he broke under extreme torture, causing the death of some patriots. His guilt was somewhat lessened by the understanding reactions of the surviving members of his group. In closing he also tells Bullet that he, too, is black—an octoroon whose great-grandmother was from Martinique. Bullet rethinks his racial attitudes and decides to coach Tamer, albeit in his own laconic, distant fashion.

One day after school Frank Verriker, with whom Bullet's sister, Lisa, ran off four years before, hails Bullet. He has driven down from Baltimore with his current girlfriend, Honey, who possesses a wealthy sugar daddy and a bright red sports car. They go to a roadhouse, and while Honey is dancing with locals, Frank talks about Lisa, who is living unmarried with their first child, Dicey, on Cape Cod. Bullet becomes so angered at this no-good whom his sister innocently loves that on leaving the roadhouse, he bashes in the hood of Honey's car with a piece of pipe.

One day while out shooting, Bullet accidentally kills the family dog, O.D. (for Old Dog). Although it is impossible for him to grieve, he feels remorse and loss. Later he again shows an unexpected emotion when he walks out in the middle of a school assembly where Tommy Leeds is being disciplined for writing an unauthorized editorial condemning the inaction of the school in the beating of Tamer.

The track team travels north for a weekend-long area track meet. Much to the coach's satisfaction, the team performs well and the combined talents of Bullet and Tamer help collect many precious points. At the end of the cross-country, which Bullet wins handily, he sees half-hidden in the crowd and trying to remain unseen, his mother. In spite of her silence, she really cares.

On March 21, 1968, Bullet's eighteenth birthday, he joins the army. Not for patriotism or commitment to a cause, but solely to escape. As a parting gesture he asks Patrice to hire Tamer as his replacement and from his savings buys the Frenchman's refurbished boat as a gift to his mother so she will have greater freedom of movement. With that, he says goodbye.

Less than two years later, now widowed Abigail answers the phone in her farmhouse and is told that her son has been killed in action in Vietnam.

Thematic Material

This novel contains a great deal of sports action and conveys the hypnotic therapeutic feelings that running often produces. It is also about personal integrity, an emotionally traumatized family, and the cruelty that parents can inflict on their children. In particular, it deals with one proud young man who knows only rejection and scorn and learns through painful experience the meaning of pity and compassion. The futility of war and the controversy concerning the Vietnam War are woven into the plot effectively. Bullet's moving death underlies the theme of war's tragic waste. Racial prejudice and its debilitating effects are important secondary themes. Above all, though, the reader will remember Bullet, a lonely young man, and his unhappy destiny.

Book Talk Material

A description of Bullet's home and school situations should interest readers, particularly those already familiar with Dicey and her family. Some important passages are: Bullet is told to cut his hair (pp. 3–5; same pp. pap.); he confronts his father with a shaved head (pp. 29–31; pp. 35–37 pap.); Mr. Walker talks about war and mercenaries in history class (pp. 58–62; pp. 70–75 pap.); the incident in the school cafeteria (pp. 62–64; pp. 75–77 pap.); and Patrice talks about his war experiences (pp. 110–114; pp. 134–138 pap.).

Additional Selections

Bullet's nephews, Dicey's brothers, James and Sammy, set out to learn more about their father, Frank Verriker, in Cynthia Voigt's *Sons from Afar* (Atheneum, 1987, $13.95).

Running is the major interest in 18-year-old Willis Pierce's lonely, spartan existence until he meets Sophie in Harry Mazer's *The Girl of His Dreams* (Crowell, 1987, $12.95). Willis originally appeared in Mazer's *The War on Villa Street* (o.p.).

A 3,000-mile foot race is staged in the middle of the depression in Tom McNab's novel *Flanagan's Run* (pap., Avon, $3.95).

Joan Benoit tells of her childhood and how she won a 1984 Olympic gold medal in the marathon in *Running Tide* (Knopf, 1987, $16.95).

An Olympic runner writes funny and irreverent memoirs in *Thirty Phone Booths to Boston* by Don Kardong (Macmillan, 1984, $14.95).

Bill Rodgers with Joe Concannon writes about many aspects of running and also gives personal and instructional information in *Marathoning* (pap., Simon, $9.95).

A teenage German girl and high-jump star learns terrible family secrets from the Nazi past in Peter Carter's *Bury the Dead* (Farrar, 1986, $14.95).

High school senior Louie loses his position on the school football team when he refuses to injure a black opponent in Chris Crutcher's *Running Loose* (Greenwillow, 1983, $10.95; pap., Dell, $2.75), and in *Zan Hagen's Marathon* (Farrar, 1984, $10.95; pap., NAL, $2.50) by R. R. Knudson an intrepid heroine tries for the Olympics.

A courageous tale of survival is told in Steven Callahan's firsthand report *Adrift: Seventy-Six Days Lost at Sea* (Houghton, 1986, $15.95).

About the Book
Booklist, March 15, 1985, p. 1052.
Bulletin of the Center for Children's Books, April 1985, p. 157.
Horn Book, May 1985, p. 32.
School Library Journal, May 1985, p. 113.
See also *Book Review Digest,* 1985, p. 1643, and *Book Review Index,* 1985, p. 631.

About the Author
Commire, Anne, ed. *Something about the Author.* Detroit: Gale, 1983. Vol. 33, p. 226.
Holtze, Sally Holmes, ed. *Fifth Book of Junior Authors and Illustrators.* New York: Wilson, 1983, pp. 320–321.
Locher, Frances C., ed. *Contemporary Authors.* Detroit: Gale, 1982. Vol. 106, p. 508.
Metzger, Linda, ed. *Contemporary Authors* (New Revision Series). Detroit: Gale, 1986. Vol. 18, p. 468.
Who's Who in America: 1986–1987 (44th edition). Chicago: Marquis Who's Who, 1986. Vol. 2, p. 2867.

10

Interesting Lives
and True Adventure

As the cliché states, truth is stranger than fiction. In this group of nonfiction works the reader is involved in a variety of geographical areas—for example, Africa, the Arctic, the United States, and Great Britain—at a variety of times from the 1930s to the present and with such fascinating people as a rock group, several writers, and a veterinarian.

Angelou, Maya. *All God's Children Need Traveling Shoes*
    Random, 1986, $15.95; pap., Bantam, $3.95

   Maya Angelou is in many ways a Renaissance woman who is an author, a playwright, and a poet, as well as a professional stage performer. She is perhaps best known for her series of autobiographical books, beginning with *I Know Why the Caged Bird Sings* (Random, 1970, $15.95; pap., Bantam, $3.95), which covers her life to age 16 and includes her being raped by her mother's boyfriend and bearing her first child. *Gather Together in My Name* (Random, 1974, $15.95; pap., Bantam, $3.95) and *Singin' and Swingin' and Gettin' Merry Like Christmas* (Random, 1976, $13.95; pap., Bantam, $3.95) continued the story through adolescence to adulthood and cover experimentation with drugs and alcohol. *The Heart of a Woman* (Random, 1981, $12.50; pap., Bantam, $3.95) deals with her participation in the civil rights movement of the 1960s, and *All God's Children Need Traveling Shoes* continues the story to the four years she spent in Ghana and includes further civil rights activities. They are read by senior high students.

Plot Summary
   Maya Angelou, poet, musician, and performer, joins a colony of some 200 black American "expatriates" in Ghana in Africa. Most of the immi-

grants chose Ghana because of its progressive outlook and its president, Kwame Nkrumah. They felt unwanted in the country of their birth and looked for a new beginning on their ancestral continent.

Maya shares a bungalow with two other expatriate women and works as an administrative assistant at the University of Ghana, where she has direct contact with African students and faculty. Although the job is rewarding, the pay is not, and so Maya decides to find a second job.

Her first assignment as a journalist for the *Ghanian Times* brings her into contact with a rude Ghanian woman who responds to her by saying, "American Negroes are always crude." Maya begins to wonder if the treatment experienced by American blacks has less to do with race than with the fact that their particular ancestors had the bad luck of being caught, sold, and treated like beasts.

Maya's experience in Ghana, in learning to love and understand the country and its people, are many and varied. She tells of being at a dance when she is approached by a tall, imposing-looking man who tells her that Sheikhali of Mali is requesting her presence at dinner that evening. Intrigued by this glimpse into the life of a culture she knows largely from technicolor movies, Maya accepts and is picked up that evening in a 1963 Coupe de Ville Cadillac by Sheikhali, who is wearing yards of gold-embroidered blue silk and a blue lace cap. It was a memorable evening.

Maya also experiences the joy of the Ghanian people in the first years of the Nkrumah government. Encouraging his people to cherish their ancestry, he singles out black Americans and West Indians as among Africa's greatest gifts to the world, which brings much gratitude from Maya and others of the black American colony. But the feeling of joy and high spirits that covers the country is changed by an attempt on Nkrumah's life. Although he is unharmed, suspicion now takes over the government. And the finger of suspicion even reaches the black colony, about whom one official says that Africans should approach all American blacks with caution, "if they must be approached at all."

When the march led by Dr. Martin Luther King in Washington, D.C., is set to begin on August 27, 1963, the community in Ghana begins its own march at midnight on August 26 to make up for the seven-hour time difference. They march in the park across from the embassy, surrounded by a much larger crowd than any of them expected. They march, sing, and think of home and of the thousands who are marching in their nation's capital.

Another high point for the black community is the arrival of Malcolm

X in Accra. The expatriates fill a house one evening in anticipation of hearing him. Malcolm X is in Africa to secure as many government contacts as possible before he takes the plight of the black American before the General Assembly of the United Nations. Maya and her friends are able to arrange influential meetings for him during his short stay in Ghana.

But despite Maya's initial joy at "being black in a black place" and the excitement of this exciting land, there comes a time when she knows that "you can't go home again," and it is time to leave. After all, as a friend tells her, "Ghana will always be there to return to."

Thematic Material

With the voice of a poet, Angelou brings alive the color, sights, and sounds of Ghana. From the background of a black American who has suffered the indignities of prejudice, she tells of her treatment in this land of her ancestors, of the government and the nature of African politics, of the yearnings of the other expatriates, of the black leaders striving to bring equal justice to their homeland, and finally of her own decision to go home. This is an intimate portrait of a black American in search of identity.

Book Talk Material

The small and large incidents that fill Maya's life in Ghana bring a special dimension to this autobiographical tale. See: Angelou's son is injured (pp. 3–9; pp. 5–9 pap.); she moves into the bungalow (pp. 29–32; pp. 29–31 pap.); her first newspaper assignment (pp. 32–36; pp. 32–35 pap.); she goes to an outdooring (pp. 44–48; pp. 43–47 pap.); and the memorable meeting with Sheikhali (pp. 62–69; pp. 62–68 pap.).

Additional Selections

Langston Hughes' autobiography about becoming a writer during the Harlem renaissance of the 1920s is *The Big Sea* (pap., Thunder's Mouth, $8.95).

Another famous black author, Richard Wright, tells of his childhood and youth in Mississippi in *Black Boy* (Harper, 1945, $18.45, pap. $3.95). Another installment is *American Hunger* (Harper, 1977, $13.45, pap. $6.95). Also use his most famous novel, *Native Son* (Harper, 1940, $18.45, pap. $4.95).

Wole Soyinka has edited a fine collection of past and present poetry in *Poems of Black Africa* (Hill & Wang, 1975, $12.95).

Alice Walker has collected her thoughts on life and her writing in a series of essays and speeches in *Living by the Word* (Harcourt, 1988, $15.95).

In Ntozake Shange's *Betsey Brown* (St. Martin's, 1985, $12.95) a 13-year-old faces prejudice when she enters an integrated school in 1959.

Gary Soto writes about growing up poor and Mexican American in *Small Faces* (Univ. of Houston, 1985, $8.00), the story of the poet's life.

A young white journalist travels 23,000 miles in southern Africa in James North's *Freedom Rising* (Macmillan, 1985, $19.95; pap., NAL, $8.95).

The civil rights movement is well chronicled in the commemoration biography *Martin Luther King, Jr.—To the Mountaintop* (Doubleday, 1984, $24.95) by William Roger Witherspoon.

About the Book
Booklist, February 1, 1986, p. 778.
Library Journal, March 15, 1986, p. 64.
New York Times Book Review, May 11, 1986, p. 14.
School Library Journal, August 1986, p. 113.
VOYA, August 1986, p. 170.
See also *Book Review Digest*, 1986, p. 52, and *Book Review Index*, 1986, p. 38.

About the Author
Bowden, Jane, ed. *Contemporary Authors*. Detroit: Gale, 1977. Vols. 65–68, p. 28.
Colby, Vineta, ed. *World Authors 1975–1980*. New York: Wilson, 1985, pp. 37–39.
Commire, Anne, ed. *Something about the Author*. Detroit: Gale, 1987. Vol. 49, pp. 35–48.
Metzger, Linda, ed. *Contemporary Authors* (New Revision Series). Detroit: Gale, 1987. Vol. 19, pp. 21–24.

Brown, Peter, and Gaines, Steven. *The Love You Make:*
An Insider's Story of The Beatles
McGraw, 1983, $14.95; pap., NAL, $4.50

One of the most amazing music phenomena of the 1960s was the Beatles. Of the many, many books written about them, this is one of the most honest and candid, combining fact and gossip in an account that is often funny but as frequently painful. Peter Brown worked directly with The Beatles as financial adviser. This book is read and enjoyed by readers in grade 9 and up.

Plot Summary

They would change the world of pop music forever, these fabulous four young men from Liverpool, England, with their (at the time) longish hair and strange new sounds. Paul, John, George, and Ringo—known as The Beatles—would become known throughout the world, and after the spectacular quartet had broken up, the name of The Beatles would remain forever etched in music annals.

This is the inside story of those creative, innovative, but not-so-innocent young men, written by Peter Brown, who was executive director of The Beatles's management company and a close personal friend of the four, and by Steven Gaines, whose credits include biographies and numerous articles on show business personalities.

When The Beatles arrived in the United States for their initial appearance on the Ed Sullivan show, their hit "I Want to Hold Your Hand" had already rocketed to the top of the music charts. It seemed that all of America wanted to see the four from Liverpool. The airport was swarming with screaming fans. On the following Sunday night in February 1964, 13 million Americans watched something new happening in the music world. Overnight they would become the most talked about phenomenon in the country.

From then until their formal breakup in 1970, The Beatles would know unbelievable adulation from fans, the dizzying heights of enormous wealth and stardom, the depths of the drug scene, a personal world of problems and messy divorces, and the satisfaction that came from breaking new ground in their chosen work. And through it all was their music— new, energizing, creative, haunting, and never to be forgotten.

Who were and are The Beatles?

There is (James) Paul McCartney, born in Liverpool June 18, 1942, to a weekend bandleader and a trained nurse. His mother died of cancer in 1955 and to help ease the loss, his father scraped together enough money to buy Paul a guitar. Picking out tunes right from the beginning, Paul discovered that he loved playing for an audience and hearing the sound of applause. In 1969 he married Linda Eastman. He was the first of The Beatles to announce leaving the group, and adjusted most quickly to solo performances and working on his own.

There is George Harrison, born February 25, 1943, to a city bus driver and a housewife. He met Paul McCartney while waiting for the school bus, and by age 14 was already a guitar fanatic. In 1966 he married Pattie Boyd with Paul in attendance. The troubled marriage, marred by a drug bust and George's infidelities, ended in divorce in 1973. In 1978 he married Olivia Trinidad Arias, a Mexican-born secretary.

There is Richard Starkey, Jr. (Ringo Starr), born July 7, 1940, the son of bakery workers. Ringo spent a sickly childhood marred by his father's desertion of the family and a burst appendix with complications that put him in the hospital for a year. But with his mother's remarriage Ringo found the only true father he would know. Ringo had played drums while in the hospital ward and later formed his own group. He took his new name because he wore so many rings on his fingers and because his drum solos were known as "Starr Time." Ringo proved to be the most fun-loving and uncomplicated of The Beatles. In 1965 he married Maureen Cox; they were divorced 10 years later and in 1981 Ringo married actress Barbara Bach.

And there was John Lennon, perhaps the best known of The Beatles for his relationship with Yoko Ono and his untimely death at the hands of an assassin. John Winston Lennon was born during an air raid on October 9, 1940, to a sailor father he rarely saw and a mother whose older sister would raise him as her own. In 1969, after a messy divorce, John married Japanese-born Yoko Ono, and on December 8, 1980, as he and his wife were returning to their New York City apartment, he was shot and killed by Mark Chapman, who thought Lennon was a "phony."

This is the complete and inside story of The Beatles, from their beginnings in Liverpool, to their joining together as a group, to their first jobs and slow recognition, to their triumphant takeover of the American music scene, on through their world tours and fantastic, unbelievable success, intermingled with their personal lives, their frustrations with each other, their romantic entanglements, their "life on the wild side" of drugs and money and unending adulation, to their breakup and choosing to go their separate ways.

Thematic Material

This story of the fabulous Beatles is made especially entertaining because it presents these four remarkable personalities as all too human, perhaps. They were not the innocent young lads that the U.S. public saw for the first time on the Ed Sullivan show. They are presented here as talented young men with hopes and dreams, who found it difficult to battle the onslaught of their own popularity, their wealth, their fans, their families, their managers and business associates, and their responsibilities. In the end the pressures were too much, and the Fabulous Four had to go their own ways, each to different destinies. But discovering that The Beatles are and were, after all, only human does not make their story any less fascinating, for nothing can ever change their music.

Book Talk Material

The Beatles in their youth and their eventual coming together can serve as an introduction to this book. See: John's early years (pp. 13–19; pp. 12–19 pap.); his first guitar and group (pp. 22–24; pp. 21–22 pap.); Paul meets John (pp. 27–30; pp. 24–26 pap.); Ringo joins the group (pp. 84–86; pp. 76–78 pap.); George becomes a Beatle (pp. 86–89; pp. 78–81 pap.); and the group signs for the Ed Sullivan show (pp. 107–109; pp. 107–111 pap.).

Additional Selections

There are many other books about The Beatles. A few are: Hunter Davies's 1968 standard work, *The Beatles* (pap., McGraw, $8.95); Philip Norman's *Shout! The Beatles in Their Generation*, a 1981 title (pap., Warner, $4.95); and Bill Harry's *Beatlemania: The History of The Beatles on Film* (pap., Avon, $9.95).

The life of John Lennon is highlighted in Anthony Fawcett's *John Lennon: One Day at a Time* (pap., Grove, $8.95), and in John Lennon's own writings, *In His Own Write* (pap., Harper, $4.95) and *A Spaniard in the Works* (pap., Harper, $5.95; combined volume, *In His Own Write and A Spaniard in the Works*, pap., NAL, $3.95).

Paul McCartney's biographies include Chris Salewicz's *McCartney* (St. Martin's, 1986, $15.95, pap. $4.50) and the somewhat unflattering *Yesterday: The Unauthorized Biography of Paul McCartney* (Doubleday, 1988, $18.95) by Chet Flippo.

The Lennon Companion edited by Elizabeth Thomson (Schirmer, 1988, $19.95), is an anthology on the Beatle phenomenon.

Some other recommended biographies of rock stars are: Philip Norman's *Symphony for the Devil: The Rolling Stones Story* (Linden, 1984, $17.95; pap., Dell, $4.50) and Eamon Dunphy's story of U2, *Unforgettable Fire* (Warner, 1988, $16.95). Michael Jackson tells his own story in *Moonwalk* (Doubleday, 1988, $15.95).

About the Book
Booklist, April 15, 1983, p. 1067.
Library Journal, April 15, 1983, p. 826.
New York Times Book Review, March 15, 1984, p. 34.
School Library Journal, November 1983, p. 101.
VOYA, October 1984, p. 214.
See also *Book Review Digest*, 1983, p. 201, and *Book Review Index*, 1983, p. 81;
    1984, p. 105.

Dahl, Roald. *Going Solo*
Farrar, 1986, $14.95; pap., Penguin, $5.95

The celebrated English author of both juvenile and adult stories popular for their display of great imagination and wit began his autobiography with the volume called simply *Boy* (Farrar, 1984, $10.95; pap., Penguin, $4.95). In it he tells about his parents, who had emigrated from Norway to live in the United Kingdom, and particularly about his gallant mother who was widowed when Roald was still a child. His experiences growing up are sometimes hilarious, sometimes painful, and often bizarre. He attended a fashionable English private school, Repton, and at graduation began work with the Shell Company. After a stint in Newfoundland, at the book's end he is being transferred to Africa.

Whereas *Boy* is episodic, *Going Solo* is a more cohesive, chronological narrative. It covers three years in the author's life, from age 22 to 25, a period extending from autumn 1938 to late 1941. The title has a double meaning because the book traces not only Dahl's years of independence but also his period of service flying in the Royal Air Force during World War II. Most of the action takes place in Africa and the eastern Mediterranean. Helpful maps plus many of the author's own photographs and letters amplify the text nicely. The book is enjoyed by both junior and senior high school students as well as adults.

Plot Summary
It is fall 1938 and Roald Dahl, age 22, is aboard the S.S. *Mantola* bound from London to Mombasa on the East Coast of Africa. His eventual destination is another coastal town farther south, Dar es Salaam, in British Tanganyika (now Tanzania), where he will assume a post with the Shell Oil Company. On board ship Roald meets an amazing group of

British eccentrics; there are Major Griffiths and his wife, who perform their daily constitutionals on deck in the buff; Miss Trefusis, whose refusal to touch food with her hands results in her peeling oranges with a knife and fork; and Dahl's cabinmate, a man with the unlikely name of U.N. Savory. His obsession with concealing the fact that he wears a wig manifests itself in such odd behavior as sprinkling the shoulders of his suit with epsom salts to feign a severe dandruff problem.

At his destination, Dahl discovers that his job involves chiefly traveling inland on safari to check on the oil company's various customers. He quickly learns to love the unspoiled countryside and marvels at the wonders of animal life present. Only one species causes him fear and loathing—the snake. On one occasion his shouts of warning narrowly save a native yard worker from being bitten by a deadly six-foot-long black mamba. On another he spots an equally deadly green mamba slithering into the home of his neighbors, the Fullers. The family escapes but not their dog, Jack. Desperate to rid their house of this intruder, they call on the services of Donald MacFarland, the snake man, whose occupation is catching snakes for zoos. In a successful scene he captures the great snake and carries it off in a cloth sack.

Once while up-country Dahl visits another English family, the Sanfords. Their evening drinks are interrupted by a loud commotion. A lion has entered the compound and is making off with the cook's wife. Mr. Sanford is able to shoot over the lion's head, and the animal, in fright, drops its prey unharmed and disappears into the jungle.

In September 1939 Britain declares war against Germany and Dahl is hastily assigned to guard the single road leading out of Dar es Salaam to prevent the German civilians from fleeing into neutral Portuguese East Africa. With a group of brave native soldiers, he lays an ambush. When the convoy of Germans arrives, a tense confrontational scene ensues. Before the Germans are turned back, their leader, a stubborn, foolhardy man, is killed.

On hearing news of the outbreak of war, Dahl's faithful personal servant, Mdisho, decides he, too, must contribute to the war effort. He steals Dahl's prize sword and beheads a wealthy, much-disliked German who had a reputation for mistreating the natives. After a stern lecture about the kinds of behavior suitable even in warfare, Dahl decides to keep the incident quiet.

Anxious to become part of the regular armed forces, Dahl travels overland to Nairobi in Kenya to join the RAF. After initial training school in Africa, he is sent for advanced instruction to Habbaniya in Iraq. There he receives his wings with distinction, but on a flight to join the Eighth Squadron in the western desert of Egypt, he is given faulty instructions and is forced to crash land. Miraculously, he survives, but a severe concussion keeps him blind for weeks in an armed forces hospital in Alexandria.

Gradually Dahl's sight returns and his severe headaches lessen. Five months after his admission to the hospital, he is discharged, and in February 1941 flies his own Mark I Hurricane to rejoin his squadron, now stationed at Elevsis aerodrome near Athens. Its total strength is only 15 planes and its mission is to protect British forces in their evacuation of Greece. The British are woefully outnumbered, 15 against a force of hundreds of German bombers and fighters, but with extraordinary courage and defiance, each day the British take to the skies and are able to inflict amazing losses on the enemy. Each day, however, they, too, suffer losses, and several of Dahl's companions are killed. He and his best friend, David Coke, survive. (This friend was killed later in the war.)

When Athens falls, the seven remaining pilots and planes retreat to Argos where because of official ineptitude, two more planes are lost. The squadron is again forced to withdraw, first to Crete and then to Palestine. There Dahl meets some refugee Jews, and through his contacts with them, he has a foreshadowing of the eventual creation of Israel.

Dahl's intense headaches return and he becomes so incapacitated that his doctor orders him to be invalided home to Britain. It is painful to leave the fight and his friends, but he can be of no use if he remains. After a long and dangerous passage on troop ships around the entire coast of Africa, he arrives safely in Liverpool and is reunited with his family.

Thematic Material

Dahl's three-year odyssey is as amazing and wondrous as any of his fictional stories. Graphic scenes of World War II in the eastern Mediterranean are unforgettable in their evocation of courage, heroism, and friendship. The acts of valor, sacrifice, and death he describes underline concepts concerning the waste and wanton destruction that war brings. In the earlier passages about Africa, the author lovingly describes the countryside and the native people whom he both respects and admires.

In addition to these lessons in sociology, geography, and history, the reader learns to savor the personality and character of the most interesting individual in the book, Roald Dahl himself.

Book Talk Material

After Roald Dahl is introduced to the readers, one or more of his shipmates aboard the S.S. *Mantola* might also be introduced: Major Griffiths (pp. 4–8; pp. 14–15 pap.); Miss Trefusis (pp. 18–21; pp. 8–11 pap.); and U.N. Savory (pp. 27–28; pp. 11–19 pap.). Other passages of interest are: the black mamba attacks (pp. 36–38; pp. 27–28 pap.); the cook's wife and the lion (pp. 44–48; pp. 35–40 pap.); and the snake man and the green mamba (pp. 50–58; pp. 41–50 pap.). Two passages involving the war are: the capture of the German civilians (pp. 66–73; pp. 57–65 pap.) and the dogfight with German bombers (pp. 136–141; pp. 135–139 pap.).

Additional Selections

J. D. Salinger, the author of *The Catcher in the Rye* (Little, 1951, $16.95; pap., Bantam, $2.95), is the subject of Ian Hamilton's *In Search of J. D. Salinger* (Random, 1988, $17.95).

Nat Hentoff's growing up involved anti-semitism and jazz in *Boston Boy* (Knopf, 1986, $15.95).

The noted young-adult writer Milton Meltzer writes about growing up in a Jewish immigrant family during the twenties and thirties in *Starting from Home: A Writer's Beginnings* (Viking, 1988, $13.95). Milton Meltzer has written about another aspect of World War II, the Holocaust, in *Never to Forget* (Harper, 1976, $13.89; pap., Dell, $3.25). This subject is also covered in Barbara Rogasky's *Smoke and Ashes* (Holiday, 1988, $16.95).

Jean Fritz, the eminent writer, returns to China, the land of her childhood, in *China Homecoming* (Putnam, 1985, $12.95).

In *And No Birds Sang* (Little, 1980, $14.45), the Canadian writer Farley Mowat writes about his disillusioning experiences as an enlistee in World War II.

Empire of the Sun (Simon, 1985, $16.95; pap., Pocket, $4.50) is J. G. Ballard's partly autobiographical novel of a boy growing up in a Japanese internment camp during World War II.

Paul Buckhill in *The Great Escape* (pap., Fawcett, $3.50) writes about a daring mass escape from a Nazi prison camp during World War II, and

Walter Lord's *Day of Infamy* (pap., Bantam, $4.50) is an hour-by-hour account of the Japanese attack on Pearl Harbor.

About the Book

Booklist, September 1, 1986, p. 3.
Horn Book, January 1987, p. 69.
Library Journal, October 15, 1986, p. 88.
New York Times Book Review, October 12, 1986, p. 12.
VOYA, February, 1987, p. 296.
See also *Book Review Digest,* 1987, pp. 417–418, and *Book Review Index,* 1986, p. 184; 1987, p. 178.

About the Author

Block, Ann, and Riley, Carolyn, eds. *Children's Literature Review.* Detroit: Gale, 1976. Vol. 1, pp. 49–52; 1984. Vol. 7, pp. 63–84.
Commire, Anne, ed. *Something about the Author.* Detroit: Gale, 1971. Vol. 1, pp. 74–76; 1982, Vol. 26, pp. 50–61.
de Montreville, Doris, and Hill, Donna, eds. *Third Book of Junior Authors.* New York: Wilson, 1972, pp. 73–74.
Ethridge, James M., and Kopala, Barbara, eds. *Contemporary Authors* (First Revision). Detroit: Gale, 1967. Vols. 1–4, pp. 223–224.
Evory, Ann, ed. *Contemporary Authors* (New Revision Series). Detroit: Gale, 1982. Vol. 6, pp. 119–121.
Kirkpatrick, D. L., ed. *Twentieth-Century Children's Writers* (2nd edition). New York: St. Martin's, 1983, pp. 216–218.
Wakeman, John, ed. *World Authors 1950–1970.* New York: Wilson, 1975, pp. 351–353.

Herriot, James. *The Lord God Made Them All*
St. Martin's, 1981, $13.95; pap., Bantam, $4.50 (same pagination)

If one were asked to name the world's most famous veterinarian, he would most probably be James Herriot. His four books, each named after a line of a hymn, continue his story as a young veterinarian in Yorkshire in the thirties through his life in the RAF during World War II and back to his practice. They are *All Creatures Great and Small* (St. Martin's, 1972, $14.95; pap., Bantam, $4.50), *All Things Bright and Beautiful* (St. Martin's, 1974, $13.95; pap., Bantam, $4.50), *All Things Wise and Wonderful* (St. Martin's, 1977, $13.95; pap., Bantam, $4.50), and *The Lord God Made Them All.* A beautiful companion piece is the richly photographed *James Herriot's Yorkshire* (St. Martin's, 1981, $18.95; pap., Bantam, $4.50). All of these are popular with both junior and senior high readers.

Plot Summary

This is the fourth of the bestselling stories of James Herriot, the country veterinarian who lives at Skeldale House on the edge of the Yorkshire dales. It completes a verse, the first three lines being the titles of previous books dealing with the same subject:

All Things Bright and Beautiful,
All Creatures Great and Small,
All Things Wise and Wonderful,
The Lord God Made Them All.

The time is the 1950s when new advances are being realized in veterinary medicine, but much else remains the same in the countryside of Yorkshire where people know hard work and the peace and solitude of the wild.

As this book opens, Dr. Herriot is just back from a stint in the RAF. The war has ended. One of his first calls—at 1:00 A.M.—comes from a Humphrey Cobb, who sobs over the phone that his little dog is dying. Off Herriot rushes to the rescue of Myrtle, a beagle who, although panting, does not seem in acute distress. He soon discovers that the trouble stems from the fact that Myrtle's bed has been placed too near the stove, and she's uncomfortably hot. But since Mr. Cobb remains unconvinced unless the doctor "does something," Herriot gives Myrtle a vitamin pill, and then everyone seems happy—at least for the time being. Herriot is to receive many calls from Mr. Cobb, who now and again takes off for a bit of enjoyment, imbibes too much, and then suffers from guilt at neglecting Myrtle.

Despite Herriot's love of his countryside and his practice, he jumps at the chance for a trip to Russia. A colleague tells him that he can take a trip as a veterinary attendant on a ship that exports animals to the USSR. His cargo is sheep, worth some £20,000. On the voyage he discovers that some of these supposedly healthy animals have developed a cough, known as husk. But it is a mild attack, and Herriot feels the animals are in generally good condition. However, after some days at sea and a particularly violent storm, he finds the sheep growing sicker. He decides to try a new wonder drug—cortisone. To his total surprise, the sheep respond within two hours and seem once again normal. This is the veterinarian's first experience with the new wonder drug.

Life may not be quite so exotic back in Yorkshire, but it is busy and fulfilling for Herriot and his wife, Helen, and their son, Jimmy, who at four years old often goes on calls with his father. And although Jimmy is quite well behaved for his age, he can be trying at times as his father learns. Having just removed a thorn from a lame dog's paw, Herriot is startled to find that his son has climbed the wisteria bush and fallen with a loud crash to the ground. He runs outside to make sure the boy is not hurt and then apologizes to the dog's owner for dashing out so quickly. The man replies that he has children of his own, and then adds, "You need nerves of steel to be a parent."

Herriot has many stories to tell of his own growth as a veterinary surgeon and of the medical advances, such as the use of penicillin, that save the lives of cattle and all manner of farm animals. At first the drug is delivered to him in small tubes, not in an injectable form. When Herriot is faced with a dying cow, he realizes that penicillin might cure it so he decides to attach the tubes to a hypodermic needle, which he injects into the cow's rump time after time, having no clear idea of how much is enough or too much. Would the drug be absorbed in this manner? In about three days he has his answer. The cow will live. And the doctor has learned about the wonders of penicillin.

Thematic Material

The Lord God Made Them All is a warm and witty collection of episodes in the life of a country veterinarian in the 1950s when the medical wonders that are much taken for granted today were new and startling developments. Any reader with a special feeling for animals will enjoy these stories of a kind and caring doctor who oftentimes has more trouble dealing with distraught owners than with sick patients. The book also gives an intimate portrait of life in the Yorkshire countryside and of the sturdy farmers and townsfolk who live there. The dedication of this veterinarian to his work and to the animals shines through these pages in every story. For all animal lovers.

Book Talk Material

As examples of the types of episodes that make up this book, see: the doctor gets hung up on a gate (pp. 1–15); Mr. Cobb and the dying

Myrtle (pp. 16–26); going to Russia (pp. 35–39); Jimmy and the wisteria (pp. 40–48); and Herriot has a close call (pp. 81–92).

Additional Selections

In *Diary of a Medical Nobody* (Severn House, 1988, $15.95), Kenneth Lane tells about his days as an English country doctor during the 1930s.

Four years as a medical student at Harvard are reported on by Perri Elizabeth Klass in *A Not Entirely Benign Procedure* (Putnam, 1987, $18.95).

The founder of the American Pet Motel in Chicago, Robert X. Leeds, tells of his experiences in *All the Comforts of Home* (Dodd, 1987, $15.95).

Another rural English doctor, Cornelius Slater, tells his story in *An Apple a Day* (Vanguard, 1988, $16.95).

John Sedgwick writes affectionately about the animals he encountered in his year at the Philadelphia Zoo in *The Peaceable Kingdom* (Morrow, 1988, $19.95).

Rory C. Foster is a wildlife veterinarian who practiced in northern Wisconsin. His two inspiring books are *Dr. Wildlife* (Watts, 1985, $14.95; pap., Ballantine, $3.50, condensed in *Juniorplots 3,* Bowker, 1987, pp. 258–262) and *I Never Met an Animal I Didn't Like* (Watts, 1987, $14.95).

Samuel Ridgway was a veterinarian for the U.S. Navy and describes his experiences in *The Dolphin Doctor* (Yankee, 1987, $12.95).

The story of a horse trainer who became a veterinarian is told in *No Job for a Lady* (pap., Ballantine, $2.25) by Phyllis Lose and Daniel Mannix.

Gerald Durrell writes about his five years on Corfu and the animals he found there in *My Family and Other Animals* (Peter Smith, 1983, $13.75; pap., Penguin, $4.95), which he continued in *Birds, Beasts and Relatives* (Peter Smith, 1983, $13.75; pap., Penguin, $4.95).

About the Book
Booklist, May 1, 1981, p. 1174.
Horn Book, October 1981, p. 563.
Library Journal, June 1, 1981, p. 1213.
School Library Journal, September 1981, p. 149.
VOYA, October 1981, p. 48.
See also *Book Review Digest,* 1981, p. 652, and *Book Review Index,* 1981, p. 594
(under Wight, James Alfred).

About the Author
Colby, Vineta, ed. *World Authors 1975–1980.* New York: Wilson, 1985, pp. 330–332.

Commire, Anne, ed. *Something about the Author.* Detroit: Gale, 1986. Vol. 45, p. 203 (under Wight, James Alfred).
Locher, Frances Carol, ed. *Contemporary Authors.* Detroit: Gale, 1979. Vols. 77–80, pp. 597–598 (under Wight, James Alfred).

Lawick-Goodall, Jane van.   *In the Shadow of Man*
pap., Houghton, $9.95

As a child growing up in England, Jane Goodall's favorite toy was a stuffed chimpanzee named Jubilee. Also as a child she vowed that one day she would study the animals of Africa. This dream has come true and she is now considered one of the foremost specialists in the area of animal behavior, particularly chimpanzees and other primates. She has been responsible for many interesting discoveries, such as that chimps fashion tools out of leaves and twigs and that they form hunting parties and eat meat. The excellent photographs in *In the Shadow of Man,* which was published in 1971, were taken by her husband, Hugo van Lawick. The book is suitable for senior high school readers.

Plot Summary

For a human being to become accepted by a group of wild animals is extraordinary, and that is the basis for this extraordinary true account of Jane Lawick-Goodall's life among the wild chimpanzees of Tanzania on the shores of Lake Tanganyika.

No creature is as close to the human being as the chimpanzee. Brain circuitry in the chimp is remarkably like that of humans, as is the structure of the blood. So it seemed natural, back in 1960, for the famed anthropologist L. S. B. Leakey to suggest to Jane Goodall, who was working for him at the time, that she undertake a long-term study of chimpanzees in an effort to throw some light on our human ancestor, stone-age man.

Chimps are found only in Africa; the group Jane would study were of Eastern or Long-haired variety. They range in rugged mountains, completely cut off from civilization. With only her mother and African assistants to accompany her, Goodall set up camp on the Gombe Stream Chimpanzee Reserve (now the Gombe National Park).

Her previous work with Leakey and in Africa, as well as a trial study of monkeys on an island in Lake Victoria, had given Jane Goodall some preparation for life in the wild. But it hadn't prepared her for disappointment. For months she tramped the jungle from dawn to dark, catching glimpses of the frightened chimpanzees, but getting no closer to beginning a study of them and their habits. Then came the magic moment when she found herself sitting quietly in the jungle next to two adult chimps who blithely ignored her and kept on with what they were doing. The fear was gone, and she was accepted.

Jane Goodall quickly learned that, like humans, chimps are very distinguishable, and she gave them names. Among the first three of her new friends were Mr. McGregor, an old, bald, and somewhat belligerent male between 30 and 40 years of age (chimps in captivity live to about age 47); Goliath, a 100-pound male with the movements of an athlete; and David Graybeard with his silvery beard who seemed less afraid of Goodall from the start than the others.

From these chimpanzees and others, Jane Goodall gradually began to learn of chimp habits and community life. Not long after her cautious acceptance into the chimp world, she had two exciting observations to report. One day as she watched David Graybeard squatting near the earth mound of a termite nest, she saw him push a grass stem into the mound hole. After he withdrew it and put the end in his mouth, Jane Goodall realized that the chimp was using the grass stem as a tool. Later, when she watched the chimps pick small twigs and strip them to use in this manner, she realized that she was watching what was actually the crude beginnings of toolmaking. Prior to this, scientists believed that only the human species were toolmakers.

On another occasion Goodall came upon a mother and youngster dining on a baby pig. Scientists believed that chimps were fruit eaters and vegetarians, perhaps supplementing their diet with insects or small rodents. But obviously they hunted and ate larger game.

So began Jane Goodall's lifelong study and love of chimpanzees. She grew to know and respect them as individuals, and to suffer with them through such tragedies as a polio epidemic, in which a number of chimps died. She learned about their mating habits and family life, including the problem of orphan chimps, and their friendships and jealousies. The lessons to be learned from chimp behavior are endless. Chimp behavior in the form of greetings, aggression, and playtime suggest a common ancestor with humans in the far distant past. And yet the absence of some human qualities in the chimpanzee gives us a sense of the uniqueness of the human species.

The thoroughness and effectiveness of Jane Goodall's study of chimps were augmented by the arrival early on of a wildlife photographer sent by Dr. Leakey. Hugo van Lawick and Jane Goodall fell in love, were married in London (after the completion of her studies at Cambridge), and spent their honeymoon with the chimps at Gombe Stream. Their son was later brought to the camp as a tiny baby, although he had to be protected from the chimps, who have been known to prey on small children.

Jane van Lawick-Goodall also writes of the inhumanity of people in the world of these creatures: of poachers who search for infant chimps, a much-prized delicacy in some areas of Africa; of those who seek chimpanzee babies for the medical research laboratories of Europe and the United States; and of the destruction of the forest, which is narrowing the natural habitat of these marvelous animals. And since chimps succumb to the same infectious diseases as do humans, their populations are ever more endangered as civilization moves nearer to them.

Thematic Material

This is a marvelous, very detailed study of animal behavior, of creatures so humanlike in many respects but so marvelously individual. It is also the study of one person's, and then a couple's, dedication to science, to understanding the nature of creatures different from ourselves. For those interested in nature and the great outdoors, the details of living in such a remote area in Tanzania will be especially fascinating; Lawick-Goodall not only describes the world of the chimps but of the natives who come to her camp out of curiosity.

Book Talk Material

Lawick-Goodall's first encounter with chimpanzees can serve as a good introduction to this book; see the first sighting of 16 (pp. 19–20); Mr. McGregor (pp. 32–33); and David and Goliath (pp. 33–37). Other interesting passages are: chimps in the rain (pp. 52–54); the chimps and Hugo come to the camp (pp. 64–78); and the mystery of Flo's sex appeal (pp. 79–88).

Additional Selections

An account of 13 years of observing mountain gorillas in central Africa is given in Dian Fossey's *Gorillas in the Mist* (Houghton, 1983, $19.95, pap. $10.95).

Fiona Sunquist and Mel Sunquist spent two years with the tigers of Nepal and wrote about them in *Tiger Moon* (Univ. of Chicago, 1988, $25.95).

To shed light on human intelligence, Shirley Strum studied the "Pump House Gang" and wrote about her observations in *Almost Human: A Journey into the World of Baboons* (Random, 1987, $22.50).

Carl Sagan's *The Dragons of Eden* (Random, 1977, $10.95; pap., Ballantine, $2.50) is subtitled "Speculations on the Evolution of Human Intelligence."

Herbert S. Terrace has written a fascinating book on animal learning in *Nim: A Chimpanzee Who Learned Sign Language* (Knopf, 1979, $15.00; pap., Pocket, $3.95).

Two interesting books about African lions are Joy Adamson's *Born Free: A Lioness of Two Worlds* (Pantheon, 1960, $11.95, pap. $7.95) and Roger Caras's *Mara Simba: The African Lion* (Henry Holt, 1985, $15.95).

The origins of humankind are explored in *Lucy* (pap., Warner, $9.95) by Donald C. Johanson and Maitland A. Edey, and in *Origins* (pap., Dutton, $8.95) by Richard E. Leakey and Roger Lewin, subtitled "What New Discoveries Reveal about the Emergence of Our Species and Its Possible Future."

Gerald Durrell and Lee Durrell give excellent guidance and simple experiments in *The Amateur Naturalist* (Knopf, 1983, $24.95).

About the Book
Booklist, January 1, 1972, pp. 374, 391; April 1, 1982, p. 664.
Horn Book, December 1, 1981, p. 629.
Library Journal, December 1, 1981, p. 4023; March 1, 1982, p. 83.
See also *Book Review Digest*, 1971, pp. 798–799; 1972, p. 767, and *Book Review Index*, 1971, p. 288; 1972, p. 279.

About the Author
Evory, Ann, ed. *Contemporary Authors* (New Revision Series). Detroit: Gale, 1981. Vol. 2, pp. 260–262 (under Goodall, Jane).

Lopez, Barry. *Arctic Dreams: Imagination and Desire in a Northern Landscape*
Scribner's, 1986, $22.95

As a result of his many expeditions to the arctic regions, Barry Lopez has produced a considerable body of writings on the subject. Perhaps his best known is *Of Whales and Men* (Scribner's, 1978, $14.95), in which he explodes the many myths surrounding wolf behavior and instead presents a sympathetic portrait of a gregarious, caring, and savage animal attuned to its environment. In *Arctic Dreams* he uses a broader canvas and by combining his own experiences with a synthesis of knowledge gained from a variety of other sources, he presents a full-range portrait of this region, a place he describes as being the size of China but having only the population of Seattle. He quotes liberally from the accounts and findings of a wide spectrum of men and women who have been touched by this northern region—explorers, fishermen, trappers, entrepreneurs, artists, writers, a variety of scientists, including biologists, anthropologists, and ethnologists, and lastly the native people themselves, the Eskimos. He discusses the land, its flora and fauna, the seasons, adaptations to the frozen land, and the many attempts of humans, past and present, to explore and understand it. The account moves easily from the concrete and factual to the philosophical and abstract. It is suitable for better readers in the senior high grades.

Plot Summary

Via various expeditions and prolonged stays in the area, Barry Lopez has explored the far northern arctic region from the Bering Strait in the West across to Baffin Island and Davis Strait in the East. Though basically desertlike in landscape, the area differs greatly in appearance during its two major seasons. In winter it is a frozen, silent, impenetrable mass, but in summer it changes to a land of gigantic, flowing icebergs, flowering tundra, rivers and waterfalls, and of an amazing collection of animal and plant life. Because the amount of solar energy is limited, the ecosystems that have developed in the far north show fewer species than in the South, but with larger numbers of individuals in each, for example, huge herds of caribou.

The musk-ox is one of the most numerous and best adapted animals found in the tundra. One of the few survivors of the ice age, it is noted for its long, glossy hair (its name in Eskimo means "animal with skin like a beard"), sometimes 25 inches in length. This helps the animal to withstand the arctic environment along with an amazing herd instinct that manifests itself in such behavior as forming a defensive "wagon train-like" circle when attacked and ceasing travel during calfing season.

The polar bear, the creature that hunts along frozen shores and from ice floes, does not hibernate in winter like its southern relations. Often massive in size (they can be 12 feet in length), they are the solitary wanderers of the arctic. After a two-year weaning period, they usually live and hunt alone. Their den habits and variety of hunting strategies reveal an unusual intelligence to the point where some scientists claim they exhibit a primitive use of tools. When foiled in hunting, they even sometimes display the very human trait of impatience by roaring or smashing pieces of ice in frustration. At present the polar bear population is endangered by the aftereffects of the increased industrial development of the area, for example, disrupted den sites and environmental poisoning.

One of the most exotic animals of the North is the narwhal, a species of whale, usually gray in color, that grows 16 feet in length, and, in the male, has a long, single, twisted tusk spiraling out from the forehead. It can reach the length of eight or nine feet. Considered the unicorn of the seas, the narwhal has been hunted commercially through the ages by those intent on satisfying the needs of curiosity collectors. Many of the world's historical notables have been presented with narwhal tusks, including Elizabeth I of England.

In a chapter on migration Lopez discusses the uncanny insights and adaptive patterns of many arctic animals and birds. He uses many examples, including the astounding travel of the snow geese, which congregate by the hundreds of thousands in basically four nesting areas in the North during the fall and fly south each year to summer at Lake Tule in northern California.

One of the most important historical migrations was that of the humans into the New World. Certain evidence of human life exists for at least 14,000 years in the North, but some archaeologists maintain that this figure could be upward of 35,000 years. Because material, including artifacts, deteriorates slowly in the arctic, many remnants of these early cultures are now being discovered.

The immediate ancestors of modern Eskimos were the Thule (pronounced too-lay) who came into ascendancy about 1000 A.D. They were superb hunters and carvers who developed an intimacy with nature, consisting partly of awe and partly of apprehension and fear, that is still a cornerstone of Eskimo culture. Through time the Eskimo has become one with nature instead of developing the adversarial relationship that is often found in Western cultures. With many examples, Eskimos are pictured as a practical, resourceful people who respect life and possess unusual insights into natural laws and phenomena.

Ice in its many formations and patterns makes up an impressive part of the landscape that produces grandeur and also a perilous environment. But ice comes in various types—freshwater and sea, for example—and ages, each having its own distinctive color and characteristics.

Another salient arctic phenomenon is the endless variation in light. Particularly spectacular is the aurora borealis, the northern lights, elongated banners or curtains of light often hundreds of miles in length and so close to the earth's surface that they appear to touch the horizon. The northern lights are caused by streams of particles flowing to the magnetic pole and emitting waves of visible light.

From an encampment on Pingole Island, a few miles off the Alaska coast, Lopez had an opportunity to view a microcosm of life in the northern wild and to ruminate on the history and the present state of the area. He describes how maps of this part of the world have been drawn by primitive Eskimos with unbelievable accuracy. He concludes with the thought that the physical landscape and its spiritual counterpart in the senses and in the memory of the Eskimo have combined to produce a relationship he calls the country of the mind.

It was, however, neither curiosity nor spiritual factors, but usually hope for financial gain, that led to the first important explorations of this region. After the initial discovery by the Irish and the Norse, it was the search for the Northwest Passage that prompted activity, principally by the English. Martin Frobisher and later John Davis explored the area during the Elizabethan Age looking for a route to the wealth of the Orient. Later such names as Henry Hudson, Sir John Barrow, and Willian Parry extended existing knowledge of the region—many losing their lives during these expeditions. The disappearance of the expedition of Sir John Franklin close to its goal in the midnineteenth century and the completion of the project by Robert McClure ended for a time the search for the passage, and attention focused on reaching the North Pole, a feat accomplished first (though controversy still surrounds this) by Robert Perry in 1909. Today the arctic's riches are being widely tapped by twentieth-century business and industry. Will this mean an end to the arctic and the unique balance of nature?

Thematic Material

In the prologue (on p. 13) Lopez states that there are three themes in his narrative: the influence of the arctic landscape on the human imagination; how a desire to put a landscape to use shapes a person's evaluation of it; and confronted by an unknown landscape, what happens to one's sense of wealth. In the first he reveals how the power and strangeness of this land have enriched and fired the human spirit and its attitude toward nature. In exploring the second theme, for example, he finds that the most telling difference between the American culture and Eskimos is that Americans have systematically separated themselves from the natural world they live in and the Eskimo has not. The third theme questions the meaning of riches—is it money and possessions, or living in moral peace with the universe? Throughout the narrative the author makes the reader feel a oneness with nature while issuing a warning that present practices and policies in the arctic could lead to its destruction. He states (on p. 405) that people must be aware of the conditions of the land where natural order prevails and thus develop a sense of dignity toward the land and its plants and creatures.

Book Talk Material

In the preface Lopez introduces the northern arctic and indicates the questions he hopes his accounts will answer (pp. xxiii–xxvii). Because the book is episodic in nature, many excellent isolated episodes can be used, for example, the seasons in the arctic are explained (pp. 21–23); the musk-ox and its habits are described (pp. 56–58); the polar bear is discussed (pp. 79–86); the exotic narwhal is introduced, including a discussion of its trunk (pp. 125–140, 143–149); and the riddle of the unicorn is presented (pp. 140–143). Other passages are: the migration of the snow goose (pp. 152–158); Eskimo history (pp. 178–203); and the expedition of John Davis (pp. 327–335).

Additional Selections

Another sort of pioneer and explorer is Chuck Yeager, the air force pilot who flew faster than sound. His two-part autobiography is *Yeager* (pap., Bantam, $4.95) and *Press On!* (Bantam, 1988, $17.95).

John Hildebrand explores the interior of Alaska during a canoe trip down the Yukon River in *Reading the River* (Houghton, 1988, $17.95).

Life among the King Island Eskimos is detailed by Vivian Senungetuk in *A Place for Winter: Paul Tiulana's Story* (CIRI Foundation, 1988, $15.95).

A history of the antarctic exploration is given in Edwin Mickleburgh's *Beyond the Frozen Sea* (St. Martin's, 1988, $22.50).

Roland Huntford also writes extensively about the polar regions. Two of his books are *The Last Place on Earth* (Atheneum, 1985, $9.95) from the television series and the biography *Shackleton* (Atheneum, 1986, $29.95; pap., Fawcett, $2.95).

A gripping account of a 1986 expedition to the North Pole by seven men and one woman is told by Will Steger and Paul Schurke in *North to the Pole* (Times, 1987, $19.95).

Jeremy Lucas tells the tragic story of the harp seals of Newfoundland in *Cry of the Seals* (Macmillan, 1984, $13.95), and in *Blueprint for a Green Planet* (Prentice, 1987, $25.95) John Seymour and Herbert Giradet lay out a guide to save the environment.

About the Book
Booklist, January 1, 1986, p. 643.
Library Journal, March 1, 1986, p. 102.
New York Times Book Review, February 16, 1986, p. 1.
See also *Book Review Digest,* 1986, pp. 998–999, and *Book Review Index,* 1986, p. 454.

About the Author
Bowden, Jane, ed. *Contemporary Authors.* Detroit: Gale, 1977. Vols. 65–68, p. 370.
Evory, Ann, ed. *Contemporary Authors* (New Revision Series). Detroit: Gale, 1982. Vol. 7, pp. 317–318.

11

The World Around Us

As ADOLESCENTS reach maturity they are able to deal more comfortably with abstractions involving place and time. This ability to deal with concepts and happenings outside their own experience is shown in expanding reading interests into the areas of science and the social studies. Books are highlighted here that explore astrophysics, paleontology, U.S. colonial history, the Vietnam War, and the land of apartheid, South Africa.

Finnegan, William. *Crossing the Line: A Year in the Land of Apartheid*
   Harper, 1986, $22.45, pap. $8.95 (same pagination)

William Finnegan, a young writer who was born in New York and raised in California, has written for several magazines including the *New Yorker*. He is also a globe-trotter whose travels (very much on the cheap) have taken him to many exotic places. As a teacher in a "colored" school in South Africa he was able to see the injustice and immorality of apartheid as few other Americans have. *Crossing the Line* has received justifiable high praise including being named as one of the 10 best nonfiction books of 1986 by *New York Times Book Review* editors. It is recommended for mature senior high readers.

Plot Summary

In his midtwenties, William Finnegan became a globe-trotter intent on circling the earth, traveling west from the United States. He survived by taking odd jobs and writing travel pieces for magazines. By early 1980 Finnegan and his traveling companion, Rachael, found themselves in South Africa with scarcely enough money to buy a car, a 1965 Opal station wagon, an absolute necessity for traveling in a land where segregation meant the affluent whites owned their own transportation, and public buses bore the sign "Non Whites Only."

In Capetown, Finnegan is interviewed and accepted for a job teaching in Grassy Park High School in one of the communities in Canal Flats, a barren, nonproductive area designated only for habitation by "colored" people. In South Africa there are four racial classifications: white, colored (mixed races), African (black natives), and Asian (Indians). Each has been assigned separate living areas, schools, and educational systems.

Beginning in late February (the start of the school year in a land where the seasons are reversed), Finnegan finds himself each morning crossing the line from an area of Victorian mansions and surf shops where he has rented rooms to the Flats, a wasteland of sand dunes, shanties, and poverty—a transition from white to black Africa, from the First World to the Third.

The school consists of several separate buildings, each containing ill-equipped classrooms with broken desks, shattered lighting fixtures, and smashed windows—no heat, no gym, no cafeteria, or any of the other facilities found in white schools situated only a few miles away. Even salary schedules are segregated, not just by education and experience, but also by race and gender, with white males earning considerably more than female teachers or those in other racial classifications.

Although coloreds form a large majority of the South African population, only a few families can afford to send their children to school and by the time children reach the junior–senior high school level, the percentage attending is even smaller. Of the very few who graduate, an even smaller number is able to gain permission to attend a university. In short, it is an educational system designed to keep an entire population in ignorance and bondage. Even the old dilapidated texts contain misinformation that falsely aggrandizes the white man's contribution to South African history.

Finnegan, who teaches English and geography to some junior high school classes, and vocational guidance and religious instruction to upperclassmen, soon becomes an outspoken but friendly member of the faculty. Only three other whites are teaching in the school: Alex, a much-respected, somewhat effete Englishman; Elizabeth Channing-Brown, a nervous, chain-smoking would-be actress; and Mr. Da Silva, who openly confesses he wants to teach in a white school and whose racial attitudes make him unpopular with both students and teachers. There are many other interesting faculty members: George Van der Heever and Mr.

Africa, the principal and vice principal; Meryl Cupido, a first-year graduate from the school; an explosive radical math teacher named Jacob; and Nelson October, another loner and radical who is bitter about the agonies of his people and is secretly trying to help organize the opposition. It is, however, very difficult to oppose effectively the regime of the Afrikaners. By using the device of divide and conquer, they have weakened the nonwhite racial groups through separation and a paralyzing use of force. Fear of detention has frightened most into submission and a feeling of hopelessness.

Finnegan also meets and enjoys his students. His radical teaching methods, which involve getting his students to think and write creatively rather than regurgitating textbooks, produce a variety of responses—from admiration to suspicion in both student and faculty member alike. One of his most outspoken and suspicious students is a rebellious, bitter senior named Clive whose first words to Finnegan in class are: "Why did you come here?" Later he becomes Finnegan's friend and shares with him news of his insurgent activities.

Just as Finnegan is adjusting to (but never accepting) conditions at Grassy Park School, the colored opposition becomes sufficiently organized to begin a student boycott demanding educational facilities and opportunities equal to those of the whites. The movement spreads to many other schools and areas. Student leaders like Clive and such faculty members as Jacob, Nelson, and Meryl lead the movement to develop an alternate curriculum, which emphasizes the study of human rights and related topics. Classes continue to be held and Bill enthusiastically contributes his teaching, but many faculty members either participate halfheartedly or sit out the boycott in the teachers' room. At the beginning of the second half of the school year, the boycott is lifted—dishearteningly little has been gained, and much has been lost both materially and spiritually.

The latter part of the school year begins in a dispirited way, but gains momentum in a frantic drive to catch up for lost time. Final exams are given, made deliberately so difficult that only enough students are passed to fill the few seats available in upper level classrooms. Finnegan is outraged at this unjust practice, but he must face reality and comply. At school's end Finnegan is filled with many conflicting emotions, partly related to a feeling of relief and partly to sorrow.

Rachael returns to the United States and Finnegan decides to hitchhike around South Africa. He is accompanied by Clive's girlfriend, Mattie, a dedicated revolutionary and white-hater who wants to make contact with underground black student groups throughout the country. They make an unusual pair, he a liberal white American and she a defiant black radical. Their travels take them to Johannesburg, Durban, through the nonwhite principality Transkei, and back to Capetown. Finnegan and Mattie meet a variety of people with widely different racial and political attitudes, but their experiences only confirm Finnegan's belief that South Africa seems inexorably destined to have a tragic future.

Thematic Material

Finnegan presents an engrossing but horrifying picture of man's inhumanity to man and a white population deluding itself to escape its guilt and wrongdoing. His multifaceted picture of life on both sides of apartheid (or "separate development" as it is known officially) is candid, humane, touching, and often humorous. He describes a society where even the most common everyday experiences are interpreted in terms of power and politics. He gives a graphic portrayal of the evil misuse of force and of the courage of the people to survive and hope under despairing conditions. The valor of the few who risk their lives to challenge injustice is well depicted. The importance of education in society and the application of a variety of educational philosophies are well presented. Finnegan gives interesting background history of the situation in South Africa, its status as of the mid-1980s, and a gloomy forecast of events to come. It is, in short, a fascinating, agonzing, and saddening eyewitness account.

Book Talk Material

This book contains a number of excellent short excerpts. Here are a few: the beginning of school and the first meeting with Clive (pp. 7–11); crossing the line to Grassy Park School, (pp. 19–21); the first faculty meeting (pp. 22–25); the classification of races in South Africa (pp. 28–30); the story of Ephraim, a handyman (pp. 138–140); and the banning of books in South Africa (pp. 142–145).

Additional Selections

Carolyn Meyer writes about her journey to South Africa in *Voices of South Africa: Growing Up in a Troubled Land* (Harcourt, 1988, $14.95).

Shirley Du Boulay presents a moving biography of a gallant South African leader in *Tutu: Voice of the Voiceless* (Eerdmans, 1988, $24.95).

The black South African singer Miriam Makeba writes about her career and her devotion to anti-apartheid activities in *Makeba: My Story* (NAL, 1988, $18.95).

For younger readers also use Jim Haskins's biography *Winnie Mandela: Life of Struggle* (Grosset, 1988, $14.95). Another fine biography for younger readers is Dorothy Hoobler and Thomas Hoobler's *Nelson and Winnie Mandela* (Watts, 1987, $11.90).

The influence of blacks is emphasized in J. D. Omer-Cooper's *History of Southern Africa* (Educational Books, 1987, $20.00).

The 1976 black uprising is recaptured in photographs and text in Peter Magubane's *Soweto: The Fruit of Fear* (Eerdmans, 1987, $29.95, pap. $14.95).

A historical account giving excellent background material to the mid-1980s is given in the American Friends Services Committee's *South Africa: Challenge and Hope* (Hill & Wang, 1987, $13.95, pap. $7.95).

A white journalist, Donald Woods, has written extensively about his career in South Africa. Two of his books are *Asking for Trouble* (Atheneum, 1987, $9.95) and the story of his friendship with *Biko* (Peter Smith, 1983, $14.50; pap., Random, $5.95), the basis for the movie *Cry Freedom.*

About the Book
Library Journal, September 1, 1986, p. 77.
See also *Book Review Index*, 1987, p. 248; 1988.

Hawking, Stephen W.   *A Brief History of Time: From the Big Bang to Black Holes*
Bantam, 1988, $18.95

Stephen W. Hawking has been called one of the greatest physicists of our age. For example, he alone changed the thinking of the scientific world with his theory of black holes. More remarkable is that he has been able to accomplish all this while being confined to a wheelchair, a victim of Lou Gehrig's disease who cannot pick up a book, hold a pen, or speak or write clearly. In *A Brief History of Time*, he tries to answer questions about the origin of the universe, what happened before that time, and where it is going. Although he has tried to simplify his concepts, the book is still a challenging one suitable only for better readers in the senior high grades.

Plot Summary

Stephen W. Hawking, who is the Lucasian Professor of Mathematics at Cambridge University, England, a post once held by Isaac Newton, is said to be the world's most brilliant theoretical physicist since Albert Einstein. Although suffering from amyotrophic lateral sclerosis, commonly known as Lou Gehrig's disease, and confined to a computerized wheelchair with a voice synthesizer, Hawking, in his midforties, continues to tackle—and explain—some of humankind's most perplexing questions.

In *A Brief History of Time*, Hawking discusses some of the questions that the average person may ask, often without hope of answering, such as how and why did the universe begin? Will it come to an end? If so, how? In readable and comprehensible terms, Hawking talks of these matters as well as how human beings arrived at a picture of what our universe is like, the concept and relationship of space and time, the often-heard term "black holes," and quantum physics.

It has long been argued by some scientists that the universe began with a so-called big bang about 10,000 million years ago. The universe, incredibly hot and of zero size, suddenly expanded in a big bang. Hawking and his colleague at the time, Roger Penrose, showed that such a theory was the correct result of the theory of relativity. When asked what the universe was like before the big bang, Hawking quoted St. Augustine who said, when asked what God did before creating the universe, that time was one of the properties of the universe itself, so before the universe was created, there was no time.

Since his work on the big bang theory, Hawking has changed his position. Largely because of the development of quantum mechanics, he argues that a big bang need not have been the inevitable result of the general theory of relativity.

Quantum mechanics deals with the very tiny. For each particle in the universe, there is an antiparticle. So there are antiworlds and antipeoples. Would you like to shake hands with your antiself? Hawking says no you wouldn't because you would both "vanish in a great flash of light."

From his work in quantum mechanics, Hawking has proposed the mathematical idea that together space and time make up a surface that has no edge or boundary. If that is so, what does that do to the human vision of God who created the universe, or at least allowed it to expand in the big bang? Such a theory, says Hawking, may have profound implications about God because if, indeed, space and time have no edge or boundary, then the universe need have no beginning or end. It just is.

Fundamental to the concept of quantum mechanics is that light is to be regarded as both a wave and a particle. If light were to be regarded only as a wave, it is not clear how it would respond to the powerful force of gravity. But if light is also to be regarded as a particle, then, scientists concluded, it should react to gravity as anything else does. This line of thinking led to the explanation of "black holes." The term was coined in 1969 by John Wheeler, an American scientist, but the idea goes back some two centuries. If a star is compact and massive enough, its gravitational field would be so strong that light could not escape from it. Any light that was emitted from the star would be dragged back by the gravity field. On earth we could not, therefore, see any light from the star, but we could detect the attraction of the star's gravity. So we know the stars are there, but we can't see them. They are what we call black holes; they are black voids in space.

Thematic Material

To follow the brilliant mind of Stephen W. Hawking as he delves into the concepts of space and time and the expanding universe is, admittedly, not the easiest of tasks. However, the author and scientist writes with much wit and excitement and with enough clarity that the good reader will at least have the impression that he or she has gained some greater knowledge of the universe around us. A good book for the scientifically curious and even for those without scientific background who find the mysteries of the universe fascinating.

Book Talk Material

Besides the relatively well known theories about the beginning of the universe (the big bang) and the evolution of black holes, readers will be interested in how scientific theories about the origin of the universe and other matters of concern developed over the ages. See, for example, how we came to develop our picture of our universe, from the theories of Aristotle (pp. 2–3), to the predictions of positions of heavenly bodies by

Ptolemy and Copernicus (pp. 3–5), to Newton's theory of gravity (pp. 5–13). See also the growth of knowledge about our expanding universe: Hubble's demonstration that ours was not the only galaxy (pp. 36–39); Friedmann's explanation of the universe (pp. 40–41); and confirmation of his work by American scientists working with microwaves (pp. 41–46).

Additional Selections

John Boslough has written his own book about the author and his theories, *Stephen Hawking's Universe* (Morrow, 1984, $12.95).

In Charles J. Caes' *Studies in Starlight* (TAB, 1988, $18.95, pap. $12.95), the reader is presented with a well-illustrated history of astronomy and introduction to astrophysics.

Physicist Paul Davies writes about new discoveries in cosmology and physics in *The Cosmic Blueprint* (Simon, 1988, $17.95). Also for advanced students is George Greenstein's *The Symbiotic Universe* (Morrow, 1988, $18.95), which concerns the amazing relationship between life and the universe.

In the historical essay *The Birth of the New Physics* by I. Bernard Cohen (Norton, 1985, $17.95, pap. $5.95) Newton's theories serve as a pivotal point.

Harold Fitzsch writes of his ideas of the universe in *The Creation of Matter* (Basic, 1984, $19.95).

Another expanding area of science biotechnology is explored in Edward Yoxen's *The Gene Business: Who Should Control Biotechnology?* (Harper, 1984, $15.95; pap., Oxford Univ., $7.95).

Carl Sagan and Ann Druyan have written a well-illustrated book on the phantom of the skies, *Comet* (Random, 1984, $24.95).

How various scientific pursuits are accomplished are outlined in Philip Morrison and Phyllis Morrison's companion to the PBS series *The Ring of Truth: An Inquiry into How We Know What We Know* (Random, 1987, $24.95), and in a series of witty essays David Quammen explores a number of science topics in *Natural Acts* (Schocken, 1985, $8.85).

About the Book

Booklist, April 1, 1988, p. 1296.
New York Times Book Review, April 3, 1988, p. 10.
See also *Book Review Index,* 1988.

Hofstadter, Richard.   *America at 1750: A Social Portrait*
   Knopf, 1971, $14.95

Richard Hofstadter, the brilliant historian, died of leukemia in 1970 at the age of 54, thus robbing America of one of its most important intellectuals. In 1956 he won the Pulitzer Prize for *The Age of Reform* (Knopf, 1955, $16.95; pap., Random, $5.95), a study of American history from Bryant to Franklin Delano Roosevelt. Perhaps his most popular work is *Anti-Intellectualism in the United States* (Knopf, 1963, $13.95; pap., Random, $8.95). In his writing he borrowed from sociology and emphasized the cultural rather than economic foundations of American history. He coined the term "paranoid style" to characterize some aspects of American politics. *America at 1750* is an important, thoughtful book suitable for better readers in the senior high grades.

Plot Summary

What was America like in 1750, nearly a century and a half after the first English settlement at Jamestown, Virginia (1607), and some 26 years before the revolution that would proclaim the United States of America? For one thing you could smell the fragrance of the pine trees about 180 nautical miles off the eastern shore. There were many forests, indeed, only few large buildings, and numerous muddy pathways that served as roads. But the American colonies in the mideighteenth century were in many ways much different from the very early landings and communities, for these colonies were now developing into what would become the first nation to be created under the influence of Protestantism, nationalism, and modern capitalism.

The central social issues of America in 1750 were slavery, white servitude, immigration, the middle-class emergence, and a religious Great Awakening. Slavery was primarily an institution of the southern colonies. By 1760 slavery would be about at its peak, with nearly 290,000 blacks in the colonies from Maryland to Georgia and about 41,000 from Delaware north. Most (60 percent) worked in the tobacco colonies of Virginia and Maryland.

Perhaps the most wicked and insidious aftermath of slavery was its destruction of the black family unit. And for the black slave there was no organization in America to sustain whatever ideas or culture the African might have retained from his or her heritage. Although some claimed that most slaves lived not unlike poor laboring men in England, there is much evidence that the lives of most slaves were far bleaker, far more cruel, far more degrading.

Perhaps a small step up from slavery was the life of white servitude. At least for some there was freedom at the end of the servitude period. There was never any time in the colonies that boasted of a sufficient supply of labor. Not everyone could afford or would morally accept owning slaves. These factors coupled with the widespread poverty and human dislocation in England at the time led to the practice of white servitude in the American colonies.

Indentured servants who survived the miserable Atlantic crossing were subjected to examination and inspection to make sure they were healthy. Their lives in the colonies depended solely on the luck of the masters they drew; some were cruel and heartless, some helpful and kind. Perhaps most telling of their condition is the most numerous crime of which indentured servants were accused—running away.

Growth in the colonies in the mideighteenth century was eagerly welcomed. In 1700 the colonies had a population of about 250,000 hardy souls; by 1750 the number had grown to 1,170,000; in another 50 years it would reach 5 million. During the early years of colonization, most of the settlers were from England. However, immigration would change the nature of the American colonies during the eighteenth century as Germans, Swiss, Scotch-Irish, Africans, and others began to enter the New World.

An important social characteristic of America in 1750 was the emergence of the middle class, defined as those not conspicuously rich or distressingly poor. The dominance of the middle class influenced every aspect of colonial life—politics, suffrage, work ethics, and religion.

Organized religion in the colonies during the early years was most notable by the number of people who were left out of it. Some may have lost their religion on the crossing and some undoubtedly found the wide open spaces of America too difficult to traverse for Sunday sermons. But religious upheavals, known as the Great Awakening, changed religious life in the colonies. It brought religion back to many of those who had lost touch and helped to restore the promises and condemnations of Christianity, especially to colonists in the South and on the frontier. Protestantism in its many forms took over and affected the character of the nation-to-be. The Great Awakening in America pointed up those qualities that set the colonies apart from the mother country—the middle-class morality, the Puritan sense of duty, and ascetic rigor.

America in 1750 was no longer the tenuous early colonies, or yet the vibrant new nation. It was a country coming to be, forming a national character of its own, which would live on in the new United States of America.

Thematic Material

This is a historical look beyond the facts and dates of history and beyond the so-often-written-about early colonial years. It is a look into the social characteristics of the colonies and the special characteristics of the people that were slowly but solidly coming together and would eventually erupt into the Declaration of Independence. This is a history book for those who find the inside details exciting.

Book Talk Material

The five main social issues concerning America in 1750 form the core of this book and should serve as a fine introduction. See: immigration changes the nature of the colonies (pp. 15–23); enduring the voyage for a period of servitude (pp. 37–49); black slavery and its effect on the family unit (p. 105); the middle class emerges (pp. 131–135); and religious awakening in the colonies (pp. 217–235).

Additional Selections

A book that explores how Americans lived in colonial times is David Freeman Hawke's *Everyday Life in Early America* (Harper, 1988, $16.95, pap. $7.95).

Two standard histories of the colonial period are Daniel J. Boorstin's *The Americans: The Colonial Experience* (Random, 1958, $15.95) and Jerome R. Reigh's *Colonial America* (Prentice, 1984, $20.95).

A personal view of the Revolution is given in Milton Meltzer's *The American Revolutionaries: A History in Their Own Words, 1750–1800* (Crowell, 1987, $12.95).

A guide to 500 important national sites is given in the well-illustrated *Reader's Digest America's Historic Places* (*Reader's Digest*, 1988, $26.95).

Using journals and other firsthand accounts, Louis Birnbaum tells of the first days of the American Revolution in *Red Dawn at Lexington* (Houghton, 1986, $18.95).

Edwin Tunis pays tribute to the people behind the beginnings of American industry in *Colonial Craftsmen* (Harper, 1976, $19.70).

Two novels set in colonial America are Murey Heidish's *Witness* (pap., Ballantine, $2.50), the story of Anne Hutchinson's fight for religious freedom, and the story of a boatload of brides sent to Virginia in 1631, Mary Johnston's classic *To Have and to Hold* (many editions available).

Robert Sobel and David B. Sicilia trace an American business phenomenon from the Industrial Revolution to the present in *The Entrepreneurs* (Houghton, 1986, $29.45).

About the Book
Booklist, December 15, 1971, p. 343.
Library Journal, January 15, 1972, p. 195.
New York Times Book Review, November 21, 1971, p. 47.
See also *Book Review Digest*, 1971, p. 634; 1972, p. 613, and *Book Review Index*, 1971, p. 232; 1972, p. 222.

About the Author
Ethridge, James M., and Kopala, Barbara, eds. *Contemporary Authors* (First Revision). Detroit: Gale, 1967. Vols. 1–4, pp. 461–462.
Evory, Ann, ed. *Contemporary Authors* (New Revision Series). Detroit: Gale, 1981. Vol. 4, pp. 305–306.
Wakeman, John, ed. *World Authors 1950–1970*. New York: Wilson, 1975, pp. 658–660.

Terry, Wallace. *Bloods: An Oral History of the Vietnam War by Black Veterans*
    Random, 1984, $17.95; pap., Ballantine, $3.95 (same pagination)

Wallace Terry, an ordained minister, also has had extensive experience in the media. He has produced documentaries and recordings on black soldiers in Vietnam, has written extensively for newspapers, and is a radio and television commentator. For two years he covered the Vietnam War for *Time* magazine and since the war has worked closely with Vietnam veterans. His account *Bloods* mixes violence and courage with the moral ambiguities that war produces. It is graphic and often horrifying and, therefore, suitable for mature readers in the senior high grades.

Plot Summary

This honest and powerful document of the courage and cowardice of black soldiers in Vietnam points up the best and the worst of the American fighting man. It is a frightening, cruel, and sometimes funny self-portrait of 20 veterans, largely from poorly educated, lower-class families, who made up a disproportionate number of the U.S. soldiers in Indochina. Although blacks make up only about 10 percent of the American population, they accounted for more than 23 percent of the U.S. fatalities in Vietnam. Not only did the black soldier have to face the enemy, as all American soldiers did, in the jungle, but he also had to face Communist propaganda, which told him not to fight against other people of color, and the racism of his own brothers-in-arms, who often waved Confederate flags on the battlefield. And when the black soldier returned from Vietnam, he was the first to be scorned and then forgotten by a country that had turned against the war—and him.

There is the story of Specialist 4 Richard J. Ford, III, of Washington, D.C., in Vietnam from June 1967 to July 1968. When he came home he felt very insecure because for the first time in a long time he wasn't carrying a weapon. He bought one as soon as he could. Not long after, while driving in a car with his wife and mother, some drunken whites in another car cut in front of him and made some insulting gesture. Ford fired at them. He just forgot where he was and started firing. After that, the army sent him for therapy at Walter Reed.

Ford received two Bronze Stars in Vietnam and was wounded three times. A high school graduate, he was drafted at age 19 and earmarked for Vietnam. Before he left, the army medical doctors said that the cartilage in his knees was too damaged for combat. They said that he'd get a desk job somewhere in the rear. He was assigned to the infantry.

Ford remembers lots of racial incidents, but not in the battlefield, he says, just when they went to the back.

Ford says his Bronze Stars were earned by accident, not valor. Once he chased one of the enemy into the bush, just one. All of a sudden three of them jumped up and started firing at him. He recalls being so scared that he just fell all the way back down the hill. But he killed all three of them, and received the Bronze Star. He also remembers another killing, this one by accident. Told to search and destroy a Vietnam village, Ford heard a noise at the back of a hut and opened up with his machine gun. He discovered that he had killed a little girl about seven years old and an elderly man. All he could think about after that was going home, but you had to keep going, he says.

Ford is home now. He survived. But if he ever sits down and thinks about it, then things aren't so good. He feels used, he says, manipulated and violated.

First Lieutenant Archie "Joe" Biggers of Colorado City, Texas, was a platoon leader in Vietnam, where he served from March 1968 to April 1969. He remembers the first man he killed; he was so big, he thought. Somehow he hadn't thought he'd be so big. He also remembers that the enemy would do anything to win. He remembers a Marine corporal trying to be friendly with a kid two or three years old. The enemy had wired explosives around the child. When the corporal walked over to be friendly, they both blew up.

When Joe Biggers arrived home, he received the cold shoulder from all sides: from Americans in general because they didn't like the war; from whites who mostly didn't care about him anyway; and from most blacks because he was an officer—which blacks aren't supposed to be. He remembers feeling bad, cold, and completely out of it.

HM2 Luther C. Benton, III, of Portsmouth, Virginia, was a hospital corpsman who didn't have to go to Vietnam because he was the only son in his family. But he wanted to go to see what it was all about; Benton figured that if his country was there, then it must be right.

One of the first things he learned was that you could order anything from back home for the war effort—air conditioners, even if the villages had no electricity, ambulances, citrus-flavored Alka Seltzer, and, of course, lots of drugs.

Benton was lucky, too; he came home, to try to forget the atrocities, the cruelty, the killing, the agony. He finished his bachelor of arts in religion. He knows that America hurt so many of its young men by sending them to Vietnam to be introduced to "prostitution, gambling, drinking, drugs, fear, terror, killing, and death." He thinks God meant him to overcome all those things.

Thematic Material

This is a powerful indictment of war—especially of the war as it was fought in Vietnam, mostly by young, undereducated, often black soldiers—and of racism, the all-pervasive evil that follows the U.S. soldier, white or black, from his hometown to a bloody battlefield. It is frightening in its honesty and cruelty. It does not spare the individual soldier, or government policies, or the people back home. It is also a tribute to the courage and strength of these men, who were lucky and smart enough to survive and strong enough to build a new life.

Book Talk Material

The fascination of this book lies in the actual stories and incidents related by the men themselves. Some strong passages are: Private First Class Reginald Edwards cries for the first time in Vietnam when he comes close to killing women and children (pp. 4–5); Richard Ford goes berserk at home (pp. 33–35); Luther Benton gets the Bronze Star (pp. 75–78); and 18-year-old Gene Woodley becomes a one-man killing machine, falls in love, then comes home and never forgets (pp. 256–265).

Additional Selections

Ernest C. Brace spent eight terrible years as a prisoner of war in North Vietnam. He tells about them in *A Code to Keep* (St. Martin's, 1988, $16.95).

From his own experiences and those of others, Stanley Karmon has written the stirring story of the war in *Vietnam: A History* (Penguin, 1984, $9.95).

A few women tell of their experiences in the Vietnam War in Kathryn Marshall's *In the Combat Zone* (Little, 1987, $17.95).

The story behind the Vietnam Veterans Memorial is told in Brent Ashabranner's *Always to Remember* (Dodd, 1988, $12.95). Letters and remembrances from the Vietnam Veterans Memorial have been collected by Laura Palmer in *Shrapnel in the Heart* (Random, 1987, $17.95).

Annette Tapert has edited a collection of servicemen's letters in *Lines of Battle: Letters from U.S. Servicemen, 1941–45* (Times, 1987, $19.95).

In *Chickenhawk* by Robert Mason (Viking, 1983, $17.95; pap., Penguin, $4.95), a helicopter pilot describes the war vividly and often gruesomely.

Philip Caputo's graphic *A Rumor of War* (Holt, 1977, $10.00; pap., Ballantine, $3.95) is an honest account of 16 months in Vietnam.

Frances Fitzgerald is highly critical of the United States's involvement in the Vietnam War in the Pulitzer-Prize-winning *Fire in the Lake* (pap., Random, $4.95).

Tom Hayden recalls being an activist during the Vietnam War days in *Reunion: A Memoir* (Random, 1988, $22.50).

About the Book
Booklist, March 15, 1985, p. 1037.
Library Journal, September 15, 1984, p. 1754.
New York Times Book Review, October 14, 1984, p. 7.
School Library Journal, August 1985, p. 89.
VOYA, April 1985, p. 68.
See also *Book Review Digest*, 1985, p. 154 (under *Bloods*), and *Book Review Index*, 1984, p. 696; 1985, p. 604.

Wilford, John Noble.   *The Riddle of the Dinosaur*
Knopf, 1985, $22.95; pap., Random, $8.95 (same pagination)

John Noble Wilford has an amazing gift of making the most complex and esoteric scientific data both fascinating and easily understood by the most uninformed layperson. In clear and concise prose, he has produced an intriguing study of paleontology as it relates primarily to the dinosaur, with substantial coverage of present-day research and theories on the subject. It is divided into three chronological parts. The first recounts the early history of fossil study from the late eighteenth century to the middle of the nineteenth, as well as beginnings of classification by a geological time scale that involves eras, periods, and epochs. In the second the history is continued through the nineteenth century and the first quarter of the twentieth. It tells of the great bone-hunting expeditions of this period. In the third, the story is continued through the mid-1980s with particular emphasis on current theories involving explanations for the extinction of the dinosaur. This book is suitable for better readers in the senior high grades.

Plot Summary
One of the first paleontologists to be involved in the study of prehistoric animal life was the French scientist Georges Cuvier, who applied principles of comparative anatomy to fossilized bones found in Paris and at other European sites around the beginning of the nineteenth century. From his findings he devised the concept of the extinction of various species. In England two other scientists, Gideon Mantell and William Buckland, though working independently, simultaneously discovered and reported on the first recognizable dinosaur fossils. These and other geological discoveries forced scientists to revise their thinking concerning

the age of the earth. Using the Bible as history, a few theologians had determined the date of creation as 9:00 A.M. October 23, 404 B.C., but geologists James Hutton and Charles Lytell, though branded as atheists, questioned this and theorized that the earth's history consists of lengthy periods of time and gradual change. William Smith, another Englishman, in turn developed principles involving the cumulative stratification of the earth's crust and the age of fossils imbedded in each of these layers.

Thus in time a geological time scale was developed. As more sophisticated devices were used to measure geological time, revised estimates of the earth's age were made. Now it is fixed at 4.6 billion years. The age of the dinosaurs was a 160-million-year period during the Mesozoic era that ended mysteriously and abruptly 75 million years ago at the beginning of the Cenozoic era. The name "dinosaur," which means literally "terrible lizard," was actually the brainchild of a haughty English paleontologist, Richard Owen, who in the midnineteenth century devised the new classification for extinct animal life.

With the dissemination of Darwin's theories of evolution and natural selection, the hunt began for a missing link that would bridge the gap between dinosaurs and present-day fauna. It was found in about 1860 in Germany in the fossilized remains of Archaeopteryx, a feathered creature that physiologically resembled both present-day birds and ancient reptiles. Interest in prehistoric life increased, flamed by intellectual debates that were spearheaded by such proevolutionists as Thomas Huxley. Soon a worldwide hunt for dinosaur remains began and systematic methods of collecting, preserving, and classifying these fossils were developed.

The western United States and Canada were particularly rich in scientific finds. Of legendary proportions was the bitter rivalry in collecting these remains between two paleontologists, Edward Cope, an independent scientist from Philadelphia, and Charles Marsh of Yale. Their so-called bone wars ruined each financially but brought tons of fossils east, principally from Colorado, enriched existing knowledge of the dinosaur immeasurably, and opened up the American West for this scientific study. They were followed by such luminaries as Charles H. Sternberg, who found the first dinosaur skeleton still wrapped in its skin; John Bell Hatcher, who found gold mines of tiny animal remains in the anthills of Wyoming; Earl Douglass; and Barnum Brown, the man who is purported to have unearthed more dinosaurs than anyone else.

At the same time such European scientists as the Frenchman Louis Dollo and Werner Janensch, a German, continued the search for fossil remains in Europe and Africa. The latter discovered Brachiosaurus, the largest dinosaur, so high it could peer over a four-story building. (In 1979 a larger one, the Ultrasaurus, was discovered by Jim Jensen in Colorado.)

In the 1920s the then-curator of the American Museum of Natural History Roy Chapman Andrews led five danger-filled expeditions into the Gobi Desert of Mongolia where they discovered such fascinating remains as well-preserved caches of dinosaur eggs.

Since World War II the principal thrust in dinosaur study has been sorting out and consolidating the facts already learned and formulating theories principally about their ways of living and about the sudden demise of these creatures.

One contemporary controversy involves the metabolic rate of dinosaurs and whether these creatures were ectotherms (cold-blooded, as present-day survivors are) or endotherms (warm-blooded, as their descendants, the birds, are). Scientists John H. Ostrow and his former student, Robert Bakkr, are present-day proponents in differing degrees of the warm-blooded theory. But this great debate continues.

Other theories involve the number and nature of the living descendants of dinosaurs. Much of this is centered on whether birds fit into this category. However, scientists do know that within the vast grouping of reptiles, there were great differences in intelligence, size, and behavior. Some, particularly the herbivorous ones, lived in colonies and developed nesting areas to take care of their young, whereas others were lone predators, carnivores who preyed on weaker species.

A vast number of theories exist on the reason for the comparatively sudden extinction of dinosaurs after so many millions of years of supremacy on the earth. One current theory, first published in 1980, was postulated by a team led by father Luis Alvarez and his son, Walter. Because stratified earth samples collected from all parts of the earth showed that in layers linked roughly to the end of the Mesozoic era, or the time of extinction, there is always a layer of rock rich in iridium, an element plentiful in meteorites, Alvarez and his son theorized that the earth was struck by a giant asteroid. Others challenge this hypothesis of mass rapid extinction by questioning why some forms of life survived and others not. An even more intriguing theory was offered by physicist Richard A. Muller and colleagues at the University of California, Berkeley. Astrophysicists have found that the earth appears to undergo a period extinction, including the one related to the period of the dinosaurs, every 26 million years. Muller and colleagues theorize that a death or rogue star, companion to our own sun, orbits that infrequently into our solar system, and by passing through a belt of asteroids causes showers of destructive meteorites to fall on the earth. The search is now on to prove the existence of such a star.

Regardless of future developments and speculations, scientists have already learned much about the dinosaur and the fragility of life. From this knowledge they should gain valuable data about how to ensure the survival of their own species.

Thematic Material

This tale of animal extinction can serve as a cautionary tale for modern humans. The author has humanized scientific processes by giving fascinating character sketches of the past and present explorers of the world of paleontology. Their intelligence, dedication, and sacrifice are inspiring, as are their endurance and physical courage. The account also shows how factual truth is arrived at by the application of the scientific method—collecting facts, devising theories, and testing them to accept or reject these hypotheses. The cumulative nature of scientitic knowledge is also demonstrated as well as the joy and excitement of discovery. The frequent serendipitous accidents in research that also have increased human knowledge are demonstrated, and lastly the book shows that there are still fascinating frontiers of discovery in the field awaiting exploration by the bold and adventurous.

Book Talk Material

Eicher's time scale, which compresses earth's history into one year, is given on page 55. The book has many wonderful self-contained episodes that will interest readers. A few are: the possible reasons for fascination with dinosaurs (pp. 65–67); Owen devises the name "dinosaur" (pp. 56–58); the work of Cuvier (pp. 17–23); Mantell and Buckland (pp. 23–30, 30–34); and Thomas Huxley defends Darwin (pp. 78–85). Chapter 6 (pp. 94–109) describes the bone wars of Cope and Marsh, and Chapter 9 (pp. 132–153) covers the Gobi Desert explorations of Andrews.

Additional Selections

Mysteries of science of the earth are explored in Lyall Watson's *The Dreams of Dragons: Riddles of Natural History* (Morrow, 1987, $15.95).

Fred Hoyle states that life did not originate on earth in *The Intelligent Universe* (Henry Holt, 1984, $18.95).

Among other topics, John Gribbin writes about the extinction of the dinosaur in *Genesis: The Origins of Man and the Universe* (pap., Dell, $8.95).

Two other excellent well-illustrated books about dinosaurs are David Lambert's *A Field Guide to Dinosaurs* (pap., Avon, $8.95) and Edwin H. Colbert's *Dinosaurs: An Illustrated History* (Hammond, 1983, $30.00, pap. $14.95).

In Ivor Noel Hume's *Martin Hundred* (pap., Dell, $10.95) an archaeologist describes the discovery and exploration of the remains of a Virginia colony of the 1600s.

Stephen Jay Gould writes about evolution with wit and intelligence in *The Flamingo's Smile* (Norton, 1985, $17.95, pap. $8.95). Also use his *Hen's Teeth and Horse's Toes* (Norton, 1983, $15.50, pap. $6.95).

The chain of evolution from the beginnings of life to the space age is discussed in Robert Jastrow's *Until the Sun Dies* (Norton, 1977, $12.95; pap., Warner, $3.95).

Annie Dillard writes about nature, divinity, and the human experience in such books as *Pilgrim at Tinker Creek* (pap., Harper, $5.95) and *Teaching a Stone to Talk* (Harper, 1982, $12.45, pap. $6.95).

About the Book
Booklist, January 15, 1986, p. 779.
Library Journal, January 1986, p. 93.
New York Times Book Review, January 12, 1986, p. 15; August 2, 1987, p. 28.
VOYA, June 1986, p. 99.
See also *Book Review Digest,* 1987, p. 1714, and *Book Review Index,* 1987, p. 817.

About the Author
Evory, Ann, ed. *Contemporary Authors* (First Revision). Detroit: Gale, 1978. Vols. 29–32, p. 752.
Metzger, Linda, ed. *Contemporary Authors* (New Revision Series). Detroit: Gale, 1985. Vol. 15, pp. 459–460.

12

Guidance and Health

Oldᴇʀ adolescents are still vulnerable to the same personal problems involving sexual awakening and puberty that younger teenagers also experience. In addition they face a host of new problems involving their future plans. In this section there is a manual on sexual self-protection, a sex guide for boys, a book on coping with family crises, and two books on life after high school—one on finding a first job and the other on getting into college.

Alexander, Sue. *Finding Your First Job*
   Dutton, 1980, $10.95

Sue Alexander is a professional writer who specializes in books for young children. She is particularly noted for her "Witch, Goblin and Ghost" books. In this compact book (it is only 73 pages in length), Alexander gives valuable tips in simple language to first-time job seekers, including many sample documents like social security forms. It is well illustrated with photographs by George Ancona and is suitable for readers in grade 9 and up.

Plot Summary
For the teenager who is not enormously wealthy (and perhaps for some who are), there will come a time, sooner or later, when he or she wants a job. This simple guide is about how to find one, the first one.

Young people want jobs for many reasons—a car, dating, new clothes, perhaps to help the family income. How do they start to find one?

The first step is the Social Security card; nobody works in the United States without one. Applications can be found at the nearest post office or Social Security office. The book has a sample application that has been filled out for teenagers to follow. (Remember, warns Alexander, it takes about six weeks to get the card after the application has been sent in.) The next step is the work permit; applications (a sample is shown in the book) can be obtained at the teenager's high school.

What kinds of jobs are open to the young reader? First, the job seeker must decide just what kind of job he or she wants and can handle, and how often he or she can work. Will this be after school? Just on weekends? Evenings? Knowing what you can handle and have time for helps in applying to the right places. What about places to apply? The author gives some helpful examples: Craig is a walking encyclopedia on current music; he applied for a job in a record store. Peggy, the reading nut, found a job in a library. Mel has a green thumb; it seemed natural to work at a flower shop. Debbie found a job at a summer day camp; she likes working with little kids.

Not every job seeker, of course, may have a special hobby or talent. That shouldn't stop you from finding a place to work, says Alexander. Some companies are noted for hiring young people to work during the summer or on weekends. Read the newspapers; note their advertisements.

Ask your friends about job opportunities; ask your parents. Look in the Yellow Pages. Ask around. Does your high school have a counselor? He or she may know of job opportunities. Depending on where you live, there may be a Youth Employment Service office, although these organizations usually have jobs for only a day or two a week or for disadvantaged young people only.

Although most "help wanted" ads are directed to adults, some do apply to teenage workers. Alexander "translates" a help wanted ad for the job seeker, so that "Gen. ofc., F/P time" becomes "General office work, Full- or part-time," and gives other helpful hints.

Sometimes knowing when to apply for a job will help to get it. If you want to work at a gas station, don't go looking early in the morning when people are trying to get to work and anxious to get gas. Lunchtime isn't the time to ask a restaurant manager if he or she needs someone. And if you don't know just what the right time is, call up and ask.

You don't have to look like you're going to a party when you apply for a job, says Alexander, but you do have to look clean and neat. That's important. And don't forget to take along the names of two or three references—no relatives—who will vouch for your honesty and trustworthiness. The references might be your clergyman, a teacher, or perhaps someone for whom you babysit.

Lots of first-time job seekers have trouble filling out applications.

There are all types of applications for all types of jobs, but they shouldn't present a problem. Alexander gives examples of various kinds of applications and how to fill them out correctly.

Next comes the all-important (and often frightening) interview. Be yourself, says Alexander. Try to relax; don't fidget. You may be asked why you want to work or what hours you want to work. Have these answers ready beforehand. And don't be afraid to ask questions yourself. Show that you're interested. Employers like potential workers who are curious and willing to work.

Once you get the job, warns Alexander, remember that your employer will expect you to be as neat and clean as you were on your interview. And you will be expected to be willing to work. Show that you are. Whatever you're asked to do on the job as it pertains to the job, do it cheerfully and as well as you know how. Willingness and efficiency will be noticed in the long run. And it's good training for your future career.

It may be difficult to get your first job, but once you do there is nothing quite like the thrill of that first paycheck—after tax deductions, of course!

Thematic Material

Aimed at the teenage reader who is looking for a first job, this is a simple and practical guide to landing that initial working experience. It covers all aspects of job hunting for the teenage market and gives examples of applications plus suggestions for job areas that the young reader might not have considered. It includes numerous photographs of young workers on the job.

Book Talk Material

This "skinny" book will be most useful to first-time job seekers in the area of filling out applications: see sending for a Social Security card and a work permit (pp. 1–5, 6–8); filling out the job application form (pp. 28–39); understanding the W-4 form (p. 50), your paycheck (pp. 55–61), and the Wage and Tax Statement (pp. 61–62).

Additional Selections

Martha C. Douglas offers ways to smooth the change from school to employment in *Go for It: How to Get Your First Good Job* (Ten Speed Press, 1983, $5.95). Another guide for job hunters is Leonard Corwen's *Your Job—Where to Find It, How to Get It* (Arco, 1981, $11.95, pap. $6.95).

Ilene Jones's *Jobs for Teenagers* (pap., Ballantine, $2.25) reviews types of jobs and gives tips on job hunting.

Go Hire Yourself an Employer (Doubleday, 1987, $9.95) by Richard K. Irish is useful for both first-time and veteran job hunters.

Jay C. Levinson has a useful guide to part-time money-making in *Five Hundred Fifty-Five Ways to Earn Extra Money* (pap., Henry Holt, $9.95).

How to explore and choose a career plus bibliographies on many careers are given in Martha P. Leape's *The Harvard Guide to Careers* (pap., Harvard, $8.95), and Anita Gates gives a rundown on careers that show projected growth in *Ninety Most Promising Careers for the '80's* (pap., Simon, $7.95). Also use Gates's *Ninety Highest Paying Careers of the '80's* (pap., Simon, $8.95).

Career Finder by Lester Schwartz and Irv Brechner (pap., Ballantine, $9.95) is a guide to 1,500 careers and how to find out which is for you.

Susan Jeffers's *Feed the Fear and Do It Anyway* (Harcourt, 1987, $14.95) outlines paths to succeed in life.

About the Book
Booklist, October 15, 1980, p. 322.
School Library Journal, March 15, 1981, p. 153.
See also *Book Review Index*, 1980, p. 8; 1981, p. 16.

About the Author
Commire, Anne, ed. *Something about the Author*. Detroit: Gale, 1977. Vol. 12, pp. 5–7.
Evory, Ann, ed. *Contemporary Authors* (New Revision Series). Detroit: Gale, 1981. Vol. 4, p. 18.
Kinsman, Clare D., ed. *Contemporary Authors*. Detroit: Gale, 1975. Vols. 53–56, p. 16.
Metzger, Linda, ed. *Contemporary Authors* (New Revision Series). Detroit: Gale, 1987. Vol. 19, pp. 17–18.

Benedict, Helen. *Safe, Strong and Streetwise: The Teenager's Guide to Preventing Sexual Assault*
Little, 1987, $14.45, pap. $5.70 (same pagination)

Helen Benedict has had wide experience in rape crisis counseling and has written widely, particularly in magazines, on the subject of sexual assault. A previous book, *Recovery: How to Survive Sexual Assault for*

Women, Men, Teenagers, Their Friends and Families (Doubleday, 1985, $15.95), deals specifically with this subject. Benedict believes that given proper guidance, young people can protect themselves better than most adults think they can. With this in mind she wrote, *Safe, Strong and Streetwise*, a practical guide to self-protection for young people. Both books are recommended for senior high collections, with *Safe, Strong and Streetwise* also of value with junior high school readers.

Plot Summary

The truth is that most young people don't grow up in a completely safe world. The sad truth is that one-third to nearly one-half of all American girls and boys are sexually molested in some way by the time they turn 18. A woman is raped *every six seconds* in America; most victims are teenage girls; 7 to 10 percent are male. The most common assault comes from those the teenager knows—adults or older teenagers. They happen every day, mostly to teenage girls. A date gets too pushy, a stranger gets too close in an elevator, and so on.

It's a grim picture, but it doesn't have to be endured. In *Safe, Strong and Streetwise*, Benedict presents the case that self-protection can become natural and it will lead to a stronger and freer life. Protecting yourself doesn't mean becoming paranoid. Being "safe, strong, and streetwise" can lead to more freedom, and more fun.

First, the reader must understand what assault is and what it means. Then he or she must understand just where that assault is likely to come from. Learning to avoid assault on the street, for instance, means first learning to avoid risky situations. The attitude that "this can't happen to me" doesn't make sense in the world today. It *can* happen, to anyone, but there are simple ways to prevent it, to lessen the risks, and this includes the painful realization for some young people that it is their own parent they may have to fear.

Does a young person have sexual rights? Sexual responsibilities? The answer is yes in both cases. Concerning sexual rights, a young person has the right to wait until he or she is ready for sex, and he or she has the right to say no. What are the sexual responsibilities? To consider another's feelings. Never to pressure a partner. Never to use sex as punishment.

Because the sober truth is that a young person is more likely to be assaulted by a friend than a stranger, Benedict urges the young reader to set up personal guidelines before an assault takes place. Decide right now just how far you want to go with sex at this time and decide right now if there is someone you know who makes you uncomfortable in his (or her) presence because of the way he touches you or makes suggestive remarks. Learn the danger signs of a potential assailant. Know what "date rape" means, and with the help of the material in this book, know how to combat it.

How do you get "streetwise?" Benedict lays down some simple, basic, and effective rules. Trust your own feelings (something's wrong with this place—get out), look alert (don't give a potential mugger a target to work on), and practice some rules of street safety—know where you're going and don't take shortcuts through strange areas, avoid vacant buildings and empty lots, carry at least enough money for a phone call, don't wait alone in a parked car.

Despite all precautions, there may come a time when the young reader must defend him- or herself. Benedict discusses nonphysical self-defense, escape, use of your voice, and some aspects of physical self-defense. If an assault does occur, you must know how to get help, the right kind, and quickly. A chapter discusses whom to talk to and how to cope with parents and friends after an assault has occurred.

At the end of the book Benedict lists numerous "safety sources" the teenager can contact for help.

Thematic Material

Although the statistics on assault make this a grim subject, Helen Benedict has not written a grim book. Instead, *Safe, Strong and Streetwise* is practical and easy to read, filled with no-nonsense suggestions that any young person can follow. It deals with subjects that no teenager wants to face—assault from family or friends, from strangers on the street, from your date after a party—but it does so in a way that is both reassuring and informative. There *is* a way to make your life safer and freer, claims Benedict, and here she clearly shows how that can be done.

Book Talk Material

The most practical sections of this guide deal directly with what the young reader can do in certain situations. Of interest are: how to handle assault by a date (pp. 51–53); how to handle group situations that turn ugly (pp. 55–56); how to handle trouble from those in authority (pp. 57–65); how to handle assault by a parent (pp. 65–67); and how to handle flashers and potential assaults (pp. 72–80).

Additional Selections

Margaret O. Hyde's book *Sexual Abuse: Let's Talk about It* (Westminster, 1987, $8.95) is a readable account that relies heavily on case studies.

Sex, health, and physical development are only three of the many topics covered in Kathy McCoy's *The New Teenage Body Book* (HP Books, 1987, $19.95, pap. $9.95).

Using a question-and-answer format, Janet R. Price outlines legal rights for public school students in *The Rights of Students* (Southern Illinois Univ., 1988, $6.95).

Rhoda McFarland uses fictionalized case histories about liquor and drugs to make telling points in *Coping with Substance Abuse* (Rosen, 1988, $12.95).

Heavy metal rocker Dee Snider gives sound advice in *Dee Snider's Teenage Survival Guide* (Doubleday, 1987, $8.95).

Sol Gordon offers good advice to troubled teens in *When Living Hurts* (Union of American Hebrew Congregations, 1985, $8.95.).

The legal, emotional, and physical results of rape are explored in Dianna Daniels Booher's *Rape: What Would You Do If. . .* (Messner, 1981, $9.79, pap. $4.95).

Andrea Medea and Kathleen Thompson have also written a useful report for women of all ages in *Against Rape* (Farrar, 1974, $8.95, pap. $4.95).

Some novels that deal with sexual abuse are Fran Arrick's *Steffie Can't Come Out to Play* (pap., Dell, $2.75), about a young girl's life as a prostitute, and a rape victim's story, *Are You in the House Alone?* (Viking, 1976, $11.95; pap., Dell, $2.95), by Richard Peck.

About the Book
Book Report, January 1987, p. 43.
Booklist, January 1, 1987, p. 702.
Bulletin of the Center for Children's Books, April 1987, p. 98.
School Library Journal, May 1987, p. 106.
VOYA, February 1987, p. 296.

Booher, Dianna Daniels. *Coping: When Your Family Falls Apart*
Messner, 1979, $9.29

Dianna Booher, an English teacher and professor of creative writing, has written widely in the field of guidance. She has written on such subjects as friendship, *Making Friends with Yourself and Other Strangers* (Messner, 1982, $9.29), love, *Love: First Aid for the Young* (Messner, 1985, $9.29), and moving, *Help, We're Moving* (Messner, 1983, $9.29). Together with *Coping*, these books are valuable with both junior and senior high school students.

Plot Summary

It is one thing to hear statistics that say the divorce rate in America is increasing. It is quite another when it is *your* father and mother who are getting the divorce. This is a basic guide for young people whose family is falling apart. It emphasizes a positive attitude and growth toward a new life.

In any family going through a divorce, certain steps will follow in a more or less general sequence. Author Booher takes young readers through these steps as they will probably experience them. First, there is hearing the news. Whether the reality of divorce follows years of fighting between parents, or whether the first mention of divorce is the child's first hint of trouble, the news is going to be a shock. In order to adjust to this new situation, says Booher to the young reader, you must do two difficult things: forgive your parent for your own sake as well as his or hers, and try to understand the situation. Understanding brings one closer to adjusting.

People go through a whole range of emotions when they experience shock. A child, upon hearing of his or her parents' divorce, might register disbelief, denial, grief, anger, or fear (who's going to take care of me?), a feeling that love has been lost, guilt (am I the cause?), embarrassment, or shame. And sometimes the reaction is simply withdrawal, from everything and everybody. But whatever the first reaction, says Booher, you can handle it so that it will move you forward, not backward, in coping with your family falling apart.

It's important for children to understand that parents, too, have second thoughts when a divorce is contemplated. They feel like failures, both as husbands or wives and as parents. They feel guilty about breaking up the family, even though they are unhappy with things as they are. They feel angry, bitter, and sad. It helps for the children in the family to know that their parents are going through these feelings, too. Perhaps second thoughts about the divorce will help all concerned to understand that the family unit was not really a happy one before. Perhaps everyone will be happier now.

Quite apart from the world of emotions that a divorce sets in motion are the all-too-real changes that will most certainly occur in most families as one parent leaves the home. Will the children stay together? Will there be money for college? Where will I live? When will I see the other parent? These questions can be frightening, especially for younger children. Booher explains such court settlements as a legal separation (the couple no longer lives together but the marriage is not legally over; often the first step toward divorce); an uncontested divorce (both parents have agreed to it); and a contested divorce (one does not want it or both cannot agree on such matters as property settlement or custody, meaning who gets the children). Obviously, a contested divorce has the most potential for upheaval and unhappiness in the family, often over the question of custody of the children.

Booher explains the different types of custody. *Joint* custody means that both parents make decisions concerning the children (religion, schooling, and such), even though they may live with one parent only. *Split* custody means that one or more of the children may live with one parent, the rest with the other. Each parent has full control over the children he or she raises. *Divided* custody means that a child may live with one parent for a certain period (say six months or during the school year) and the rest of the time (vacations and holidays, or the other six months) with the other parent. *Sole* custody means that one parent has responsibility for the child all the time.

When a divorce takes place, warns Booher, parents may, sometimes without realizing it, play games with their children. Children of divorced families should be aware of these games, understand what causes them, and know how to react. Sometimes one parent will try to "poison" the child against the other parent ("your mother's a lousy housekeeper; it's a wonder you have clean clothes to wear"); will use the child as a scapegoat, pouring all the anger and frustration of the divorce on the child's shoulders; will make the child into a messenger ("tell your dad you need something new") or a spy ("is your mother dating?"), or any of a number of games that parents can play, and that Booher has solutions for.

But children, warns Booher, can play games, too. The most common are *bribery* ("Mom, if you don't let me go on the ski trip, I'll spend the holidays with Dad"), *destroy* (steal, run away from home, set fire to things), and *poor me* (a play for sympathy that friends, and parents, too, tire of quickly).

After a look at the possibilities of parents' dating and remarriage, which is often a shock to the children, Booher talks about the end result of all this knowledge about coping when the family falls apart—turning the bad into good. Taking the obvious pain of divorce and making it work for you by turning your life toward something better than you ever thought you could have, even before you heard the word. For in the end, Booher says to young readers, " . . . you have no choice but to accept the past and make it into something useful in your growth toward maturity. Because at times friends and family will fail you, you must take responsibility for your own happiness."

Thematic Material

Dianna Booher has written an easy-to-read, uncomplicated guide for the young reader who is trying to survive the very real disaster of divorce. Step by step, she outlines the probable happenings and emotions that the family will experience and must endure. Learning to handle the anger, fear, and anxiety is a very real problem for young people, and this practical book can help them face what might well be the greatest challenge of their young lives.

Book Talk Material

For young people who might have to face the agony of a family that will be split by divorce, two areas will serve as an excellent introduction to this guide; see hearing the news (pp. 11–25) and the types of child custody that the court might decree (pp. 46–47). Other passages of interest are: experiencing first reactions to the news (pp. 17–29) and games children play (pp. 71–76).

Additional Selections

Interviews with youngsters ages 12 to 18, plus general information, are included in Paula McGuire's *Putting It Together: Teenagers Talk about Family Breakup* (Delacorte, 1987, $15.95).

Harold H. Bloomfield and Leonard Falder use case studies in *Making Peace with Your Parents* (Random, 1983, $15.95; pap., Ballantine, $3.95) to help readers sort out their feelings toward parents.

Single parent families are explored in Sara Gilbert's *How to Live with a Single Parent* (Lothrop, 1982, $11.88).

Varieties of family structures and how they are evolving are discussed in Kathlyn Gay's *Changing Families: Meeting Today's Challenges* (Enslow, 1988, $13.50).

Good advice on how to get along with parents is given in Joyce Vedral's *My Parents Are Driving Me Crazy* (pap., Ballantine, $2.50).

Two self-help books to work through the divorce experience are William V. Arnold's *When Your Parents Divorce* (pap., Westminster, $6.95) and *The Kids' Book of Divorce*, edited by Eric E. Rofas (Little, 1985, $14.95).

A historical and contemporary view of the various configurations of *The American Family* is given in Richard Worth's book (Watts, 1984, $10.90).

Two novels about divorce are Merrill Joan Gerber's *Please Don't Kiss Me Now* (pap., NAL, $1.95) and Sue Ellen Bridgers's *Notes for Another Life* (Knopf, 1981, $9.95; pap., Bantam, $2.25; condensed in *Juniorplots 3*, Bowker, 1987, pp. 9–12).

About the Book
Booklist, February 1, 1980, p. 767.
School Library Journal, February 1980, p. 63.
See also *Book Review Index*, 1980, p. 53.

About the Author
Commire, Anne, ed. *Something about the Author*. Detroit: Gale, 1983. Vol. 33, pp. 43–44.
Locher, Frances Carol, ed. *Contemporary Authors*. Detroit: Gale, 1982. Vol. 103, pp. 50–51.

Gale, Jay. *A Young Man's Guide to Sex*
Holt, 1984, $14.95

Jay Gale holds a Ph.D. and is a practicing psychologist and sex therapist. He has taught many courses in human sexuality and sex therapy and now teaches at the Irving School of Medicine at the University of California at Irvine. His book for teenage males covers all topics related to understanding one's body and mind. It is particularly strong in referral material indicating where help can be obtained. It contains brief coverage (two pages) on AIDS and has a useful glossary of terms. It is suitable for high school readers.

Plot Summary

Despite the generally permissive sexual attitudes that abound in the 1980s and the air of sexual sophistication that many teenagers profess, the truth is all too evident (in part through the increasing number of teenage pregnancies) that a large percentage of America's youth is woefully ill-informed about sex in general and their own sexuality in particular. This guide, written by a clinical psychologist and sex therapist, is addressed to teenage boys.

In one way or another and to one degree or another, most teenage boys are preoccupied with sex. This is not unusual. Their bodies are changing; they are developing into adult males. In 13 chapters, each with suggestions and guidelines, Dr. Gale talks frankly and reassuringly to the young male reader.

Chapter 1 discusses the art of talking about sex—with friends; with parents. Open and honest discussion about sexual feelings can lead to understanding; bragging about sex "with the guys" more often than not leads to confusion.

In Chapter 2, Gale discusses stages in the life of the young male, most importantly puberty, which the reader has already entered or is about to. He discusses the various body changes the young man may be experiencing—rapid growth, growth of pubic hair, change in vocal cords, the occurrence of (sometimes embarrassing) erections, ejaculation, and orgasm, and the feelings and fantasies that are part of this maturation process.

In Chapter 3 the myths and realities of masturbation are discussed, as well as its benefits and, for some, the associated guilt. From touching yourself, Gale discusses touching others in Chapter 4. For the young man (and young woman) who indulges in "making out" or "petting," there are responsibilities to be aware of, for they go along with the fun. This is the time when the teenager must be prepared to make decisions regarding sex, and these decisions may have important results for him or her in the coming years.

Part of a teenager's responsibility must be to understand what can occur as a result of a decision to engage in sex. What can, and too often does, occur is an unwanted pregnancy. In Chapter 5, Gale frankly discusses how pregnancy occurs in the female as a result of intercourse, and this entails how to prevent such pregnancy if engaging in sex. Condoms are discussed with detailed illustrations of their use. Gale also talks about various forms of female contraception.

Chapter 6 covers the act of sexual intercourse, the intense feelings and nervous tension that often accompany the first such encounter. On the more somber side is a look at teenage sex and the law. Chapter 7 covers factors that can affect the penis—such as alcohol and drugs, illness and disease, worry, and other feelings.

In today's atmosphere of fear about AIDS (Acquired Immune Deficiency Syndrome), Chapter 8 on sexually transmitted diseases will be of great interest to the young reader. Besides a discussion of how AIDS is transmitted or acquired, the chapter also covers more common complaints such as gonorrhea, herpes, syphilis, infections of the urethra, venereal warts, and hepatitis.

Chapters 9 through 11 tackle such areas as truth and fiction about sex, myths that get passed down from generation to generation and the truth; what happens as a sexual relationship continues; and understanding the female body.

Many teenage boys have agonizing questions concerning their own sexuality. Am I too sexual? Am I different? What is a homosexual? A transsexual? Chapter 12 covers these areas, as well as answering what may be difficult subjects for the young reader to voice. What if I ejaculate too quickly? What does it mean to be impotent? What if I don't satisfy my partner?

Chapter 13 deals with the harsh reality of an unplanned pregnancy. All options are discussed: abortion, adoption, marriage, and being a teenage father. An appendix directs the reader to finding help in all the areas discussed in the first 13 chapters.

Thematic Material

This is an accurate and comprehensive guide written in language directed toward the young male with the intention of being reassuring and nonjudgmental. Recognizing that sex is a complicated subject even for the not-so-young, Gale makes sense of this complexity with easy-to-understand explanations of body functions and emotional roller coasters. In a practical and sensitive manner, this guide covers any area in which the teenager might have questions concerning his body and his mind. The illustrations are detailed and helpful, as is the where-to-find-it material in the appendix.

Book Talk Material

Depending upon specific areas of concern or confusion, the reader will find the following passages helpful: ejaculation and orgasm, what they mean and signify (pp. 24–26); the myths and realities of masturbation (pp. 33–35); becoming sexual with girls (pp. 48–50); how and why to use a condom (pp. 61–65); experiencing intercourse (pp. 76–80); and AIDS and other sexually acquired diseases (pp. 99–123).

Additional Selections

Questions and answers on all matters sexual, including AIDS, are contained in the Boston Children's Hospital's *What Teenagers Want to Know about Sex* (Little, 1988, $16.95).

Alan E. Nourse has produced a thorough, detailed work for teenagers in *Birth Control* (Watts, 1988, $12.90), as has Jacqueline Voss in *A Young Woman's Guide to Sex* (Henry Holt, 1987, $16.95).

Frances Hanckel and John Cunningham's book *A Way of Love, A Way of Life* (Lothrop, 1978, $11.88) has the subtitle "A Young Person's Introduction to What It Means to Be Gay."

John Langone discusses what is love and what is not in *Like, Love, Lust: A View of Sex and Sexuality* (Little, 1980, $9.95; pap., Avon, $2.25).

An excellent compilation of standard information is given in Eric W. Johnson's *Love and Sex in Plain Language* (Harper, 1985, $14.95).

Interviews with 15 women are included in Paula McGuire's *It Won't Happen to Me: Teenagers Talk about Pregnancy* (Delacorte, 1983, $14.95; pap., Dell, $7.95), and Jane Claypool Miner talks about being a teenage parent in *Young Parents* (Messner, 1985, $9.79).

Nissa Simon has written a reassuring book explaining puberty in *Don't Worry, You're Normal* (pap., Harper, $4.95).

Two standard books on the subject of sex by Wardell B. Pomeroy are *Boys and Sex* (Delacorte, 1981, $13.95; pap., Dell, $2.95) and *Girls and Sex* (Delacorte, 1981, $13.95; pap., Dell, $2.95).

About the Book

Booklist, August 1984, p. 1605; November 15, 1985, p. 485.
School Library Journal, November 1984, p. 130.
VOYA, February 1985, p. 344.
See also *Book Review Digest,* 1985, p. 569, and *Book Review Index,* 1984, p. 260; 1985, p. 223.

Leana, Frank C.   *Getting into College*
pap., Hill & Wang, $7.95

Beginning in the junior year, and often earlier, college-bound students are plagued with anxieties concerning the pressures of being admitted into the college of their choice. *Getting into College* is a simple, straightforward manual that gives step-by-step guidance. It is suitable for senior high school students.

Plot Summary

From Maine to Hawaii, says Frank C. Leana, the process of getting into college is the same. And whereas where a teenager goes to college may not be the most important decision of his or her life, it certainly is one of the most important. The aim of this guide is to acquaint students and parents with the process of applying to college and to help teenagers assure themselves of getting into the college of their choice.

In Part 1, Getting Ready, the author covers the junior year, test time, the senior year, and college possibilities. To get into the college of your choice, says Leana, look to your high school record, make sure that by your junior year you are taking courses with college in mind. Such courses include a minimum four years of English, three years of math and of a foreign language, two years of history and two or more of a lab science, plus elective courses in art, art history, theater, or music. Make sure your schedule doesn't take too much of your time and that you are not overextended. Colleges look for young people who are organized, don't spread themselves too thin, and know how to divide their time.

Test time discusses the PSAT (Preliminary Scholastic Aptitude Test), the SAT (Scholastic Aptitude Test), the ACT (American College Test), as well as achievement tests.

The senior year is a time for talks with high school college counselors and with parents. A crucial conference, advises Leana, takes place no later than November of your senior year. It should include your parents, your counselor, and you. If you are not satisfied with the advice of your counselor or feel that you need more specialized help, turn to such publications as *The College Handbook, Barron's Profiles of American Colleges,* and college catalogs themselves for help in making your decisions. Private educational consultants are available, too, although they are expensive.

Part 2 deals with "getting there." What do you look for on your first campus visit (always call for an appointment; never arrive unannounced)? What questions do you ask? How can you judge if you'll be happy there? What can you expect at the college admitting office? How should you act on your personal interview? What should you wear? These and many more topics are discussed and questions answered.

When you have finally completed such background basics, you must get down to the all-important application itself. Leana gives detailed advice on filling out applications and includes such helpful information as what teachers to ask for recommendations. Most colleges will ask that a personal essay be included with the application, and Leana warns that this is a crucial part of the application process. He discusses four types of personal essays. Also included are sample student essays to help the reader decide on the best approach for him or her.

Also covered in Part 2 are factors in your acceptance that are beyond your control, such as the college's geographical distribution, your major, your athletic ability, how sex or minority status may affect your admission, and other factors. Three sample admissions cases are detailed and analyzed. What can you expect and when in the way of a response from the college of your choice? How do you respond?

If, after following all of the advice given in this book, you get into the college of your choice, or perhaps your second or third choice, what about finances? (As the author points out, colleges generally will accept the applicant they want regardless of financial status. The decision to admit a student is different from the decision to grant aid.) In these days of skyrocketing college tuition and expenses, many would-be college students will need financial aid. What is available? How does one apply? The author discusses college deferred payment plans (at Wellesley, for instance, you can pay on a monthly basis); four kinds of federal and state aid including grants and loans; the free service academies for qualified students; and state scholarship programs.

The book concludes with a calendar of application procedures beginning in October of the junior year with the PSAT test and ending in May of the senior year with Advanced Placement examinations. From the beginning of this process until its successful conclusion, Leana takes the would-be college student down the path to acceptance.

Thematic Material

This is a straightforward, down-to-earth, practical guide for the teenager who is interested in getting into college. It starts with preparation in the junior year and ends with a discussion of financial aid. Simply written in a step-by-step fashion, it should answer most of the major and minor questions the young reader might have about getting into colleges and may calm some anxieties about beginning what may seem to be an awesome process.

Book Talk Material

At one time or another the teenager interested in going to college will need to read about some topics covered in this book. Examples include: how to select high school courses with college in mind (pp. 10–11); how to evaluate what you can offer to a college (pp. 15–16); how to correct high school mistakes while there is still time (pp. 16–19); making the frightening prospect of tests less frightening (pp. 20–30); and how to respond during a college interview (pp. 66–68).

Additional Selections

George Ehrenhaft has written a useful manual, *Writing Your Way into College: Composing a Successful Application Essay* (Barrons, 1987, $6.95), and on the same subject is *The Admissions Essay: Stop Worrying and Start Writing* (Lyle Stuart, 1987, $7.95) by Helen W. Power and Robert Di Antonio.

An extremely useful guide is Patricia Mulcrone's *The New GED: How to Prepare for the High School Equivalency Examination* (Contemporary, 1987, $9.95).

Edward B. Fiske and colleagues have written two important guides for the college bound, *The Best Buys in College Education* (Times, 1987, $10.95) and *Selective Guide to Colleges* (Times, 1987, $10.95).

Paulo de Oliveira and Steve Cohen's book *Getting In!* (pap., Workman, $5.95) has the subtitle "The First Comprehensive Step-by-Step Strategy Guide to Acceptance at the College of Your Choice."

The subtitle "The Survival Manual for High School Students and Their Parents" describes Melody Martin's *Getting Off to College* (pap., Simon, $7.95).

Two useful guides to taking the SATs are Samuel C. Brownstein's *How to Prepare for the Scholastic Aptitude Test* (Barrons, 1986, $23.95, pap. $8.95) and Marcia Laurence's *How to Take the SAT* (pap., NAL, $7.95).

Good financial guidance is given in Gene R. Hawes's *The College Money Book* (pap., Macmillan, $12.95) and the annual publication of the College

Entrance Examination Board *The College Cost Book* (pap., The Board, $10.95).

About the Book
Booklist, October 1, 1980, p. 202.
See also *Book Review Index,* 1980, p. 299; 1981, p. 330.

AUTHOR INDEX

Author and titles fully discussed in *Seniorplots* and those cited in the text and in "Additional Selections" are included in this index. An asterisk (*) precedes those titles for which full summaries and discussions appear.

Abercrombie, Barbara, *Run for Your Life*, 215
Abrahams, Peter, *Mine Boy*, 138
Adams, Douglas, *Dirk Gently's Holistic Detective Agency*, 171
  The Hitchhiker's Guide to the Galaxy, 171
Adamson, Joy, *Born Free: A Lioness of Two Worlds*, 292
Agee, James, *A Death in the Family*, 44
Aiken, Joan, *If I Were You*, 24
  Midnight Is a Place, 152
Alben, Alex, *Our Man in Mongoa*, 248
Alexander, Lloyd, *The Drackenberg Adventure*, 212
  The El Dorado Adventure, 212
  The Illyrian Adventure, 212
Alexander, Sue, *Finding Your First Job*, 318
Allen, Benedict, *Who Goes Out in the Midday Sun?*, 256
Allen, Maury, *Jackie Robinson: A Life Remembered*, 253
Allman, William F. *See* Schrier, Eric W.
Ambler, Eric, *A Coffin for Dimitrios*, 224
  Journey into Fear, 224
American Friends Services Commit-

tee, *South Africa: Challenge and Hope*, 302
Anderson, Sherwood, *Winesburg, Ohio*, 117
Angell, Judie, *One Way to Ansonia*, 81
Angelou, Maya, *All God's Children Need Traveling Shoes*, 274
  Gather Together in My Name, 274
  The Heart of a Woman, 274
  I Know Why the Caged Bird Sings, 274
  Singin' and Swingin' and Gettin' Merry Like Christmas, 274
Arnold, Mark Alan. *See* Windling, Terri
Arnold, William V., *When Your Parents Divorce*, 328
Arnow, Harriette, *The Dollmaker*, 95
  Hunter's Horn, 44
Arrick, Fran, *Steffie Can't Come Out to Play*, 324
  Tunnel Vision, 72
Ashabranner, Brent, *Always to Remember*, 312
Asimov, Isaac, *The Collapsing Universe*, 165
  Foundation, 165
  Foundation and Empire, 165
  Isaac Asimov Presents the Best Fantasy of the 19th Century, 198

100 Great Fantasy Short Stories, 198
Prelude to Foundation, 165
The Realm of Numbers, 165
Second Foundation, 165
Asimov, Janet, *Mind Transfer,* 167
Atwood, Margaret, *The Handmaid's Tale,* 125
Auel, Jean, *Clan of the Cave Bear,* 135
Austen, Jane, *Emma,* 130
Pride and Prejudice, 130
Avi, *A Place Called Ugly,* 232
Sometimes I Think I Hear My Name, 232
*Wolf Rider: A Tale of Terror, 232
Ayres, Alex, ed., *The Wit and Wisdom of Mark Twain,* 117

Babson, Marion, *The Twelve Deaths of Christmas,* 240
Baehr, Consuelo Saah, *Daughters,* 63
Baird, Thomas, *Finding Fever,* 215
Walk Out a Brother, 73
Baldwin, James, *Go Tell It on the Mountain,* 1, 72
*If Beale Street Could Talk, 1
Ball, John, *In the Heat of the Night,* 125
Ballantyne, Sheila, *Imaginary Crimes,* 95
Ballard, J. G., *Empire of the Sun,* 284
Balzac, Honoré de, *Old Goriot,* 117
Banks, Lynne Reid, *The Writing on the Wall,* 215
Barnao, Jack, *Hammer Locke,* 59
Barnard, Robert, *The Skeleton in the Grass,* 244
Barnberger, Michael, *The Green Road Home,* 268
Barrett, William E., *The Lilies of the Field,* 85
Beagle, Peter S., *A Fine and Private Place,* 202
The Last Unicorn, 202
Bear, Greg, *Eon,* 91
The Forge of God, 176
The Infinity Concerto, 176
Bell, Clare, *Ratha's Creature,* 198
Bellamy, Edward, *Looking Backward,* 198

Bellow, Saul, *The Adventures of Augie March,* 100
Benedict, Helen, *Recovery: How to Survive Sexual Assault for Women, Men, Teenagers, Their Friends and Families,* 321
*Safe, Strong and Streetwise: The Teenager's Guide to Preventing Sexual Assault, 321
Benedict, Rex, *Run for Your Sweet Life,* 28
Bennett, Jay, *The Dangling Witness,* 235
Benoit, Joan, *Running Tide,* 272
Bentford, Gregory, *Against Infinity,* 171
Timescape, 171
Berger, Thomas, *Arthur Rex,* 159
Biggle, Lloyd, Jr., *The Quallsford Inheritance,* 152
Birnbaum, Louis, *Red Dawn at Lexington,* 308
Bishop, Michael, *No Enemy but Time,* 220
Bisson, Terry, *Nat Turner,* 112
Blish, James, *Welcome to Mars,* 176
Blockson, Charles, *The Underground Railroad,* 163
Bloomfield, Harold H., and Leonard Falder, *Making Peace with Your Parents,* 327
Bograd, Larry, *Travelers,* 37
Boissard, Janine, *Christmas Lessons,* 77
A Matter of Feeling, 77
A Time to Choose, 24
Bond, Nancy, *The Best of Enemies,* 49
A Place to Come Back To, 49
Booher, Dianna Daniels, **Coping: When Your Family Falls Apart,* 324
Help, We're Moving, 325
Love: First Aid for the Young, 325
Making Friends with Yourself and Other Strangers, 325
Rape: What Would You Do If. . . , 324
Boorstin, Daniel J., *The Americans: The Colonial Experience,* 308
Borland, Hal, *When the Legend Dies,* 64
Boslough, John, *Stephen Hawking's Universe,* 305
Bosse, Malcolm, *Captives of Time,* 159

Boston Children's Hospital, *What Teenagers Want to Know about Sex*, 331
Boswell, Thomas, *How Life Imitates the World Series*, 264
Boulle, Pierre, *Planet of the Apes*, 211
Bowden, Nina, *Devil By the Sea*, 235
Brace, Ernest C., *A Code to Keep*, 312
Bradbury, Ray, *The Stories of Ray Bradbury*, 167
The Toynbee Convector, 167
Bradley, Marion Zimmer, *Hawkmistress!*, 194
Bradshaw, Gillian, **The Beacon at Alexandria*, 131
The Beekeeper's Daughter, 135
Brechner, Irv. *See* Schwartz, Lester
Brent, Madeleine, *Stormswift*, 244
Bridgers, Sue Ellen, *Notes for Another Life*, 41, 328
Permanent Connections, 41
*Sara Will, 41
Brin, David, **The Postman*, 87
Startide Rising, 87
Sundiver, 87
The Uplift War, 87
Brink, Andre, *Rumors of Rain*, 139
Brinkley, William, *The Last Ship*, 91
Bronte, Charlotte, *Jane Eyre*, 244
Brooks, Bruce, **Midnight Hour Encores*, 45
The Moves Make the Man, 45
Brooks, Sara, *You May Plow Here*, 113
Brooks, Terry, *The Black Unicorn*, 190
The Elfstones of Shannara, 190
*Magic Kingdom for Sale—Sold!, 190
The Sword of Shannara, 190
The Wishsong of Shannara, 190
Brown, Dee, *Conspiracy of Knaves*, 163
Kildeer Mountain, 163
Brown, Joe D., *Paper Moon*, 117
Brown, Peter, and Steven Gaines, **The Love You Make: An Insider's Story of The Beatles*, 277
Brown, Rosellen, *Tender Mercies*, 95
Brownstein, Samuel C., *How to Prepare for the Scholastic Aptitude Test*, 334
Brunner, John, *Stand on Zanzibar*, 210
Buchan, Stuart, *Guys Like Us*, 85
Buck, Pearl, *The Good Earth*, 155
Buckhill, Paul, *The Great Escape*, 284

Bunting, Eve, *Will You Be My Posslq?*, 28
Burch, Jennings Michael, *They Cage the Animals at Night*, 21
Burgess, Anthony, *A Clockwork Orange*, 211
The Clockwork Testament, 211
Burns, Olive Ann, *Cold Sassy Tree*, 8
Butler, Octavia, *Dawn*, 91
Butler, Samuel, *The Way of All Flesh*, 99
Butterworth, W. E., *Flunking Out*, 28
Butterworth, William, *The Butterfly Revolution*, 53

Caes, Charles J., *Studies in Starlight*, 305
Callahan, Steven, *Adrift: Seventy-Six Days Lost at Sea*, 273
Calvert, Patricia, *Yesterday's Daughter*, 49
Cameron, Peter, *One Way or Another*, 40
Camus, Albert, *The Plague*, 142
Capote, Truman, *Breakfast at Tiffany's*, 130
One Christmas, 129
The Thanksgiving Visitor, 129
Caputo, Philip, *A Rumor of War*, 312
Caras, Roger, *Mara Simba: The African Lion*, 292
Card, Orson Scott, *Seventh Son*, 176
Carillo, Charles, *Shepherd Avenue*, 95
Carter, Alden R., *Growing Season*, 28
Carter, Peter, *Bury the Dead*, 273
Cash, Johnny, *Man in White*, 135
Cassedy, Sylvia, *Behind the Attic Wall*, 207
Chalker, Jack L., *Web of the Chosen*, 180
Chambers, Aidan, *Breaktime*, 37
Chappell, Fred, *I Am One of You Forever*, 7
Cherryh, C. J., *Angel with the Sword*, 184
The Dreamstone, 184
The Tree of Swords and Jewels, 184
Childress, Alice, *Rainbow Jordan*, 4

Christie, Agatha, *The Mousetrap and Other Plays*, 32
Christopher, John, *City of Gold and Lead*, 188
   Pool of Fire, 188
   The White Mountain, 188
Clapp, Patricia, *Witch's Children: A Story of Salem*, 142
Clark, Mary Higgins, *Stillwatch*, 236
   Weep No More, My Lady, 236
   Where Are the Children?, 236
Clark, Walter Van Tilberg, *The Ox Bow Incident*, 117
Clarke, Arthur C., *Rendezvous with Rama*, 168
   2001: A Space Odyssey, 168
   2010: Odyssey Two, 168
   2061: Odyssey Three, 171
Clavell, James, *Children's Story*, 189
Clemeau, Carol, *The Ariadne Clue*, 240
Clement, Hal, *Still River*, 172
Coetzee, J. M., *Life and Times of Michael K*, 139
Cohen, Barbara, and Bahija Lovejoy, *Seven Daughters and Seven Sons*, 135
Cohen, I. Bernard, *The Birth of the New Physics*, 305
Cohen, Steve. *See* de Oliveira, Paulo
Colbert, Edwin H., *Dinosaurs: An Illustrated History*, 317
Cole, Brock, *The Goats*, 230
College Entrance Examination Board, *The College Cost Book*, 335
Conover, Ted, *Rolling Nowhere*, 59
Conrad, Pam, *Prairie Songs*, 24
Conroy, Pat, *The Prince of Tides*, 92
   The Water Is Wide, 92
Cook, Glen, *Doomstalker*, 185
Cook, Robin, *Coma*, 220
   Mortal Fear, 220
Cooney, Caroline B., *Don't Blame the Music*, 85
Cormier, Robert, *Beyond the Chocolate War*, 50
   The Chocolate War, 50
Corwen, Leonard, *Your Job—Where to Find It, How to Get It*, 320
Crawford, Charles, *Letter Perfect*, 54
   Split Time, 36

Crichton, Michael, *The Andromeda Strain*, 216
   The Great Train Robbery, 152
   Sphere, 216
   The Terminal Man, 216
Cross, Gillian, *Chartbreaker*, 40
Crutcher, Chris, *The Crazy Horse Electric Game*, 55
   Running Loose, 55, 273
   Stotan!, 55
Cullan, Brian, *What Niall Saw*, 91
Cunningham, E. V., *The Wabash Factor*, 248
Cunningham, John. *See* Hanckel, Francis
Curry, Jane Louise, *Me, Myself and I*, 235
Cussler, Clive, *Raise the Titanic*, 227
   Treasure, 227

Dahl, Roald, *Boy*, 281
   Going Solo, 281
Dann, Patty, *Mermaids*, 121
Daugherty, Lynn B., *Why Me?*, 21
Davies, Hunter, *The Beatles*, 280
Davies, Paul, *The Cosmic Blueprint*, 305
Davis, Jenny, *Good-bye and Keep Cold*, 25
Deaver, Julie Reece, *Say Goodnight Gracie*, 68
Deighton, Len, *The Berlin Game*, 227
   Goodbye Mickey Mouse, 227
   The Ipcress File, 227
de Jenkins, Lyll Becerra, *The Honorable Prison*, 215
Delorio, Ella Cara, *Waterlily*, 64
DeMille, Nelson, *The Charm School*, 224
de Oliveira, Paulo, and Steve Cohen, *Getting In!*, 334
de Villiers, Marq, *White Tribe Dreaming*, 103
Di Antonio, Robert. *See* Power, Helen W.
Dick, Philip K., *Blade Runner*, 176
   The Man in the High Castle, 91
Dickens, Charles, *Bleak House*, 96
   Hard Times, 96
   Little Dorrit, 96

The Mystery of Edwin Drood, 152
A Tale of Two Cities, 108
Dickinson, Peter, *The Gift,* 207
Tulku, 230
Dickson, Gordon R., *Dorsai!,* 176
Dillard, Annie, *An American Childhood,*
121
Pilgrim at Tinker Creek, 317
Teaching a Stone to Talk, 317
Dixon, Jeanne, *The Tempered Wind,* 8
Doctorow, E. L., *World's Fair,* 32
Doherty, Berlie, *Granny Was a Buffer
Girl,* 64
Doig, Ivan, *English Creek,* 230
Donaldson, Stephen R., *Lord Foul's
Bane,* 194
Dorris, Michael, **A Yellow Raft in Blue
Water,* 59
Douglas, Martha C., *Go for It: How to
Get Your First Good Job,* 320
Douglas, Paul Harding, *The Essential
AIDS Fact Book,* 17
Downey, Brigitte, *Nellie,* 44
Doyle, Sir Arthur Conan, *The Hound
of the Baskervilles,* 152
Drabble, Margaret, *The Millstone,*
81
Druyan, Ann. *See* Sagan, Carl, and
Ann Druyan
Du Boulay, Shirley, *Tutu: Voice of the
Voiceless,* 301
Dumas, Alexander, *The Count of Monte
Cristo,* 108
The Three Musketeers, 108
du Maurier, Daphne, *My Cousin Ra-
chel,* 240
*Myself When Young: The Shaping of a
Writer,* 240
*Rebecca, 240
Duncan, Lois, *I Know What You Did
Last Summer,* 215
Locked in Time, 215
Dunphy, Eamon, *Unforgettable Fire,*
280
Durrell, Gerald, *Birds, Beasts and Rela-
tives,* 288
My Family and Other Animals, 288
Durrell, Gerald, and Lee Durrell, *The
Amateur Naturalist,* 292
Durrell, Lee. *See* Durrell, Gerald, and
Lee Durrell

Dygard, Thomas J., *The Rookie Arrives,*
264

Eberhart, Mignon G., *Postmark Mur-
der,* 244
Three Days for Emeralds, 244
Edey, Maitland A. *See* Johanson, Don-
ald C.
Ehrenhaft, George, *Writing Your Way
into College: Composing a Successful
Application Essay,* 334
Ellison, Harlan, *Dangerous Visions,* 168
More Dangerous Visions, 168
Ellison, Ralph, *Invisible Man,* 4
Emecheta, Buchi, *The Bride Price,* 103

Fairbairn, Ann, *Five Smooth Stones,* 4
Falder, Leonard. *See* Bloomfield, Har-
old H.
Fante, John, *1933 Was a Bad Year,* 264
Farmer, Philip J., *Dayworld,* 168
Farris, John, *The Uninvited,* 240
Fast, Julius, *What Should We Do about
Davey?,* 32
Faulkner, William, *Intruder in the Dust,*
117
Fawcett, Anthony, *John Lennon: One
Day at a Time,* 280
Ferris, Jean, *Invincible Summer,* 17
Looking for Home, 85
Finn, Doug, *Heart of a Family,* 68
Finnegan, William, **Crossing the Line:
A Year in the Land of Apartheid,* 298
Fiske, Edward B., *The Best Buys in Col-
lege Education,* 334
Selective Guide to Colleges, 334
Fitzgerald, Frances, *Fire in the Lake,*
312
Fitzsch, Harold, *The Creation of Matter,*
305
Fleischman, Paul, *Rear-View Mirrors,*
68
Flippo, Chet. *Yesterday: The Unautho-
rized Biography of Paul McCartney,*
280
Follett, Ken, *Eye of the Needle,* 224
The Key to Rebecca, 224

Forsyth, Frederick, *The Day of the Jackal, 221
The Devil's Alternative, 221
The Odessa File, 221
Forward, Robert L., Dragon's Egg, 172
Starquake, 172
Fossey, Dian, Gorillas in the Mist, 291
Foster, Alan Dean, Spellsinger, 206
Starman, 176
To the Vanishing Point, 176
Foster, Rory C., Dr. Wildlife, 288
I Never Met an Animal I Didn't Like, 288
Fox, Paula, *The Moonlight Man, 65
The Slave Dancer, 65
Francis, Dick, *Bolt, 245
Break In, 245
Whip Hand, 245
Frank, Elizabeth Bales, Cooder Cutlas, 12
Frank, Pat, Alas, Babylon, 210
Fraser, Sylvia, My Father's House: A Memoir of Incest and of Healing, 21
French, Michael, Soldier Boy, 28
The Throwing Season, 264
Fritz, Jean, China Homecoming, 284
Frommer, Harvey, Jackie Robinson, 253
Fugard, Athol, Master Harold and the Boys, 103
Fuller, Jack, Fragments, 146

Gaines, Ernest, The Autobiography of Miss Jane Pitman, 112
A Gathering of Old Men, 112
In My Father's House, 4
Gaines, Steven. See Brown, Peter
Gale, Jay, *A Young Man's Guide to Sex, 328
Gallo, Donald R., Sixteen, 85
Galsworthy, John, The Forsyte Saga, 100
Gans, Ernest K., The Aviator, 231
Fate Is the Hunter, 231
Garden, Nancy, Annie on My Mind, 76
Gardner, John (American), Grendel, 198
Gardner, John (English), No Deals, Mr. Bond, 224

Scorpius, 224
Gardner, Sandra, Teenage Suicide, 72
Garfield, Brian, Necessity, 220
Garfield, Leon, The Mystery of Edwin Drood, 152
The Wedding Ghost, 152
Garner, Alan, Red Shift, 207
Gates, Anita, Ninety Highest Paying Careers of the '80's, 321
Ninety Most Promising Careers for the '80's, 321
Gay, Kathlyn, Changing Families: Meeting Today's Challenges, 327
George, Jean Craighead, Julie of the Wolves, 230
Gerber, Merrill Joan, Marry Me Tomorrow, 28
Please Don't Kiss Me Now, 328
Gibbons, Stella, Cold Comfort Farm, 8
Gilbert, Sara, How to Live with a Single Parent, 327
Gilman, Dorothy, The Amazing Mrs. Polifax, 239
Mrs. Polifax and the Golden Triangle, 239
Gingher, Marianne, Bobby Rex's Greatest Hits, 7
Gino, Carol, Rusty's Story, 21
Giradet, Herbert. See Seymour, John
Girion, Barbara, A Tangle of Roots, 73
Godden, Rumer, The Dark Horse, 248
Thursday's Children, 85
Golding, William, Lord of the Flies, 54
Goldis, Al, and Rick Wolff, Breaking into the Big Leagues, 260
Goldman, William, The Princess Bride, 194
Gordimer, Nadine, *July's People, 100
Lifetimes: Under Apartheid, 103
Gordon, Alison, Foul Ball!, 256
Gordon, Mary, Final Payments, 121
Gordon, Ruth, Under All Silences, 25
Gordon, Sheila, *Waiting for the Rain: A Novel of South Africa, 136
Gordon, Sol, When Living Hurts, 324
Gould, Stephen Jay, The Flamingo's Smile, 317
Hen's Teeth and Horse's Toes, 317
Gowlart, Ron, The Great British Detective, 152

Graber, Richard, *Doc*, 77
Greeley, Andrew M., *The Magic Cup*, 198
Greenberg, Jan, *No Dragons to Slay*, 58
Greenberg, Joanne, *I Never Promised You a Rose Garden*, 5
  In This Sign, 5
  Of Such Small Differences, 7
  *Simple Gifts, 5
Greenberg, Martin. *See* Pronzini, Bill
Greene, Constance C., *The Love Letters of J. Timothy Owen*, 40
Greene, Graham, *The Heart of the Matter*, 142
  The Human Factor, 227
Greenstein, George, *The Symbiotic Universe*, 305
Gribbin, John, *Genesis: The Origins of Man and the Universe*, 317
Grunwald, Lisa, *Summer*, 49
Guest, Judith, **Ordinary People*, 69
  Second Heaven, 21
Guy, David, *Second Brother*, 59
Guy, Rosa, *The Friends*, 12
  My Love, My Love; or, the Peasant Girl, 12

Hailey, Elizabeth F., *A Woman of Independent Means*, 81
Halberstam, David, *The Amateurs*, 267
Haley, Alex, *Roots*, 112
Hall, Lynn, *Flyaway*, 68
Hall, Lynn, and Thomas Modl, eds., *AIDS*, 17
Hamilton, Ian, *In Search of J. D. Salinger*, 284
Hamilton, Virginia, *Anthony Burns: The Defeat and Triumph of a Fugitive Slave*, 112
  *A Little Love, 8
  M. C. Higgins the Great, 8
  Sweet Whispers, Brother Rush, 9
  A White Romance, 9
Hamsun, Knut, *Growth of the Soil*, 99
Hanckel, Frances, and John Cunningham, *A Way of Love, A Way of Life*, 331
Harris, Mark, *Bang the Drum Slowly*, 264

Harris, Rosemary, *Summer of the Wild Rose*, 81
Harrison, Harry, *West of Eden*, 167
Harry, Bill, *Beatlemania: The History of The Beatles on Film*, 280
Hart, Bruce, and Carole Hart, *Breaking Up Is Hard to Do*, 28
Hart, Carole. *See* Hart, Bruce
Haseley, Dennis, *The Counterfeiter*, 28
Haskins, Jim, *Winnie Mandela: Life of Struggle*, 302
Havemann, Ernst, *Bloodsong*, 139
  Bloodsong and Other Stories of South Africa, 103
Hawes, Gene R., *The College Money Book*, 334
Hawke, David Freeman, *Everyday Life in Early America*, 308
Hawking, Stephen W., **A Brief History of Time: From the Big Bang to Black Holes*, 302
Hayden, Tom, *Reunion: A Memoir*, 312
Hayden, Tony, *The Sunflower Effect*, 95
Heggen, Thomas, *Mister Roberts*, 146
Heidish, Murey, *Witness*, 309
Heinlein, Robert A., *Citizen of the Galaxy*, 172
  *Stranger in a Strange Land, 172
Heller, Joseph, *Catch 22*, 211
Hemingway, Ernest, *A Farewell to Arms*, 146
Hemphill, Paul, *Me and the Boy*, 37
Hentoff, Nat, *Boston Boy*, 284
Herbert, Frank, *Children of Dune*, 167
  Dune, 167
Herbert, James, *The Fog*, 220
Hermes, Patricia, *A Solitary Secret*, 21
  A Time to Listen: Preventing Youth Suicide, 72
Herriot, James, *All Creatures Great and Small*, 285
  All Things Bright and Beautiful, 285
  All Things Wise and Wonderful, 285
  *The Lord God Made Them All, 285
Hersey, John, *The Wall*, 147
Higgins, Jack, *The Eagle Has Landed*, 224
  *Solo, 224
Highwater, Jamake, *Legend Days*, 64

Hildebrand, John, *Reading the River*, 296

Hill, Douglas, *Day of the Starwind*, 180
Galactic Warlord, 180
Planet of the Warlord, 180

Hillerman, Tony, *Skinwalkers*, 64
A Thief of Time, 64

Hilton, James, *Goodbye, Mr. Chips*, 195
*Lost Horizon, 195
Random Harvest, 195

Hoffman, Alice, *At Risk*, 16
Illumination Night, 44

Hofstadter, Richard, *The Age of Reform*, 306
*America at 1750: A Social Portrait, 306
Anti-Intellectualism in the United States, 306

Holland, Isabelle, *A Death at St. Anselm's*, 248
Summer of My First Love, 76

Hollander, Zander, *The Complete Handbook of Pro Hockey*, 268

Holt, Victoria, *Bride of Pendorric*, 152
The India Fan, 244
Mistress of Mellyn, 152
The Time of the Hunter's Moon, 244

Honig, Donald, *The American League: An Illustrated History*, 260
The National League: An Illustrated History, 260

Hoobler, Dorothy, and Thomas Hoobler, *Nelson and Winnie Mandela*, 302

Hoobler, Thomas. *See* Hoobler, Dorothy

Hoover, H. M., *The Delikon*, 181
The Lost Star, 181

Hope, Christopher, *A Separate Development*, 138

Hough, John, *The Conduct of the Game*, 264
A Player for a Moment, 256

Household, Geoffrey, *Rogue Justice*, 223
Rogue Male, 223
Watcher in the Shadows, 223

Howe, Irving, *World of Our Fathers*, 81

Howker, Janni, *Isaac Campion*, 68
The Nature of the Beast, 40

Hoyle, Fred, *The Intelligent Universe*, 317

Hudson, W. H., *Green Mansions*, 198

Huggan, Isabel, *The Elizabeth Stories*, 44

Hughes, Langston, *The Big Sea*, 276

Hughes, Monica, *The Keeper of the Isis Light*, 189

Hughes, Terence, *The Day They Stole the Queen Mary*, 248

Hugo, Victor, **The Hunchback of Notre Dame*, 104
Les Misérables, 104
Notre Dame de Paris, 104

Hume, Ivor Noel, *Martin Hundred*, 317

Humphrey, Josephine, *Rich in Love*, 76

Huntford, Roland, *The Last Place on Earth*, 296
Shackleton, 297

Hurmence, Belinda, *Tancy*, 163

Hurston, Zora Neale, *Their Eyes Were Watching God*, 164

Huxley, Aldous, *Brave New World*, 198

Hyde, Margaret O., *Sexual Abuse: Let's Talk about It*, 324

Irish, Richard K., *Go Hire Yourself an Employer*, 321

Irvine, Lucy, *Runaway*, 12

Irving, John, *The World According to Garp*, 211

Irwin, Hadley, *Abbey, My Love*, 21

Jackson, Michael, *Moonwalk*, 280

Jackson, Shirley, *The Haunting of Hill House*, 252
We Have Always Lived in the Castle, 252

James, Bill, *The Bill James Historical Baseball Abstract*, 256

James, P. D., *The Black Tower*, 252

James, Peter, *Possession*, 252

Janus, Christopher G., *Miss Fourth of July*, 125

Jastrow, Robert, *Until the Sun Dies*, 317
Jeffers, Susan, *Feed the Fear and Do It Anyway*, 321
Johanson, Donald C., and Maitland A. Edey, *Lucy*, 292
Johnson, Annabel, and Edgar Johnson, *Alien Music*, 177
The Danger Quotient, 177
Prisoner of Psi, 177
Johnson, Edgar. *See* Johnson, Annabel
Johnson, Eric W., *Love and Sex in Plain Language*, 331
Johnston, Mary, *To Have and to Hold*, 309
Johnston, Norma, *The Potter's Wheel*, 64
Jones, Diana Wynne, *Howl's Moving Castle*, 194
Jones, Douglas C., *Elkhorn Tavern*, 117
Gone the Dreams and Dancing, 164
Roman, 117
Jones, Ilene, *Jobs for Teenagers*, 321
Jones, Toeckey, *Go Well, Stay Well*, 138

Kafka, Franz, *The Trial*, 142
Kahn, Joan, *Ready or Not: Here Come 14 Frightening Stories*, 235
Kantor, MacKinlay, *Andersonville*, 164
Kardong, Don, *Thirty Phone Booths to Boston*, 273
Karmon, Stanley, *Vietnam: A History*, 312
Karoly, Bela. *See* Retton, Mary Lou
Katz, Michael, *Murder Off the Glass*, 259
Katz, William, *Face Maker*, 220
Kaufman, Pamela, *Shield of Three Lions*, 135
Kazimiroff, Theodore L., *The Last Algonquin*, 64
Kellogg, Marjorie, *Tell Me That You Love Me, Junie Moon*, 125
Kemelman, Harry, *Friday the Rabbi Slept Late*, 248
Kerr, M. E., *Dinky Hocker Shoots Smack*, 13
Fell, 13

Gentlehands, 13
If I Love You, Am I Trapped Forever?, 13
Night Kites, 13
Kherdian, David, *The Road from Home: The Story of an Armenian Girl*, 155
Kiely, Benedict, *Proxopera*, 103
Kincaid, Jamaica, *Annie John*, 4
King, Stephen, *Carrie*, 252
Christine, 252
Kinsella, W. P., *The Iowa Baseball Confederacy*, 259
Shoeless Joe, 257
Kirkwood, James, *Good Times, Bad Times*, 54
Klass, David, *Breakaway Run*, 58
Klass, Perri Elizabeth, *A Not Entirely Benign Procedure*, 288
Klein, Norma, *My Life as a Body*, 36
Knowles, John, *Peace Breaks Out*, 54
A Separate Peace, 54
Knudson, R. R., *Zan Hagen's Marathon*, 273
Knudson, R. R., and May Swenson, eds., *American Sports Poems*, 268
Koertge, Ron, *The Arizona Kid*, 17
Koestler, Arthur, *Darkness at Noon*, 155
Koontz, Dean R., *Watchers*, 235
Korman, Gordon, *A Semester in the Life of a Garbage Bag*, 40
Son of Interflux, 40
Kotzwinkle, William, *Trouble in Bugland*, 215
Kram, Mark, *Miles to Go*, 264
Kropp, Lloyd, *Greencastle*, 4
Kurtz, Katherine, *Deryni Checkmate*, 176
Deryni Rising, 176
Kyer, Duncan, *The Dancing Men*, 54

Lackey, Mercedes, *Arrows of the Queen*, 194
Lamb, Wendy, *The Ground Zero Club and Other Prize-Winning Plays*, 32
Lambert, David, *A Field Guide to Dinosaurs*, 317
Lane, Kenneth, *Diary of a Medical Nobody*, 288

Langone, John, *AIDS: The Facts*, 17
  *Like, Love, Lust: A View of Sex and
  Sexuality*, 331
Laure, Jason, *South Africa: Coming of
  Age under Apartheid*, 138
Laurence, Marcia, *How to Take the
  SAT*, 334
Lawick-Goodall, Jane van, **In the
  Shadow of Man*, 289
Lawrence, Louise, *Moonwind*, 185
Leakey, Richard E., and Roger Lewin,
  Origins, 292
Leana, Frank C., **Getting into College*,
  332
Leape, Martha P., *The Harvard Guide
  to Careers*, 321
Le Carré, John, *The Little Drummer
  Girl*, 227
Lee, Harper, *To Kill a Mockingbird*,
  125
Lee, Mildred, *The People Therein*, 44
Lee, Tanith, *The Storm Land*, 185
Leeds, Robert X., *All the Comforts of
  Home*, 288
LeGuin, Ursula K., *The Dispossessed*,
  185
  The Lathe of Heaven, 185
  Very Far Away from Anywhere Else,
  202
Lehrman, Robert, *Juggling*, 17
Lelyveld, Joseph, *Move Your Shadow:
  South Africa, Black and White*, 139
L'Engle, Madeleine, *The Arm of the
  Starfish*, 73
  *A House Like a Lotus, 73
  A Ring of Endless Light, 73
Lennon, John, *In His Own Write*, 280
  A Spaniard in the Works, 280
Lerner, Alan Jay, *Camelot*, 160
Leroux, Gaston, *Phantom of the Opera*,
  108
Lesley, Craig, *Winterkill*, 64
Lessing, Doris, *African Stories*, 103
Lester, Julius, *This Strange New Feel-
  ing*, 113
Levchenko, Stanislav, *On the Wrong
  Side*, 224
LeVert, John, *The Flight of the Casso-
  wary*, 121
Levin, Ira, *Deathtrap*, 32

Levinson, Jay C., *Five Hundred Fifty-
  Five Ways to Earn Extra Money*, 321
Levoy, Myron, *A Shadow Like a Leop-
  ard*, 4
Lewin, Roger. *See* Leakey, Richard E.
Lewis, Sinclair, *Babbitt*, 130
  Main Street, 130
Lipsyte, Robert, *The Contender*, 260
Llewellyn, Richard, *How Green Was My
  Valley*, 99
Llywelyn, Morgan, *Grania: She-King of
  the Irish Seas*, 159
Lopez, Barry, **Arctic Dreams: Imagina-
  tion and Desire in a Northern Land-
  scape*, 292
  Of Whales and Men, 292
Lord, Walter, *Day of Infamy*, 285
Lose, Phyllis, and Daniel Mannix, *No
  Job for a Lady*, 288
Lovejoy, Bahija. *See* Cohen, Barbara
Lovell, Marc, *Good Spies Don't Grow on
  Trees*, 8
Lucas, Jeremy, *Cry of the Seals*, 297
Luciano, Ron, *The Fall of the Roman
  Umpire*, 256
  Strike Two, 256
  The Umpire Strikes Back, 256
Ludlum, Robert, *The Bourne Identity*,
  226
  The Icarus Agenda, 226
  The Rhineman Exchange, 226

MacInnes, Helen, *Above Suspicion*, 245
  Cloak of Darkness, 244
  Message from Malaga, 245
MacIvoy, R. A., *Tea with the Black Drag-
  on*, 202
MacKinnon, Bernie, *The Meantime*, 85
MacLaverty, Bernard, *Cal*, 104
MacLean, Alistair, *Force 10 from
  Navarone*, 227
  The Guns of Navarone, 227
  Ice Station Zebra, 227
MacLean, John, **Mac*, 18
Magorian, Michelle, *Good Night, Mr.
  Tom*, 21
Magubane, Peter, *Soweto: The Fruit of
  Fear*, 302

Mahy, Margaret, *The Catalogue of the Universe*, 120
  The Changeover, 198
  The Haunting, 198
  Memory, 44
  *The Tricksters, 198
Mailer, Norman, *The Naked and the Dead*, 147
Makeba, Miriam, *Makeba: My Story*, 302
Malamud, Bernard, *The Assistant*, 260
  The Fixer, 260
  *The Natural, 260
Malmgren, Dallin, *The Whole Nine Yards*, 85
Maloney, Ray, *The Impact Zone*, 59
Malory, Thomas, *Tales of King Arthur*, 159
Manes, Stephen, *The Obnoxious Jerks*, 54
Mango, Karin N., *Somewhere Green*, 49
Mannix, Daniel. *See* Lose, Phyllis
Markandaya, Kamala, *Nectar in a Sieve*, 125
Marsh, Ngaio, *Light Thickens*, 248
Marshall, Catherine, *Christy*, 22
  *Julie, 21
  A Man Called Peter, 21
  Mr. Jones, Meet the Master, 21
Marshall, Kathryn, *In the Combat Zone*, 312
Martin, George R., and Lisa Tuttle, *Wildhaven*, 185
Martin, Melody, *Getting Off to College*, 334
Mason, Bobbie Ann, *In Country*, 146
Mason, Robert, *Chickenhawk*, 312
Massie, Robert K., *Nicholas and Alexandra*, 155
Mathabane, Mark, *Kaffir Boy*, 138
Mathis, Sharon Bell, *A Teacup Full of Roses*, 12
Matsubara, Hisako, *Cranes at Dusk*, 77
Matthews, John, and Bob Stewart, *Warriors of Arthur*, 159
Mays, Willie, *Say Hey*, 256
Mazer, Harry, *City Light*, 28
  The Girl of His Dreams, 272
  The War on Villa Street, 272
Mazer, Norma Fox, *After the Rain*, 44

McCaffrey, Anne, *Dragonflight*, 181
  Dragonsong, 181
  *Moreta: Dragonlady of Pern, 181
  Nerilka's Story, 181
McCaig, Donald, *Nop's Trials*, 58
McClanahan, Ed, *The Natural Man*, 49
McCoy, Kathy, *The New Teenage Body Book*, 324
McCullers, Carson, *The Heart Is a Lonely Hunter*, 125
McCullough, Colleen, *Tim*, 121
McFaddan, Cyra, *Rain or Shine*, 68, 268
McFarland, Rhoda, *Coping with Substance Abuse*, 324
McGuire, Paula, *It Won't Happen to Me: Teenagers Talk about Pregnancy*, 331
  Putting It Together: Teenagers Talk about Family Breakup, 327
McInerny, Ralph, *The Basket Case*, 248
McIntyre, Vonda N., *The Bride*, 108
  Dreamsnake, 185
  Superluminal, 185
McKillip, Patricia A., *Fool's Run*, 184
McKinley, Robin, *Beauty*, 202
  The Blue Sword, 207
  The Hero and the Crown, 206
McNab, Tom, *Flanagan's Run*, 272
Meaney, Dee Morrison, *Iseult*, 159
Medea, Andrea, and Kathleen Thompson, *Against Rape*, 324
Medoff, Mark, *Children of a Lesser God*, 142
Meltzer, Milton, *The American Revolutionaries: A History in Their Own Words, 1750–1800*, 308
  Never to Forget, 284
  Starting from Home: A Writer's Beginnings, 284
Mersand, Joseph, ed., *Three Comedies of American Family Life*, 32
Meyer, Carolyn, *Denny's Tapes*, 85
  Voices of South Africa: Growing Up in a Troubled Land, 301
Meyer, Nicholas E., *The West End Horror*, 152
Michener, James A., *Sports in America*, 268

Mickleburgh, Edwin, *Beyond the Frozen Sea*, 296
Miklowitz, Gloria, *Goodbye Tomorrow*, 16
Miller, Arthur, **The Crucible*, 139
  Death of a Salesman, 139
Millis, Walter M., *A Canticle for Leibowitz*, 168
Mills, Kay, *A Place in the News*, 25
Miner, Jane Claypool, *Young Parents*, 331
Mitchell, Margaret, *Gone with the Wind*, 163
Modl, Thomas. *See* Hall, Lynn, and Modl, Thomas
Momaday, N. Scott, *House Made of Dawn*, 64
Morrison, Philip, and Phyllis Morrison, *The Ring of Truth: An Inquiry into How We Know What We Know*, 305
Morrison, Phyllis. *See* Morrison, Philip
Morrison, Toni, **Beloved*, 108
  The Bluest Eyes, 108
  Song of Solomon, 109
  Sula, 109
  Tar Baby, 108
Mowat, Farley, *Lost in the Barrens*, 231
  And No Birds Sang, 284
Mulcrone, Patricia, *The New GED: How to Prepare for the High School Equivalency Examination*, 334
Munn, H. Warner, *Merlin's Godson*, 194
  Merlin's Ring, 194
Munro, Alice, *Lives of Girls and Women*, 121
Murphy, Gloria, *Blood Ties*, 252
Murphy, Jim, *Death Run*, 231
Murphy, Shirley Rousseau, *The Ivory Lyre*, 203
  The Joining of the Stone, 203
  *Nightpool, 203
  The Ring of Fire, 203
Myers, Walter Dean, *Crystal*, 12
  *Fallen Angels, 143
  Hoops, 143
  Motown and Didi: A Love Story, 12
  The Outside Shot, 143

Nathan, Robert, *Portrait of Jennie*, 198
Navratilova, Martina, *Martina*, 256
Naylor, Gloria, *Mama Day*, 94
Naylor, Phyllis Reynolds, *The Keeper*, 25
  A String of Chances, 25
  Unexpected Pleasures, 12
  *The Year of the Gopher, 25
Neufeld, John, *Sleep, Two, Three, Four*, 189
Niven, Larry, *Ringworld*, 176
  Ringworld Engineers, 176
Nixon, Joan Lowery, *The Dark and Deadly Pool*, 235
  The Séance, 235
Noonan, Michael, *McKenzie's Boots*, 146
Norman, Philip, *Shout! The Beatles in Their Generation*, 280
  Symphony for the Devil: The Rolling Stones Story, 280
North, James, *Freedom Rising*, 277
Nourse, Alan E., *Birth Control*, 331

Oates, Joyce Carol, *Them*, 125
O'Brien, Tim, *Going after Cacciato*, 146
O'Dell, Scott, *The Castle in the Sea*, 216
  The Spanish Smile, 216
O'Flaherty, Lian, *The Informer*, 142
O'Hara, John, *Appointment in Samarra*, 130
Oldham, June, *Grow Up, Cupid*, 40
Olshan, Joseph, *A Warmer Season*, 36
Omer-Cooper, J. D., *History of Southern Africa*, 302
Omond, Roger, *The Apartheid Handbook*, 139
Oneal, Zibby, *In Summer Light*, 68
O'Neill, Eugene, *Ah! Wilderness*, 32
  Nine Plays by Eugene O'Neill, 32
Orwell, George, *Animal Farm*, 211
  Down and Out in Paris and London, 99
  1984, 91
Orzy, Baroness, *The Scarlet Pimpernel*, 108
Oyler, Chris, *Go Toward This Light*, 16

Packard, William, *The Art of the Playwright*, 33

Palmer, Laura, *Shrapnel in the Heart*, 312

Parini, Jay, *The Patch Boys*, 44

Pascoe, Elaine, *South Africa: Troubled Land*, 138

Pasternak, Boris, *Doctor Zhivago*, 155

Paton, Alan, *Ah, but Your Land Is Beautiful*, 103
Cry, the Beloved Country, 103

Paulsen, Gary, *The Crossing*, 20
Dogsong, 227
*Hatchet, 227
The Island, 228
Tracker, 227

Pearson, Diane, *Summer of the Barshinskeys*, 155

Peck, Richard, *Amanda/Miranda*, 80
Are You in the House Alone?, 324
Princess Ashley, 49
Remembering the Good Times, 72

Pei, Lowry, *Family Resemblances*, 72, 129

Penman, Sharon Kay, *Falls the Shadow*, 159

Peters, Elizabeth, *The Deeds of the Disturber*, 239
The Mummy Case, 239

Petersen, P. J., *Nobody Else Can Walk It for You*, 231

Petry, Ann, *Tituba of Salem Village*, 142

Pfeffer, Susan Beth, *The Year without Michael*, 76

Phillip, Neil, *The Tale of Sir Gawain*, 159

Pierce, Meredith Ann, *The Darkangel*, 197
A Gathering of Gargoyles, 197

Plain, Belva, *Evergreen*, 78
*The Golden Cup, 78
Tapestry, 78

Plath, Sylvia, *The Bell Jar*, 94

Plautus, *Menaechmi*, 113

Plimpton, George, *Bogey Man*, 265
*The Open Net, 265
Out of My League, 265
Paper Lion, 265

Pohl, Frederick, *Gateway*, 172

Polnasznek, Frank, *505 Hockey Questions Your Friends Can't Answer*, 268

Pomerance, Bernard, *The Elephant Man*, 108

Pomeroy, Wardell B., *Boys and Sex*, 331
Girls and Sex, 331

Porte, Barbara Ann, **I Only Made Up the Roses*, 82

Portis, Charles, *True Grit*, 117

Potok, Chaim, *The Chosen*, 264
Davita's Harp, 81

Powell, Randy, *My Underrated Year*, 54

Power, Helen W., and Robert Di Antonio, *The Admissions Essay: Stop Worrying and Start Writing*, 334

Powers, John R., *Do Black Patent Leather Shoes Really Reflect Up?*, 40

Price, Janet R., *The Rights of Students*, 324

Pringle, Laurence, *Nuclear War*, 91

Pronzini, Bill, and Martin Greenberg, eds., *Prime Suspects*, 252
Suspicious Characters, 252

Pullman, Philip, **The Ruby in the Smoke*, 147
The Shadow in the North, 148

Quammen, David, *Natural Acts*, 305

Redford, Dorothy, *Somerset Homecoming*, 112

Reigh, Jerome R., *Colonial America*, 308

Remarque, Erich Maria, *All Quiet on the Western Front*, 146

Renault, Mary, *Fire from Heaven*, 135
The King Must Die, 135

Rendell, Ruth, *From Doon with Death*, 249
*Heartstones, 249
The Veiled One, 252

Retton, Mary Lou, and Bela Karoly, *Mary Lou: Creating an Olympic Champion*, 268

Richter, Conrad, *A Light in the Forest*, 64

Ridgway, Samuel, *The Dolphin Doctor*, 288

Rinaldi, Ann, *Time Enough for Drums*, 152

Roberts, John Maddox, *Spacer: Window of the Mind*, 180

Robinson, Margaret A., *Courting Emma Howe*, 24

Robinson, Spider, *Callahan's Crosstime Saloon*, 172

Rodgers, Bill, *Marathoning*, 273

Rodowsky, Colby, *Julie's Daughter*, 49

Rofas, Eric E., ed., *The Kids' Book of Divorce*, 328

Rogasky, Barbara, *Smoke and Ashes*, 284

Rolvaag, O. E., *Giants in the Earth*, 99

Rosen, Richard, *Fadeaway*, 259

Rostkowski, Margaret, *After the Dancing Days*, 77

Roth, Arthur, *Two for Survival*, 231

Roth, Henry, *Call It Sleep*, 81

Rumsey, Tim, *Pictures from a Trip*, 17

Rylant, Cynthia, *A Fine White Dust*, 49

Sagan, Carl, *Contact*, 220
The Dragons of Eden, 292

Sagan, Carl, and Ann Druyan, *Comet*, 305

Saint-Exupery, Antoine de, *The Little Prince*, 194

St. George, Judith, *Do You See What I See?*, 235

Salewicz, Chris, *McCartney*, 280

Salinger, J. D., *The Catcher in the Rye*, 284

Samson, Joan, *The Auctioneer*, 142

Sanders, Scott R., *Bad Man's Ballad*, 117

Santiago, Danny, *Famous All Over Town*, 58

Sargent, Pamela, *Alien Child*, 180

Saroyan, William, *My Name Is Aram*, 7

Schell, Jonathan, *The Fate of the Earth*, 91

Schewel, Amy. *See* Smith, Marisa

Schieber, Phyllis, *Strictly Personal*, 36

Schlee, Ann, *Ask Me No Questions*, 99

Schmidt, Michael, *Green Island*, 53

Schrier, Eric W., and William F. Allman, *Newton at the Bat*, 268

Schurke, Paul. *See* Steger, Will

Schwandt, Stephen, *Holding Steady*, 68

Schwartz, Lester, and Irv Brechner, *Career Finder*, 321

Scoppetone, Sandra, *The Late Great Me*, 21

Sebestyen, Ouida, *Words by Heart*, 85

Sedgwick, John, *The Peaceable Kingdom*, 288

Senungetuk, Vivian, *A Place for Winter: Paul Tiulana's Story*, 296

Severin, Tim, *The Ulysses Voyage*, 135

Seymour, John, and Herbert Giradet, *Blueprint for a Green Planet*, 297

Shakespeare, *A Comedy of Errors*, 113

Shange, Ntozake, *Betsey Brown*, 277

Shannon, Mike, *The Best of Spitball*, 259

Shaw, Diana, *Gone Hollywood*, 215
Lessons in Fear, 215

Shaw, Irwin, *The Young Lions*, 147

Shea, Michael, *Polyphemus*, 108

Shelley, Mary W., *Frankenstein*, 108

Shoemaker, Bill, *Shoemaker*, 248

Sholokhov, Mikhail, *And Quiet Flows the Don*, 155
The Don Flows Home to the Sea, 155

Shriver, Pam, *Passing Shots*, 268

Shute, Nevil, *On the Beach*, 91

Sicilia, David B. *See* Sobel, Robert

Siegel, Robert, *Alpha Centauri*, 194

Silgbee, Peter, *Love among the Hiccups*, 28

Sillitoe, Alan, *The Loneliness of the Long Distance Runner*, 264

Silone, Ignazio, *Bread and Wine*, 155

Silverberg, Robert, *Lord Valentine's Castle*, 171
Majipoor Chronicles, 171

Simon, Neil, *Biloxi Blues*, 29
Brighton Beach Memoirs, 29
Broadway Bound, 29

Come Blow Your Horn, 29

Simon, Nissa, *Don't Worry, You're Normal,* 331

Simpson, Dorothy, *Element of Doubt,* 252

Sinclair, Upton, *The Jungle,* 99

Singer, Isaac Bashevis, *In My Father's Court,* 81

Sioracchini, Peter, *The Urge to Die: Why Young People Commit Suicide,* 72

Sjowall, Maj, and Wahloo, Per, *The Laughing Policeman,* 248

Slater, Cornelius, *An Apple a Day,* 288

Sleator, William, *The Boy Who Reversed Himself,* 188

The Duplicate, 186

House of Stairs, 186

Interstellar Pig, 188

*Singularity, 186

Small, David, *The River in Winter,* 49

Smith, Betty, *Tomorrow Will Be Better,* 24

A Tree Grows in Brooklyn, 24

Smith, Marisa, and Amy Schewel, eds., *The Actor's Book of Movie Monologues,* 32

Smith, Martin Cruz, *Nightwing,* 220

Snider, Dee, *Dee Snider's Teenage Survival Guide,* 324

Sobel, Robert, and David B. Sicilia, *The Entrepreneurs,* 309

Solzhenitsyn, Alexandr, *The Gulag Archipelago,* 153

*One Day in the Life of Ivan Denisovich, 153

Somtow, S. P., *The Shattered Horse,* 135

Soto, Gary, *Small Faces,* 277

Soyinka, Wole, ed., *Poems of Black Africa,* 277

Speare, Elizabeth, *The Witch of Blackbird Pond,* 142

Springer, Nancy, *The Hex Witch of Seldom,* 202

Stafford, Jean, *The Mountain Lion,* 72

Steger, Will, and Paul Schurke, *North to the Pole,* 297

Steinbeck, John, *The Grapes of Wrath,* 125

Sterling, Dorothy, *We Are Your Sisters,* 113

Stevenson, Robert Louis, *Doctor Jekyll and Mr. Hyde,* 108

Stewart, Bob. *See* Matthews, John

Stewart, George R., *Earth Abides,* 91

Stewart, Mary, *The Crystal Cave,* 156

The Hollow Hills, 156

The Last Enchantment, 156

Madame Will You Talk?, 156

*The Wicked Day, 156

Stoker, Bran, *Dracula,* 108

Stone, Bruce, *Half Nelson, Full Nelson,* 260

Strand, Peter, *Shadowland,* 236

Stratton, Barbara, *You Never Lose,* 264

Strum, Shirley, *Almost Human: A Journey into the World of Baboons,* 292

Styron, William, *The Confessions of Nat Turner,* 112

Sulzberger, C. L., *Fathers and Children,* 37

Sunquist, Fiona, and Mel Sunquist, *Tiger Moon,* 291

Sunquist, Mel. *See* Sunquist, Fiona

Swanwick, Michael, *In the Drift,* 210

Swarthout, Glendon, *Bless the Beasts and Children,* 58

Sweeney, Joyce, *Center Line,* 68

Swenson, May. *See* Knudson, R. R., and May Swenson

Swindells, Robert, *Staying Up,* 40

Switzer, Ellen, *Greek Myths,* 135

Talbert, Marc, *Dead Birds Singing,* 59

Tapert, Annette, *Lines of Battle: Letters from U.S. Servicemen, 1941–45,* 312

Tarkington, Booth, *The Magnificent Ambersons,* 130

Terkel, Studs, *Hard Times,* 100

Terrace, Herbert S., *Nim: A Chimpanzee Who Learned Sign Language,* 292

Terris, Susan, *Nell's Quilt,* 81

Terry, Wallace, **Bloods: An Oral History of the Vietnam War by Black Veterans,* 309

Theroux, Paul, *The Mosquito Coast,* 95

Thesman, Jean, *The Last April Dancers,* 68

Thomas, Joyce, *Bright Shadow*, 4
  Marked by Fire, 4
  Water Girl, 4
Thompson, Julian F., *Simon Pure*, 40
  The Taking of Mariasburg, 8
Thompson, Kathleen. *See* Medea, Andrea
Thomson, Elizabeth, ed., *The Lennon Companion*, 280
Thorn, John, *The Game for All America*, 256
Tiburzi, Bonnie, *Takeoff!*, 268
Tiptree, James, *The Starry Rift*, 189
Tirone, Mary-Ann, *The Book of Phoebe*, 8
Tolkien, J. R. R., *The Fellowship of the Ring*, 206
  Lord of the Rings, 206
Townsend, John Rowe, **Downstream*, 33
Townsend, Sue, **The Adrian Mole Diaries*, 37
  The Growing Pains of Adrian Mole, 38
  The Secret Diary of Adrian Mole, Aged 13 3/4, 38
Trevor, Elleston, *Death Watch*, 220
Trevor, William, *Fools of Fortune*, 129
Truman, Margaret, *Murder in the CIA*, 239
Tunis, Edwin, *Colonial Craftsmen*, 309
Tuttle, Lisa. *See* Martin, George R.
Twain, Mark, *A Connecticut Yankee in King Arthur's Court*, 113
  Huckleberry Finn, 113
  *Puddn'head Wilson, 113
  Tom Sawyer, 113
  The Wit and Wisdom of Mark Twain, 117
Tyler, Anne, *If Morning Ever Comes*, 117
  *A Slipping-Down Life, 117

Ungar, Douglas, *El Yanqui*, 121
Updike, John, *Rabbit Run*, 130
Ure, Jean, *The Other Side of the Fence*, 36
  What If They Saw Me Now?, 40
  You Win Some, You Lose Some, 40
Uris, Leon, *Trinity*, 104

Vedral, Joyce, *My Parents Are Driving Me Crazy*, 328
Vidal, Gore, *Burr*, 163
  Lincoln, 163
Villarreal, José Antonio, *Pocho*, 4
Vinge, Joan D., *Psion*, 180
Voigt, Cynthia, *Homecoming*, 269
  *The Runner, 269
  Sons from Afar, 272
Vonnegut, Kurt, Jr., **Cat's Cradle*, 207
  Slaughterhouse 5, 207
Voss, Jacqueline, *A Young Woman's Guide to Sex*, 331

Wahloo, Per. *See* Sjowall, Maj
Wain, John, *The Free Zone Starts Here*, 77
Walker, Alice, **The Color Purple*, 121
  Living by the Word, 277
  Meridian, 121
  The Third Life of Grange Copeland, 121
Walker, Margaret, *How I Wrote "Jubilee,"* 160
  *Jubilee, 160
Wallin, Luke, *In the Shadow of Wind*, 25
Walsh, Jill P., *A Chance Child*, 202
Wangerin, Walter, Jr., *The Book of the Dunn Cow*, 211
Watson, Lyall, *The Dreams of Dragons: Riddles of Natural History*, 316
Waugh, Evelyn, *The Loved One*, 108
Wells, H. G., *The Invisible Man*, 189
  The Island of Dr. Moreau, 189
  Seven Science Fiction Novels, 189
  The Time Machine, 189
Wells, Rosemary, *When No One Was Looking*, 260
Welty, Eudora, *The Bride of Innisfallen*, 126
  A Curtain of Green, 126
  Losing Battles, 126
  *The Optimist's Daughter, 126
Wersba, Barbara, *Beautiful Losers*, 12
  Fat, 12
  Love Is a Crooked Thing, 12
  Run Softly, Go Fast, 73

Westall, Robert, *Futuretrack 5*, 189
Westheimer, David, *Von Ryan's Express*, 224
Wharton, William, *Birdy*, 121
A Midnight Clear, 155
White, T. H., *The Once and Future King*, 159
Whitney, Phyllis A., *Feather on the Moon*, 239
Rainsong, 239
Spindrift, 239
Wicker, Tom, *Unto This Hour*, 163
Wiesel, Elie, *Dawn*, 156
Night, 156
Wieseltier, Leon, *Nuclear War, Nuclear Peace*, 91
Wilford, John Noble, **The Riddle of the Dinosaur*, 313
Wilhelm, Kate, *Oh, Susannah!*, 121
Willard, Nancy, *Things Invisible to See*, 95
Williams, Tennessee, *The Glass Menagerie*, 142
Windling, Terri, and Mark Alan Arnold, eds., *Elsewhere, Volume 3*, 194
Witherspoon, William Roger, *Martin Luther King, Jr.—To the Mountaintop*, 277
Woiwode, Larry, *Beyond the Bedroom Door*, 95
Wolf, Gary, *Who Censored Roger Rabbit?*, 220
Wolff, Rick. *See* Goldis, Al
Wood, Robert, *Dodger Dogs to Fenway Franks*, 256
Woods, Donald, *Asking for Trouble*, 302
Biko, 302

Wooley, Persia, *Child of the Northern Spring*, 159
Worth, Richard, *The American Family*, 328
Wouk, Herman, *The Caine Mutiny*, 147
Wrede, Patricia C., *Daughter of Witches*, 206
The Harp of Imach Thyssel, 206
Wright, Richard, *American Hunger*, 276
Black Boy, 276
Native Son, 276
Wrightson, Patricia, *The Dark Bright Water*, 202
Wyss, Thelma Hatch, *Here at the Scenic-Vu Motel*, 54

Yeager, Chuck, *Press On!*, 296
Yeager, 296
Yep, Laurence, *Liar, Liar*, 235
Monster Makers, Inc., 181
Yolen, Jane, *Dragon's Blood*, 206
The Gift of Sarah Baker, 44
Yoxen, Edward, *The Gene Business: Who Should Control Biotechnology?*, 305

Zahn, Timothy, *Spinneret*, 168
Zelazny, Roger, *Changeling*, 202
The Last Defender of Camelot, 202
Zindel, Paul, *The Amazing and Death-Defying Diary of Eugene Dingman*, 36
The Effects of Gamma Rays on Man-in-the-Moon Marigolds, 142

TITLE INDEX

Titles fully discussed and summarized in *Seniorplots* as well as those cited in the text and in "Additional Selections" are included in this index. An asterisk (*) precedes those titles for which full summaries and discussions appear.

Abbey, My Love, Hadley Irwin, 21

Above Suspicion, Helen MacInnes, 245

The Actor's Book of Movie Monologues, Marisa Smith and Amy Schewel, eds., 32

The Admissions Essay: Stop Worrying and Start Writing, Helen W. Power and Robert Di Antonio, 334

*The Adrian Mole Diaries, Sue Townsend, 37

Adrift: Seventy-Six Days Lost at Sea, Steven Callahan, 273

The Adventures of Augie March, Saul Bellow, 100

African Stories, Doris Lessing, 103

After the Dancing Days, Margaret Rostkowski, 77

After the Rain, Norma Fox Mazer, 44

Against Infinity, Gregory Bentford, 171

Against Rape, Andrea Medea and Kathleen Thompson, 324

The Age of Reform, Richard Hofstadter, 306

Ah, but Your Land Is Beautiful, Alan Paton, 103

Ah! Wilderness, Eugene O'Neill, 32

AIDS, Lynn Hall and Thomas Modl, eds., 17

AIDS: The Facts, John Langone, 17

Alas, Babylon, Pat Frank, 210

Alien Child, Pamela Sargent, 180

Alien Music, Annabel Johnson and Edgar Johnson, 177

All Creatures Great and Small, James Herriot, 285

*All God's Children Need Traveling Shoes, Maya Angelou, 274

All Quiet on the Western Front, Erich Maria Remarque, 146

All the Comforts of Home, Robert X. Leeds, 288

All Things Bright and Beautiful, James Herriot, 285

All Things Wise and Wonderful, James Herriot, 285

Almost Human: A Journey into the World of Baboons, Shirley Strum, 292

Alpha Centauri, Robert Siegel, 194

Always to Remember, Brent Ashabranner, 312

Amanda/Miranda, Richard Peck, 80

The Amateur Naturalist, Gerald Durrell and Lee Durrell, 292

The Amateurs, David Halberstam, 267

The Amazing and Death-Defying Diary of Eugene Dingman, Paul Zindel, 36

The Amazing Mrs. Polifax, Dorothy Gilman, 239

*America at 1750: A Social Portrait, Richard Hofstadter, 306

An American Childhood, Annie Dillard, 121

The American Family, Richard Worth, 328

American Hunger, Richard Wright, 276

The American League: An Illustrated History, Donald Honig, 260

The American Revolutionaries: A History in Their Own Words, 1750–1800, Milton Meltzer, 308

American Sports Poems, R. R. Knudson and May Swenson, eds., 268

The Americans: The Colonial Experience, Daniel J. Boorstin, 308

And No Birds Sang, Farley Mowat, 284

And Quiet Flows the Don, Mikhail Sholokhov, 155

Andersonville, MacKinlay Kantor, 164

The Andromeda Strain, Michael Crichton, 216

Angel with the Sword, C. J. Cherryh, 184

Animal Farm, George Orwell, 211

Annie John, Jamaica Kincaid, 4

Annie on My Mind, Nancy Garden, 76

Anthony Burns: The Defeat and Triumph of a Fugitive Slave, Virginia Hamilton, 112

Anti-Intellectualism in the United States, Richard Hofstadter, 306

The Apartheid Handbook, Roger Omond, 139

An Apple a Day, Cornelius Slater, 288

Appointment in Samarra, John O'Hara, 130

*Arctic Dreams: Imagination and Desire in a Northern Landscape, Barry Lopez, 292

Are You in the House Alone?, Richard Peck, 324

The Ariadne Clue, Carol Clemeau, 240

The Arizona Kid, Ron Koertge, 17

The Arm of the Starfish, Madeleine L'Engle, 73

Arrows of the Queen, Mercedes Lackey, 194

The Art of the Playwright, William Packard, 33

Arthur Rex, Thomas Berger, 159

Ask Me No Questions, Ann Schlee, 99

Asking for Trouble, Donald Woods, 302

The Assistant, Bernard Malamud, 260

At Risk, Alice Hoffman, 16

The Auctioneer, Joan Samson, 142

The Autobiography of Miss Jane Pitman, Ernest Gaines, 112

The Aviator, Ernest K. Gans, 231

Babbitt, Sinclair Lewis, 130

Bad Man's Ballad, Scott R. Sanders, 117

Bang the Drum Slowly, Mark Harris, 264

The Basket Case, Ralph McInerny, 248

*The Beacon at Alexandria, Gillian Bradshaw, 131

Beatlemania: The History of The Beatles on Film, Bill Harry, 280

The Beatles, Hunter Davies, 280

Beautiful Losers, Barbara Wersba, 12

Beauty, Robin McKinley, 202

The Beekeeper's Daughter, Gillian Bradshaw, 135

Behind the Attic Wall, Sylvia Cassedy, 207

The Bell Jar, Sylvia Plath, 94

*Beloved, Toni Morrison, 108

The Berlin Game, Len Deighton, 227

The Best Buys in College Education, Edward B. Fiske, 334

The Best of Enemies, Nancy Bond, 49

The Best of Spitball, Mike Shannon, 259

Betsey Brown, Ntozake Shange, 277

Beyond the Bedroom Door, Larry Woiwode, 95

*Beyond the Chocolate War, Robert Cormier, 50

Beyond the Frozen Sea, Edwin Mickleburgh, 296

The Big Sea, Langston Hughes, 276

Biko, Donald Woods, 302

The Bill James Historical Baseball Abstract, Bill James, 256

Biloxi Blues, Neil Simon, 29

Birds, Beasts and Relatives, Gerald Durrell, 288

Birdy, William Wharton, 121

Birth Control, Alan E. Nourse, 331

The Birth of the New Physics, I. Bernard Cohen, 305

Black Boy, Richard Wright, 276

The Black Tower, P. D. James, 252

The Black Unicorn, Terry Brooks, 190

Blade Runner, Philip K. Dick, 176

Bleak House, Charles Dickens, 96

Bless the Beasts and Children, Glendon Swarthout, 58

Blood Ties, Gloria Murphy, 252

*Bloods: An Oral History of the Vietnam War by Black Veterans, Wallace Terry, 309

Bloodsong, Ernst Havemann, 139

Bloodsong and Other Stories of South Africa, Ernst Havemann, 103

The Blue Sword, Robin McKinley, 207

Blueprint for a Green Planet, John Seymour and Herbert Giradet, 297

The Bluest Eyes, Toni Morrison, 108

Bobby Rex's Greatest Hits, Marianne Gingher, 7

Bogey Man, George Plimpton, 265

*Bolt, Dick Francis, 245

The Book of Phoebe, Mary-Ann Tirone, 8

The Book of the Dunn Cow, Walter Wangerin, Jr., 211

Born Free: A Lioness of Two Worlds, Joy Adamson, 292

Boston Boy, Nat Hentoff, 284

The Bourne Identity, Robert Ludlum, 226

Boy, Roald Dahl, 281

The Boy Who Reversed Himself, William Sleator, 188

Boys and Sex, Wardell B. Pomeroy, 331

Brave New World, Aldous Huxley, 198

Bread and Wine, Ignazio Silone, 155

Break In, Dick Francis, 245

Breakaway Run, David Klass, 58

Breakfast at Tiffany's, Truman Capote, 130

Breaking into the Big Leagues, Al Goldis and Rick Wolff, 260

Breaking Up Is Hard to Do, Bruce Hart and Carole Hart, 28

Breaktime, Aidan Chambers, 37

The Bride, Vonda N. McIntyre, 108

The Bride of Innisfallen, Eudora Welty, 126

Bride of Pendorric, Victoria Holt, 152

The Bride Price, Buchi Emecheta, 103

*A Brief History of Time: From the Big Bang to Black Holes, Stephen W. Hawking, 302

Bright Shadow, Joyce Thomas, 4

*Brighton Beach Memoirs, Neil Simon, 29

Broadway Bound, Neil Simon, 29

Burr, Gore Vidal, 163

Bury the Dead, Peter Carter, 273

The Butterfly Revolution, William Butterworth, 53

The Caine Mutiny, Herman Wouk, 147

Cal, Bernard MacLaverty, 104

Call It Sleep, Henry Roth, 81

Callahan's Crosstime Saloon, Spider Robinson, 172

Camelot, Alan Jay Lerner, 160

A Canticle for Leibowitz, Walter M. Millis, 168

Captives of Time, Malcolm Bosse, 159

Career Finder, Lester Schwartz and Irv Brechner, 321

Carrie, Stephen King, 252

The Castle in the Sea, Scott O'Dell, 216

The Catalogue of the Universe, Margaret Mahy, 120

Catch 22, Joseph Heller, 211

The Catcher in the Rye, J. D. Salinger, 284

*Cat's Cradle, Kurt Vonnegut, Jr., 207

Center Line, Joyce Sweeney, 68

A Chance Child, Jill P. Walsh, 202

Changeling, Roger Zelazny, 202

The Changeover, Margaret Mahy, 198

Changing Families: Meeting Today's Challenges, Kathlyn Gay, 327

The Charm School, Nelson DeMille, 224

Chartbreaker, Gillian Cross, 40

Chickenhawk, Robert Mason, 312

Child of the Northern Spring, Persia Wooley, 159

Children of a Lesser God, Mark Medoff, 142

Children of Dune, Frank Herbert, 167

Children's Story, James Clavell, 189

China Homecoming, Jean Fritz, 284

The Chocolate War, Robert Cormier, 50

The Chosen, Chaim Potok, 264

Christine, Stephen King, 252

Christmas Lessons, Janine Boissard, 77

Christy, Catherine Marshall, 22

Citizen of the Galaxy, Robert A. Heinlein, 172

City Light, Harry Mazer, 28

City of Gold and Lead, John Christopher, 188

Clan of the Cave Bear, Jean Auel, 135

Cloak of Darkness, Helen MacInnes, 244

A Clockwork Orange, Anthony Burgess, 211

The Clockwork Testament, Anthony Burgess, 211

A Code to Keep, Ernest C. Brace, 312

A Coffin for Dimitrios, Eric Ambler, 224

Cold Comfort Farm, Stella Gibbons, 8

Cold Sassy Tree, Olive Ann Burns, 8

The Collapsing Universe, Isaac Asimov, 165

The College Cost Book, College Entrance Examination Board, 335

The College Money Book, Gene R. Hawes, 334

Colonial America, Jerome R. Reigh, 308

Colonial Craftsmen, Edwin Tunis, 309

*The Color Purple, Alice Walker, 121

Coma, Robin Cook, 220

Come Blow Your Horn, Neil Simon, 29

A Comedy of Errors, Shakespeare, 113

Comet, Carl Sagan and Ann Druyan, 305

The Complete Handbook of Pro Hockey, Zander Hollander, 268

The Conduct of the Game, John Hough, 264

The Confessions of Nat Turner, William Styron, 112

A Connecticut Yankee in King Arthur's Court, Mark Twain, 113

Conspiracy of Knaves, Dee Brown, 163

Contact, Carl Sagan, 220

The Contender, Robert Lipsyte, 260

Cooder Cutlas, Elizabeth Bales Frank, 12

*Coping: When Your Family Falls Apart, Dianna Daniels Booher, 324

Coping with Substance Abuse, Rhoda McFarland, 324

The Cosmic Blueprint, Paul Davies, 305

The Count of Monte Cristo, Alexander Dumas, 108

The Counterfeiter, Dennis Haseley, 28

Courting Emma Howe, Margaret A. Robinson, 24

Cranes at Dusk, Hisako Matsubara, 77

*The Crazy Horse Electric Game, Chris Crutcher, 55

The Creation of Matter, Harold Fitzsch, 305

The Crossing, Gary Paulsen, 20

*Crossing the Line: A Year in the Land of Apartheid, William Finnegan, 298

*The Crucible, Arthur Miller, 139

Cry of the Seals, Jeremy Lucas, 297

Cry, the Beloved Country, Alan Paton, 103

Crystal, Walter Dean Myers, 12

The Crystal Cave, Mary Stewart, 156

A Curtain of Green, Eudora Welty, 126

The Dancing Men, Duncan Kyer, 54

*The Danger Quotient, Annabel Johnson and Edgar Johnson, 177

Dangerous Visions, Harlan Ellison, 168

The Dangling Witness, Jay Bennett, 235

Daphne Du Maurier's Classics of the Macabre, 244

The Dark and Deadly Pool, Joan Lowery Nixon, 235

The Dark Bright Water, Patricia Wrightson, 202

The Dark Horse, Rumer Godden, 248

The Darkangel, Meredith Ann Pierce, 197

Darkness at Noon, Arthur Koestler, 155

Daughter of Witches, Patricia C. Wrede, 206

Daughters, Consuelo Saah Baehr, 63
Davita's Harp, Chaim Potok, 81
Dawn, Octavia Butler, 91
Dawn, Elie Wiesel, 156
Day of Infamy, Walter Lord, 285
*The Day of the Jackal, Frederick Forsyth, 221
Day of the Starwind, Douglas Hill, 180
The Day They Stole the Queen Mary, Terence Hughes, 248
Dayworld, Philip J. Farmer, 168
Dead Birds Singing, Marc Talbert, 59
A Death at St. Anselm's, Isabelle Holland, 248
A Death in the Family, James Agee, 44
Death of a Salesman, Arthur Miller, 139
Death Run, Jim Murphy, 231
Death Watch, Elleston Trevor, 220
Deathtrap, Ira Levin, 32
Dee Snider's Teenage Survival Guide, Dee Snider, 324
The Deeds of the Disturber, Elizabeth Peters, 239
The Delikon, H. M. Hoover, 181
Denny's Tapes, Carolyn Meyer, 85
Deryni Checkmate, Katherine Kurtz, 176
Deryni Rising, Katherine Kurtz, 176
Devil By the Sea, Nina Bowden, 235
The Devil's Alternative, Frederick Forsyth, 221
Diary of a Medical Nobody, Kenneth Lane, 288
Dinky Hocker Shoots Smack, M. E. Kerr, 13
Dinosaurs: An Illustrated History, Edwin H. Colbert, 317
Dirk Gently's Holistic Detective Agency, Douglas Adams, 171
The Dispossessed, Ursula K. LeGuin, 185
Do Black Patent Leather Shoes Really Reflect Up?, John R. Powers, 40
Do You See What I See?, Judith St. George, 235
Doc, Richard Graber, 77
Doctor Jekyll and Mr. Hyde, Robert Louis Stevenson, 108
Dr. Wildlife, Rory C. Foster, 288
Doctor Zhivago, Boris Pasternak, 155

Dodger Dogs to Fenway Franks, Robert Wood, 256
Dogsong, Gary Paulsen, 227
The Dollmaker, Harriette Arnow, 95
The Dolphin Doctor, Samuel Ridgway, 288
The Don Flows Home to the Sea, Mikhail Sholokhov, 155
Don't Blame the Music, Caroline B. Cooney, 85
Don't Worry, You're Normal, Nissa Simon, 331
Doomstalker, Glen Cook, 185
Dorsai!, Gordon R. Dickson, 176
Down and Out in Paris and London, George Orwell, 99
*Downstream, John Rowe Townsend, 33
The Drackenberg Adventure, Lloyd Alexander, 212
Dracula, Bran Stoker, 108
Dragonflight, Anne McCaffrey, 181
Dragon's Blood, Jane Yolen, 206
Dragon's Egg, Robert L. Forward, 172
The Dragons of Eden, Carl Sagan, 292
Dragonsong, Anne McCaffrey, 181
The Dreams of Dragons: Riddles of Natural History, Lyall Watson, 316
Dreamsnake, Vonda N. McIntyre, 185
The Dreamstone, C. J. Cherryh, 184
Dune, Frank Herbert, 167
The Duplicate, William Sleator, 186

The Eagle Has Landed, Jack Higgins, 224
Earth Abides, George R. Stewart, 91
The Effects of Gamma Rays on Man-in-the-Moon Marigolds, Paul Zindel, 142
*The El Dorado Adventure, Lloyd Alexander, 212
Element of Doubt, Dorothy Simpson, 252
The Elephant Man, Bernard Pomerance, 108
The Elfstones of Shannara, Terry Brooks, 190
The Elizabeth Stories, Isabel Huggan, 44

Elkhorn Tavern, Douglas C. Jones, 117

Elsewhere, Volume 3, Terri Windling and Mark Alan Arnold, eds., 194

Emma, Jane Austen, 130

Empire of the Sun, J. G. Ballard, 284

English Creek, Ivan Doig, 230

The Entrepreneurs, Robert Sobel and David B. Sicilia, 309

Eon, Greg Bear, 91

The Essential AIDS Fact Book, Paul Harding Douglas, 17

Evergreen, Belva Plain, 78

Everyday Life in Early America, David Freeman Hawke, 308

Eye of the Needle, Ken Follett, 224

Face Maker, William Katz, 220

Fadeaway, Richard Rosen, 259

The Fall of the Roman Umpire, Ron Luciano, 256

Fallen Angels, Walter Dean Myers, 143

Falls the Shadow, Sharon Kay Penman, 159

Family Resemblances, Lowry Pei, 72, 129

Famous All Over Town, Danny Santiago, 58

A Farewell to Arms, Ernest Hemingway, 146

Fat, Barbara Wersba, 12

Fate Is the Hunter, Ernest K. Gans, 231

The Fate of the Earth, Jonathan Schell, 91

Fathers and Children, C. L. Sulzberger, 37

Feather on the Moon, Phyllis A. Whitney, 239

Feed the Fear and Do It Anyway, Susan Jeffers, 321

Fell, M. E. Kerr, 13

The Fellowship of the Ring, J. R. R. Tolkien, 206

A Field Guide to Dinosaurs, David Lambert, 317

Final Payments, Mary Gordon, 121

Finding Fever, Thomas Baird, 215

Finding Your First Job, Sue Alexander, 318

A Fine and Private Place, Peter S. Beagle, 202

A Fine White Dust, Cynthia Rylant, 49

Fire from Heaven, Mary Renault, 135

Fire in the Lake, Frances Fitzgerald, 312

Five Hundred Fifty-Five Ways to Earn Extra Money, Jay C. Levinson, 321

505 Hockey Questions Your Friends Can't Answer, Frank Polnasznek, 268

Five Smooth Stones, Ann Fairbairn, 4

The Fixer, Bernard Malamud, 260

The Flamingo's Smile, Stephen Jay Gould, 317

Flanagan's Run, Tom McNab, 272

The Flight of the Cassowary, John LeVert, 121

Flunking Out, W. E. Butterworth, 28

Flyaway, Lynn Hall, 68

The Fog, James Herbert, 220

Fools of Fortune, William Trevor, 129

Fool's Run, Patricia A. McKillip, 184

Force 10 from Navarone, Alistair MacLean, 227

The Forge of God, Greg Bear, 176

The Forsyte Saga, John Galsworthy, 100

Foul Ball!, Alison Gordon, 256

Foundation, Isaac Asimov, 165

Foundation and Empire, Isaac Asimov, 165

Fragments, Jack Fuller, 146

Frankenstein, Mary W. Shelley, 108

The Free Zone Starts Here, John Wain, 77

Freedom Rising, James North, 277

Friday the Rabbi Slept Late, Harry Kemelman, 248

The Friends, Rosa Guy, 12

From Doon with Death, Ruth Rendell, 249

Futuretrack 5, Robert Westall, 189

Galactic Warlord, Douglas Hill, 180

The Game for All America, John Thorn, 256

Gateway, Frederick Pohl, 172

Gather Together in My Name, Maya Angelou, 274

A Gathering of Gargoyles, Meredith Ann Pierce, 197

A Gathering of Old Men, Ernest Gaines, 112

The Gene Business: Who Should Control Biotechnology?, Edward Yoxen, 305

Genesis: The Origins of Man and the Universe, John Gribbin, 317

Gentlehands, M. E. Kerr, 13

Getting In!, Paulo de Oliveira and Steve Cohen, 334

*Getting into College, Frank C. Leana, 332

Getting Off to College, Melody Martin, 334

Giants in the Earth, O. E. Rolvaag, 99

The Gift, Peter Dickinson, 207

The Gift of Sarah Baker, Jane Yolen, 44

The Girl of His Dreams, Harry Mazer, 272

Girls and Sex, Wardell B. Pomeroy, 331

The Glass Menagerie, Tennessee Williams, 142

Go for It: How to Get Your First Good Job, Martha C. Douglas, 320

Go Hire Yourself an Employer, Richard K. Irish, 321

Go Tell It on the Mountain, James Baldwin, 1, 72

Go Toward This Light, Chris Oyler, 16

Go Well, Stay Well, Toeckey Jones, 138

The Goats, Brock Cole, 230

Going after Cacciato, Tim O'Brien, 146

*Going Solo, Roald Dahl, 281

*The Golden Cup, Belva Plain, 78

Gone Hollywood, Diana Shaw, 215

Gone the Dreams and Dancing, Douglas Jones, 164

Gone with the Wind, Margaret Mitchell, 163

Good-bye and Keep Cold, Jenny Davis, 25

The Good Earth, Pearl Buck, 155

Good Night, Mr. Tom, Michelle Magorian, 21

Good Spies Don't Grow on Trees, Marc Lovell, 8

Good Times, Bad Times, James Kirkwood, 54

Goodbye Mickey Mouse, Len Deighton, 227

Goodbye, Mr. Chips, James Hilton, 195

Goodbye Tomorrow, Gloria Miklowitz, 16

Gorillas in the Mist, Dian Fossey, 291

Grania: She-King of the Irish Seas, Morgan Llywelyn, 159

Granny Was a Buffer Girl, Berlie Doherty, 64

The Grapes of Wrath, John Steinbeck, 125

The Great British Detective, Ron Gowlart, 152

The Great Escape, Paul Buckhill, 284

The Great Train Robbery, Michael Crichton, 152

Greek Myths, Ellen Switzer, 135

Green Island, Michael Schmidt, 53

Green Mansions, W. H. Hudson, 198

The Green Road Home, Michael Barnberger, 268

Greencastle, Lloyd Kropp, 4

Grendel, John Gardner, 198

The Ground Zero Club and Other Prize-Winning Plays, Wendy Lamb, 32

Grow Up, Cupid, June Oldham, 40

The Growing Pains of Adrian Mole, Sue Townsend, 38

Growing Season, Alden R. Carter, 28

Growth of the Soil, Knut Hamsun, 99

The Gulag Archipelago, Alexandr Solzhenitsyn, 153

The Guns of Navarone, Alistair MacLean, 227

Guys Like Us, Stuart Buchan, 85

Half Nelson, Full Nelson, Bruce Stone, 260

Hammer Locke, Jack Barnao, 59

The Handmaid's Tale, Margaret Atwood, 125

*Hard Times, Charles Dickens, 96

Hard Times, Studs Terkel, 100

The Harp of Imach Thyssel, Patricia C. Wrede, 206

The Harvard Guide to Careers, Martha P. Leape, 321

*Hatchet, Gary Paulsen, 227

The Haunting, Margaret Mahy, 198
The Haunting of Hill House, Shirley Jackson, 252
Hawkmistress!, Marion Zimmer Bradley, 194
The Heart Is a Lonely Hunter, Carson McCullers, 125
Heart of a Family, Doug Finn, 68
The Heart of a Woman, Maya Angelou, 274
The Heart of the Matter, Graham Greene, 142
*Heartstones, Ruth Rendell, 249
Help, We're Moving, Dianna Daniels Booher, 325
Hen's Teeth and Horse's Toes, Stephen Jay Gould, 317
Here at the Scenic-Vu Motel, Thelma Hatch Wyss, 54
The Hero and the Crown, Robin McKinley, 206
The Hex Witch of Seldom, Nancy Springer, 202
History of Southern Africa, J. D. Omer-Cooper, 302
The Hitchhiker's Guide to the Galaxy, Douglas Adams, 171
Holding Steady, Stephen Schwandt, 68
The Hollow Hills, Mary Stewart, 156
Homecoming, Cynthia Voigt, 269
The Honorable Prison, Lyll Becerra de Jenkins, 215
Hoops, Walter Dean Myers, 143
The Hound of the Baskervilles, Sir Arthur Conan Doyle, 152
*A House Like a Lotus, Madeleine L'Engle, 73
House Made of Dawn, N. Scott Momaday, 64
House of Stairs, William Sleator, 186
How Green Was My Valley, Richard Llewellyn, 99
How I Wrote "Jubilee," Margaret Walker, 160
How Life Imitates the World Series, Thomas Boswell, 264
How to Live with a Single Parent, Sara Gilbert, 327
How to Prepare for the Scholastic Aptitude Test, Samuel C. Brownstein, 334

How to Take the SAT, Marcia Laurence, 334
Howl's Moving Castle, Diana Wynne Jones, 194
Huckleberry Finn, Mark Twain, 113
The Human Factor, Graham Greene, 227
*The Hunchback of Notre Dame, Victor Hugo, 104
Hunter's Horn, Harriette Arnow, 44

I Am One of You Forever, Fred Chappell, 7
I Know What You Did Last Summer, Lois Duncan, 215
I Know Why the Caged Bird Sings, Maya Angelou, 274
I Never Met an Animal I Didn't Like, Rory C. Foster, 288
I Never Promised You a Rose Garden, Joanne Greenberg, 5
*I Only Made Up the Roses, Barbara Ann Porte, 82
The Icarus Agenda, Robert Ludlum, 226
Ice Station Zebra, Alistair MacLean, 227
*If Beale Street Could Talk, James Baldwin, 1
If I Love You, Am I Trapped Forever?, M. E. Kerr, 13
If I Were You, Joan Aiken, 24
If Morning Ever Comes, Anne Tyler, 117
Illumination Night, Alice Hoffman, 44
The Illyrian Adventure, Lloyd Alexander, 212
Imaginary Crimes, Sheila Ballantyne, 95
The Impact Zone, Ray Maloney, 59
In Country, Bobbie Ann Mason, 146
In His Own Write, John Lennon, 280
In My Father's Court, Isaac Bashevis Singer, 81
In My Father's House, Ernest J. Gaines, 4
In Search of J. D. Salinger, Ian Hamilton, 284
In Summer Light, Zibby Oneal, 68

In the Combat Zone, Kathryn Marshall, 312

In the Drift, Michael Swanwick, 210

In the Heat of the Night, John Ball, 125

In the Shadow of Man, Jane van Lawick-Goodall, 289

In the Shadow of Wind, Luke Wallin, 25

In This Sign, Joanne Greenberg, 5

The India Fan, Victoria Holt, 244

The Infinity Concerto, Greg Bear, 176

The Informer, Lian O'Flaherty, 142

The Intelligent Universe, Fred Hoyle, 317

Interstellar Pig, William Sleator, 188

Intruder in the Dust, William Faulkner, 117

Invincible Summer, Jean Ferris, 17

Invisible Man, Ralph Ellison, 4

The Invisible Man, H. G. Wells, 189

The Iowa Baseball Confederacy, W. P. Kinsella, 259

The Ipcress File, Len Deighton, 227

Isaac Asimov Presents the Best Fantasy of the 19th Century, Isaac Asimov, 198

Isaac Campion, Janni Howker, 68

Iseult, Dee Morrison Meaney, 159

The Island, Gary Paulsen, 228

The Island of Dr. Moreau, H. G. Wells, 189

It Won't Happen to Me: Teenagers Talk about Pregnancy, Paula McGuire, 331

The Ivory Lyre, Shirley Rousseau Murphy, 203

Jackie Robinson, Harvey Frommer, 253

Jackie Robinson: A Life Remembered, Maury Allen, 253

Jane Eyre, Charlotte Bronte, 244

Jobs for Teenagers, Ilene Jones, 321

John Lennon: One Day at a Time, Anthony Fawcett, 280

The Joining of the Stone, Shirley Rousseau Murphy, 203

Journey into Fear, Eric Ambler, 224

Jubilee, Margaret Walker, 160

Juggling, Robert Lehrman, 17

Julie, Catherine Marshall, 21

Julie of the Wolves, Jean Craighead George, 230

Julie's Daughter, Colby Rodowsky, 49

July's People, Nadine Gordimer, 100

The Jungle, Upton Sinclair, 99

Kaffir Boy, Mark Mathabane, 138

The Keeper, Phyllis Reynolds Naylor, 25

The Keeper of the Isis Light, Monica Hughes, 189

The Key to Rebecca, Ken Follett, 224

The Kids' Book of Divorce, Eric E. Rofas, ed., 328

Kildeer Mountain, Dee Brown, 163

The King Must Die, Mary Renault, 135

The Last Algonquin, Theodore L. Kazimiroff, 64

The Last April Dancers, Jean Thesman, 68

The Last Defender of Camelot, Roger Zelazny, 202

The Last Enchantment, Mary Stewart, 156

The Last Place on Earth, Roland Huntford, 296

The Last Ship, William Brinkley, 91

The Last Unicorn, Peter S. Beagle, 202

The Late Great Me, Sandra Scoppetone, 21

The Lathe of Heaven, Ursula K. LeGuin, 185

The Laughing Policeman, Maj Sjowall and Per Wahloo, 248

Legend Days, Jamake Highwater, 64

The Lennon Companion, Elizabeth Thomson, ed., 280

Lessons in Fear, Diana Shaw, 215

Letter Perfect, Charles Crawford, 54

Liar, Liar, Laurence Yep, 235

Life and Times of Michael K, J. M. Coetzee, 139

Lifetimes: Under Apartheid, Nadine Gordimer, 103

A Light in the Forest, Conrad Richter, 64

Light Thickens, Ngaio Marsh, 248

Like, Love, Lust: A View of Sex and Sexuality, John Langone, 331

The Lilies of the Field, William E. Barrett, 85

Lincoln, Gore Vidal, 163

Lines of Battle: Letters from U.S. Servicemen, 1941–45, Annette Tapert, 312

Little Dorrit, Charles Dickens, 96

The Little Drummer Girl, John Le Carré, 227

*A Little Love, Virginia Hamilton, 8

The Little Prince, Antoine de Saint-Exupery, 194

Lives of Girls and Women, Alice Munro, 121

Living by the Word, Alice Walker, 277

Locked in Time, Lois Duncan, 215

The Loneliness of the Long Distance Runner, Alan Sillitoe, 264

Looking Backward, Edward Bellamy, 198

Looking for Home, Jean Ferris, 85

Lord Foul's Bane, Stephen R. Donaldson, 194

*The Lord God Made Them All, James Herriot, 285

Lord of the Flies, William Golding, 54

Lord of the Rings, J. R. R. Tolkien, 206

Lord Valentine's Castle, Robert Silverberg, 171

Losing Battles, Eudora Welty, 126

*Lost Horizon, James Hilton, 195

Lost in the Barrens, Farley Mowat, 231

The Lost Star, H. M. Hoover, 181

Love among the Hiccups, Peter Silgbee, 28

Love and Sex in Plain Language, Eric W. Johnson, 331

Love: First Aid for the Young, Dianna Daniels Booher, 325

Love Is a Crooked Thing, Barbara Wersba, 12

The Love Letters of J. Timothy Owen, Constance C. Greene, 40

*The Love You Make: An Insider's Story of The Beatles, Peter Brown and Steven Gaines, 277

The Loved One, Evelyn Waugh, 108

Lucy, Donald C. Johanson and Maitland A. Edey, 292

M. C. Higgins the Great, Virginia Hamilton, 8

*Mac, John MacLean, 18

Madame Will You Talk?, Mary Stewart, 156

The Magic Cup, Andrew M. Greeley, 198

*Magic Kingdom for Sale—Sold!, Terry Brooks, 190

The Magnificent Ambersons, Booth Tarkington, 130

Main Street, Sinclair Lewis, 130

Majipoor Chronicles, Robert Silverberg, 171

Makeba: My Story, Miriam Makeba, 302

Making Friends with Yourself and Other Strangers, Dianna Daniels Booher, 325

Making Peace with Your Parents, Harold H. Bloomfield and Leonard Falder, 327

Mama Day, Gloria Naylor, 94

A Man Called Peter, Catherine Marshall, 21

The Man in the High Castle, Philip K. Dick, 91

Man in White, Johnny Cash, 135

Mara Simba: The African Lion, Roger Caras, 292

Marathoning, Bill Rodgers, 273

Marked by Fire, Joyce Thomas, 4

Marry Me Tomorrow, Merrill Joan Gerber, 28

Martin Hundred, Ivor Noel Hume, 317

Martin Luther King, Jr.—To the Mountaintop, William Roger Witherspoon, 277

Martina, Martina Navratilova, 256

Mary Lou: Creating an Olympic Champion, Mary Lou Retton and Bela Karoly, 268

Master Harold and the Boys, Athol Fugard, 103

A Matter of Feeling, Janine Boissard, 77

McCartney, Chris Salewicz, 280

McKenzie's Boots, Michael Noonan, 146

Me and the Boy, Paul Hemphill, 37

Me, Myself and I, Jane Louise Curry, 235

The Meantime, Bernie MacKinnon, 85
Memory, Margaret Mahy, 44
Menaechmi, Plautus, 113
Meridian, Alice Walker, 121
Merlin's Godson, H. Warner Munn, 194
Merlin's Ring, H. Warner Munn, 194
Mermaids, Patty Dann, 121
Message from Malaga, Helen MacInnes, 245
A Midnight Clear, William Wharton, 155
*Midnight Hour Encores, Bruce Brooks, 45
Midnight Is a Place, Joan Aiken, 152
Miles to Go, Mark Kram, 264
The Millstone, Margaret Drabble, 81
Mind Transfer, Janet Asimov, 167
Mine Boy, Peter Abrahams, 138
Les Misérables, Victor Hugo, 104
Miss Fourth of July, Christopher G. Janus, 125
Mr. Jones, Meet the Master, Catherine Marshall, 21
Mister Roberts, Thomas Heggen, 146
Mistress of Mellyn, Victoria Holt, 152
Mrs. Polifax and the Golden Triangle, Dorothy Gilman, 239
Monster Makers, Inc., Laurence Yep, 181
*The Moonlight Man, Paula Fox, 65
Moonwalk, Michael Jackson, 280
Moonwind, Louise Lawrence, 185
More Dangerous Visions, Harlan Ellison, 168
*Moreta: Dragonlady of Pern, Anne McCaffrey, 181
Mortal Fear, Robin Cook, 220
The Mosquito Coast, Paul Theroux, 95
Motown and Didi: A Love Story, Walter Dean Myers, 12
The Mountain Lion, Jean Stafford, 72
The Mousetrap and Other Plays, Agatha Christie, 32
Move Your Shadow: South Africa, Black and White, Joseph Lelyveld, 139
The Moves Make the Man, Bruce Brooks, 45
The Mummy Case, Elizabeth Peters, 239
Murder in the CIA, Margaret Truman, 239

Murder Off the Glass, Michael Katz, 259
My Cousin Rachel, Daphne du Maurier, 240
My Family and Other Animals, Gerald Durrell, 288
My Father's House: A Memoir of Incest and of Healing, Sylvia Fraser, 21
My Life as a Body, Norma Klein, 36
My Love, My Love; or, the Peasant Girl, Rosa Guy, 12
My Name Is Aram, William Saroyan, 7
My Parents Are Driving Me Crazy, Joyce Vedral, 328
My Underrated Year, Randy Powell, 54
Myself When Young: The Shaping of a Writer, Daphne du Maurier, 240
The Mystery of Edwin Drood, Leon Garfield, 152

The Naked and the Dead, Norman Mailer, 147
Nat Turner, Terry Bisson, 112
The National League: An Illustrated History, Donald Honig, 260
Native Son, Richard Wright, 276
*The Natural, Bernard Malamud, 260
Natural Acts, David Quammen, 305
The Natural Man, Ed McClanahan, 49
The Nature of the Beast, Janni Howker, 40
Necessity, Brian Garfield, 220
Nectar in a Sieve, Kamala Markandaya, 125
Nellie, Brigitte Downey, 44
Nell's Quilt, Susan Terris, 81
Nelson and Winnie Mandela, Dorothy Hoobler and Thomas Hoobler, 302
Nerilka's Story, Anne McCaffrey, 181
Never to Forget, Milton Meltzer, 284
The New GED: How to Prepare for the High School Equivalency Examination, Patricia Mulcrone, 334
The New Teenage Body Book, Kathy McCoy, 324
Newton at the Bat, Eric W. Schrier and William F. Allman, 268
Nicholas and Alexandra, Robert K. Massie, 155
Night, Elie Wiesel, 156

*Night Kites, M. E. Kerr, 13
*Nightpool, Shirley Rousseau Murphy, 203
Nightwing, Martin Cruz Smith, 220
Nim: A Chimpanzee Who Learned Sign Language, Herbert S. Terrace, 292
Nine Plays by Eugene O'Neill, Eugene O'Neill, 32
1984, George Orwell, 91
1933 Was a Bad Year, John Fante, 264
Ninety Highest Paying Careers of the '80's, Anita Gates, 321
Ninety Most Promising Careers for the '80's, Anita Gates, 321
No Deals, Mr. Bond, John Gardner, 224
No Dragons to Slay, Jan Greenberg, 58
No Enemy but Time, Michael Bishop, 220
No Job for a Lady, Phyllis Lose and Daniel Mannix, 288
Nobody Else Can Walk It for You, P. J. Petersen, 231
Nop's Trials, Donald McCaig, 58
North to the Pole, Will Steger and Paul Schurke, 297
A Not Entirely Benign Procedure, Perri Elizabeth Klass, 288
Notes for Another Life, Sue Ellen Bridgers, 41, 328
Notre Dame de Paris, Victor Hugo, 104
Nuclear War, Laurence Pringle, 91
Nuclear War, Nuclear Peace, Leon Wieseltier, 91

The Obnoxious Jerks, Stephen Manes, 54
The Odessa File, Frederick Forsyth, 221
Of Such Small Differences, Joanne Greenberg, 7
Of Whales and Men, Barry Lopez, 292
Oh, Susannah!, Kate Wilhelm, 121
Old Goriot, Honoré de Balzac, 117
On the Beach, Nevil Shute, 91
On the Wrong Side, Stanislav Levchenko, 224
The Once and Future King, T. H. White, 159
One Christmas, Truman Capote, 129

*One Day in the Life of Ivan Denisovich, Alexandr Solzhenitsyn, 153
100 Great Fantasy Short Stories, Isaac Asimov, 198
One Way or Another, Peter Cameron, 40
One Way to Ansonia, Judie Angell, 81
*The Open Net, George Plimpton, 265
*The Optimist's Daughter, Eudora Welty, 126
*Ordinary People, Judith Guest, 69
Origins, Richard E. Leakey and Roger Lewin, 292
The Other Side of the Fence, Jean Ure, 36
Our Man in Mongoa, Alex Alben, 248
Out of My League, George Plimpton, 265
The Outside Shot, Walter Dean Myers, 143
The Ox Bow Incident, Walter Van Tilberg Clark, 117

Paper Lion, George Plimpton, 265
Paper Moon, Joe D. Brown, 117
Passing Shots, Pam Shriver, 268
The Patch Boys, Jay Parini, 44
Peace Breaks Out, John Knowles, 54
The Peaceable Kingdom, John Sedgwick, 288
The People Therein, Mildred Lee, 44
Permanent Connections, Sue Ellen Bridgers, 41
Phantom of the Opera, Gaston Leroux, 108
Pictures from a Trip, Tim Rumsey, 17
Pilgrim at Tinker Creek, Annie Dillard, 317
A Place Called Ugly, Avi, 232
A Place for Winter: Paul Tiulana's Story, Vivian Senungetuk, 296
A Place in the News, Kay Mills, 25
A Place to Come Back To, Nancy Bond, 49
The Plague, Albert Camus, 142
Planet of the Apes, Pierre Boulle, 211
Planet of the Warlord, Douglas Hill, 180
A Player for a Moment, John Hough, 256

Please Don't Kiss Me Now, Merrill Joan Gerber, 328

Pocho, José Antonio Villarreal, 4

Poems of Black Africa, Wole Soyinka, ed., 277

Polyphemus, Michael Shea, 108

Pool of Fire, John Christopher, 188

Portrait of Jennie, Robert Nathan, 198

Possession, Peter James, 252

The Postman, David Brin, 87

Postmark Murder, Mignon G. Eberhart, 244

The Potter's Wheel, Norma Johnston, 64

Prairie Songs, Pam Conrad, 24

Prelude to Foundation, Isaac Asimov, 165

Press On!, Chuck Yeager, 296

Pride and Prejudice, Jane Austen, 130

Prime Suspects, Bill Pronzini and Martin Greenberg, eds., 252

The Prince of Tides, Pat Conroy, 92

Princess Ashley, Richard Peck, 49

The Princess Bride, William Goldman, 194

Prisoner of Psi, Annabel Johnson and Edgar Johnson, 177

Proxopera, Benedict Kiely, 103

Psion, Joan D. Vinge, 180

Puddn'head Wilson, Mark Twain, 113

Putting It Together: Teenagers Talk about Family Breakup, Paula McGuire, 327

The Quallsford Inheritance, Lloyd Biggle, Jr., 152

Rabbit Run, John Updike, 130

Rain or Shine, Cyra McFaddan, 68, 268

Rainbow Jordan, Alice Childress, 4

Rainsong, Phyllis A. Whitney, 239

Raise the Titanic, Clive Cussler, 227

Random Harvest, James Hilton, 195

Rape: What Would You Do If . . . , Dianna Daniels Booher, 324

Ratha's Creature, Clare Bell, 198

Reader's Digest America's Historic Places, 308

Reading the River, John Hildebrand, 296

Ready or Not: Here Come 14 Frightening Stories, Joan Kahn, 235

The Realm of Numbers, Isaac Asimov, 165

Rear-View Mirrors, Paul Fleischman, 68

Rebecca, Daphne du Maurier, 240

Recovery: How to Survive Sexual Assault for Women, Men, Teenagers, Their Friends and Families, Helen Benedict, 321

Red Dawn at Lexington, Louis Birnbaum, 308

Red Shift, Alan Garner, 207

Remembering the Good Times, Richard Peck, 72

Rendezvous with Rama, Arthur C. Clarke, 168

Reunion: A Memoir, Tom Hayden, 312

The Rhineman Exchange, Robert Ludlum, 226

Rich in Love, Josephine Humphrey, 76

The Riddle of the Dinosaur, John Noble Wilford, 313

The Rights of Students, Janet R. Price, 324

A Ring of Endless Light, Madeleine L'Engle, 73

The Ring of Fire, Shirley Rousseau Murphy, 203

The Ring of Truth: An Inquiry into How We Know What We Know, Philip Morrison and Phyllis Morrison, 305

Ringworld, Larry Niven, 176

Ringworld Engineers, Larry Niven, 176

The River in Winter, David Small, 49

The Road from Home: The Story of an Armenian Girl, David Kherdian, 155

Rogue Justice, Geoffrey Household, 223

Rogue Male, Geoffrey Household, 223

Rolling Nowhere, Ted Conover, 59

Roman, Douglas C. Jones, 117

The Rookie Arrives, Thomas J. Dygard, 264

Roots, Alex Haley, 112

*The Ruby in the Smoke, Philip Pullman, 147

A Rumor of War, Philip Caputo, 312

Rumors of Rain, Andre Brink, 139

Run for Your Life, Barbara Abercrombie, 215

Run for Your Sweet Life, Rex Benedict, 28

Run Softly, Go Fast, Barbara Wersba, 73

Runaway, Lucy Irvine, 12

*The Runner, Cynthia Voigt, 269

Running Loose, Chris Crutcher, 55, 273

Running Tide, Joan Benoit, 272

Rusty's Story, Carol Gino, 21

*Safe, Strong and Streetwise: The Teenager's Guide to Preventing Sexual Assault, Helen Benedict, 321

*Sara Will, Sue Ellen Bridgers, 41

Say Goodnight Gracie, Julie Reece Deaver, 68

Say Hey, Willie Mays, 256

The Scarlet Pimpernel, Baroness Orzy, 108

Scorpius, John Gardner, 224

The Séance, Joan Lowery Nixon, 235

Second Brother, David Guy, 59

Second Foundation, Isaac Asimov, 165

Second Heaven, Judith Guest, 21

The Secret Diary of Adrian Mole, Aged 13 3/4, Sue Townsend, 38

Selective Guide to Colleges, Edward B. Fiske, 334

A Semester in the Life of a Garbage Bag, Gordon Korman, 40

A Separate Development, Christopher Hope, 138

A Separate Peace, John Knowles, 54

Seven Daughters and Seven Sons, Barbara Cohen and Bahija Lovejoy, 135

Seven Science Fiction Novels, H. G. Wells, 189

Seventh Son, Orson Scott Card, 176

Sexual Abuse: Let's Talk about It, Margaret O. Hyde, 324

Shackleton, Roland Huntford, 297

The Shadow in the North, Philip Pullman, 148

A Shadow Like a Leopard, Myron Levoy, 4

Shadowland, Peter Strand, 236

The Shattered Horse, S. P. Somtow, 135

Shepherd Avenue, Charles Carillo, 95

Shield of Three Lions, Pamela Kaufman, 135

*Shoeless Joe, W. P. Kinsella, 257

Shoemaker, Bill Shoemaker, 248

Shout! The Beatles in Their Generation, Philip Norman, 280

Shrapnel in the Heart, Laura Palmer, 312

Simon Pure, Julian F. Thompson, 40

*Simple Gifts, Joanne Greenberg, 5

Singin' and Swingin' and Gettin' Merry Like Christmas, Maya Angelou, 274

*Singularity, William Sleator, 186

Sixteen, Donald R. Gallo, 85

The Skeleton in the Grass, Robert Barnard, 244

Skinwalkers, Tony Hillerman, 64

Slaughterhouse 5, Kurt Vonnegut, Jr., 207

The Slave Dancer, Paula Fox, 65

Sleep, Two, Three, Four, John Neufeld, 189

*A Slipping-Down Life, Anne Tyler, 117

Small Faces, Gary Soto, 277

Smoke and Ashes, Barbara Rogasky, 284

Soldier Boy, Michael French, 28

A Solitary Secret, Patricia Hermes, 21

*Solo, Jack Higgins, 224

Somerset Homecoming, Dorothy Redford, 112

Sometimes I Think I Hear My Name, Avi, 232

Somewhere Green, Karin N. Mango, 49

Son of Interflux, Gordon Korman, 40

Song of Solomon, Toni Morrison, 109

Sons from Afar, Cynthia Voigt, 272

South Africa: Challenge and Hope, American Friends Services Committee, 302

South Africa: Coming of Age under Apartheid, Jason Laure, 138

South Africa: Troubled Land, Elaine Pascoe, 138

Soweto: The Fruit of Fear, Peter Magubane, 302

Spacer: Window of the Mind, John Maddox Roberts, 180

A Spaniard in the Works, John Lennon, 280

The Spanish Smile, Scott O'Dell, 216

Spellsinger, Alan Dean Foster, 206

*Sphere, Michael Crichton, 216

Spindrift, Phyllis A. Whitney, 239

Spinneret, Timothy Zahn, 168

Split Time, Charles Crawford, 36

Sports in America, James A. Michener, 268

Stand on Zanzibar, John Brunner, 210

Starman, Alan Dean Foster, 176

Starquake, Robert L. Forward, 172

The Starry Rift, James Tiptree, 189

Startide Rising, David Brin, 87

Starting from Home: A Writer's Beginnings, Milton Meltzer, 284

Staying Up, Robert Swindells, 40

Steffie Can't Come Out to Play, Fran Arrick, 324

Stephen Hawking's Universe, John Boslough, 305

Still River, Hal Clement, 172

Stillwatch, Mary Higgins Clark, 236

The Stories of Ray Bradbury, Ray Bradbury, 167

The Storm Land, Tanith Lee, 185

Stormswift, Madeleine Brent, 244

Stotan!, Chris Crutcher, 55

*Stranger in a Strange Land, Robert A. Heinlein, 172

Strictly Personal, Phyllis Schieber, 36

Strike Two, Ron Luciano, 256

A String of Chances, Phyllis Reynolds Naylor, 25

Studies in Starlight, Charles J. Caes, 305

Sula, Toni Morrison, 109

Summer, Lisa Grunwald, 49

Summer of My First Love, Isabelle Holland, 76

Summer of the Barshinskeys, Diane Pearson, 155

Summer of the Wild Rose, Rosemary Harris, 81

Sundiver, David Brin, 87

The Sunflower Effect, Tony Hayden, 95

Superluminal, Vonda N. McIntyre, 185

Suspicious Characters, Bill Pronzini and Martin Greenberg, eds., 252

Sweet Whispers, Brother Rush, Virginia Hamilton, 9

The Sword of Shannara, Terry Brooks, 190

The Symbiotic Universe, George Greenstein, 305

Symphony for the Devil: The Rolling Stones Story, Philip Norman, 280

Takeoff!, Bonnie Tiburzi, 268

The Taking of Mariasburg, Julian F. Thompson, 8

The Tale of Sir Gawain, Neil Phillip, 159

A Tale of Two Cities, Charles Dickens, 108

Tales of King Arthur, Thomas Malory, 159

Tancy, Belinda Hurmence, 163

A Tangle of Roots, Barbara Girion, 73

Tapestry, Belva Plain, 78

Tar Baby, Toni Morrison, 108

Tea with the Black Dragon, R. A. MacIvoy, 202

Teaching a Stone to Talk, Annie Dillard, 317

A Teacup Full of Roses, Sharon Bell Mathis, 12

Teenage Suicide, Sandra Gardner, 72

Tell Me That You Love Me, Junie Moon, Marjorie Kellogg, 125

The Tempered Wind, Jeanne Dixon, 8

Tender Mercies, Rosellen Brown, 95

The Terminal Man, Michael Crichton, 216

The Thanksgiving Visitor, Truman Capote, 129

Their Eyes Were Watching God, Zora Neale Hurston, 164

Them, Joyce Carol Oates, 125

They Cage the Animals at Night, Jennings Michael Burch, 21

A Thief of Time, Tony Hillerman, 64

Things Invisible to See, Nancy Willard, 95

The Third Life of Grange Copeland, Alice Walker, 121

Thirty Phone Booths to Boston, Don Kardong, 273

This Strange New Feeling, Julius Lester, 113

Three Comedies of American Family Life, Joseph Mersand, ed., 32

Three Days for Emeralds, Mignon G. Eberhart, 244

The Three Musketeers, Alexander Dumas, 108

The Throwing Season, Michael French, 264

Thursday's Children, Rumer Godden, 85

Tiger Moon, Fiona Sunquist and Mel Sunquist, 291

Tim, Colleen McCullough, 121

Time Enough for Drums, Ann Rinaldi, 152

The Time Machine, H. G. Wells, 189

The Time of the Hunter's Moon, Victoria Holt, 244

A Time to Choose, Janine Boissard, 24

A Time to Listen: Preventing Youth Suicide, Patricia Hermes, 72

Timescape, Gregory Bentford, 171

Tituba of Salem Village, Ann Petry, 142

To Have and to Hold, Mary Johnston, 309

To Kill a Mockingbird, Harper Lee, 125

To the Vanishing Point, Alan Dean Foster, 176

Tom Sawyer, Mark Twain, 113

Tomorrow Will Be Better, Betty Smith, 24

The Toynbee Convector, Ray Bradbury, 167

Tracker, Gary Paulsen, 227

Travelers, Larry Bograd, 37

Treasure, Clive Cussler, 227

A Tree Grows in Brooklyn, Betty Smith, 24

The Tree of Swords and Jewels, C. J. Cherryh, 184

The Trial, Franz Kafka, 142

The Tricksters, Margaret Mahy, 198

Trinity, Leon Uris, 104

Trouble in Bugland, William Kotzwinkle, 215

True Grit, Charles Portis, 117

Tulku, Peter Dickinson, 230

Tunnel Vision, Fran Arrick, 72

Tutu: Voice of the Voiceless, Shirley Du Boulay, 301

The Twelve Deaths of Christmas, Marion Babson, 240

Two for Survival, Arthur Roth, 231

2001: A Space Odyssey, Arthur C. Clarke, 168

2010: Odyssey Two, Arthur C. Clarke, 168

2061: Odyssey Three, Arthur C. Clarke, 171

The Ulysses Voyage, Tim Severin, 135

The Umpire Strikes Back, Ron Luciano, 256

Under All Silences, Ruth Gordon, 25

The Underground Railroad, Charles Blockson, 163

Unexpected Pleasures, Phyllis Reynolds Naylor, 12

Unforgettable Fire, Eamon Dunphy, 280

The Uninvited, John Farris, 240

Until the Sun Dies, Robert Jastrow, 317

Unto This Hour, Tom Wicker, 163

The Uplift War, David Brin, 87

The Urge to Die: Why Young People Commit Suicide, Peter Sioracchini, 72

The Veiled One, Ruth Rendell, 252

Very Far Away from Anywhere Else, Ursula K. LeGuin, 202

Vietnam: A History, Stanley Karmon, 312

Voices of South Africa: Growing Up in a Troubled Land, Carolyn Meyer, 301

Von Ryan's Express, David Westheimer, 224

The Wabash Factor, E. V. Cunningham, 248

Waiting for the Rain: A Novel of South Africa, Sheila Gordon, 136

Walk Out a Brother, Thomas Baird, 73

The Wall, John Hersey, 147

The War on Villa Street, Harry Mazer, 272

A Warmer Season, Joseph Olshan, 36

Warriors of Arthur, John Matthews and Bob Stewart, 159

Watcher in the Shadows, Geoffrey Household, 223

Watchers, Dean R. Koontz, 235

Water Girl, Joyce Thomas, 4

The Water Is Wide, Pat Conroy, 92

Waterlily, Ella Cara Delorio, 64

The Way of All Flesh, Samuel Butler, 99

A Way of Love, A Way of Life, Frances Hanckel and John Cunningham, 331

We Are Your Sisters, Dorothy Sterling, 113

We Have Always Lived in the Castle, Shirley Jackson, 252

Web of the Chosen, Jack L. Chalker, 180

The Wedding Ghost, Leon Garfield, 152

Weep No More, My Lady, Mary Higgins Clark, 236

Welcome to Mars, James Blish, 176

The West End Horror, Nicholas E. Meyer, 152

West of Eden, Harry Harrison, 167

What If They Saw Me Now?, Jean Ure, 40

What Niall Saw, Brian Cullan, 91

What Should We Do about Davey?, Julius Fast, 32

What Teenagers Want to Know about Sex, Boston Children's Hospital, 331

When Living Hurts, Sol Gordon, 324

When No One Was Looking, Rosemary Wells, 260

When the Legend Dies, Hal Borland, 64

When Your Parents Divorce, William V. Arnold, 328

Where Are the Children?, Mary Higgins Clark, 236

Whip Hand, Dick Francis, 245

The White Mountain, John Christopher, 188

A White Romance, Virginia Hamilton, 9

White Tribe Dreaming, Marq de Villiers, 103

Who Censored Roger Rabbit?, Gary Wolf, 220

Who Goes Out in the Midday Sun?, Benedict Allen, 256

The Whole Nine Yards, Dallin Malmgren, 85

Why Me?, Lynn B. Daugherty, 21

The Wicked Day, Mary Stewart, 156

Wildhaven, George R. Martin and Lisa Tuttle, 185

Will You Be My Posslq?, Eve Bunting, 28

Winesburg, Ohio, Sherwood Anderson, 117

Winnie Mandela: Life of Struggle, Jim Haskins, 302

Winterkill, Craig Lesley, 64

The Wishsong of Shannara, Terry Brooks, 190

The Wit and Wisdom of Mark Twain, Alex Ayres, ed., 117

The Witch of Blackbird Pond, Elizabeth Speare, 142

Witch's Children: A Story of Salem, Patricia Clapp, 142

Witness, Murey Heidish, 309

Wolf Rider: A Tale of Terror, Avi, 232

A Woman of Independent Means, Elizabeth F. Hailey, 81

Words by Heart, Ouida Sebestyen, 85

The World According to Garp, John Irving, 211

World of Our Fathers, Irving Howe, 81

World's Fair, E. L. Doctorow, 32

The Writing on the Wall, Lynne Reid Banks, 215

Writing Your Way into College: Composing a Successful Application Essay, George Ehrenhaft, 334

El Yanqui, Douglas Ungar, 121

Yeager, Chuck Yeager, 296

The Year of the Gopher, Phyllis Reynolds Naylor, 25

The Year without Michael, Susan Beth Pfeffer, 76

*A Yellow Raft in Blue Water, Michael Dorris, 59

Yesterday: The Unauthorized Biography of Paul McCartney, Chet Flippo, 280

Yesterday's Daughter, Patricia Calvert, 49

You May Plow Here, Sara Brooks, 113

You Never Lose, Barbara Stratton, 264

You Win Some, You Lose Some, Jean Ure, 40

The Young Lions, Irwin Shaw, 147

*A Young Man's Guide to Sex, Jay Gale, 328

Young Parents, Jane Claypool Miner, 331

A Young Woman's Guide to Sex, Jacqueline Voss, 331

Your Job—Where to Find It, How to Get It, Leonard Corwen, 320

Zan Hagen's Marathon, R. R. Knudson, 273

SUBJECT INDEX

This brief listing includes only those titles fully summarized and discussed in the book. Additional titles relating to these subjects can be found in the "Additional Selections" that accompany the discussion of the books listed here. Unless otherwise noted with the label nonfiction, the subject headings refer to fictional treatment of the subject.

Abandoned Children
Brooks, Bruce. *Midnight Hour Encores,* 45

Adolescence—Nonfiction
Benedict, Helen. *Safe, Strong and Streetwise: The Teenager's Guide to Preventing Sexual Assault,* 321
Booher, Dianna Daniels. *Coping: When Your Family Falls Apart,* 324
Gale, Jay. *A Young Man's Guide to Sex,* 328

Adultery
du Maurier, Daphne. *Rebecca,* 240
Plain, Belva. *The Golden Cup,* 78
Townsend, John Rowe. *Downstream,* 33
Townsend, Sue. *The Adrian Mole Diaries,* 37

Adventure Stories
Alexander, Lloyd. *The El Dorado Adventure,* 212
Bradshaw, Gillian. *The Beacon at Alexandria,* 131
Crichton, Michael. *Sphere,* 216

Forsyth, Frederick. *The Day of the Jackal,* 221
Higgins, Jack. *Solo,* 224
Hugo, Victor. *The Hunchback of Notre Dame,* 104
Myers, Walter Dean. *Fallen Angels,* 143
Paulsen, Gary. *Hatchet,* 227
Pullman, Philip. *The Ruby in the Smoke,* 147

Adventure Stories—Nonfiction
Dahl, Roald. *Going Solo,* 281
Lopez, Barry. *Arctic Dreams: Imagination and Desire in a Northern Landscape,* 292

Africa
Gordimer, Nadine. *July's People,* 100
Gordon, Sheila. *Waiting for the Rain: A Novel of South Africa,* 136

Africa—Nonfiction
Angelou, Maya. *All God's Children Need Traveling Shoes,* 274
Dahl, Roald. *Going Solo,* 281

Africa—Nonfiction (cont.)
Finnegan, William. *Crossing the Line: A Year in the Land of Apartheid,* 298
Lawick-Goodall, Jane van. *In the Shadow of Man,* 289

AIDS
Kerr, M. E. *Night Kites,* 13

Alcoholism
Fox, Paula. *The Moonlight Man,* 65
Townsend, Sue. *The Adrian Mole Diaries,* 37

Animal Stories
Murphy, Shirley Rousseau. *Nightpool,* 203

Animal Stories—Nonfiction
Herriot, James. *The Lord God Made Them All,* 285
Lawick-Goodall, Jane van. *In the Shadow of Man,* 289

Apartheid
Gordimer, Nadine. *July's People,* 100
Gordon, Sheila. *Waiting for the Rain,* 136

Apartheid—Nonfiction
Finnegan, William. *Crossing the Line: A Year in the Land of Apartheid,* 298

Arctic Regions—Nonfiction
Lopez, Barry. *Arctic Dreams: Imagination and Desire in a Northern Landscape,* 292

Arthurian Legends
Stewart, Mary. *The Wicked Day,* 156

Assassinations
Forsyth, Frederick. *The Day of the Jackal,* 221
Higgins, Jack. *Solo,* 224

Astrophysics—Nonfiction
Hawking, Stephen W. *A Brief History of Time: From the Big Bang to Black Holes,* 302

Authors
Fox, Paula. *The Moonlight Man,* 65
Kinsella, W. P. *Shoeless Joe,* 257

Authors—Nonfiction
Dahl, Roald. *Going Solo,* 281

Baseball
Crutcher, Chris. *The Crazy Horse Electric Game,* 55
Kinsella, W. P. *Shoeless Joe,* 257
Malamud, Bernard. *The Natural,* 260

Baseball—Nonfiction
Allen, Maury. *Jackie Robinson: A Life Remembered,* 253

Basketball
Crutcher, Chris. *The Crazy Horse Electric Game,* 55

The Beatles—Nonfiction
Brown, Peter, and Gaines, Steven. *The Love You Make: An Insider's Story of The Beatles,* 277

Bigotry
Miller, Arthur. *The Crucible,* 139

Biography
Allen, Maury. *Jackie Robinson: A Life Remembered,* 253
Brown, Peter, and Gaines, Steven. *The Love You Make: An Insider's Story of The Beatles,* 277
Dahl, Roald. *Going Solo,* 281
Terry, Wallace. *Bloods: An Oral History of the Vietnam War by Black Veterans,* 309

Birth Control—Nonfiction
Benedict, Helen. *Safe, Strong and Streetwise: The Teenager's Guide to Preventing Sexual Assault,* 321
Gale, Jay. *A Young Man's Guide to Sex,* 328

Blacks
Baldwin, James. *If Beale Street Could Talk,* 1
Gordimer, Nadine. *July's People,* 100

Gordon, Sheila. *Waiting for the Rain: A Novel of South Africa*, 136

Hamilton, Virginia. *A Little Love*, 8

Morrison, Toni. *Beloved*, 108

Myers, Walter Dean. *Fallen Angels*, 143

Porte, Barbara Ann. *I Only Made Up the Roses*, 82

Twain, Mark. *Puddn'head Wilson*, 113

Walker, Alice. *The Color Purple*, 121

Walker, Margaret. *Jubilee*, 160

Blacks—Nonfiction

Allen, Maury. *Jackie Robinson: A Life Remembered*, 253

Angelou, Maya. *All God's Children Need Traveling Shoes*, 274

Finnegan, William. *Crossing the Line: A Year in the Land of Apartheid*, 298

Terry, Wallace. *Bloods: An Oral History of the Vietnam War by Black Veterans*, 309

Boy-Girl Relationships

Brooks, Bruce. *Midnight Hour Encores*, 45

Cormier, Robert. *Beyond the Chocolate War*, 50

Kerr, M. E. *Night Kites*, 13

L'Engle, Madeleine. *A House Like a Lotus*, 73

MacLean, John. *Mac*, 18

Mahy, Margaret. *The Tricksters*, 198

Naylor, Phyllis Reynolds. *The Year of the Gopher*, 25

Pullman, Philip. *The Ruby in the Smoke*, 147

Simon, Neil. *Brighton Beach Memoirs*, 29

Townsend, John Rowe. *Downstream*, 33

Townsend, Sue. *The Adrian Mole Diaries*, 37

Tyler, Anne. *A Slipping-Down Life*, 117

Boy-Girl Relationships—Nonfiction

Benedict, Helen. *Safe, Strong and Streetwise: The Teenager's Guide to Preventing Sexual Assault*, 321

Gale, Jay. *A Young Man's Guide to Sex*, 328

Bribery

Malamud, Bernard. *The Natural*, 260

Brothers

Kerr, M. E. *Night Kites*, 13

Simon, Neil. *Brighton Beach Memoirs*, 29

Sleator, William. *Singularity*, 186

Twain, Mark. *Puddn'head Wilson*, 113

Brothers and Sisters

Conroy, Pat. *The Prince of Tides*, 92

Dickens, Charles. *Hard Times*, 96

Naylor, Phyllis Reynolds. *The Year of the Gopher*, 25

Porte, Barbara Ann. *I Only Made Up the Roses*, 82

California

Clark, Mary Higgins. *Weep No More, My Lady*, 236

Canada

Fox, Paula. *The Moonlight Man*, 65

Central America

Alexander, Lloyd. *The El Dorado Adventure*, 212

Child Abuse

MacLean, John. *Mac*, 18

Walker, Alice. *The Color Purple*, 121

Chimpanzees—Nonfiction

Lawick-Goodall, Jane van. *In the Shadow of Man*, 289

Civil Rights—Nonfiction

Allen, Maury. *Jackie Robinson: A Life Remembered*, 253

Angelou, Maya. *All God's Children Need Traveling Shoes*, 274

Finnegan, William. *Crossing the Line: A Year in the Land of Apartheid*, 298

Terry, Wallace. *Bloods: An Oral History of the Vietnam War by Black Veterans*, 309

Civil War

Gordimer, Nadine. *July's People*, 100

Walker, Margaret. *Jubilee*, 160

Colleges and Universities—Nonfiction
Leana, Frank C. *Getting into College*, 332

Colonial History
Miller, Arthur. *The Crucible*, 139

Colonial History—Nonfiction
Hofstadter, Richard. *America at 1750: A Social Portrait*, 306

Colorado
Greenberg, Joanne. *Simple Gifts*, 5

Coming-of-Age
Brooks, Bruce. *Midnight Hour Encores*, 45
Crutcher, Chris. *The Crazy Horse Electric Game*, 55
Dorris, Michael. *A Yellow Raft in Blue Water*, 59
Fox, Paula. *The Moonlight Man*, 65
Hamilton, Virginia. *A Little Love*, 8
Kerr, M. E. *Night Kites*, 13
L'Engle, Madeleine. *A House Like a Lotus*, 73
Mahy, Margaret. *The Tricksters*, 198
Naylor, Phyllis Reynolds. *The Year of the Gopher*, 25
Simon, Neil. *Brighton Beach Memoirs*, 29
Townsend, John Rowe. *Downstream*, 33
Townsend, Sue. *The Adrian Mole Diaries*, 37
Tyler, Anne. *A Slipping-Down Life*, 117

Communism
Solzhenitsyn, Alexandr. *One Day in the Life of Ivan Denisovich*, 153

Courage
Alexander, Lloyd. *The El Dorado Adventure*, 212
Bradshaw, Gillian. *The Beacon at Alexandria*, 131
Murphy, Shirley Rousseau. *Nightpool*, 203

Myers, Walter Dean. *Fallen Angels*, 143
Pullman, Philip. *The Ruby in the Smoke*, 147
Walker, Alice. *The Color Purple*, 121
Walker, Margaret. *Jubilee*, 160

Courage—Nonfiction
Dahl, Roald. *Going Solo*, 281
Terry, Wallace. *Bloods: An Oral History of the Vietnam War by Black Veterans*, 309

Crime—Nonfiction
Benedict, Helen. *Safe, Strong and Streetwise: The Teenager's Guide to Preventing Sexual Assault*, 321

Death and Dying
Avi. *Wolf Rider: A Tale of Terror*, 232
Bridgers, Sue Ellen. *Sara Will*, 41
Guest, Judith. *Ordinary People*, 69
L'Engle, Madeleine. *A House Like a Lotus*, 73
Myers, Walter Dean. *Fallen Angels*, 143
Voigt, Cynthia. *The Runner*, 269
Welty, Eudora. *The Optimist's Daughter*, 126

Death and Dying—Nonfiction
Dahl, Roald. *Going Solo*, 281
Terry, Wallace. *Bloods: An Oral History of the Vietnam War by Black Veterans*, 309

Depressions (Economic)
Marshall, Katherine. *Julie*, 21
Plain, Belva. *The Golden Cup*, 78
Simon, Neil. *Brighton Beach Memoirs*, 29

Detective Stories
Forsyth, Frederick. *The Day of the Jackal*, 221
Twain, Mark. *Puddn'head Wilson*, 113

Detention Camps
Solzhenitsyn, Alexandr. *One Day in the Life of Ivan Denisovich*, 153

Dinosaurs—Nonfiction
Wilford, John Noble. *The Riddle of the Dinosaur*, 313

Divorce
Brooks, Bruce. *Midnight Hour Encores*, 45
Fox, Paula. *The Moonlight Man*, 65
Paulsen, Gary. *Hatchet*, 227
Porte, Barbara Ann. *I Only Made Up the Roses*, 82

Divorce—Nonfiction
Booher, Dianna Daniels. *Coping: When Your Family Falls Apart*, 324

Doctors
Bradshaw, Gillian. *The Beacon at Alexandria*, 131

Dragons
McCaffrey, Anne. *Moreta: Dragonlady of Pern*, 181
Murphy, Shirley Rousseau. *Nightpool*, 203

Drugs
Pullman, Philip. *The Ruby in the Smoke*, 147

Drugs—Nonfiction
Brown, Peter, and Gaines, Steven. *The Love You Make: An Insider's Story of The Beatles*, 277
Terry, Wallace. *Bloods: An Oral History of the Vietnam War by Black Veterans*, 309

Education
Dickens, Charles. *Hard Times*, 96

Educational Guidance
Naylor, Phyllis Reynolds. *The Year of the Gopher*, 25

Educational Guidance—Nonfiction
Leana, Frank C. *Getting into College*, 332

Educational Testing—Nonfiction
Leana, Frank C. *Getting into College*, 332

Egypt
Bradshaw, Gillian. *The Beacon at Alexandria*, 131

England
Dickens, Charles. *Hard Times*, 96
du Maurier, Daphne. *Rebecca*, 240
Francis, Dick. *Bolt*, 245
Higgins, Jack. *Solo*, 224
Pullman, Philip. *The Ruby in the Smoke*, 147
Rendell, Ruth. *Heartstones*, 249
Stewart, Mary. *The Wicked Day*, 156
Townsend, John Rowe. *Downstream*, 33
Townsend, Sue. *The Adrian Mole Diaries*, 37

England—Nonfiction
Brown, Peter, and Gaines, Steven. *The Love You Make: An Insider's Story of The Beatles*, 277
Hawking, Stephen W. *A Brief History of Time: From the Big Bang to Black Holes*, 302

Environmental Concerns—Nonfiction
Lopez, Barry. *Arctic Dreams: Imagination and Desire in a Northern Landscape*, 292

Eskimos—Nonfiction
Lopez, Barry. *Arctic Dreams: Imagination and Desire in a Northern Landscape*, 292

Families
Bridgers, Sue Ellen. *Sara Will*, 41
Conroy, Pat. *The Prince of Tides*, 92
Crutcher, Chris. *The Crazy Horse Electric Game*, 55
Dickens, Charles. *Hard Times*, 96
Dorris, Michael. *A Yellow Raft in Blue Water*, 59
Fox, Paula. *The Moonlight Man*, 65

Families (cont.)
Francis, Dick. *Bolt*, 245
Gordimer, Nadine. *July's People*, 100
Gordon, Sheila. *Waiting for the Rain: A Novel of South Africa*, 136
Greenberg, Joanne. *Simple Gifts*, 5
Guest, Judith. *Ordinary People*, 69
Hamilton, Virginia. *A Little Love*, 8
Johnson, Annabel, and Johnson, Edgar. *The Danger Quotient*, 177
Kerr, M. E. *Night Kites*, 13
L'Engle, Madeleine. *A House Like a Lotus*, 73
MacLean, John. *Mac*, 18
Mahy, Margaret. *The Tricksters*, 198
Marshall, Catherine. *Julie*, 21
Morrison, Toni. *Beloved*, 108
Naylor, Phyllis Reynolds. *The Year of the Gopher*, 25
Plain, Belva. *The Golden Cup*, 78
Porte, Barbara Ann. *I Only Made Up the Roses*, 82
Rendell, Ruth. *Heartstones*, 249
Simon, Neil. *Brighton Beach Memoirs*, 29
Townsend, John Rowe. *Downstream*, 33
Townsend, Sue. *The Adrian Mole Diaries*, 37
Voigt, Cynthia. *The Runner*, 269
Walker, Alice. *The Color Purple*, 121
Walker, Margaret. *Jubilee*, 160
Welty, Eudora. *The Optimist's Daughter*, 126

Families—Nonfiction
Allen, Maury. *Jackie Robinson: A Life Remembered*, 253
Angelou, Maya. *All God's Children Need Traveling Shoes*, 274
Booher, Dianna Daniels. *Coping: When Your Family Falls Apart*, 324
Brown, Peter, and Gaines, Steven. *The Love You Make: An Insider's Story of The Beatles*, 277
Lawick-Goodall, Jane van. *In the Shadow of Man*, 289

Fantasy
Brooks, Terry. *Magic Kingdom for Sale—Sold!*, 190

Hilton, James. *The Lost Horizon*, 195
Kinsella, W. P. *Shoeless Joe*, 257
McCaffrey, Anne. *Moreta: Dragonlady of Pern*, 181
Mahy, Margaret. *The Tricksters*, 198
Murphy, Shirley Rousseau. *Nightpool*, 203
Vonnegut, Kurt, Jr. *Cat's Cradle*, 207

Fathers and Daughters
Brooks, Bruce. *Midnight Hour Encores*, 45
Fox, Paula. *The Moonlight Man*, 65
Hamilton, Virginia. *A Little Love*, 8
Marshall, Catherine. *Julie*, 21
Rendell, Ruth. *Heartstones*, 249
Tyler, Anne. *A Slipping-Down Life*, 117
Welty, Eudora. *The Optimist's Daughter*, 126

Fathers and Sons
Avi. *Wolf Rider: A Tale of Terror*, 232
Conroy, Pat. *The Prince of Tides*, 92
Crutcher, Chris. *The Crazy Horse Electric Game*, 55
Kerr, M. E. *Night Kites*, 13
Stewart, Mary. *The Wicked Day*, 156
Townsend, John Rowe. *Downstream*, 33
Voigt, Cynthia. *The Runner*, 269

Floods
Marshall, Catherine. *Julie*, 21

France
Forsyth, Frederick. *The Day of the Jackal*, 221
Hugo, Victor. *The Hunchback of Notre Dame*, 104

Friendship
Alexander, Lloyd. *The El Dorado Adventure*, 212
Bridgers, Sue Ellen. *Sara Will*, 41
Brooks, Terry. *Magic Kingdom for Sale—Sold!*, 190
Cormier, Robert. *Beyond the Chocolate War*, 50
Crutcher, Chris. *The Crazy Horse Electric Game*, 55
Francis, Dick. *Bolt*, 245

Gordon, Sheila. *Waiting for the Rain: A Novel of South Africa,* 136

Heinlein, Robert A. *Stranger in a Strange Land,* 172

Johnson, Annabel, and Johnson, Edgar. *The Danger Quotient,* 177

Kerr, M. E. *Night Kites,* 13

L'Engle, Madeleine. *A House Like a Lotus,* 73

Mahy, Margaret. *The Tricksters,* 198

Myers, Walter Dean. *Fallen Angels,* 143

Townsend, John Rowe. *Downstream,* 33

Tyler, Anne. *A Slipping-Down Life,* 117

Voigt, Cynthia. *The Runner,* 269

Walker, Alice. *The Color Purple,* 121

Walker, Margaret. *Jubilee,* 160

Welty, Eudora. *The Optimist's Daughter,* 126

Friendship—Nonfiction

Angelou, Maya. *All God's Children Need Traveling Shoes,* 274

Brown, Peter, and Gaines, Steven. *The Love You Make: An Insider's Story of The Beatles,* 277

Finnegan, William. *Crossing the Line: A Year in the Land of Apartheid,* 298

Georgia

Hamilton, Virginia. *A Little Love,* 8

Walker, Margaret. *Jubilee,* 160

Ghana—Nonfiction

Angelou, Maya. *All God's Children Need Traveling Shoes,* 274

Greece

Higgins, Jack. *Solo,* 224

L'Engle, Madeleine. *A House Like a Lotus,* 73

Grief

Bridgers, Sue Ellen. *Sara Will,* 41

Guest, Judith. *Ordinary People,* 69

Grooming—Nonfiction

Alexander, Sue. *Finding Your First Job,* 318

Guidance—Nonfiction

Alexander, Sue. *Finding Your First Job,* 318

Benedict, Helen. *Safe, Strong and Streetwise: The Teenager's Guide to Preventing Sexual Assault,* 321

Booher, Dianna Daniels. *Coping: When Your Family Falls Apart,* 324

Gale, Jay. *A Young Man's Guide to Sex,* 328

Leana, Frank C. *Getting into College,* 332

Guilt

Conroy, Pat. *The Prince of Tides,* 92

Guest, Judith. *Ordinary People,* 69

MacLean, John. *Mac,* 18

Morrison, Toni. *Beloved,* 108

Welty, Eudora. *The Optimist's Daughter,* 126

Historical Fiction

Alexander, Lloyd. *The El Dorado Adventure,* 212

Bradshaw, Gillian. *The Beacon at Alexandria,* 131

Dickens, Charles. *Hard Times,* 96

Hugo, Victor. *The Hunchback of Notre Dame,* 104

Miller, Arthur. *The Crucible,* 139

Morrison, Toni. *Beloved,* 108

Pullman, Philip. *The Ruby in the Smoke,* 147

Stewart, Mary. *The Wicked Day,* 156

Twain, Mark. *Puddn'head Wilson,* 13

Walker, Margaret. *Jubilee,* 160

Homosexuality

Kerr, M. E. *Night Kites,* 13

Plain, Belva. *The Golden Cup,* 78

Horses and Horse Racing

Francis, Dick. *Bolt,* 245

Humorous Stories

Greenberg, Joanne. *Simple Gifts,* 5

Naylor, Phyllis Reynolds. *The Year of the Gopher,* 25

Porte, Barbara Anne. *I Only Made Up the Roses,* 82

Humorous Stories (cont.)
Simon, Neil. *Brighton Beach Memoirs*, 29
Townsend, Sue. *The Adrian Mole Diaries*, 37

Humorous Stories—Nonfiction
Plimpton, George. *The Open Net*, 265

Ice Hockey—Nonfiction
Plimpton, George. *The Open Net*, 265

Indians of North America
Dorris, Michael. *A Yellow Raft in Blue Water*, 59

Industrial Revolution
Dickens, Charles. *Hard Times*, 96

Interplanetary Travel
Asimov, Isaac. *Foundation*, 165
Clarke, Arthur C. *Rendezvous with Rama*, 168
Heinlein, Robert A. *Stranger in a Strange Land*, 172

Interracial Marriages
Porte, Barbara Ann. *I Only Made Up the Roses*, 82

Iowa
Kinsella, W. P. *Shoeless Joe*, 257

Jews
Plain, Belva. *The Golden Cup*, 78
Simon, Neil. *Brighton Beach Memoirs*, 29

Jobs and Work—Nonfiction
Alexander, Sue. *Finding Your First Job*, 318

Journalism
Marshall, Catherine. *Julie*, 21

Juvenile Delinquency
Crutcher, Doris. *The Crazy Horse Electric Game*, 55

Kentucky
Morrison, Toni. *Beloved*, 108

King Arthur
Stewart, Mary. *The Wicked Day*, 156

Lesbianism
L'Engle, Madeleine. *A House Like a Lotus*, 73
Walker, Alice. *The Color Purple*, 121

Lies and Lying
Avi. *Wolf Rider: A Tale of Terror*, 232
Dickens, Charles. *Hard Times*, 96
Twain, Mark. *Puddn'head Wilson*, 113

Loners
Tyler, Anne. *A Slipping-Down Life*, 117
Voigt, Cynthia. *The Runner*, 269

Long Island
Kerr, M. E. *Night Kites*, 13

Magicians
Cormier, Robert. *Beyond the Chocolate War*, 50

Marriages
Clark, Mary Higgins. *Weep No More, My Lady*, 236
Conroy, Pat. *The Prince of Tides*, 92
du Maurier, Daphne. *Rebecca*, 240

Maryland
Voigt, Cynthia. *The Runner*, 269

Massachusetts
Cormier, Robert. *Beyond the Chocolate War*, 50
Miller, Arthur. *The Crucible*, 139

Middle Ages
Stewart, Mary. *The Wicked Day*, 156

Minnesota
Naylor, Phyllis Reynolds. *The Year of the Gopher*, 25

Mississippi
Welty, Eudora. *The Optimist's Daughter*, 126

Missouri
Twain, Mark. *Puddn'head Wilson*, 113

Montana
Dorris, Michael. *A Yellow Raft in Blue Water,* 59

Mothers and Daughters
Brooks, Bruce. *Midnight Hour Encores,* 45
Dorris, Michael. *A Yellow Raft in Blue Water,* 59
Morrison, Toni. *Beloved,* 108

Mothers and Sons
Conroy, Pat. *The Prince of Tides,* 92
Guest, Judith. *Ordinary People,* 69
Murphy, Shirley Rousseau. *Nightpool,* 203
Twain, Mark. *Puddn'head Wilson,* 113
Voigt, Cynthia. *The Runner,* 269

Murder
Clark, Mary Higgins. *Weep No More, My Lady,* 236
Conroy, Pat. *The Prince of Tides,* 92
du Maurier, Daphne. *Rebecca,* 240
Francis, Dick. *Bolt,* 245
Hugo, Victor. *The Hunchback of Notre Dame,* 104
Morrison, Toni. *Beloved,* 108
Pullman, Philip. *The Ruby in the Smoke,* 147
Rendell, Ruth. *Heartstones,* 249
Twain, Mark. *Puddn'head Wilson,* 113

Music
Brooks, Bruce. *Midnight Hour Encores,* 45
Higgins, Jack. *Solo,* 224
Kerr, M. E. *Night Kites,* 13
Tyler, Anne. *A Slipping-Down Life,* 117

Music—Nonfiction
Angelou, Maya. *All God's Children Need Traveling Shoes,* 274
Brown, Peter, and Gaines, Steven. *The Love You Make: An Insider's Story of The Beatles,* 277

Mystery Stories
Avi. *Wolf Rider: A Tale of Terror,* 232
Clark, Mary Higgins. *Weep No More, My Lady,* 236

du Maurier, Daphne. *Rebecca,* 240
Francis, Dick. *Bolt,* 245
Higgins, Jack. *Solo,* 224
Pullman, Philip. *The Ruby in the Smoke,* 147
Rendell, Ruth. *Heartstones,* 249

New York City
Baldwin, James. *If Beale Street Could Talk,* 1
Clark, Mary Higgins. *Weep No More, My Lady,* 236
Conroy, Pat. *The Prince of Tides,* 92
Kerr, M. E. *Night Kites,* 13
Malamud, Bernard. *The Natural,* 260
Plain, Belva. *The Golden Cup,* 78
Simon, Neil. *Brighton Beach Memoirs,* 29

New York City—Nonfiction
Allen, Maury. *Jackie Robinson: A Life Remembered,* 253

New Zealand
Mahy, Margaret. *The Tricksters,* 198

Nova Scotia
Fox, Paula. *The Moonlight Man,* 65

Nuclear Holocaust
Brin, David. *The Postman,* 87
Johnson, Annabel, and Johnson, Edgar. *The Danger Quotient,* 177

Occupational Guidance
Naylor, Phyllis Reynolds. *The Year of the Gopher,* 25

Occupational Guidance—Nonfiction
Alexander, Sue. *Finding Your First Job,* 318

Ohio
Hamilton, Virginia. *A Little Love,* 8
Morrison, Toni. *Beloved,* 108

Oregon
Brin, David. *The Postman,* 87

Otters
Murphy, Shirley Rousseau. *Nightpool,* 203

Paleontology—Nonfiction
Wilford, John Noble. *The Riddle of the Dinosaur*, 313

Paris
Hugo, Victor. *The Hunchback of Notre Dame*, 104

Philadelphia
Alexander, Lloyd. *The El Dorado Adventure*, 212

Photography
Pullman, Philip. *The Ruby in the Smoke*, 147

Plays
Miller, Arthur. *The Crucible*, 139
Simon, Neil. *Brighton Beach Memoirs*, 29

Political Activism
Gordimer, Nadine. *July's People*, 100
Gordon, Sheila. *Waiting for the Rain: A Novel of South Africa*, 136

Political Activism—Nonfiction
Angelou, Maya. *All God's Children Need Traveling Shoes*, 274
Finnegan, William. *Crossing the Line: A Year in the Land of Apartheid*, 298

Political Persecution
Solzhenitsyn, Alexandr. *One Day in the Life of Ivan Denisovich*, 153

Poverty
Baldwin, James. *If Beale Street Could Talk*, 1
Dickens, Charles. *Hard Times*, 96
Dorris, Michael. *A Yellow Raft in Blue Water*, 59
Morrison, Toni. *Beloved*, 108
Walker, Alice. *The Color Purple*, 121

Poverty—Nonfiction
Finnegan, William. *Crossing the Line: A Year in the Land of Apartheid*, 298

Pregnancy
Baldwin, James. *If Beale Street Could Talk*, 1
Bridgers, Sue Ellen. *Sara Will*, 41

Pregnancy—Nonfiction
Gale, Jay. *A Young Man's Guide to Sex*, 328

Prehistoric Life—Nonfiction
Wilford, John Noble. *The Riddle of the Dinosaur*, 313

Prejudice. *See* Political Persecution; Racial Prejudice; Religious Persecution; Sexual Prejudice

Prisons
Baldwin, James. *If Beale Street Could Talk*, 1
Hugo, Victor. *The Hunchback of Notre Dame*, 104

Psychiatry
Avi. *Wolf Rider: A Tale of Terror*, 232
Conroy, Pat. *The Prince of Tides*, 92
Guest, Judith. *Ordinary People*, 69
MacLean, John. *Mac*, 18

Puberty—Nonfiction
Gale, Jay. *A Young Man's Guide to Sex*, 328

Racial Prejudice
Baldwin, James. *If Beale Street Could Talk*, 1
Dorris, Michael. *A Yellow Raft in Blue Water*, 59
Gordimer, Nadine. *July's People*, 100
Gordon, Sheila. *Waiting for the Rain: A Novel of South Africa*, 136
Hamilton, Virginia. *A Little Love*, 8
Morrison, Toni. *Beloved*, 108
Myers, Walter Dean. *Fallen Angels*, 143
Twain, Mark. *Puddn'head Wilson*, 113
Voigt, Cynthia. *The Runner*, 269
Walker, Alice. *The Color Purple*, 121
Walker, Margaret. *Jubilee*, 160

Racial Prejudice—Nonfiction
Allen, Maury. *Jackie Robinson: A Life Remembered,* 253
Angelou, Maya. *All God's Children Need Traveling Shoes,* 274
Finnegan, William. *Crossing the Line: A Year in the Land of Apartheid,* 298
Terry, Wallace. *Bloods: An Oral History of the Vietnam War by Black Veterans,* 309

Ranch Life
Greenberg, Joanne. *Simple Gifts,* 5

Rape
Conroy, Pat. *The Prince of Tides,* 92
MacLean, John. *Mac,* 18

Rape—Nonfiction
Benedict, Helen. *Safe, Strong and Streetwise: The Teenager's Guide to Preventing Sexual Assault,* 321

Religion
Heinlein, Robert A. *Stranger in a Strange Land,* 172
Hilton, James. *Lost Horizon,* 195

Religious Persecution
Miller, Arthur. *The Crucible,* 139

Roman Empire
Bradshaw, Gillian. *The Beacon at Alexandria,* 131

Romance
Baldwin, James. *If Beale Street Could Talk,* 1
Bradshaw, Gillian. *The Beacon at Alexandria,* 131
Bridgers, Sue Ellen. *Sara Will,* 41
Francis, Dick. *Bolt,* 245
Hamilton, Virginia. *A Little Love,* 8
Heinlein, Robert A. *Stranger in a Strange Land,* 172
Higgins, Jack. *Solo,* 224
Mahy, Margaret. *The Tricksters,* 198
Malamud, Bernard. *The Natural,* 260
Marshall, Catherine. *Julie,* 21
Plain, Belva. *The Golden Cup,* 78

Running
Voigt, Cynthia. *The Runner,* 269

Russia
Solzhenitsyn, Alexandr. *One Day in the Life of Ivan Denisovich,* 153

Russia—Nonfiction
Herriot, James. *The Lord God Made Them All,* 285

Salem Witch Trials
Miller, Arthur. *The Crucible,* 139

School Stories
Cormier, Robert. *Beyond the Chocolate War,* 50
Crutcher, Chris. *The Crazy Horse Electric Game,* 55
Dickens, Charles. *Hard Times,* 96
MacLean, John. *Mac,* 18
Townsend, Sue. *The Adrian Mole Diaries,* 37
Voigt, Cynthia. *The Runner,* 269

School Stories—Nonfiction
Finnegan, William. *Crossing the Line: A Year in the Land of Apartheid,* 298

Science—Nonfiction
Hawking, Stephen W. *A Brief History of Time: From the Big Bang to Black Holes,* 302
Wilford, John Noble. *The Riddle of the Dinosaur,* 313

Science Fiction
Asimov, Isaac. *Foundation,* 165
Brin, David. *The Postman,* 87
Clarke, Arthur C. *Rendezvous with Rama,* 168
Crichton, Michael. *Sphere,* 216
Johnson, Annabel, and Johnson, Edgar. *The Danger Quotient,* 177
Sleator, William. *Singularity,* 186
Vonnegut, Kurt, Jr. *Cat's Cradle,* 207

Sex Education—Nonfiction
Benedict, Helen. *Safe, Strong and*

Sex Education—Nonfiction (cont.)
Streetwise: The Teenager's Guide to Preventing Sexual Assault, 321
Gale, Jay. *A Young Man's Guide to Sex,* 328

Sexual Abuse
MacLean, John. *Mac,* 18
Walker, Alice. *The Color Purple,* 121

Sexual Abuse—Nonfiction
Benedict, Helen. *Safe, Strong and Streetwise: The Teenager's Guide to Preventing Sexual Assault,* 321

Sexual Prejudice
Alexander, Lloyd. *The El Dorado Adventure,* 212
Bradshaw, Gillian. *The Beacon at Alexandria,* 131
Marshall, Catherine. *Julie,* 21

Sisters
Mahy, Margaret. *The Tricksters,* 198
Rendell, Ruth. *Heartstones,* 249

Slavery
Morrison, Toni. *Beloved,* 108
Twain, Mark. *Puddn'head Wilson,* 113
Walker, Margaret. *Jubilee,* 160

Soccer
MacLean, John. *Mac,* 18

South Africa
Gordimer, Nadine. *July's People,* 100
Gordon, Sheila. *Waiting for the Rain: A Novel of South Africa,* 136

South Africa—Nonfiction
Finnegan, William. *Crossing the Line: A Year in the Land of Apartheid,* 298

South Carolina
Conroy, Pat. *The Prince of Tides,* 92
L'Engle, Madeleine. *A House Like a Lotus,* 73

Space
Asimov, Isaac. *Foundation,* 165
Clarke, Arthur C. *Rendezvous with Rama,* 168

Space—Nonfiction
Hawking, Stephen W. *A Brief History of Time: From the Big Bang to Black Holes,* 302

Sports Stories
Crutcher, Chris. *The Crazy Horse Electric Game,* 55
Kinsella, W. P. *Shoeless Joe,* 257
Malamud, Bernard. *The Natural,* 260
Voigt, Cynthia. *The Runner,* 269

Sports Stories—Nonfiction
Allen, Maury. *Jackie Robinson: A Life Remembered,* 253
Plimpton, George. *The Open Net,* 265

Stepfathers
Porte, Barbara Ann. *I Only Made Up the Roses,* 82

Suicide
Baldwin, James. *If Beale Street Could Talk,* 1
Conroy, Pat. *The Prince of Tides,* 92
Guest, Judith. *Ordinary People,* 69
Plain, Belva. *The Golden Cup,* 78

Supernatural
Hilton, James. *Lost Horizon,* 195
Mahy, Margaret. *The Tricksters,* 198

Survival Stories
Brin, David. *The Postman,* 87
Gordimer, Nadine. *July's People,* 100
Paulsen, Gary. *Hatchet,* 227

Tanzania—Nonfiction
Lawick-Goodall, Jane van. *In the Shadow of Man,* 289

Tennessee
Hamilton, Virginia. *A Little Love,* 8

Tibet
Hilton, James. *Lost Horizon,* 195

Time—Nonfiction
Hawking, Stephen W. *A Brief History of Time: From the Big Bang to Black Holes,* 302

Time Travel
Johnson, Annabel, and Johnson, Edgar. *The Danger Quotient,* 177
Sleator, William. *Singularity,* 186

Track Activities
Voigt, Cynthia. *The Runner,* 269

UFOs
Clarke, Arthur C. *Rendezvous with Rama,* 168

Underwater Adventure
Crichton, Michael. *Sphere,* 216

U.S. History
Miller, Arthur. *The Crucible,* 139
Morrison, Toni. *Beloved,* 108
Myers, Walter Dean. *Fallen Angels,* 143
Twain, Mark. *Puddn'head Wilson,* 113
Walker, Margaret. *Jubilee,* 160

U.S. History—Nonfiction
Hofstadter, Richard. *America at 1750: A Social Portrait,* 306
Terry, Wallace. *Bloods: An Oral History of the Vietnam War by Black Veterans,* 309

Universe—Nonfiction
Hawking, Stephen W. *A Brief History of Time: From the Big Bang to Black Holes,* 302

Unmarried Mothers
Baldwin, James. *If Beale Street Could Talk,* 1
Bridgers, Sue Ellen. *Sara Will,* 41

Venereal Disease—Nonfiction
Gale, Jay. *A Young Man's Guide to Sex,* 328

Veterinarians—Nonfiction
Herriot, James. *The Lord God Made Them All,* 285

Victorian Age
Dickens, Charles. *Hard Times,* 96

Pullman, Philip. *The Ruby in the Smoke,* 147

Vietnam War
Myers, Walter Dean. *Fallen Angels,* 143
Voigt, Cynthia. *The Runner,* 269

Vietnam War—Nonfiction
Terry, Wallace. *Bloods: An Oral History of the Vietnam War by Black Veterans,* 309

War
Myers, Walter Dean. *Fallen Angels,* 143
Plain, Belva. *The Golden Cup,* 78
Solzhenitsyn, Alexandr. *One Day in the Life of Ivan Denisovich,* 153
Stewart, Mary. *The Wicked Day,* 156
Voigt, Cynthia. *The Runner,* 269

War—Nonfiction
Dahl, Roald. *Going Solo,* 281
Terry, Wallace. *Bloods: An Oral History of the Vietnam War by Black Veterans,* 309

Washington (state)
Brin, David. *The Postman,* 87
Crutcher, Chris. *The Crazy Horse Electric Game,* 55
Dorris, Michael. *A Yellow Raft in Blue Water,* 59

Wilderness Stories
Paulsen, Gary. *Hatchet,* 227

Wildlife—Nonfiction
Dahl, Roald. *Going Solo,* 281
Lawick-Goodall, Jane van. *In the Shadow of Man,* 289
Lopez, Barry. *Arctic Dreams: Imagination and Desire in a Northern Landscape,* 292

Witchcraft
Brooks, Terry. *Magic Kingdom for Sale—Sold!,* 190

Witchcraft (cont.)
McCaffrey, Anne. *Moreta: Dragonlady of Pern,* 181
Miller, Arthur. *The Crucible,* 139

World War I
Plain, Belva. *The Golden Cup,* 78

World War II
Solzhenitsyn, Alexandr. *One Day in the Life of Ivan Denisovich,* 153

World War II—Nonfiction
Dahl, Roald. *Going Solo,* 281